A HANDBOOK
on
THE REVELATION TO JOHN

The Handbooks in the **UBS Handbook Series** are in-depth commentaries providing valuable exegetical, historical, cultural, and linguistic information on the books of the Bible. They are prepared primarily to assist practicing Bible translators as they carry out the important task of putting God's Word into the many languages spoken in the world today. The text is discussed verse by verse and is accompanied by running text in at least one modern English translation.

Over the years church leaders and Bible readers have found the UBS Handbooks to be useful for their own study of the Scriptures. Many of the issues Bible translators must address when trying to communicate the Bible's message to modern readers are the ones Bible students must address when approaching the Bible text as part of their own private study and devotions.

The Handbooks will continue to be prepared primarily for translators, but we are confident that they will be useful to a wider audience, helping all who use them to gain a better understanding of the Bible message.

Helps for Translators

A HANDBOOK ON

The Revelation to John

by Robert G. Bratcher
and Howard A. Hatton

UBS Handbook Series

United Bible Societies
New York

Books in the series of **Helps for Translators** may be ordered from a national Bible Society, or from either of the following centers:

United Bible Societies
European Production Fund
W-7000 Stuttgart 80
Postfach 81 03 40
Germany

United Bible Societies
1865 Broadway
New York, New York 10023
U.S.A.

L.C. Cataloging-in-Publication Data

Bratcher, Robert G.
    A handbook on the Revelation to John / by Robert G. Bratcher and Howard A. Hatton.
        p.   cm. — (UBS handbook series) (Helps for translators)
    Includes bibliographical references and index.
    ISBN 0-8267-0174-4
    1. Bible. N.T. Revelation—Commentaries.   2. Bible. N.T. Revelation—Translating. I. Hatton, Howard, 1929-   . II. Title.
III. Title: Revelation to John.   IV. Series.   V. Series: Helps for translators.
BS2825.3.B69 1993
228'.077—dc20
                                                    92-33639
                                                        CIP

ABS-1993-750-EB-1-104926

Contents

CONTENTS

Map and Illustrations

Preface

A Handbook on the Revelation to John, like other Handbooks in the UBS Handbook Series, concentrates on exegetical information important for translators, and it attempts to indicate possible solutions for translational problems related to language or culture. The authors do not consciously attempt to provide help that other theologians and scholars may seek but which is not directly related to the translation task. Such information is normally sought elsewhere. However, many church leaders and interested Bible readers have found these Handbooks useful and informative, and we hope that this volume will be no exception.

The Revised Standard Version (RSV) and the Today's English Version (TEV) are shown at the beginning of each section so that the translator may compare the two approaches to structure of the discourse and to paragraph division. The two versions are shown again at the beginning of the comments on each verse, so that they may be compared in detail. However, the discussion follows RSV, and quotations of RSV words and phrases from the verse under discussion are printed in **boldface** so that the translator can easily locate desired information. TEV is kept before the translator as one of several possible models for a meaningful translation. Quotations from TEV and other translations, as well as quotations from elsewhere in RSV, are displayed within quotation marks.

A limited Bibliography is included for the benefit of those who are interested in further study. Furthermore, a Glossary is provided that explains technical terms according to their usage in this volume. The translator may find it useful to read through the Glossary in order to become aware of the specialized way in which certain terms are used. An Index gives the location by page number of some of the important words and subjects discussed in the Handbook, especially where the Handbook provides the translator with help in rendering these concepts into the receptor language.

The publication of *A Handbook on the Revelation to John* is part of a plan to complete those Handbooks in the series that will cover New Testament books. Meanwhile work on Handbooks for the books of the Old Testament continues. The editor of the United Bible Societies' Handbook Series will be happy to receive comments from translators and others who use these books, so that future volumes may benefit and may better serve the needs of the readers.

Abbreviations Used in This Volume

General Abbreviations, Bible Texts, Versions, and Other Works Cited
(For details see Bibliography)

A.D.	Anno Domini (the Year of our Lord)	NEB	New English Bible
		NIV	New International Version
ASV	American Standard Version	NJB	New Jerusalem Bible
AT	An American Translation (Goodspeed)	NRSV	New Revised Standard Version
B.C.	Before Christ	Phps	Phillips
Brc	Barclay	REB	Revised English Bible
BRCL	Brazilian Portuguese common language version	RNAB	Revised New American Bible
		RSV	Revised Standard Version
FRCL	French common language version	SPCL	Spanish common language version
GECL	German common language version	TEV	Today's English Version
		TNT	Translator's New Testament
IDB	Interpreter's Dictionary of the Bible	TOB	*Traduction œcuménique de la Bible*
KJV	King James Version	UBS	United Bible Societies
Mft	Moffatt		

Books of the Bible

Gen	Genesis	Zeph	Zephaniah
Exo	Exodus	Hag	Haggai
Lev	Leviticus	Zech	Zechariah
Num	Numbers	Matt	Matthew
Deut	Deuteronomy	Rom	Romans
Josh	Joshua	1,2 Cor	1,2 Corinthians
1,2 Sam	1,2 Samuel	Gal	Galatians
1,2 Kgs	1,2 Kings	Eph	Ephesians
1,2 Chr	1,2 Chronicles	Phil	Philippians
Est	Esther	Col	Colossians
Psa	Psalms	1,2 Thes	1,2 Thessalonians
Isa	Isaiah	1,2 Tim	1,2 Timothy
Jer	Jeremiah	Heb	Hebrews
Ezek	Ezekiel	Rev	Revelation
Dan	Daniel		

Translating the Revelation to John

Given the unique nature of this book in the New Testament canon, it may be helpful to bring to the attention of the translator several matters that are normally not dealt with in a Translator's Handbook.

A. Author

The writer is John (1.1,4,9; 22.8), who in early church tradition was identified as the apostle John, son of Zebedee. But nowhere in the book is this identification made; the twelve apostles are mentioned only once (21.14). The writer regards himself as a prophet (22.9) and his task as that of prophesying (10.11); the book itself is a "prophetic" book (22.7,10,19). In the course of time this John was identified as John the Elder (that is, the Presbyter) or some other John, otherwise unknown to us. In modern times he is often referred to as John the Seer.

The translation of the book itself will not be affected by the opinion of the translator about the author's identity, except that in no case is the author to be called the "Apostle" (as in the Douay Version) or "St. John the Divine" (as in the King James Version).

B. Place and Date of Writing

John is in exile on the island of Patmos (1.9), which is in the Aegean Sea (eastern Mediterranean), some 100 kilometers (62 miles) southwest of Ephesus. Patmos was used as a prison by the Roman authorities, and John had been placed there, he says, "because I had proclaimed God's word and the truth that Jesus revealed" (1.9, Today's English Version [TEV]).

Opinions vary as to the time the book was written. Most scholars take it to be either during the latter years of Nero's reign (A.D. 54–68) or the latter years of Domitian's reign (81–96), both of whom persecuted Christians. The majority of scholars favor the time of Domitian.

C. Nature of the Book

This is an apocalypse (1.1), that is, a book that deals with eschatological matters, events that take place at the end of human history. There are apocalyptic passages elsewhere (such as Daniel 7–12, and Mark 13 and parallels), but this is the one biblical book that is thoroughly apocalyptic. The first part, the letters to the seven churches, serves as an introduction to the book.

The message is presented in a series of visions, which include bizarre events and places, and unusual figures—celestial, human, and animal—all of which are symbols that represent some person or event that relates to the life and destiny of first-century Christians in an important way. The translator should keep firmly in mind that, above all, this book was meant to meet the spiritual needs of its immediate readers. This implies that most, if not all, of the symbols and figures were understood by them.

Modern translators, however, are far removed from those first readers and cannot be certain that they understand all the seer's visions. There are various interpretations: some understand the book to be referring to things of the past; others, to the time of the writer or to the time from the writer to the end of history; others take the book to refer completely to the time of the End, that is, the end of human history. All these interpretations depend in some measure on how 1.19 and 20.1-8 are understood. On the other hand there have been those who have seen the book as pure allegory, without any relation to a particular period in human history; but very few take this position nowadays. Whatever may be the interpretation preferred, full force must be given to the author's insistence that the things he is describing will take place soon (1.4; 22.7,10,12,20).

Regardless of the interpretation adopted, it seems quite evident that chapters 2–3 have to do with "the things that are now" and chapters 4–22 with "the things that will happen afterward" (1.19).

D. Translating the Book

Fortunately the translator need not understand completely the meaning of all the symbols, signs, events, animals, and numbers; the translator's sole task is to translate them as literally, clearly, and specifically as possible, without interpreting them. Since the purpose of a dynamic equivalence translation is to allow its readers to understand the text as well as did the readers of the original, the objection may be raised that the translator must supply some clues as to the meaning of the various symbols. To this argument the only response is that we as translators are quite uncertain as to their precise reference and would be doing the readers a disservice by introducing interpretation into the text. In some cases the author himself gives the explanation. The notorious prostitute in chapter 17 is "that great city that is built near many rivers" (17.1), that is, "Babylon the Great" (18.2); there are "seven hills, on which the woman sits" (17.9), which makes it clear that "Babylon" is Rome; but nowhere does the name Rome appear in the book. And there are other clues that help the modern reader identify with a high degree of certainty the historical figures represented by the various symbolic beings and names (see, for example, 11.8).

E. Vocabulary, Grammar, and Style

The reader of the Greek text will notice how unusual, not to say bizarre, is the author's Greek. It is filled with substandard Greek expressions and peculiarities. Swete comments: "The Apocalypse of John stands alone among Greek literary writings in its disregard for the ordinary rules of syntax. . . . The book seems openly and deliberately to defy the grammarian" (page cxx). Should not this serious disregard for common grammatical norms be apparent in a modern translation? In principle the answer to this question should be an unqualified yes, but in practice the matter is not that simple.

To take one example: at 1.4 the description of God goes as follows in Greek: "the one-being, the he-was, and the one-coming." The first and third phrases are the nominative masculine forms of the present participle of the verbs "to be" and "to come," with the masculine definite article—a proper and common way of describing someone. But for the second phrase, which describes God's eternal existence in the past, there is no comparable participle of the imperfect tense of the verb "to be"; consequently the phrase consists of the definite article "the" and the third person singular of the imperfect tense of the verb "he was," forming the ungrammatical "the he-was." For the modern reader that expression is not only substandard but wrong, and the writer would get a failing grade in school for such an error.

But one must ask whether it was also strange for the readers or listeners at that time. It may well be that this had become a standard liturgical phrase, or else it may be that the kind of semitic Greek used in the book was fairly common among Christians of that day.

It seems therefore that the translator's task is to represent the meaning of the Greek in correct, standard language, and not to reproduce the substandard Greek often found in the book. At least such is the recommendation of this Handbook.

1. The vocabulary consists of 870 common Greek words and 44 proper nouns (as listed in Swete's "Index of Greek words," pages 311-323). Of the common words, 107 appear nowhere else in the Greek New Testament; of the proper nouns, 18 likewise do not appear elsewhere in the New Testament.

The book deals with an unusually broad range of objects and beings for which precise equivalents in other languages will sometimes be difficult to find. These include the following:

a. Plants: fig tree (6.13), palm branches (7.9), olive trees (11.4), grain harvest (14.15), grapes (14.18), wheat and barley (6.6), olive oil and wine (6.6).

b. Animals: lion (5.5), lamb (5.6), eagle (8.13), leopard (13.2), bear (13.2), frogs (16.13), cattle and sheep (18.13), horse (6.2). There are also mythical creatures: the dragon (13.2) and two beasts (13.1,11).

c. Natural phenomena: thunder and lightning (4.5), earthquake (6.12), hail (8.7).

d. Weights, measures, money: quart (6.6), denarius (6.6), stadia (14.20); hundred-weight (16.21); "height of a horse's bridle" (14.20).

e. Artifacts: lampstand (1.12), lamp (18.23), throne (4.2), torches (4.5), scroll (5.1); rod of iron (2.27), crown worn by kings and conquerors (4.4,10; 6.2; 9.7; 12.1; 14.14), diadem (12.3; 13.1; 19.12), a victor's laurel wreath (2.10; 3.11); bow (6.2), sword (1.16), chariot (9.9), breastplate (9.9); balance (6.5), seal (7.2), censer (8.3), key (9.1), measuring rod (11.1); shaft (9.1), chain (20.1), millstone (18.21), wine press (14.19); ark of the covenant (11.19), sickle (14.14), robe (6.11), sackcloth (11.3). And see the additional items in the long list of products and goods in 18.12-13.

f. Musical instruments: harp (5.8), flute and trumpet (18.22).

g. Stones: jasper, carnelian, and emerald (4.3); crystal (4.6); pearls (17.4). And see others in the list in 21.19-20.

3

h. Other substances: sulfur (9.17), incense (5.8), wormwood (8.11).

2. As for grammar and style, the translator will have to deal with the following matters:

a. Repetition

In a number of places words or phrases are repeated as a matter of style, and a translator must decide whether this repetition in the receptor language will function the same way it does in the Greek text. That is, if the repetition in the Greek text is a way of emphasizing the importance of what is being said, will a similar repetition in the receptor language also make for emphasis? In some languages repetition may have precisely the opposite effect. Notice the following examples: 10.6 "who created heaven and what is in it, the earth and what is in it, and the sea and what is in it"; 11.5 "if any one would harm them . . . if any one would harm them"; 12.9 "the great dragon was thrown down . . . he was thrown down to the earth, and his angels were thrown down with him"; 19.18 "to eat the flesh of kings, the flesh of captains, the flesh of mighty men, the flesh of horses and their riders, and the flesh of all men."

b. The Use of the Passive Voice of the Verb

In many passages the passive form of the verb is used, and so the actor, or agent, is not identified. In languages where verbs do not have a passive form, the active voice must be used and the actor identified. And even in languages that do have the passive form of the verb, it may be helpful to use the active voice, with the actor made explicit, if it seems quite obvious that the implied actor of the passive verb in the Greek text is God. In many instances it is God or an angel who is the implied agent of the verb. Notice the following examples: 6.11 "they were told"; 12.5 "her child was caught up to God"; 12.9 "the great dragon was thrown down"; 14.1 "his name and his Father's name were written on their foreheads"; 14.20 "the wine press was trodden outside the city."

The verb "to give" is used in its passive form in many passages, in the following contexts: (1) an object is given to someone: 6.2,4b,11; 8.2,3; 9.1; 11.1; 12.14; 13.5a; (2) authority or power is given someone: 6.8; 9.3; 13.5b,7b; power to perform miracles: 13.14; power or right to judge: 20.4; (3) with the meaning "allotted": 11.2; (4) meaning "allowed," "permitted": 6.4a; 7.2; 9.5; 13.7a,15; 16.8; 19.8.

In a large number of instances the receptors of the action of "giving" are enemies of God, and the use of the passive voice emphasizes that God is in control, and that all the events that take place obey God's plan and purpose. The forces of evil operate only with God's permission. God allows or causes these things to happen.

c. The Impersonal Third Person Plural of an Active Verb

Like the passive form of the verb, the impersonal third plural of the active voice also conceals the subject. Sometimes it is not clear in the Greek text that there actually is a concealed subject, and sometimes it is difficult, if not impossible, to identify the subject. The following verbal phrases may all have an unidentified subject: 3.9 "they will know"; 10.11 "they say"; 12.6 "they nourish"; 13.16 "they give"; 16.15 "they see"; 18.14 "they will not find"; 21.26 "they will bring" (see the discussion under the individual passages).

d. Explanatory "And"

Sometimes the conjunction "and" (Greek *kai*) is not used in the normal way of introducing another item in a list, but explains or defines the item that precedes it ("epexegetic," or explanatory use of *kai*). For example, in 1.19 "So then, write what you see and what is and what will happen after this," the first "and" (after "what you see") means "that is," "namely," and what follows explains what comes before. The meaning is "So then, write what you see, that is, what is now and what will happen later." There is no complete unanimity on all instances of the epexegetic *kai* (as it is called), but the matter is raised in the Handbook in those passages where the possibility exists. For example, in 6.11 "until the number was completed of their fellow servants and of their brothers," the meaning is "until the number was completed of their fellow servants, that is, their Christian brothers." And in 2.26 "He who conquers, that is, he who keeps my works." In the following passages it is probable that the "and" is epexegetic: 1.14; 1.19; 2.2; 2.26; 6.11; 11.18; 13.2; 16.11; 17.4; 17.6; 18.24; 19.5; 19.16; 20.4; 20.9; 21.27.

The compound phrase "the word of God and the testimony of Jesus" is used a number of times, and there is a strong possibility that the "and" is explanatory. See the comments on 1.2; 1.9; 6.9; 12.17; and 20.4 (and see also the similar 14.12). In these passages, according to this Handbook, "the testimony of Jesus" means "the testimony that Jesus gave," that is, the message that Jesus proclaimed, or the truth that Jesus revealed.

e. Change of Tenses

Sometimes there is a sudden change from the past or future tense of the verb to the present tense; usually the Revised Standard Version (RSV) makes this change. Often it is difficult to understand what this unexpected change of tenses means, and a translator must decide what will be the effect of such a change in the text of the receptor language. See the following passages: 13.11-14; 13.15-16; 14.2-3; 21.24.

f. Lack of Conjunction

Sometimes two words or phrases appear together without any conjunction joining them; this is called *asyndeton,* which means "the absence of what joins together." In many instances the second word or phrase serves to define or in some way modify the first one. For example, in 1.6 "he made us a kingdom, priests to his God and Father" probably means "he made us a kingdom of priests who serve . . ." (see similar passages in 5.10 and 20.6). In 10.7 "as he announced to his servants the prophets," the meaning is "as he announced to the prophets, who are his servants." In 11.18 there is another instance of this construction, and also the use of the epexegetic "and." The literal translation of this verse is "And the time came for you to give the reward to your servants the prophets and to the saints and to those fearing

5

your name." RSV is surely wrong in its translation; it is most probable that the text means "The time has come for you to give the reward to your servants, that is, the prophets, and to all your people, that is, those who fear your name" (see TEV). The following passages may contain further instances of asyndeton: 1.6; 2.13; 2.14; 10.7; 11.18; 13.6; 14.3; 20.8. In 17.17 this kind of construction goes beyond joined pairs of words or phrases.

g. Unexpected Exhortations or Warnings

In several places the narrative is interrupted by a warning or a promise or an exhortation. Care must be taken with these passages, and if possible the speaker should be identified. Sometimes it seems to be the writer himself; at other times it is clearly the exalted Christ or an angel. See the following passages: 1.7; 13.9-10; 13.18; 14.12; 16.15; 18.20; 18.24; 22.7; 22.12-13. In the following passages a beatitude interrupts the narrative: 1.3; 14.13; 16.15; 19.9; 20.6; 22.7; 22.14.

h. Inversion of Order of Events

In some passages two events are placed in what seems to be the reverse order; the technical name for this is *hysteron-proteron,* which means "last (is) first." For example, in 10.9 the angel commands John to eat the scroll, and adds: "it will be sour in your stomach, but in your mouth it will be sweet as honey" (see verse 10 "it tasted like sweet honey in my mouth . . . and it was sour in my stomach"). Other instances of this may be found in 5.2; 5.5; 10.4; and perhaps in 22.14 and 22.19 (see discussion of these passages).

F. Translating the Poetry of Revelation

Other Handbooks in this series have addressed the problem of translating passages in Hebrew poetical style into modern languages. These are: *A Handbook on the Book of Amos, A Handbook on the Book of Psalms,* and the forthcoming *A Handbook on the Book of Job.* Here in The Revelation to John the task is not as clear or simple for translators.

Modern English translations such as RSV, TEV, NIV, NEB, and others appear to agree that certain passages in Revelation are in poetic style or are heightened rhetoric in the Greek, and so have printed these passages using indented lines to indicate that these can be considered to be poetry. These passages seem to fall into three general types:

1. SONGS: 4.8; 5.9-10; 5.12; 5.13; 7.15-17; 15.3-4;
2. Words of PRAISE and ADORATION: 4.11; 7.12; 11.15; 11.17-18; 19.1-2; 19.5; 19.6b-8;
3. Words of CONDEMNATION and WOE; 18.2-3; 18.4-8; 18.16-17a; 18.19-20.

Other passages in the Greek text that are included are either too short or for other reasons are deemed to be not true poetic style by the authors of this Handbook; for example, 1.7; 2.26b-27; 3.7; 7.10; 7.12; 10.5b-6; 12.10-12; 16.5-6; 16.7; 18.10; 18.14; 19.3.

Before a translator can make a decision about how to translate the poetic sections in The Revelation to John, he or she must first of all investigate whether any subject matter at all appears in poetic form in the receptor language. However, if poetry does exist, do songs, words of praise, or words of condemnation normally appear as poetry in the receptor language? Translators should consult with people who have the reputation of being competent poets in the community. In the Handbook on the Book of Amos, page 15, the authors suggest the following:

> Here are some questions the translator can ask himself and literary specialists: What do people write poems about in this language? Are all subjects equally suitable for poetry? . . . .
>
> Of course, it may well be that within the culture of which this language is an expression, various types of biblical subject matter simply do not exist at all. But the translator still needs to think about the poetry that does exist in order to help decide whether or not these new subjects would be appropriate within poetic tradition.

The translator with the help of experts needs to look at all the different forms or types of poetry that exist in his or her language. Some languages have a large range of poetic forms; others are very limited, and in some languages there may be no poetry at all, as we have suggested above.

If, after this research, a translator and the translation committee decide to translate these passages in Revelation into poetry, it must also be decided who will do this translation. As the Handbook on the Book of Amos says on page 16:

> Very often it will have to be someone different from the person who translates the prose passages . . . . Can people who have this skill be included in the translation team? . . . To be successful, the translation of poetry must be done by a skillful person. Such a person has to be sought out, and the search may be difficult.

The poem in the receptor language must contain all the ideas (meaning) and the purpose of the original; but often it cannot carry over all the devices used in the original poetic structure. In the case of these passages in Revelation, this structure does not contain, either in the Greek or in English translations, any external rhyming patterns, even though these normally appear in SONGS, the first classification above. However, poems in many languages demand external rhyming patterns, even though they do not appear in either the Greek or in TEV and RSV. The structural devices that often appear are: (1) repetition of words and phrases; for example, in Revelation 4.8, where the word "holy" is repeated three times; and (2) multiple synonyms, where in this same passage and in several other songs the words "honor," "glory," and "praise" appear in a row as synonyms.

To sum up, the translator poet should have the same meaning, and if at all possible the same emphasis and feeling, of the original. However, the words, word pictures, and other rhetorical devices in the Greek will often have to be quite different in the receptor language.

When translating these passages in Revelation into poetry, the poet translator must be cautious in using TEV and RSV. These passages in the English, as we have noted above, are not in true English poetic form, especially the songs. These English translations have simply used indented lines of varying length, often beginning with capital letters. But this is not true English poetry.

HOW TO TRANSLATE INTO POETRY: *A Handbook on the Book of Amos*, page 19, says:

> The first step in translating into the poetry of any language is to make a simple translation of the ideas of the original into meaningful prose, without being too concerned with the poetic form. As that is done, the translator should keep track of the kinds of images used, the kinds of emotion that he wants to reproduce. This step is necessary in order to make sure that the meaning is preserved. After that, the same translator, or someone else who is more skilled in poetic style, can take this prose translation and restructure it into the poetic form of the language.
>
> We suggest this procedure because it is easier for a poet to work within his own language as he tries to sense the feeling and rhythm that will make a suitable poem.

The authors of *A Handbook on The Revelation to John* recommend that poet translators follow this same procedure.

G. Outline of Revelation

Commentaries and Study Bibles differ considerably in the outlines they provide for this book. Most of them reflect the content of the book itself: the letters to the seven churches in chapters 2–3 and the visions in chapters 4–22. Some commentators take the book to be a drama and are able to discover seven acts and, sometimes, seven scenes in each act. The following outline is rather brief but does allow the reader to follow the succession of visions to the climactic vision of the new heaven, the new earth, and the new Jerusalem.

Title: The Revelation to John

Like the titles of all other New Testament books, this title was not originally part of the book; it was added later, derived from 1.1.

In Greek the title includes the genitive phrase "of John": "(The) Revelation of John," as many translate it (New English Bible [NEB], Revised English Bible [REB], Moffatt [Mft], American Translation [AT], Phillips [Phps]). In this case "of John" means "given by John," that is, John revealed it. This is possible inasmuch as 1.2 says that John "bore witness . . . to all that he saw" (RSV). But the genitive phrase may be understood to mean "given (by God) to John," that is, God revealed it to John (so TEV, New Revised Standard Version [NRSV], New Jerusalem Bible [NJB], Brazilian Portuguese common language translation [BRCL], Barclay [Brc]). The Revised New American Bible (RNAB) has "The Book of Revelation," and the New International Version (NIV) "Revelation"; Spanish common language translation (SPCL) and *Traduction œcuménique de la bible* (TOB) have "The Apocalypse." Some languages require a verbal phrase instead of the abstract noun "Revelation." The title may then be, for example, "A message is revealed to John by God," "God reveals a message to John," or "John receives a message from God." In many languages that have had the New Testament for quite some time, the title of the book may have to follow the traditional rendering, "Revelation" or "Apocalypse." As a rule the exact meaning of the word "Apocalypse" is not clear to readers today; therefore, if the word must be retained as the name of the book, it may be well to do what the French common language translation (FRCL) has done, "Apocalypse or Revelation given to John"; see also BRCL "Apocalypse, or The Revelation of God to John." God revealed it to Jesus Christ, who passed it on by means of his angel to John, who transmitted it in writing to the seven churches in the Roman province of Asia.

Some traditional Bibles have ". . . of St. John the Divine" (so the King James Version [KJV]). This, however, is not to be done; the additional phrase was not part of the original form of the name of the book.

For the identification of John see the introduction, "Translating the Revelation to John," page 1.

A. Prologue

A-1. Opening Words 1.1-3

REVISED STANDARD VERSION

TODAY'S ENGLISH VERSION

1 The revelation of Jesus Christ, which God gave him to show to his servants what must soon take place; and he made it known by sending his angel to his servant John, 2 who bore witness to the word of God and to the testimony of Jesus Christ, even to all that he saw. 3 Blessed is he who reads aloud the words of the prophecy, and blessed are those who hear, and who keep what is written therein; for the time is near.

1 This book is the record of the events that Jesus Christ revealed. God gave him this revelation in order to show to his servants what must happen very soon. Christ made these things known to his servant John by sending his angel to him, 2 and John has told all that he has seen. This is his report concerning the message from God and the truth revealed by Jesus Christ. 3 Happy is the one who reads this book, and happy are those who listen to the words of this prophetic message and obey what is written in this book! For the time is near when all these things will happen.

SECTION HEADING: it may be helpful to have a section heading; something like "Introduction" (FRCL, TOB) or "Prologue" (NJB, NIV) may be used, or even "The first words," "The beginning words," or "Introducing this book."

1.1-2   RSV   TEV

1 The revelation of Jesus Christ, which God gave him to show to his servants what must soon take place; and he made it known by sending his angel to his servant John, 2 who bore witness to the word of God and to the testimony of Jesus Christ, even to all that he saw.

1 This book is the record of the events that Jesus Christ revealed. God gave him this revelation in order to show to his servants what must happen very soon. Christ made these things known to his servant John by sending his angel to him, 2 and John has told all that he has seen. This is his report concerning the message from God and the truth revealed by Jesus Christ.

The book begins with an incomplete sentence; the opening phrase **The revelation of Jesus Christ** is the subject, but it has no finite verb following it. The word **revelation** (or "apocalypse") occurs only here in the book, and the related verb "to reveal" is not used. The verb means "to uncover," "to disclose," "to make known." The verb and the noun are used in several senses: (1) to reveal, "uncover," what has previously been hidden or unknown (Luke 12.2; John 12.38); (2) in particular, of a message from God, without a human bearer of the message, which reveals something hitherto unknown (Matt 11.25; 16.17; Gal 1.16; 2.2); (3) in a specialized sense, the making known of important events and persons related to the end of this age and the beginning of the new age (2 Thes 2.3,6,8; 1 Peter 1.7,13; 4.13). In this passage the word refers to the visions recorded in the book. As 1.10 makes clear, it was through God's Spirit that John was enabled to see those visions of things present and things future (1.19).

The revelation of Jesus Christ means that Jesus Christ disclosed, made known, the visions recorded in the book. It was God who chose Jesus Christ to make this disclosure, **which God gave to him to show to his servants**; and the visions that John sees portray events that will happen in the near future.

The complete name **Jesus Christ** appears in two other passages (1.2,5); elsewhere "Jesus" is used without "Christ" (eleven times).

To show to his servants: the verb **to show**, in connection with the noun **revelation**, means "to reveal," "to make known," "to disclose," or "cause to see." The noun **servants** here is used in the general sense of all believers, all followers of Jesus Christ, those who will hear this account being read (verse 3). In 2.20 they are servants of Christ; here and in 7.3; 19.2,5; 22.3,6 they are servants of God. In a more restricted sense God's servants in 10.7 and 11.18 are Christian prophets.

The verb form translated **must** points to God as the cause, the motivating force that determines what has to happen (see the verb used in 4.1; 10.11; 11.5 ["he is doomed"]; 13.10; 17.10; 20.3; 22.6). If necessary this may be made explicit by making God the subject of the verb: "to show his servants what he (God) has decided will happen soon."

Soon: this indicates that the events portrayed in the visions will take place within the lifetime of John, a relatively short period of time (see 2.16; 3.11; 22.6). The final events (20.7–22.5) are to take place after the period of one thousand years (20.1-6). And the book closes with the Lord's promise "I am coming soon" (22.12,20).

And he made it known: the subject, **he**, is Jesus Christ; **it** is the **revelation** that God gave him. The verb **made . . . known** translates a verb that is related to the noun "sign, symbol" and means, in a strict sense, "to reveal (or, make known) by means of signs." In ancient Greek stories it is often used of messages from the gods to humankind. This includes figurative or symbolic language, as well as symbols of people and events. In John 12.33 the same verb, translated "to show," is used when Jesus indicates, by means of figurative language, what kind of death he will soon experience, as he refers back to "be lifted up" in verse 32. In John 18.32 the verb refers back to the Jews' statement in verse 31 that they could not execute a criminal, thereby indicating that Jesus would be crucified—which was the Roman method of execution. In Acts 11.28 the verb is used of a prediction of future events, "foretold"; and the general sense "to make known," "to make explicit," is found in Acts 25.27, where it is rendered "indicate." It is possible that here in 1.1 the verb means "to make known by means of signs or symbols," but the majority of translations have simply "to make known," "to reveal." However, in certain languages it will be necessary to express this phrase as "cause to see."

By sending his angel: the word "angel" in Hebrew and Greek means "messenger" and is used both of earthly and heavenly messengers. Here **his angel** is a heavenly messenger, but there is no clear indication as to what particular angel it is. Many different angels appear in the visions, which begin at chapter 4. They appear singly, or in groups of three (14.6-12), four (7.1-8), and seven (two groups: 14.6-20 and chapters 15-16). In 10.1-11 "another mighty angel" tells John that he must prophesy again. In chapter 17 one of the seven angels who had the seven bowls of God's wrath comes to John and explains to him the vision of the notorious prostitute and the red beast. In 19.9-10 "the angel" is probably the one of chapter 17. And in 21.9 one of that same group of seven angels comes to John and shows him the new Jerusalem. The angel stays with John until his concluding statement in 22.6-11, with his commission to John to write the book and send it out. The final endorsement is given by Jesus, in 22.16: "I Jesus have sent my angel to you with this testimony for the churches" (see also 22.6). Here in 1.1, then, the phrase must be translated "his (that is, of Jesus Christ) angel," even though his identity is not known. **His angel** may be rendered in many languages as "his heavenly messenger."

The clauses **he made it known . . . by sending** may be translated as NJB has done: "he sent his angel to make it known to his servant John"; BRCL "Christ sent his angel so that his servant John would know these things"; AT "He sent and communicated it by his angel to his slave John." One may also translate this sentence as "He had (caused) his messenger to go to his servant John and make this message known to him."

The Greek noun translated **servant** often has the meaning "slave"; but in keeping with the Old Testament use of the word, "servant" is the best translation of it into English. Such terms as "employee" or "aide" are not appropriate in English, and most European languages use the equivalent of "servant" (as distinguished from "slave"). The noun "servants" may be adequate in many languages, but where it is not, a verbal phrase may be used; for example, "those who serve (or, those who worship) him (Jesus Christ)." Certain languages must maintain a clear distinction between a person who works for a fixed salary and one who is a personal attendant supported by his master, but who does not have a fixed salary. It is this latter term that should be used in this context if it is necessary to make a distinction. In some languages one may say "those who serve him," "those who are his people," or "those who follow him." John is here identified as the servant of Jesus Christ; in this context it indicates that John is a prophet (see "your brethren the prophets" in 22.8-9). The phrase "his servants the prophets" appears in 10.7, and "thy servants the prophets" in 11.18. "In the Spirit" in 1.10 is a technical term for prophetic inspiration; and in 10.8-11 John is told "You must prophesy again . . . ." So John, as a prophet, is God's chosen messenger to proclaim God's message to the churches (1.11,19; 22.10,16).

In verse 2 the subject of **who bore witness** is John. The Greek verb "to bear witness" is used also in 22.16,18,20 (translated "testimony," "warn," and "testifies"; for the noun "witness" or "testimony," see below). The verb normally means to testify, or to report something orally; here, however, John's **witness** is the book of Revelation itself. In 1.11 he is told "Write what you see in a book and send it to . . . ," and in 22.7,9,10,18a reference is made to "the words of the prophecy of this book" (see also 22.18a,19a,b). So a translation such as "told all that he has seen" (TEV) or "wrote down all that he saw" is appropriate here.

The compound object of the verb is "the word of God and the witness of Jesus Christ, the things he [John] saw." Considering the last phrase first: "the things he saw" is in apposition to "the word of God and the witness of Jesus Christ," referring to the visions that John saw. See 1.12 "I turned to see," and 1.19 "write what you see." The first person form "I saw" appears forty-five times in the narrative section of the book.

The visions John had, **all that he saw,** had to do with (1) **the word of God** and (2) **the testimony of Jesus Christ**.

In this context **the word of God** means the message or messages God sends to John by means of the visions and the warnings and instructions given by various angels. In a broad sense it is the truth or truths that God, by means of Jesus Christ, made known to the prophet John. Alternative translation models are "the message that comes from God" or "the message sent by God."

The precise meaning of **the testimony of Jesus Christ** is debated. It may mean "the witness, or testimony, about Jesus Christ" or "the witness, or testimony, given by Jesus Christ." A similar phrase "the testimony of Jesus" appears in the Greek of 1.9; 12.17; 19.10 (twice); 20.4. In other contexts the noun "testimony" refers to the testimony given by the subject of the phrase (6.9; 11.7; 12.11). And in 20.4, "those who had been beheaded because of the testimony of Jesus and because of the word of God," the meaning is clear: it is the witness or testimony those martyrs had given about Jesus. Here, then, the meaning is most likely the same: "the testimony about Jesus Christ" or "the things that had been revealed (shown) concerning Jesus Christ." In Greek the phrase "who testified about . . . the testimony of Jesus Christ" is not natural, but such unnatural usage occurs frequently in this book.

The translation of the single Greek (incomplete) sentence 1.1-2 must bring out clearly and naturally the relations between the various words, phrases, and clauses, so as to make sense for the readers.

(1) In English the use of an incomplete sentence is most unnatural, but some translations have it (RSV, NRSV, RNAB, NIV, NJB, Mft, AT; so also TOB). It is easy enough to have a complete sentence, such as TEV "This book is the record of the events that . . ."; FRCL "In this book are presented the events that . . ."; the German common language translation (GECL), more simply, "This is the revelation that . . ."; REB "This is the revelation of Jesus Christ . . ."; and Phps "This is a Revelation from Jesus Christ . . . ." BRCL has "In this book are written the things that . . . ." Phps and REB are the simplest. In certain languages it will be necessary to use an active verb and say, for example, "In this book John has written the things that . . . ."

(2) The meaning of the abstract noun **revelation** must often be expressed by a verbal phrase, "the events that Jesus Christ revealed" (so FRCL; TEV), or even "the truth that Jesus Christ revealed." In languages that require an object for the verb "revealed," one may translate "the events that Jesus Christ caused me to see."

(3) The verb **gave** has as its object **The revelation**, and it may not be natural to use the verb with the object "the events" or "the truth." Therefore it may be helpful to restructure, using two sentences, in which **gave** appears in the second sentence, as in TEV "God gave him this revelation . . ."; FRCL is similar, "God gave him the task of revealing them" (that is, "the events" of the first sentence). In certain languages it will be impossible to speak about "giving revelation." In such cases one may render this clause as "God caused Jesus Christ to make known these events" or "God let Jesus Christ see these things in order to make them known to . . . ."

(4) The ultimate recipients of the revelation are the servants of Jesus Christ. The noun **servants** may be adequate in many languages, but where it is not, a verbal

phrase may be used, "those who serve (or, worship) God" (see the comment above on the translation of **servants**).

(5) By means of his angel, which he sent to his servant John, Jesus Christ made this revelation known to John. It may be well to have a complete sentence for the second part of verse 1, as follows: "Jesus Christ made this revelation known to his servant John by sending his angel to him," or "Jesus Christ let his servant John know about these events through his messenger (angel) which he sent to him," or "Jesus Christ sent his messenger to his servant John to tell him (make known to him) the message . . . ." In languages that use modal verbs such as "come" or "go" to show the direction of the action and who or what is the center of focus of the action, one may say ". . . sent his messenger (to come) to his servant . . ." or "sent his messenger (to go) to his servant . . . ." The choice depends upon who the translator feels is in focus here, Jesus or John. John appears to be the focus of attention here, because from this sentence on John is the one telling about all that he has seen. A translation should not try to anticipate here the means used to reveal to John the message from God, that is, the visions John saw. An alternative translation may be "Jesus Christ sent his angel to his servant John to make known to him the message from God."

(6) John reported all that he saw, that is, the visions that are recorded in his book. By doing this John gave his testimony about God's word, that is, the truth God made known, and about the message, or the events, that Jesus Christ revealed. This verse (2) may be rendered as FRCL has done: "John has told all that he saw. He reports here the message that came from God and the truths (or, the events) revealed by Jesus Christ" (so also BRCL). REB has ". . . John, who in telling all that he saw has borne witness to the word of God and to the testimony of Jesus Christ." SPCL is a bit different: ". . . John, who has told the truth of all that he saw, and is witness of God's message confirmed by Jesus Christ." And TOB has ". . . his servant John, who has attested as Word of God and testimony of Jesus Christ all that he has seen."

An alternative translation model for these two verses is the following:

> In this book John records the events that Jesus Christ made known. God caused Jesus to see these things in order to let his followers (servants) know the things that would happen very soon (in the near future). Jesus sent his messenger (angel) to his servant John to tell him (make known to him) this message. John has told all that he saw. He records the message that came from God and the events that Jesus Christ made known.

1.3 RSV	TEV
Blessed is he who reads aloud the words of the prophecy, and blessed are those who hear, and who keep what is written therein; for the time is near.	Happy is the one who reads this book, and happy are those who listen to the words of this prophetic message and obey what is written in this book! For the time is near when all these things will happen.

In this verse the writer congratulates the person who will read and those who will hear the book being read; they are to be congratulated indeed if they obey the book's message, for all the things reported in the book will take place in the near future.

Blessed: the word is used in six other passages: 14.13; 16.15; 19.9; 20.6; 22.7,14 (see especially 22.7, "Blessed is he who keeps the words of the prophecy of this book"). The word, known especially from its use in the Beatitudes of Matthew 5.3-11, is in Greek an adjective, not the passive participle of the verb "to bless." The Greek *makarios* is the equivalent of the Hebrew *'ashrey* (see Psa 1.1). It is not only a statement, "Such a person is happy," but expresses also a wish, "May such a person be happy." So in some languages it will need to be expressed as "May (let) happiness come to the person who . . . ." This word indicates God's, or a person's, approval of someone. In English, at least, **Blessed** (RSV, NRSV, NIV, NJB, RNAB, Mft, AT) is not the best word to use, since it means (or should mean) "God has blessed (or, will bless) such a person." "Happy" is used by a number of translations (TEV, Phps, FRCL, TOB) but seems somewhat inadequate. SPCL has "Fortunate"; Brc "God's joy (will come to) . . . ," and GECL "Happiness without end (belongs to) . . . ." Perhaps the best equivalent in English is "How fortunate is the person who . . . !"

He who reads aloud: the pronoun **he** (TEV "the one") in many languages will be rendered as "the person." The phrase **who reads aloud** refers to the person who will read the book to the people assembled in church to worship. Translators in many languages will need to render this phrase in a similar way to RSV, by employing a word or expression that means "reading in public"; for example, "read with a loud voice," "read so everyone can hear," or even "read this book to the congregation (or, to the assembled believers)."

The words of the prophecy: this literal translation fails to indicate that the author means the book itself (to which **what is written therein** refers). See the same phrase in 22.7,10,18, and a similar one in 22.19. The phrase means "these prophetic words," "this prophetic message." Modern translations have rendered it in similar ways: TEV "the words of this prophetic message"; REB "the words of this prophecy"; GECL "this prophetic word." In this context the noun "prophecy" does refer to things in the future, but not exclusively so; the inspired interpretation of present events is also included (see 1.19, which refers to "what is [now] and what is to take place"). Perhaps some readers in English will understand the word **prophecy** in this context to have a present and future meaning, but many others will not. Translators in many other languages will need an expression such as "listen to the words of this message about present and future events," to carry the meaning of **prophecy** in this context.

Those who hear, and who keep: this is one group of people, not two. TEV "those who listen . . . and obey"; NIV "those who hear it and take to heart what is written in it"; REB ". . . and happy those who listen if they take to heart what is here written." The latter is a legitimate rendering of the phrase, inasmuch as only those who do obey the message are to be congratulated, and not simply those who hear but do not obey.

The verb "to keep" means "to pay attention to," "to heed," "to obey" (see its use in 3.8,10a; 12.17; 14.12; 22.7,9).

The time is near: the Greek word that appears here (*kairos*) is regularly used in the New Testament of a time, or occasion, that God chooses to act on behalf of his people; see 11.18, and in 22.10 see the exact same statement. Here it means the time when the events foretold in the book will take place. FRCL has "the chosen moment," RNAB "the appointed time," REB "the time of fulfillment." Something like "The time is near when all these things will take place" may be the best way to translate this. Or, more extensively, "Before long, at the time that God has already chosen, all these things will happen" or "The time that God has already chosen for all these things to happen is coming very soon."

An alternative translation model is:

> Happy is the person who reads to the congregation this message (that came) from God, and happy are those who listen to it and obey what it says. For the time when God will make all these things happen is very near.

A-2. Greetings   1.4-8

RSV

4 John to the seven churches that are in Asia:

Grace to you and peace from him who is and who was and who is to come, and from the seven spirits who are before his throne, 5 and from Jesus Christ the faithful witness, the first-born of the dead, and the ruler of kings on earth.

To him who loves us and has freed us from our sins by his blood 6 and made us a kingdom, priests to his God and Father, to him be glory and dominion for ever and ever. Amen. 7 Behold, he is coming with the clouds, and every eye will see him, every one who pierced him; and all tribes of the earth will wail on account of him. Even so. Amen.

8 "I am the Alpha and the Omega," says the Lord God, who is and who was and who is to come, the Almighty.

TEV

Greetings to the Seven Churches

4 From John to the seven churches in the province of Asia:

Grace and peace be yours from God, who is, who was, and who is to come, and from the seven spirits in front of his throne, 5 and from Jesus Christ, the faithful witness, the first to be raised from death and who is also the ruler of the kings of the world.

He loves us, and by his sacrificial death he has freed us from our sins 6 and made us a kingdom of priests to serve his God and Father. To Jesus Christ be the glory and power forever and ever! Amen.

7 Look, he is coming on the clouds! Everyone will see him, including those who pierced him. All peoples on earth will mourn over him. So shall it be!

8 "I am the first and the last," says the Lord God Almighty, who is, who was, and who is to come.

In this section John sends greetings to seven churches in the Roman province of Asia, to whom the book will be sent (verses 4-5a). After confessing Christ's glory and power (verses 5b-6), John announces Christ's coming in power (verse 7) and ends with a word from God (verse 8).

SECTION HEADING: if a complete sentence is a more natural way to phrase a heading, something like "John sends greetings to the seven churches" may be used; if it is helpful to identify the seven churches, the heading may read "John writes to the seven churches in (the Roman province of) Asia."

4 John to the seven churches that are in Asia:

Grace to you and peace from him who is and who was and who is to come, and from the seven spirits who are before his throne, 5 and from Jesus Christ the faithful witness, the first-born of the dead, and the ruler of kings on earth.

4 From John to the seven churches in the province of Asia:

Grace and peace be yours from God, who is, who was, and who is to come, and from the seven spirits in front of his throne, 5 and from Jesus Christ, the faithful witness, the first to be raised from death and who is also the ruler of the kings of the world.

This sentence in Greek also lacks a main verb (as both RSV and TEV show), and in some languages it may be better to supply a verb: "I, John, write to the seven churches . . . ." In other languages it is more appropriate style to restructure the sentence and say "To the seven churches in the province of Asia. From John."

Asia was the Roman province in what is now southwestern Turkey. Its most important city was Ephesus. The **seven churches** are named in verse 11 (see also the map, page 36). There were other churches in Asia: in Colossae (Col 1.2), Hierapolis (Col 4.13), Troas (Acts 20.5; 2 Cor 2.12), and possibly others. It is impossible to tell why these seven churches are listed and why they are called **the seven churches,** as though there were no other churches in Asia. In the New Testament the primary reference of "church" is to a group of believers. So in certain languages the term may be translated as "gathering (group) of believers," or even "group of people who believe in Jesus Christ."

This book is filled with groups of seven; in all, the number seven occurs fifty-four times. In the Bible the number seven indicates totality, completeness; commentators point to the seven nations in Ezekiel 25–32, representing all the Gentiles. So it may be assumed that the writer addresses his book to all Christians of his day, or at least to all Christians in the Roman province of Asia.

What follows is a typical Christian greeting used in letters: **Grace to you and peace** is the way Paul invariably begins his letters (see Rom 1.7; 1 Cor 1.3; 2 Cor 1.2, and others). Although there is no verb in the Greek text, the sentence is a normal way in Greek of expressing a wish: "May grace and peace be given to you by . . ." or "May you receive grace and peace from . . . ."

Grace is God's constant love for his people, a love affirmed by and guaranteed in the covenant he made with them, in which he promised always to bless and protect them. This very important word appears many times in the New Testament, and it is not always easy to find a natural way of expressing the meaning of the term other than to use the word "love," usually strengthened by an adjective. In the Old Testament the equivalent word *chesed* is usually translated "steadfast love" by RSV and "constant love" by TEV (see Psa 13.5). Some languages will find it useful to have a fuller definition of the word in a glossary, as BRCL does. **Peace** is not only the lack of external conflict and hostility, but also the presence of an inner sense of well-being, security, and wholeness. It results from faithful obedience to God's commands and receiving his consequent blessings. Peace in some languages may be expressed idiomatically; for example, "live in coolness and happiness" or "have a cool heart." In other languages this clause may be expanded as "May you receive love and peace from God." Other languages will require a preposed expression of prayer or request; for example, "I pray (ask) that you receive love and peace from God" or "I pray that God will show you his love and peace."

What follows is an invocation to the triune God, usually spoken of as "Father, Son, and Holy Spirit" (see Matt 28.19). Here the term "Father" is not used and should not appear in a translation. God is spoken of as **him who is and who was and who is to come**; TEV, like others, has "from God, who is . . . ." The threefold phrase describes God as the eternal one (see 1.8; 4.8; 11.17; 16.5). The first one, **[he] who is**, is the translation of the divine title in the Greek Septuagint translation of Exodus 3.14, where the title in Hebrew is "I AM" (see RSV). The Greek phrase uses the nominative form of the present participle, with the definite article, "the being (one)," as though it were a proper noun; Mft represents this by "grace be to you and peace from HE WHO IS AND WAS AND IS COMING, and . . . ." This rendering is somewhat awkward and should not be imitated. The second phrase is **[he] who was**, which in Greek is the finite form of the imperfect of the verb "to be" in the third person, "he was," with the definite article "the" (there is no participial form of the imperfect tense of the verb). The two phrases declare God's eternal existence and may be expressed by ". . . God, who exists now and has always existed" or ". . . God, who now lives and has always lived." The third phrase, **who is to come**, expresses not only God's living forever but also God's continued activity on behalf of his people—God as Judge and Redeemer.

The phrase **the seven spirits who are before his throne** (see also 3.1; 4.5; 5.6) is a way of speaking of the Holy Spirit; the number seven is probably used in the sense of totality, completeness. As already stated, "seven" plays a very important role in this book. Unless this is the first New Testament book to be translated (a most unlikely possibility), the translation of "spirit" will have already been determined. The main thing to avoid is a word that indicates a ghost, or an evil or malevolent spirit, or the (human) spirit that survives a person's death, or even the "soul stuff" (or, vital force) that is understood in certain cultures to inhabit plants, animals or even humans. It is also important not to borrow a term from some other language that will be practically meaningless to the reader or even give the wrong meaning. The translation of the phrase in this verse must be quite literal; as with all other symbolic figures and events in this book, the translation must accurately represent them without trying to interpret them. The translation should not say or imply "seven Holy Spirits," nor should the word "angels" be used.

The word **throne** identifies God as the supreme ruler of the world, attended by the seven spirits, who are at his service. In some languages **throne** is rendered as "sacred chair," and in others as "the high chief's chair" or "the place where one sits to govern." In the phrase **who are before his throne**, translators in certain languages will want to state the bodily position (standing, sitting, or bowing) of these spirits. However, this information is not at all certain. In fact in 5.6 the seven spirits are referred to as "the seven eyes" of the Lamb. Thus the translator in this context will try to keep the translation vague.

Jesus Christ is described by three phrases: (1) **the faithful witness**: this means that the testimony about God and God's will for humankind that Jesus is going to give John in the visions reported in this book is true, or reliable, and can be believed. If a distinction can be drawn between the two, the word refers more to the reliability of Jesus Christ as a witness than to the truth, the reliability, of his

19

testimony. In other words the witness of Jesus Christ can be trusted. Some languages will require an expanded phrase; for example, "the one who reveals the truth about God faithfully (or, in a way that can be trusted)." In 3.14 the title is expanded to "the faithful and true witness." (2) Jesus Christ is **the firstborn of the dead**, that is, the first one to "be born" to a new life by being raised from death. The use of "first" indicates that there are and will be others to be "born." The phrase is similar to the one used in Colossians 1.18. The element "first" may refer to Jesus as "the firstborn Son," as TEV translates it; so also FRCL "the firstborn Son, the first to have been transferred from death to life." GECL has "the first one of all the dead who has been born to new life," and SPCL translates "who was the first one to rise from death." (3) Jesus Christ is **the ruler of kings on earth**, which indicates his power over all earthly rulers (see 17.14; 19.16). Where the concept of **kings** is difficult to express, the translation may say "the great chief," "the great one," or in certain languages, "the fat (or, large) one," or even "big (or, older) brother with uplifted name." And the phrase **the ruler of kings on earth** may be expressed as "the supreme ruler of all the world" or "the one who has power over all people on earth." **Christ** here is used as part of the name of Jesus, rather than a title meaning the "Messiah."

The one sentence, verses 4-5a, is in the form of a wish, or a prayer, and the appropriate equivalent form in a given language should be used. SPCL translates "Receive grace and peace from the one who . . . ." FRCL and BRCL have "May grace and peace be given you by God, who . . . ," and GECL has "I wish for you grace and peace from God, who . . . ."

An alternative translation model for verses 4-5a is:

> I, John, write to the seven groups of believers (churches) in the province of Asia.
>
> I pray that you may receive love and peace from God. He is the one who lives and has always lived, and who is coming (or, about to come). May you receive love and peace from the seven spirits in front of God's throne, and from Jesus Christ, the one who reveals the truth about God faithfully. He was the first one to rise from death, and who also rules over all the kings (high chiefs) all over the world.

1.5b-6	RSV	TEV

RSV	TEV
5b To him who loves us and has freed us from our sins by his blood 6 and made us a kingdom, priests to his God and Father, to him be glory and dominion for ever and ever. Amen.	5b He loves us, and by his sacrificial death he has freed us from our sins 6 and made us a kingdom of priests to serve his God and Father. To Jesus Christ be the glory and power forever and ever! Amen.

This one sentence in Greek is a doxology, that is, the giving of praise to Christ, confessing his greatness and might (see other doxologies in 5.12,13; 7.10; see also 2 Tim 4.18b; Heb 13.21b; 1 Peter 4.11b). It lacks a verb, and most English translations use the form **To him . . . be . . .** (RSV, NRSV, REB, RNAB, NIV); but there are other ways of restructuring the text (see below).

This doxology is addressed to Jesus Christ, not to God; if necessary the translation can make this explicit; for example, "To Jesus, the one who loves us," or in a similar way to TEV, "He loves us . . . ."

Him who loves us: the use of the Greek present participle "the one loving us" emphasizes the continual, never-ending love of Jesus Christ for all his people. The Greek verb *agapaō* occurs again at 3.9 (and see the noun *agapē* at 2.40); another Greek verb, *phileō*, is used at 3.19.

Loves: the word for "love" in some languages has very little to do with feelings of mercy or compassion, which are components of the word used in this verse, and thus it is often expressed idiomatically; for example, "His (Jesus') heart (or, insides) is warm for us" or "He holds us in his heart." The pronoun **us** includes all followers of Jesus Christ, even though the writer has in mind particularly his readers, the people of the churches to whom he will send his book.

And has freed us from our sins by his blood: the background of this description of redemption is the Old Testament sacrificial system, in which an animal was offered as the means of achieving the forgiveness of sins. The blood shed when the animal was killed represented the life being offered. In this passage **his blood** is a way of speaking of Christ's sacrificial death on the cross. For similar language see Romans 5.9; Ephesians 2.16; Colossians 1.20; 1 Peter 1.18-19; 1 John 1.7. Most cultures are familiar with the concept of sin, that it refers to a violation of the teachings, laws, and traditions of the culture, or that it is an offense against some deity. In certain languages sinfulness or **sins** will be best expressed as "going the wrong way," "wrong actions," or "evil deeds," while in others one may translate "deeds that go against God" or "actions done in disobedience against (that disobey) God."

Has freed us: some Greek manuscripts and ancient versions have "washed us"; NJB has followed this reading. However, there is better textual evidence for "freed" than for "washed," and most modern translations have "freed." The statement **freed us from our sins** may mean freed us from the penalty, or consequences, of our sins (see Gal 3.13; Eph 1.7; Col 1.14). It seems more likely, however, that here the author means that Christ's death has freed us from the power of our sins, from the domination of sin in our lives (as Paul develops at length in Rom 6.16-23). In some languages this phrase will be rendered "has caused us to escape from the power of our sins," or "has prevented our sins from having control (power) over us anymore," or even "has helped us to be able to refrain from sinning."

The preposition **by** may indicate the price paid for the freedom, as at 5.9, where "the blood" is the price paid. But it may indicate the means, the instrument, by which the freedom was achieved—and that is how most translations render it. In certain languages that use modal words to express instrumentality or cause, one may express this as "used his blood (death) to free us . . . ."

As elsewhere, **blood** here is a way of speaking of Christ's sacrificial death on the cross for the salvation of the world. So BRCL "by means of his death on the cross"; FRCL "by his death." SPCL has "by shedding his blood," and GECL "he has poured out his blood."

And made us a kingdom, priests to his God and Father: the literal rendition of RSV makes for an unnatural sentence in English. The meaning is better brought out by TEV "a kingdom of priests," the kingdom established by God and Christ, in which the followers of Christ serve as priests (see Exo 19.6 "and you shall be to me a kingdom of priests and a holy nation"; and in 1 Peter 2.9 "a royal priesthood, a holy nation" reflects the Greek Septuagint translation of Exo 19.6). The RSV literal **priests to** has been improved in NRSV to "priests serving . . . ." In any society, especially one that has a large established religion, priests are a professional minority, the duly authorized mediators between the people and God or gods. However, in so-called animistic societies it may be difficult to find a suitable word for **priest**. The shaman or the medicine man is the closest equivalent and would not be recommended in translation. In certain languages one may use a descriptive phrase; for example, "sacrificer to God," or "go-between," or "a person who contacts God for others." A number of different expressions for **priest** are used in various languages. The important thing is that the term chosen designates the correct function of **priest** in this context, namely, that in the coming kingdom all believers are **priests**, and every believer has a direct and constant access to God (see Heb 10.19-22). Where the concept of **kingdom** may be difficult to represent, the word for "people" or "nation" will serve, since here the idea of a king as head of the country is not in focus, but rather a unified group of people who have a common identity.

To his God and Father: the preposition **to** here is a way of saying "serve." In the phrase **God and Father**, care must be taken that the two refer to one being, not to two. The possessive **his God** may cause a problem if somehow **his** seems exclusive—that is, the God of Jesus Christ alone and of no one else. If there is a problem, in some languages it will be helpful to restructure the phrase and say "God his Father." As for **his . . . Father**, there should be no problem, inasmuch as it is clear here and elsewhere in the New Testament that God is the Father of Jesus Christ in a special way. Other ways of translating the whole phrase are "to serve God, who is his Father" or "to serve God, who is the Father of Jesus."

To him be glory and dominion for ever and ever: **to him** repeats the opening words of the sentence (verse 5b) in order to continue the statement that began there. If necessary, either at the beginning or here, or even in both places, "Jesus Christ" may be named in order to avoid any ambiguity. The wish expressed by **to him be** is in effect a prayer, that **for ever and ever** Jesus Christ will continue to have **glory and dominion**. As elsewhere, **glory** is a difficult term to translate. It represents basically the shining light of the divine presence, manifested particularly in God's (and Christ's) acts on behalf of his people. Some translations may wish to treat this as a technical term, with an explanation in the glossary. In this context it means the greatness and the consequent fame, or honor, associated with Christ's **dominion**, that is, his power as ruler of the world (Louw and Nida, *Greek-English Lexicon of the New Testament*, 76.13; 87.4; 87.23).

For ever and ever translates what is literally "to the ages of the ages," a typical Semitic expression meaning "for all time to come" or "for all eternity." This phrase occurs thirteen times in this book.

Amen is the Hebrew word meaning "So be it" or "May it happen this way," a fitting conclusion to a prayer.

RSV and others (NRSV, NIV, REB, RNAB, TOB) have reproduced the Greek text, using one sentence for verses 5b-6. This makes for a long and fairly difficult passage to read, and it is recommended that a translation imitate TEV and others (BRCL,

SPCL, FRCL, GECL, NJB), with a declarative statement first, "He loves us and . . . ," followed by the prayer, or wish, "To him be . . ." or "May he have . . . ."

An alternative translation model for this passage is:

> He (Jesus) loves us. He has used his death (blood) as a sacrifice to help us escape from the power of our sins. Because of this we have become a family (tribe, nation) of priests who serve God, his Father. May Jesus Christ therefore receive glory and power always. So be it!

1.7 RSV	TEV
Behold, he is coming with the clouds, and every eye will see him, every one who pierced him; and all tribes of the earth will wail on account of him. Even so. Amen.	Look, he is coming on the clouds! Everyone will see him, including those who pierced him. All peoples on earth will mourn over him. So shall it be!

The opening interjection **Behold** is a way of calling the attention of the reader to what follows. RSV often translates the same Greek command elsewhere in Revelation by the archaic English term "Lo!" It may be translated "Look" (TEV, NRSV, NIV, REB, NJB), or "See" (AT, Phps), or "Pay attention" (GECL). Some translations do not have a distinct word to represent it (SPCL). But in a number of Asian and African languages where particles such as this are an essential part of discourse, translators should use an appropriate particle here as an attention-getter. And in certain languages it is more natural style for commands such as this to employ a first person inclusive plural pronoun; for example, "Let us look . . . ."

He is coming with the clouds: the subject is Jesus Christ, and this will need to be made explicit in many languages. The figure of "coming with the clouds" goes back to Daniel 7.13 and appears a number of times in the Gospels (Matt 24.30; 26.64; Mark 13.26; 14.62), "with (upon, in) the clouds"; Luke 21.27 has "in a cloud." This describes the return of the glorified Christ to the world, and **the clouds** are, so to speak, his means of transportation (see Psa 104.3b). The present tense "he comes" describes the event as taking place in the immediate future; the translation should not say he is coming now, at the time of this event. Translators need to decide which preposition, "with" or "upon," is more natural in their languages.

Every eye will see him, every one who pierced him: these words reflect Zechariah 12.10. The statement "Everyone will see him" is followed in the Greek by "and those who pierced him." Here the Greek "and" serves to mark an explanation, emphasizing in particular one group that will see him. Most translations have "even those who . . ." (NIV, RNAB, NJB, TOB, BRCL, NRSV, FRCL); SPCL, REB, TEV have "including those who . . . ," and GECL "especially those who . . . ." In certain languages it will be necessary to render this phrase as "all those people who . . . ." The verb "to pierce" means here to put to death by the thrust of a sword or a spear. John 19.34 describes how the Roman soldier pierced the side of Jesus with his spear, but uses a different verb from the one used here. At John 19.37, however, the quotation from Zechariah 12.10 has the same verb for "pierce" that is used here (the verb appears nowhere else in the New Testament). The figure here is used of those responsible for Jesus' death, either the Jewish religious leaders in Jerusalem or the Roman authorities, or all of them. In many languages it will be necessary to make explicit the instrument used in the "piercing" and say, for example, "all those who had (caused) him (to be) pierced with a spear" or "all those who caused people to kill him by piercing him with a spear."

All tribes of the earth will wail on account of him: this is a way of speaking of all the inhabitants of the world: "all the peoples of the world" (REB). Here **wail** means to weep loudly, but it is not clear whether the weeping is caused by remorse or repentance over what they did, or by fear or despair over what is about to happen. Commentators are divided on the question, and most translations are not specific. Commentators who prefer the idea of fear or despair point to 18.9 and Matthew 24.30, and this is probably the meaning intended. TEV, NJB "mourn over him" represents sorrow; REB, SPCL, Brc have "lament in remorse." One may also say "weep over (because of) him with a loud voice."

Even so. Amen. This is a double confirmation, using the Greek term *nai,* "yes," "indeed," and the Hebrew term *'amen.* In certain languages this double affirmation may be expressed as "It will be like this for sure. So be it!"

1.8

RSV	TEV
"I am the Alpha and the Omega," says the Lord God, who is and who was and who is to come, the Almighty.	"I am the first and the last," says the Lord God Almighty, who is, who was, and who is to come.

This verse brings to an end this section. God's statement confirms what is said in verse 7.

I am the Alpha and the Omega: **Alpha** is the first letter of the Greek alphabet (A), and **Omega** is the last (Ω). Used of God they indicate the beginning and the end, God's eternal existence and sovereignty (see 21.6; in 22.13 the words are used of Christ; and see Isa 41.4; 44.6).

Some Greek manuscripts and early versions add "the beginning and the end" as in 21.6; but these words are not genuine here.

To transliterate the Greek letters may not make much sense in some languages, no more than the equivalent first and last letters of that language's alphabet. Something like "the first and the last" or "the beginning and the end" may be used; or else, "I cause all things to begin, and I bring all things to an end."

Who is and who was and who is to come: see the translation comments on verse 4.

Lord: for the translation of **Lord** and "LORD," see *A Handbook on the Book of Ruth,* page 10; *A Handbook on the Book of Jonah,* pages 6,19; and *A Handbook on the Book of Amos,* page 66. In the Old Testament the Hebrew equivalent of the English expression "the Lord" replaced the name of God, which is rendered in English as "Yahweh" or "Jehovah." However, for the most part the term in the New Testament refers to Jesus Christ. In many languages, in this context terms for "Lord" or "LORD" are often rendered "Chief, God," "Elder Brother, God," or "The one who Rules, God," but here it will be helpful to simply say "God," since the term for "Lord" may refer specifically to Jesus Christ.

The Almighty: "the All-powerful." This title occurs eight more times in Revelation and appears in 2 Corinthians 6.18. A translation may imitate TEV, FRCL, SPCL, and others and join the title to "the Lord God" instead of having it alone at the end of the sentence. **Almighty** is variously translated as "who has the power," "who is all powerful," or "who is the strongest of all."

An alternative translation model for this verse is:

"I am the one who causes all things to begin and brings all things to an end," says (the Lord) God who is all powerful (Almighty), who exists now, has always existed, and lives for ever.

A-3. Introductory Vision 1.9-20

RSV

9 I John, your brother, who share with you in Jesus the tribulation and the kingdom and the patient endurance, was on the island called Patmos on account of the word of God and the testimony of Jesus. 10 I was in the Spirit on the Lord's day, and I heard behind me a loud voice like a trumpet 11 saying, "Write what you see in a book and send it to the seven churches, to Ephesus and to Smyrna and to Pergamum and to Thyatira and to Sardis and to Philadelphia and to Laodicea."

12 Then I turned to see the voice that was speaking to me, and on turning I saw seven golden lampstands, 13 and in the midst of the lampstands one like a son of man, clothed with a long robe and with a golden girdle round his breast; 14 his head and his hair were white as white wool, white as snow; his eyes were like a flame of fire, 15 his feet were like burnished bronze, refined as in a furnace, and his voice was like the sound of many waters; 16 in his right hand he held seven stars, from his mouth issued a sharp two-edged sword, and his face was like the sun shining in full strength.

17 When I saw him, I fell at his feet as though dead. But he laid his right hand upon me, saying, "Fear not, I am the first and the last, 18 and the living one; I died, and behold I am alive for evermore, and I have the keys of Death and Hades. 19 Now write what you see, what is and what is to take place hereafter. 20 As for the mystery of the seven stars which you saw in my right hand, and the seven golden lampstands, the seven stars are the angels of the seven churches and the seven lampstands are the seven churches.

TEV

A Vision of Christ

9 I am John, your brother, and as a follower of Jesus I am your partner in patiently enduring the suffering that comes to those who belong to his Kingdom. I was put on the island of Patmos because I had proclaimed God's word and the truth that Jesus revealed. 10 On the Lord's day the Spirit took control of me, and I heard a loud voice, that sounded like a trumpet, speaking behind me. 11 It said, "Write down what you see, and send the book to the churches in these seven cities: Ephesus, Smyrna, Pergamum, Thyatira, Sardis, Philadelphia, and Laodicea."

12 I turned around to see who was talking to me, and I saw seven gold lampstands, 13 and among them there was what looked like a human being, wearing a robe that reached to his feet, and a gold band around his chest. 14 His hair was white as wool, or as snow, and his eyes blazed like fire; 15 his feet shone like brass that has been refined and polished, and his voice sounded like a roaring waterfall. 16 He held seven stars in his right hand, and a sharp two-edged sword came out of his mouth. His face was as bright as the midday sun. 17 When I saw him, I fell down at his feet like a dead man. He placed his right hand on me and said, "Don't be afraid! I am the first and the last. 18 I am the living one! I was dead, but now I am alive forever and ever. I have authority over death and the world of the dead. 19 Write, then, the things you see, both the things that are now and the things that will happen afterward. 20 Here is the secret meaning of the seven stars that you see in my right hand, and of the seven gold lampstands: the seven stars are the angels of the seven churches, and the seven lampstands are the seven churches.

In this initial vision (1.9-20) the glorified Christ (that is, the risen Christ who now dwells in heavenly glory) appears to John and commissions him to write what he sees and to send the book to the seven churches of the Roman province of Asia (verses 9-11). After a description of Christ (verses 12-16) John is told the meaning of the seven stars and the seven gold lampstands (verses 17-20).

SECTION HEADING: TEV "A Vision of Christ." The Greek noun translated "vision" appears with this meaning in 9.17 only (see also Acts 2.17). As used in the Section Heading, it is a means by which God makes known future events or otherwise transmits a message to a person. The Section Heading may avoid the word "vision" altogether and say something like "John sees the risen (or, glorified) Christ" or "The risen Christ appears to John."

1.9   RSV   TEV

I John, your brother, who share with you in Jesus the tribulation and the kingdom and the patient endurance, was on the island called Patmos on account of the word of God and the testimony of Jesus.

I am John, your brother, and as a follower of Jesus I am your partner in patiently enduring the suffering that comes to those who belong to his Kingdom. I was put on the island of Patmos because I had proclaimed God's word and the truth that Jesus revealed.

The author introduces himself, **I John, your brother**. He uses no titles or other identification, which implies he is well known to his readers. He is a **brother** of all those to whom he writes, that is, a fellow Christian, a fellow believer in Jesus Christ. If the referent of the plural **your** must be made explicit, something like "all of you to whom I am sending this book" may be used. This becomes clear, of course, in verse 11, and so may not be needed.

Who share with you in Jesus: he states he has had, or is having, the same experiences they have had (see similar language in Phil 4.14). The phrase **in Jesus** means "as a follower of Jesus," "as a believer in Jesus," or even "as a Christian." Another way of expressing this phrase is "who as a fellow believer in Jesus share . . . ."

The tribulation and the kingdom and the patient endurance: the events or the experiences these nouns represent are of different natures and are not easily or naturally joined together as objects of the verb: "sharing in the suffering and reign and endurance." The **tribulation**, or "suffering," or "persecution," is that which the followers of Christ are called upon to experience before the coming of Christ (see its use in 7.14). It may also be expressed as a complete clause: "I suffer the same difficulties that you are experiencing," "I am persecuted just as you are," or in languages that avoid the passive one may say "People persecute me just as they do you." The **kingdom** here has a future reference, the coming Kingdom in which God and Christ will reign completely over the world (11.15; 12.10). Other ways of expressing the clause **share . . . kingdom** are "with you who are citizens of (belong to) Christ's (God's) kingdom" or "with you who have God ruling over you." John and his fellow believers must wait with **patient endurance** for the coming of the Kingdom. This quality is praised in the letters to Ephesus (2.2,3), Thyatira (2.19), and

26

Philadelphia (3.10); see also 13.10; 14.12. Caird (page 20) comments: "*Ordeal* and *sovereignty* are obverse and reverse of the one calling; for those who endure with Christ also reign with him, and reign in the very midst of their *ordeal*." **Patient endurance** may be variously rendered as "willingness to put up with for a long time," "never give up," "have a big heart towards." **Patient endurance** may also be rendered as "endure with long hearts." In certain languages it will be helpful to join the ideas of **tribulation** and **patient endurance**, keeping **kingdom** separate, and say "I am together with you in God's kingdom, but also in patiently enduring the suffering."

Was on the island called Patmos: the past tense **was** implies that he is no longer there. TEV has "I was put (on the island of Patmos)" on the assumption that he had been sent there as a prisoner (so also REB, FRCL, Translator's New Testament [TNT]). If translators follow this interpretation, in certain languages it will be necessary to avoid a passive expression and say "they put me on the island of Patmos," where "they" is an unknown agent. **Patmos** is a small island some sixteen kilometers long and nine kilometers wide (ten miles by six miles), in the Aegean Sea (eastern Mediterranean), about one hundred kilometers southwest of Ephesus. It was used by the Romans as a penal colony.

On account of the word of God and the testimony of Jesus: the same two noun phrases appeared already in verse 2 (which see). There are several possible interpretations of **on account . . . Jesus**, but the most likely one is the one given by TEV (so also FRCL, RNAB, TNT, Brc, Phps).

The verse is a fairly long and complex sentence in Greek, and it is recommended that a translation have at least two sentences. The following may serve as a model: "I, your Christian brother John, have, like you, patiently endured the suffering that is ours as followers of Jesus as we await the coming of the Kingdom." Or, less freely, as SPCL has: "I, John, am your brother, and because of my union with Jesus I share with you in the Kingdom of God, in the sufferings, and in the strength to endure them," or even "I, John, who am your fellow believer in Christ, am persecuted as you are. I am a citizen of the Kingdom of God as you are, and I must patiently endure my troubles just as you do."

The second sentence is more easily translated in simple and natural language: "I had been sent to the island of Patmos because I had preached God's message and the truth revealed by Jesus." If the passive "I had been sent to (or, put on) the island of Patmos . . ." raises the question as to who had sent him there, it may be well to avoid it by saying simply "I was on the island . . . ," or perhaps "I was a prisoner on the island . . ." (BRCL). But in certain languages one may avoid the passive and say "They sent me to the island of Patmos," where "They" is an unknown agent.

1.10 RSV	TEV
I was in the Spirit on the Lord's day, and I heard behind me a loud voice like a trumpet	On the Lord's day the Spirit took control of me, and I heard a loud voice, that sounded like a trumpet, speaking behind me.

In Greek verses 10-11 are one sentence; but it is easy to make two sentences, as TEV has done, inasmuch as verse 11 begins with the present participle "saying."

I was in the Spirit: this expression describes being possessed by God's Spirit (as also in 4.2; 17.3; 21.10). FRCL has "the Holy Spirit took hold of me," SPCL "I was overcome by the power of the Spirit," and TOB "I was seized by the Spirit." But NJB has "I was in ecstasy," and AT and Brc "I fell into a trance." This is possible but seems less likely. The idea of "ecstasy" or "trance" is better expressed by the Greek noun *ekstasis,* which does not occur here (see Acts 10.10; 11.5; 22.17). RNAB "I was caught up in spirit" and NRSV "I was in the spirit" do not make much sense in English. For many translators it will be essential here to translate **Spirit** as "God's Spirit" and say, for example, "God's Spirit took control . . . ," "God's Spirit came upon me," "God's Spirit led me," or "I fell under the power of God's Spirit," or even idiomatically, "I was grabbed by the Holy Spirit." For other comments on the translation of **Spirit**, see verse 4.

Lord's day: this is the Christian day of worship, the first day of the week, the day of Christ's resurrection (see Acts 20.7; 1 Cor 16.2). Only here in the New Testament is the expression **the Lord's day** used, but it is found in early Christian literature: *Didache* 14 (the end of the first century), and Ignatius' *Letter to the Magnesians* 19 (early second century). The same adjective that is translated **the Lord's** is used in the phrase "the Lord's Supper" (1 Cor 11.20).

I heard behind me a loud voice like a trumpet: as one commentator puts it: "loud and clear." The comparison may be expressed variously: "as loud as a trumpet" (RNAB), or "like a trumpet blast" (SPCL), or even "as loud as the sound of a trumpet," or "that sounded like the loud noise that a trumpet makes." In certain languages that employ ideophones, here is a good place to use one for the sound that a trumpet makes. A **trumpet** in the Old Testament was a ram's horn, but in New Testament times it was most likely a metal instrument something like a modern trumpet. In cultures where trumpets don't exist, one may use a general word for an animal "horn" (not the horn of an automobile), or else any other kind of loud musical instrument. However, it may be necessary in certain cultures that do not use wind instruments at all to transliterate the English word "trumpet" and have a glossary note describing this instrument.

The text here does not say whose voice it is, but the speaker is clearly identified in the following verses. Another translation model for this final sentence is "I heard a loud voice like the sound of a trumpet, speaking (coming) from behind me . . . ."

1.11	RSV	TEV

saying, "Write what you see in a book and send it to the seven churches, to Ephesus and to Smyrna and to Pergamum and to Thyatira and to Sardis and to Philadelphia and to Laodicea."	It said, "Write down what you see, and send the book to the churches in these seven cities: Ephesus, Smyrna, Pergamum, Thyatira, Sardis, Philadelphia, and Laodicea."

As suggested above, a period can be placed at the end of verse 10, and verse 11 can begin, as TEV has it, "It said" (or, "The voice said"). Not until the next verse does John turn around to discover who is speaking to him.

Write what you see in a book: the unfortunate order of words in RSV has been corrected in NRSV, "Write in a book what you see." The phrase **what you see** includes all the visions John will see, as recorded in the book. In this case the **book** is most likely a papyrus scroll. In certain languages the phrase **what you see** will be expressed as "all the things you see (will be seeing)," and the full clause may be expressed as "Write an account (report) of all the things that you see . . . ."

There is no way of knowing why these seven churches in the Roman province of Asia were chosen. The order in which the cities are named may indicate the route to be followed by the messenger taking the book to them. The first one on the list, **Ephesus**, was the most important city in the Roman province of Asia. (See the locations of the seven cities on the map, page 36.) For the translation of **churches** see the comments on verse 4. The phrase **to the seven churches** may also be expressed as "to the groups of Christians (or, people who follow Christ) and who live in these seven cities."

1.12	RSV	TEV
	Then I turned to see the voice that was speaking to me, and on turning I saw seven golden lampstands,	I turned around to see who was talking to me, and I saw seven gold lampstands,

In the Greek text verses 12-16 are one sentence (so RSV but not NRSV); but the break between verses is quite natural, so that the following discussion will proceed one verse at a time.

I turned to see the voice: this is what the Greek text says, but it is clear that the meaning is "to see the person" or "to see who was speaking to me" (NJB). NRSV, RNAB, and REB "to see whose voice it was that spoke to me" is unnecessarily wordy.

And on turning I saw: again RSV follows literally the Greek form, which began the verse with the finite verb "I turned (to see)," followed here by the aorist participle "having turned (I saw)."

Seven golden lampstands: the lamp in these **lampstands** was an oil lamp, which consisted of a shallow clay bowl full of olive oil, with a wick lying in the oil; one end of the wick extended onto a lip of the bowl, where the oil in the wick burned so that its flame provided light. A translation must avoid giving the impression that electric light bulbs or wax candles were the source of light. The **lampstands** themselves were either made of gold or, more likely, were gold plated. Each lampstand, it is assumed, had several lamps on it. **Lampstands** may in certain languages be rendered as "lamp holders," "things on which lamps are placed," or even "poles that have lamps on top."

LAMPSTANDS

1.13   RSV   TEV

and in the midst of the lampstands one like a son of man, clothed with a long robe and with a golden girdle round his breast;	and among them there was what looked like a human being, wearing a robe that reached to his feet, and a gold band around his chest.

If the sentence seems too long and unwieldy, a translation can easily place a full stop at the end of verse 12 and begin a new sentence in verse 13 (FRCL, REB, BRCL).

In the midst of the lampstands: this can be stated "among the lampstands," "standing among them," or "in the middle of them." They may have been arranged in a row or in a circle, and in certain languages this will have to be made explicit. If the translator determines that the lampstands were in a circle, one may say "standing with the lampstands in a circle around him." However, if it is decided that the lampstands were in a row, one may say, for example, "Standing in the middle of the row of lampstands."

One like a son of man: what John sees is a figure that appears to be a human being. From what follows, the reader knows that this one is the glorified Christ. The phrase **a son of man** reflects Daniel 7.13, which RSV translates "there came one like a son of man." The title that in the Gospels Jesus uses of himself, "the Son of Man," is also obviously related to Daniel 7.13, but it does not seem likely that here the author means "one like the Son of Man" (as NRSV has it). In English, at least, "a son of man" (NIV, RNAB), or "a Son of man" (NJB), or even "a Son of Man" (Phps) means nothing. Many translations are like TEV: "a figure like a man" (Brc), "a being like a man" (AT), "One who resembled a human being" (Mft), "someone with a human appearance" (SPCL), "a being that looked like a man" (BRCL), "a figure like a man" (REB). It is recommended that translations follow one of these renderings.

Clothed with a long robe: this is a single piece of clothing that reaches to the feet, a vestment indicating dignity and rank. In some languages one must say "a long cloth outer garment."

A golden girdle round his breast: this is better translated by NRSV "a golden sash across his chest." It is impossible to determine what this "sash" or "band" (TEV) was made of; perhaps linen, with the use of much gold thread, or else a gold metal band. It served to keep the robe in place. NRSV "a golden sash across his chest" gives the picture of a sash coming down diagonally from one shoulder to the waist. Whatever it was, it was definitely not a belt around the waist (as NJB has it). If in a certain language one must state whether the sash was gold-colored or was actually made out of gold, it should be translated clearly one way or the other; for example, "a gold-colored band (sash)" or "a sash made of (the metal) gold."

An alternative translation model for this verse is the following:

A being who looked like a man was standing in the middle of the lampstands. He was wearing a robe (a long cloth outer garment) that reached to his feet, and a gold-colored sash across his chest.

1.14   RSV   TEV

his head and his hair were white as white wool, white as snow; his eyes were like a flame of fire,	His hair was white as wool, or as snow, and his eyes blazed like fire;

The description of the figure's head and eyes is like that of Daniel 7.9; 10.6.

His head and his hair: this is a way of saying "the hair on his head"; it is not to be thought that the skin of his head was white as snow; see TNT, RNAB "The hair of his head"; but in most languages one may say simply "hair."

White as white wool, white as snow: this is unnecessarily wordy, and something like "as white as wool, as white as snow" is sufficient; or, as REB has it, "as white as snow-white wool"; SPCL "were white as wool, or as snow." In a given language the appropriate model for whiteness must be used (see the Handbook on Matthew, 28.3). In some languages "egret's feathers" will be appropriate; in others, "cotton" or "cotton-wool." If no such model exists, something like "very, very white" may be used, or an ideophone.

His eyes were like a flame of fire: this can be said "his eyes blazed (or, shone) like fire." TNT "his eyes were blazing like fire." The figure is probably related to Daniel 10.6 (see the figure also in 2.18; 19.12). As commentators note, this is generally understood to represent fierce opposition to enemies.

1.15   RSV   TEV

his feet were like burnished bronze, refined as in a furnace, and his voice was like the sound of many waters;	his feet shone like brass that has been refined and polished, and his voice sounded like a roaring waterfall.

His feet were like burnished bronze, refined as in a furnace: this describes the appearance of the figure's feet; it does not say or imply that his feet were made of metal. The exact metal indicated by the Greek word translated **burnished bronze** is in doubt; the Greek word occurs only here and in 2.18, and nowhere else in Greek literature. The Arndt and Gingrich Lexicon has this entry: "Name of a metal or alloy, the exact nature of which is unknown." Swete says it was a mixed metal of great brilliance. Most translations have "bronze" or "brass"; TNT has "precious metal." The precise word **burnished** may be too high level for the average reader (it means "polished").

Refined as in a furnace: the process of refining metal ore involves a furnace, where the heat consumes the impurities and the liquid metal flows into a mold. Once the bronze artifact has been made, then it is polished so as to shine. A translation should not give the impression that the bronze was first polished and then refined in a furnace, as REB, for example, may imply: "like burnished bronze refined in a furnace." NIV's "like bronze glowing in a furnace" is not a satisfactory translation, nor is "as the finest bronze glows in a furnace" (Phps). Translators in many languages will need to make all of this information explicit and say, for example, "shone like bronze that has been refined (melted down to get rid of impurities) and then polished."

His voice was like the sound of many waters: see Ezek 43.2. The **many waters** may be a waterfall or the roaring sea. RNAB has "the sound of rushing water," FRCL "giant waterfalls" (also SPCL, BRCL), REB "a mighty torrent." The figure, of course, indicates the volume of sound, not its quality. One may also say "his voice was loud like . . . ."

1.16   RSV   TEV

in his right hand he held seven stars, from his mouth issued a sharp two-edged sword, and his face was like the sun shining in full strength.	He held seven stars in his right hand, and a sharp two-edged sword came out of his mouth. His face was as bright as the midday sun.

The same subject, "one like a son of man," continues in this verse, and the simple repetition of **his** throughout verses 13-16 should be adequate. However, in certain languages it will be helpful to reintroduce the subject, "one who looked like a human being," of verse 13 and say "The one who looked like a human being held . . . ."

In his right hand he held seven stars: the regular word for "star" should be used without any attempt to designate an object in the shape of a star. As verse 20 explains, these stars represent the "angels" of the seven churches.

From his mouth issued a sharp two-edged sword: where **sword** is not known, something like "knife," "large knife," "war knife," or even "a large knife like a machete," will be used; but a knife that has been sharpened on both sides may be a strange item to speak of, unless something like "a sharp knife that cuts on both sides" can be said. This sword represents the word, the message, of the glorified Christ (see Eph 6.17; Heb 4.12). Where RSV has **issued** TEV says "came out (of)." The image is that of a sword that extends from Christ's mouth, pointing straight out. It seems that only the blade of the sword protruded from Christ's mouth, and in languages where this information needs to be made explicit, one may say "the blade of a sharp two-edged sword (knife) protruded from . . . ," otherwise readers may get the picture that a complete sword—handle and blade—was extending out of Christ's mouth.

His face was like the sun shining in full strength: this simile should offer no great difficulty: "shone as bright as the noonday sun." See TNT "shone like the sun at mid-day"; BRCL "his face was shining like the noonday sun." In certain languages one does not speak about "mid-day" or "noon," but rather, like the Greek, refers to the "sun in full force" or "the sun at its highest point in the sky."

An alternative translation model for this verse is:

> The one who looked like a human being held seven stars in his right hand, and a sharp large knife (sword) that cuts on both sides protruded from his mouth. His face shone as bright as the sun when it reaches its highest point in the sky.

1.17-18   RSV   TEV

RSV	TEV
17 When I saw him, I fell at his feet as though dead. But he laid his right hand upon me, saying, "Fear not, I am the first and the last, 18 and the living one; I died, and behold I am alive for evermore, and I have the keys of Death and Hades.	17 When I saw him, I fell down at his feet like a dead man. He placed his right hand on me and said, "Don't be afraid! I am the first and the last. 18 I am the living one! I was dead, but now I am alive forever and ever. I have authority over death and the world of the dead.

When I saw him, I fell at his feet as though dead: John's reaction is like those of others in the Bible who were suddenly confronted by the presence of the Almighty; see Ezekiel 1.28; Daniel 8.17; 10.9; Matthew 17.6; Acts 26.14. The verb **fell** here does not mean that he collapsed to the ground in a dead faint, but that he prostrated himself at the feet of the glorified Christ, with forehead and body touching the ground in an act of worship and reverence, and lay there as though he were dead. Other ways of expressing **fell** are "bowed down low to the ground" or "spread myself flat on the ground." **At his feet** in certain languages will be rendered as "near his feet," "by his feet," or even "in front of his feet" or "in front of him."

As though dead may also be expressed as "without moving," "as if I was dead," or "completely rigid like a person who has died."

Both with his gesture (**he laid his right hand upon me**) and with his words (**Fear not**), the resurrected and glorified Christ reassures John, commissions him to write (verse 19), and explains the meaning of the seven stars and the seven lampstands (verse 20). In some languages the clause **he laid his right hand upon me** will be rendered as "he stretched out his right hand and placed it on me."

Fear not will often be expressed as "stop being afraid." **Fear** is rendered idiomatically in many languages; for example, "heart (or, liver) trembles," "liver shivers," "heart (liver) falls," or even "his heart came outside" (Chewa).

I am the first and the last: the meaning is the same as "I am the Alpha and the Omega" of verse 8.

The living one: this is also a divine title, and a translation may wish to make this explicit. It is used by the resurrected Christ, who had been raised from death and now lives forever. This phrase can also be expressed as "the one who has life" or "the one who gives life."

I died, and behold I am alive for evermore: the meaning of the first statement, in this context, is better expressed by TEV "I was dead" (also NRSV, REB, NJB).

Behold: this translates an interjection that calls attention to what follows (see 1.7); it occurs twenty-six times in this book. It is not represented by a verbal equivalent in various translations (thus FRCL, SPCL, BRCL, REB). NRSV has "and see," which at least is not obsolete, as **behold** is. A translator must decide if a distinct word is necessary in order to emphasize what follows. **I am alive for evermore** can also be rendered as "I have life that never ends." For the translation of the phrase **for evermore**, see the comments on 1.6, where the Greek for "for ever and ever" is the same expression as **for evermore** in this verse.

I have the keys of Death and Hades: keys are the symbol of authority, and by having been raised from death, the glorified Christ has the power over death and the world of the dead; he has the power to leave people in death or to open the gates of Hades (see Isa 38.10; Matt 16.18 [RSV footnote]) and let its inhabitants leave. This, of course, is a figure for the power to bring the dead to life. In some languages it will be possible to keep the symbol **keys** and say, for example, "I have the keys that give me the power to open the place where dead people are (the land of the dead) and bring them to life again." In cultures where keys do not exist, one may say "the things that open or close doors" or "the power to open doors." **Death**: in languages where one cannot talk about "power over death," one may say "power to raise people from death" or "power to cause dead people to be alive again." **Hades** (also 6.8; 20.13,14) is the Greek equivalent of Sheol, the Hebrew word for the world of the dead, which was sometimes pictured as an underground city, whose locked gates prevented the dead from leaving. It should not be translated "hell," that is, the place of punishment, which in the New Testament is called "Gehenna." SPCL has joined the two terms, "I have the keys of the kingdom of death," which a translation may choose to imitate.

An alternative translation model for this verse is:

> I am the one who is the source of (or, who gives) life. I was dead, but now I am alive for all time to come. I have the keys that give me the power to open or close the place where dead people are (or, the land of the dead) and bring them to life again.

1.19

RSV	TEV
Now write what you see, what is and what is to take place hereafter.	Write, then, the things you see, both the things that are now and the things that will happen afterward.

The command is the same as the one in verse 11, and it will be helpful in certain languages to say "write in the book (record) the things . . ." or "you must write in the book the things . . . ." The direct object **what you see** includes everything John will see and then record in the book. The two clauses that follow are not additional items but define explicitly the nature of what John will see: things present and things future, "both that which is happening now as well as that which will happen afterward" (FRCL; similarly SPCL, TEV). NJB shortens and combines the three into two: "Now write down all that you see of present happenings and what is still to come." The auxiliary verb "will" in "that will happen afterward" (TEV) translates a Greek verb that at times seems to express divine authority. The Arndt and Gingrich Lexicon defines this use of it as follows: "concerning an action that necessarily follows a divine decree, *is destined, must, will certainly.*"

An alternative translation model for this verse is:

> You must write (record) in the book all the things that you are seeing right now, and the things that will happen in the future (afterwards).

1.20   RSV   TEV

As for the mystery of the seven stars which you saw in my right hand, and the seven golden lampstands, the seven stars are the angels of the seven churches and the seven lampstands are the seven churches.	Here is the secret meaning of the seven stars that you see in my right hand, and of the seven gold lampstands: the seven stars are the angels of the seven churches, and the seven lampstands are the seven churches.

As for (TEV "Here is") points forward to the content of this verse, and translators should choose a word or phrase that functions in this way; for example, "The following is about . . ." or "What I say next is about . . . ."

The mystery of the seven stars: the Greek word for **mystery** here means "the secret meaning" (TEV, FRCL, RNAB, REB, BRCL, AT, Brc, Phps). In the New Testament a **mystery** is a secret truth or event that is not grasped by the human mind but is disclosed by God (see Eph 3.1-11). The Arndt and Gingrich Lexicon defines it as follows: "The secret thoughts, plans, and dispensations of God that are hidden from the human reason . . . and hence must be revealed to those for whom they are intended." It may also be expressed as "that which was not known before." The genitive phrase **of the seven stars** means "about the seven stars" or "concerning the seven stars"; it does not mean "belonging to the seven stars." This whole clause may be expressed as "The following is the secret meaning concerning (of) the seven stars."

You saw: this is how the great majority of translations render the verb; TEV, GECL, and BRCL have "you see." A decision for either the past or the present tense must be made in the light of the context. The latter seems to be the most likely, as John was obviously still seeing these things.

For the translation of **lampstands** see the comments on verse 12.

The angels of the seven churches: every one of the seven letters in chapters 2–3 begins "To the angel of the church in . . . ." There is no unanimity on what or whom the "angel" represents: either the pastor (or, presbyters) of the church, or some other representative of the church, or the guardian angel of each church, or, as Beasley-Murray puts it, "the heavenly counterparts of the earthly congregations." Most probably it refers to the heavenly guardian or representative of each church, just as there are of nations (Dan 10.13,20; 12.1) and individuals (Matt 18.10; Acts 12.15). In certain languages it will not be appropriate to say "angels of"; rather, translators must make the role of the angels explicit and say "the seven stars represent (stand for) the angels (heavenly messengers) who guard (watch over) the seven churches."

The word "angel" appears seventy-seven times in this book and, with the possible exception of "the angels of the seven churches," is always specifically a supernatural messenger, either of God or of Satan. Regardless of the interpretation readers will give, the translation should use the same word used elsewhere in the Bible to speak of God's heavenly messengers. On the translation of **angels** see verse 1. And for the translation of **churches** see verse 4.

Instead of following the order of the Greek sentence, a translation may say "This is what the seven stars . . . and the seven lampstands mean . . ." or "The meaning of . . . is this."

MAP LOCATING THE SEVEN CHURCHES OF ASIA MINOR

B. The Letters to the Seven Churches

(2.1–3.22)

B-1. The Message to Ephesus   2.1-7

RSV

1 "To the angel of the church in Ephesus write: 'The words of him who holds the seven stars in his right hand, who walks among the seven golden lampstands.
2 "'I know your works, your toil and your patient endurance, and how you cannot bear evil men but have tested those who call themselves apostles but are not, and found them to be false; 3 I know you are enduring patiently and bearing up for my name's sake, and you have not grown weary. 4 But I have this against you, that you have abandoned the love you had at first. 5 Remember then from what you have fallen, repent and do the works you did at first. If not, I will come to you and remove your lampstand from its place, unless you repent. 6 Yet this you have, you hate the works of the Nicolaitans, which I also hate. 7 He who has an ear, let him hear what the Spirit says to the churches. To him who conquers I will grant to eat of the tree of life, which is in the paradise of God.'

TEV

The Message to Ephesus

1 "To the angel of the church in Ephesus write:
"This is the message from the one who holds the seven stars in his right hand and who walks among the seven gold lampstands. 2 I know what you have done; I know how hard you have worked and how patient you have been. I know that you cannot tolerate evil men and that you have tested those who say they are apostles but are not, and have found out that they are liars. 3 You are patient, you have suffered for my sake, and you have not given up. 4 But this is what I have against you: you do not love me now as you did at first. 5 Think how far you have fallen! Turn from your sins and do what you did at first. If you don't turn from your sins, I will come to you and take your lampstand from its place. 6 But this is what you have in your favor: you hate what the Nicolaitans do, as much as I do.
7 "If you have ears, then, listen to what the Spirit says to the churches!
"To those who win the victory I will give the right to eat the fruit of the tree of life that grows in the Garden of God.

SECTION HEADING: TEV "The Message to Ephesus" may also be expressed as "The special words to the Christians in the city of Ephesus" or "The one who is like a human being gives a message to the Christians in Ephesus."

2.1   RSV

"To the angel of the church in Ephesus write: 'The words of him who holds the seven stars in his right hand, who walks among the seven golden

TEV

"To the angel of the church in Ephesus write:
"This is the message from the one who holds the seven stars in his right

lampstands.   **hand and who walks among the seven gold lampstands.**

It should be noticed that the speaker continues to be the glorified Christ, who at 1.17 begins to speak to John and continues to do so to the end of chapter 3.

Since this is the beginning of a new chapter, it will be helpful in some languages to say "And then he said to me . . ." or "The one whose form was like that of a human being then said to me . . . ." A translator may also wish to introduce the speaker at the beginning of each of the seven letters, but it is not easy to decide how to identify him. "He said to me" is about the only way of doing this; it is not appropriate in this context to say "The risen Christ said to me" or "Jesus Christ said to me." But each letter begins by identifying the speaker in terms of the description in 1.12-16, so the reader of the text is told at once who the speaker is.

Notice that RSV has two levels of quotation marks, using double and single marks, and translators in certain languages may wish to follow this system. TEV, however, has only the double quotation marks throughout. NRSV is like TEV. A translator should use the system that is easiest for the readers to understand.

To the angel of the church in Ephesus: for **the angel** see the comment at 1.20. In this context **angel** more likely refers to a person who represents the church. Thus translators may render **the angel of the church** as "the representative of the church . . . ," or even "messenger of the church."

Write: a more natural order for a command in English and other languages is to begin with the verb: "Write this message (or, letter) to . . . ," "You must write . . . ," or "I want (or, command) you to write . . . ."

Ephesus was the most important city in the Roman province of Asia; it was a busy seaport, had a thriving commerce, and was the center of the cult of the goddess Artemis (see Acts 19.27,35), and also a place where magical arts were practiced (Acts 19.19). As the book of Acts shows, it soon became a very important center of Christian activity, and at the time of the writing of this letter, it may have been the most important Christian church in the Roman empire.

In many languages it will be necessary to identify Ephesus as a city. In some cultures, however, there are no human settlements that are the equivalent of cities. People live in villages or small groups of houses, often without protective walls or fences. In such cases it will be necessary to refer to a city as "a large (or, chief) village" or "a large group of houses surrounded by a strong wall."

The words of: RSV's incomplete sentence follows the form of the Greek text; TEV has a complete sentence, with the use of "This is the message from . . ."; one may also say "The following is what the one who . . . says."

Who holds the seven stars in his right hand: see 1.16.

Who walks among the seven golden lampstands: see 1.12-13. Here the added information **walks** is given, implying that he watches and takes care of the churches.

An alternative translation model for this verse is the following:

> He said to me, "I want you to write a letter to the representative of God's group of people in the city of Ephesus, as follows:

" 'The one who holds the seven stars in his right hand and who walks among the seven lampstands says the following words (sends this message) to you . . . .' "

2.2 RSV	TEV
" 'I know your works, your toil and your patient endurance, and how you cannot bear evil men but have tested those who call themselves apostles but are not, and found them to be false;	I know what you have done; I know how hard you have worked and how patient you have been. I know that you cannot tolerate evil men and that you have tested those who say they are apostles but are not, and have found out that they are liars.

Many languages have different forms for the singular and the plural second person pronouns and corresponding verb forms. In this letter the formal addressee is "the angel of the church," singular, whereas the actual addressees are the members of the various churches, plural. Translators must decide whether or not they can follow the Greek of these letters and use the second person singular. In some languages (such as Spanish, Portuguese, French) the second person plural is normally used. In languages that have the same form for the singular and the plural (such as English), it may be well, after the address "to the angel of the church . . . ," to start the letter itself with something like "I know what you Christians in Ephesus have done . . . ."

I know can be variously translated as "I am aware of" or "It has come to my attention."

Your works: here and elsewhere (2.19; 3.1,8,15) **works** are not just specific deeds but the manner of life, the behavior of these people: "I know the life that you have lived" (Brc), which is more inclusive than "I know what you have done" (AT, Phps, TEV). Some, like SPCL and FRCL, say "all that you have done." The rest of the verse and verse 3 cite specific matters included in this opening general statement.

Your toil: here **toil** means their persistent and painful struggles to maintain their Christian profession. FRCL has "the pain you have taken." The general "how hard you have worked" (TEV, Phps) may not be specific enough; the terms used should not imply working hard for a living. Consequently something like "I know how hard you have worked as Christians (or, as believers in Jesus Christ)," "I know that you have had a difficult time in following Christ as you should," or ". . . in doing your Christian duties."

For **patient endurance** see 1.9. As elsewhere in this book (2.3,19; 3.10; 14.12) this is the endurance of suffering and persecution that Christians were experiencing, and were to experience in the future.

Notice that in Greek the possessive pronoun **your** comes only after **patient endurance**, so that **toil** and **patient endurance** are governed by the one pronoun and may be taken to refer not to two separate matters but to two aspects of the one characteristic being praised: "I know how patient you have been as you have worked hard at your Christian duties." Most translations, however, take it for granted that two distinct qualities are being praised: the first one is taken up in the rest of verse

2 and the second one in verse 3. Some ancient manuscripts and early versions have the possessive **your** after **toil** also.

And how you cannot bear evil men: TEV begins a new sentence here, repeating "I know that"; NRSV does the same. "To bear" means to tolerate, to put up with. **Cannot bear** is expressed idiomatically in certain languages as "don't have a big heart towards" or "have a small heart towards." It means that one opposes the people indicated.

These **evil men** include all kinds of people, men and women alike, whom the (true) believers in Ephesus could not tolerate, and of whom the "false apostles" are a specific example. It is not possible to identify them with certainty. Most commentators take them to be the same as the Nicolaitans in verse 6 (see also 2.14,20-24) and identify them as teachers, in or out of the churches, who were spreading false doctrines. Most languages are quite rich in words and expressions for "bad" people, and no particular caution is needed except to make sure that the term used refers to bad moral or spiritual qualities, not to shameful physical characteristics or disgraceful social behavior.

But have tested those who call themselves apostles but are not: the verb "to test" means to apply certain procedures in order to determine the truth or falsity of a claim. The kind of test to be applied varies according to the situation. In the case of the people who claimed to be **apostles**, the test probably involved noticing their behavior and their teachings, and perhaps seeking information about them from other churches. Another way of translating **tested those who . . .** is "tried to find out the genuineness (validity) of those who . . . ." Here **apostles** is not used in the restricted sense of the twelve apostles of Jesus, but in the broader sense of people sent to be traveling Christian teachers, like Paul and Barnabas, who were genuine apostles (and see also the false apostles on whom Paul pours such scorn in 2 Cor 11.5,13; 12.11). In some languages **apostles** in this context may be translated as "Christ's messengers."

And found them to be false: as a result of such tests, the people at Ephesus had decided that the claims of these people to be authentic apostles were lies. RNAB has a good translation, "and discovered that they are impostors" (so also AT). One may also say "and found that they were not what they said they were," or even "and found that they were lying."

It is recommended that, unlike RSV, this verse be divided up into two or three complete sentences, like NJB, TEV, NRSV, and other modern translations.

An alternative translation model for this verse is:

> I know how you have lived your life. I know how very hard you have worked as Christians and how you have put up with difficulties. I know that you cannot tolerate wicked people. You have tried to find out the genuineness of those people who say that they are Christ's messengers (apostles), and you have found that they are lying.

2.3   RSV   TEV

I know you are enduring patiently and   You are patient, you have suffered for
bearing up for my name's sake, and you   my sake, and you have not given up.
have not grown weary.

I know you are enduring patiently: the Greek text does not have **I know** at
the beginning of the verse (see TEV), but a translation may choose to include it for
a more natural transition. This statement repeats what was said in verse 2.

And bearing up for my name's sake: here the same verb "to bear" used in
verse 2 appears, but in a different sense; it is practically synonymous with **enduring
patiently**. Here "to bear up" implies suffering of some sort; so FRCL "you have
suffered," SPCL and BRCL "you have suffered greatly."

For my name's sake: as in many other places in the Bible, "name" stands for
the person, and here the person is Christ. They are suffering for Christ's sake, that
is, they are suffering because they are determined to be faithful Christians. This
indicates persecution, either the occasional kind inflicted by a pagan society, or else
the official organized persecution started by the authorities.

And you have not grown weary: they had not given up, they had not
renounced their faith. It is to be noticed that the Greek verb here is related to the
noun "toil" of verse 2, implying here "not to tire of toil," meaning "haven't tired of
following me." Other ways of translating this clause are "and you have never given
up following me" or "and your hearts have always remained strong as you follow
me."

2.4   RSV   TEV

But I have this against you, that you   But this is what I have against you: you
have abandoned the love you had at   do not love me now as you did at first.
first.

But I have this against you: this is a word of censure. The phrase "to have
against" reflects quite faithfully the Greek idiom, which is carried over also into
Spanish, French, and Portuguese. Otherwise something like "But there is something
in you I disapprove of" can be used, or "But I have this criticism to make of you,"
or "But I must scold you about something."

You have abandoned the love you had at first: this love may be their love
for one another as Christians, or their love for Christ. Some commentators point out
that the praise lavished on them in verses 2-3 assumes that they had continued to
love Christ with the same fervor they had had at the first. Some translations (TEV,
FRCL, BRCL) explicitly have Christ as the object of that love; most commentators,
however, favor the fellow believers as the object of their love (so Mft). This kind of
love expresses itself in helping one another in the Christian life, in being loyal to one
another, and acting always in the best interests of the whole body of believers. TOB
has "the fervor," that is, the enthusiasm they had shown when they first became
Christians. On the translation of **love** see 1.5b.

41

At first: this means "when you became Christians," "at the beginning of your Christian life," or even "when you first believed in me."

In translating this passage, if a noun for "love" is used, no object is usually required; for example, "your love" or "the love you had." But if an event word is used (which is generally preferable), it is recommended that something like the following be said: "you no longer love one another as you did when you became Christians" or "your hearts (or, livers) are no longer warm towards one another . . . ."

An alternative translation model for this verse is:

> But I must scold (criticize) you about this: you no longer love your fellow Christians as you did when you first believed in me.

2.5   RSV   TEV

RSV	TEV
Remember then from what you have fallen, repent and do the works you did at first. If not, I will come to you and remove your lampstand from its place, unless you repent.	Think how far you have fallen! Turn from your sins and do what you did at first. If you don't turn from your sins, I will come to you and take your lampstand from its place.

The earnest warning to **repent** is emphasized by the use of the verb twice. The church in Ephesus runs the danger of being no church at all because of this lack of Christian love.

Remember then from what you have fallen: the present tense of the imperative **Remember** stresses a continuous state of mind: "Keep on remembering," "Keep on thinking about," or "Never forget." The command is that they keep in mind what they used to be when they became Christians. The literal representation of the figure **from what you have fallen** may give the wrong impression of an actual place; this is how NJB can be understood: "Think where you were before you fell." RSV's rendering can have a similar meaning. So it is better to render this clause as "Remember how far you have fallen" (AT, Phps, RNAB). The verb "to fall" is also used of moral or spiritual downfall in Romans 11.11; 1 Corinthians 10.12. In English the verb "to backslide" is used by some Christian groups to designate Christians who have committed serious crimes.

Repent: this can be rendered "change your ways," "Turn from your sins" (TEV), "turn your back on sinning," or "stop sinning." The aorist imperative designates a decisive act: "change your attitude" (FRCL); "turn back to God" (SPCL). There are various ways of expressing repentance, and a translator should use one that denotes a thorough, radical change, and not just a temporary feeling of regret or remorse that does not include a determination to abandon the sin. A translator should consult the Handbooks on Matthew 3.2 and Mark 1.4 for further comments on the translation of the word **repent**. See 1.5b of this Handbook for ways to translate "sin," or "sinfulness."

And do the works you did at first: as in verse 2, **the works** here is a way of speaking of their way of life, their Christian behavior. Brc has "live again the life you lived, when you first became Christians," and FRCL "act as you did at the beginning." REB "do as once you did" is too brief and vague.

In the warning, for emphasis, the text has **If not** at the beginning of the sentence, followed by **unless you repent** at the end. In many languages it will be stylistically more natural to combine the two, as NJB does, "or else, if you will not repent, ..." However, in other languages it will be sufficient to say "If you will not do this."

I will come to you and remove your lampstand from its place: this "coming" of Christ is not the final coming in glory, but his immediate coming to punish these unfaithful believers. In certain languages, if Christ is considered the focus of attention, **come** should be translated as "go"; for example, "I will go to you." The threat **remove your lampstand** means the end of this community of believers as a church. The figurative language must not be abandoned in translation. The question as to *where* the lampstand will be moved to is not addressed by the text. See 1.12 on the translation of **lampstand**. **Its place** may also be expressed as "where it was standing."

An alternative translation model for this verse is:

> Never forget (Remember) how far you have fallen into sin! You must stop sinning and live your life as you did when you first believed in me. If you continue sinning, I will come (go) to you and punish you by taking away your lampstand from where it has been standing (situated).

2.6   RSV   TEV

Yet this you have, you hate the works of the Nicolaitans, which I also hate.   But this is what you have in your favor: you hate what the Nicolaitans do, as much as I do.

Here is one more word of praise, perhaps to soften the severity of the censure in verse 5.

Yet this you have: "But you have this in your favor," "This, however, is to your credit," "But I will praise you for this," or "Here is a good thing that you are doing."

You hate the works of the Nicolaitans: they also appear in 2.15, in the letter to Pergamum. The word means "the followers of Nicolaus," but there is no way of deciding who this Nicolaus was, if indeed he was a real person and not a fictitious character. Aside from what is said about the Nicolaitans here and in 2.14-15 (and perhaps in 2.20,24), there is no precise information on their origin or activities. Most commentators see them as Gnostic teachers who, on the basis of their doctrine that the material and spiritual realms are completely separate, taught that immoral conduct does not affect the spiritual life. **Hate** may be expressed as "despise," "not like to look at," or idiomatically in some languages as "heart is not warm towards." Here **the works**, as in the other instances (verses 2,5), mean everything they do and are.

Which I also hate: it is well to have this come at the end, to make for the proper emphasis. TEV "as much as I do" is a possible way of making the comparison.

2.7   RSV   TEV

RSV	TEV
He who has an ear, let him hear what the Spirit says to the churches. To him who conquers I will grant to eat of the tree of life, which is in the paradise of God.'	"If you have ears, then, listen to what the Spirit says to the churches! "To those who win the victory I will give the right to eat the fruit of the tree of life that grows in the Garden of God.

He who has an ear, let him hear what the Spirit says to the churches: this injunction appears in all seven letters. It is much like Christ's saying, found in all three Synoptic Gospels (see Matt 13.9; Mark 4.9; Luke 8.8). It is addressed to all believers in Ephesus, all of whom are hearing the letter being read to them. The exclusively masculine **He who has** is easily dealt with by the use of the plural, "Those who have . . . ."

The literal **who has an ear**, taken to the extreme, can sound ridiculous. Which of the two ears? Is there anyone who doesn't have an ear? The organ of hearing, "ear," represents here the sense of hearing. So it is better to translate "If you can hear." Or, as REB has it, "You have ears, so hear . . . ," or "You can hear can't you, so listen." Or note AT "Let anyone who can hear listen to . . . ," or Phps "Let every listener hear . . . ." The meaning of "let" in such a context is a way of phrasing a command, an order, in English; it does not mean permission.

For **the Spirit** a translation may need to say "the Holy Spirit" or "the Spirit of God." And the message, **what . . . says to the churches** is precisely the message of the letters and of the whole book. A given letter is addressed not only to one particular church, but to all the churches. God's Spirit speaks to them through the risen Christ. On the translation of **Spirit** or "Holy Spirit," see 1.10, and on **churches** see 1.4.

To him who conquers: this is not what the Spirit is saying to the churches but is a continuation of the words of the risen Christ. The military figure "to conquer" (see also 2.11,17,26; 3.5; 12.11; 21.7) has no direct object; what is implied is all that is opposed to the Christian faith. The Christian life is seen as a combat against the forces of evil. If an object is required, perhaps "forces of evil" can be used. The exclusively male rendering of RSV can be easily remedied by using the plural form, "To those who conquer . . . ." **Conquers** may also be expressed as "has the victory over" or "defeats."

I will grant to eat of the tree of life, which is in the paradise of God: the risen Christ promises spiritual food, the food of eternal life in the coming Kingdom of God or Christ. **I will grant to eat** is not a natural expression in modern English; NRSV is better, "I will give permission to eat," and REB "I will give the right to eat." The imagery is drawn from Genesis 2.9; 3.22,24 (see also Rev 22.2,14). The phrase **of the tree** means "the fruits of the tree." The **tree of life** is "the life-giving tree" or "the tree that gives life," not "the tree that lives (forever)," as a literal translation may suggest.

The tree grows **in the paradise of God**, that is, in the garden of Eden, a symbol of heaven (as in the Septuagint of Ezek 28.13; 31.8). The Greek word translated **paradise** means a garden, or a fruit orchard, and became a way of speaking of heaven (see Luke 23.43; 2 Cor 12.3).

Alternative translation models for this verse are:

> You can hear, can't you? Then listen to what (the things that) the Spirit of God says to the churches.
>
> To those people who defeat the forces of evil, I will give permission (allow) to eat the fruit from the tree that gives life, which grows in the heavenly Garden of God.

Or:

> You have ears, so you must listen to what the Spirit of God says to the groups of God's people.
>
> I will give those people who are victorious over the forces of evil the right to eat the fruit . . . .

B-2. The Message to Smyrna   2.8-11

RSV

8 "And to the angel of the church in Smyrna write: 'The words of the first and the last, who died and came to life.

9 "'I know your tribulation and your poverty (but you are rich) and the slander of those who say that they are Jews and are not, but are a synagogue of Satan. 10 Do not fear what you are about to suffer. Behold, the devil is about to throw some of you into prison, that you may be tested, and for ten days you will have tribulation. Be faithful unto death, and I will give you the crown of life. 11 He who has an ear, let him hear what the Spirit says to the churches. He who conquers shall not be hurt by the second death.'

TEV

The Message to Smyrna

8 "To the angel of the church in Smyrna write:

"This is the message from the one who is the first and the last, who died and lived again. 9 I know your troubles; I know that you are poor—but really you are rich! I know the evil things said against you by those who claim to be Jews but are not; they are a group that belongs to Satan! 10 Don't be afraid of anything you are about to suffer. Listen! The Devil will put you to the test by having some of you thrown into prison, and your troubles will last ten days. Be faithful to me, even if it means death, and I will give you life as your prize of victory.

11 "If you have ears, then, listen to what the Spirit says to the churches!

"Those who win the victory will not be hurt by the second death.

SECTION HEADING: TEV "The Message to Smyrna." See heading at 2.1.

2.8   RSV   TEV

"**And to the angel of the church in Smyrna write: 'The words of the first**

"**To the angel of the church in Smyrna write:**

and the last, who died and came to life.   **"This is the message from the one who is the first and the last, who died and lived again.**

The same opening formula is used in 2.1, with the exception of **And** at the beginning (it also appears in the next five letters). The name **Smyrna** means "myrrh"; it was a prosperous seaport city and had many Jewish residents. Sweet points out that it was the only one of the seven cities where Christianity never died out.

The words of: see the comments at 2.1.

The first and the last: see the comments at 1.17.

Who died and came to life: see the comments at 1.18. Here, instead of the continuative present "I am living," the Greek text has the aorist "I lived," that is, "I came (back) to life," "[I] lived again" (TEV), "I returned to life," or "I became alive again."

In light of the imminent persecution and the possible martyrdom of some of the believers (verse 10), the phrases used of Christ have special significance for the Christians in Smyrna.

2.9   RSV   TEV

" **'I know your tribulation and your poverty (but you are rich) and the slander of those who say that they are Jews and are not, but are a synagogue of Satan.**   I know your troubles; I know that you are poor—but really you are rich! I know the evil things said against you by those who claim to be Jews but are not; they are a group that belongs to Satan!

I know your tribulation and your poverty: for **I know** see the comments at 2.2. The translation here should do the same for **your** and **you** as in the letter to Ephesus. For **tribulation** see the comments at 1.9. The **poverty** John speaks of is material and may have been the result of their possessions having been confiscated by the authorities; but there is no evidence for this. The word **poverty** occurs in this book only here; the adjective "poor," in a literal sense, appears in 13.16. In some languages words for **poverty** or "poor" are often lacking. This is often the case where only certain people in a culture own material things. In such cases one may say "you have nothing" or "you are like those who live far from the chief's compound."

(But you are rich): this parenthetical statement turns the situation around; they may be poor materially but are rich spiritually (see 3.18; 1 Cor 4.8). The situation in Laodicea is exactly the contrary; they boast that they are rich but are in fact poor (3.17-18).

If possible the translation should preserve the seeming contradiction in the text. If, however, a literal translation will mislead the reader, the translation can say "I know that you have been persecuted and that you are poor. But in spiritual matters (matters of the heart) you are really rich."

The slander of those who say that they are Jews and are not: the text doesn't specify what kind of slander this was, but it probably consisted of false accusations made by their enemies for the purpose of getting them into trouble with the Roman authorities. The noun translated here as **slander** appears also in 13.1,5,6; 17.3. Its related Greek verb, "to blaspheme," "to curse" (13.6; 16.9,11,21) always has God as object. In translating this phrase it should be made clear that these false accusations were directed against the believers in Smyrna. REB has "I know how you are slandered by," and FRCL "I know the evil things they say about you."

Their detractors falsely claim to be **Jews**. What does this mean? We must keep in mind the fact that John, the writer of Revelation, is himself a Jew. The term may be used in the literal sense of people of the Jewish race, and given the large number of Jews in Smyrna, it is probable that these are Jews. But in denying their claim to be "Jews," John is using the word in the extended sense of "God's (chosen) people," which Jews claimed to be. For him it is the Christians, and not the Jews, who are the chosen people (see Paul's definition of authentic Jews in Rom 2.28-29; 9.8; Gal 6.15-16). John's position is that Christians are the true people of God. If translators feel that translating **Jews** literally will give the wrong impression to readers, it will be helpful to say "those who say (claim) to be God's people, but are not."

These Jews in the ethnic sense are not Jews in the spiritual sense (also 3.9); they are **a synagogue of Satan**. John purposely uses the Jewish term **synagogue** (also 3.9), the name for a group of Jews meeting in one place for religious purposes. The phrase **of Satan** means either that they belong to Satan, or else that they serve Satan instead of serving God (see John 8.44).

Satan, the Hebrew word for "adversary," "opponent," is the name given to the Devil, the ruler of all evil spiritual forces, and "the synagogue of Satan" stands in opposition to "the synagogue of Yahweh" (thus the Septuagint translation of Num 16.3; 20.4). **Satan** is used in the New Testament as a proper noun, and translators should transliterate it, writing it in the way in which it would be pronounced in their own language. The word used to translate **synagogue** should not be a building or a place but a group, "an assembly," "a congregation" (FRCL, SPCL); NJB has "members of the synagogue of Satan."

An alternative translation model for this verse is:

> I know (am aware of) the troubles you are undergoing. I know that you have few material possessions—but you are rich in things of the heart (or, spirit). I know about those who claim that they are God's chosen people (Jews), but are not. They say evil things about you, but they are really members of a group that belongs to Satan.

2.10 RSV | TEV

Do not fear what you are about to suffer. Behold, the devil is about to throw some of you into prison, that you may be tested, and for ten days you will have tribulation. Be faithful unto death, and I will give you the crown of life.

Don't be afraid of anything you are about to suffer. Listen! The Devil will put you to the test by having some of you thrown into prison, and your troubles will last ten days. Be faithful to me, even if it means death, and I will give you life as your prize of victory.

After the praise (verse 9) comes the warning (verse 10); there is no condemnation.

Do not fear what you are about to suffer: often the word **fear** is expressed in certain languages idiomatically as "heart (or, liver) falls." **What (you . . . suffer)** means "the things . . . ," or "anything (you . . . suffer)" (TEV). The Greek auxiliary verb translated **are about to** may carry the overtones of the divine will and plan; what is happening to them is in accordance with God's will. In translation it is not advisable, however, to explicitly make God the subject; something like "you will certainly (or, surely) suffer" is preferable. This clause may also be rendered as "Do not be afraid (let your heart fall) as you think about the things that you will certainly suffer."

Behold: see comments at 1.7. NRSV has "Beware."

The devil is about to throw some of you into prison: the Devil is the same as Satan, the ruler of the forces of evil; the name means "accuser" or "slanderer." In cultures where Christianity is known only a recent, a suitable term for **the devil** (Satan) may not yet have been agreed upon by the Christian community. Translators in concurrence with the churches should carefully select a term that adequately translates the Biblical idea of "Devil." Often in some cultures people recognize an evil supernatural spirit being who is active in the universe. The term used for this being may be a good translation of **the devil** if it refers to a spirit of demonic origin. In other cultures people talk about the "chief" or "head" of the evil or bad spirits. The title for this bad spirit can almost certainly be employed for **the devil** in the present context. However, if a suitable term cannot be found, then the name "Satan" should be used in contexts where that proper noun appears.

Throw some of you into prison: if at all possible the translation should be quite literal, "the Devil is going to," unless the readers may be led to think that the Devil, in person, will arrest these Christians and lead them off to prison; in this case something like "the Devil will cause your enemies to throw some of you into prison" or "the Devil will have some of you thrown into prison" is preferable.

The verb **throw** does not mean that someone will actually pick the Christians up physically and throw them into a prison. If translating **throw** literally gives this wrong meaning, one may say "arrest some of you and put you into prison" or "cause some of you to be arrested and put into prison." **Prison** or "jail (gaol)": most societies have a place where criminals or wrongdoers are confined. Translators should use that term here. If, however, in a certain culture criminals are not kept in a prison but are turned over to their families or relatives to watch over, then one can express this clause as "arrest some of you so that you may be punished."

That you may be tested: it should be noticed that it is the jailing itself of some of these Christians that is the "test," so it may be better to translate "and in this way you will be tested." The use of the verb "to test" here is different from its use in verse 2; here the purpose is either their enemies' attempt to get them to renounce their Christian faith, or else (which is more likely) it is part of the divine plan to test the genuineness of their faith. Notice that all the believers in Smyrna will be tested by the jailing of some of them, and not only those who would actually be thrown into prison. Translators in languages that do not use the passive will have to decide who is the agent of the action in this context, enemies or God; for example, "in order that your [plural] enemies may test you" or "in order that God may test you [plural]." Either agent is possible, but if translators pick God as the agent, they should avoid giving the impression to readers that God is in league with Satan (see the second translation model at the end of the comments on this verse).

And for ten days you will have tribulation: in apocalyptic literature **ten days** stands for a short, limited amount of time. Some commentators connect the phrase to Daniel 1.14. For **tribulation** see the comments at 1.9. Other ways of phrasing this clause are "and you will go through hard times for ten days" or "and you will suffer trials for a short time."

Be faithful unto death, and I will give you the crown of life: the injunction **Be faithful** means "Be loyal to your Christian commitment," "Be faithful Christians," "Be faithful to me," or "Never give up believing in me," that is, acknowledge me as your Lord and obey me. The adjective **faithful** is used of believers in 2.13; 17.14; of Jesus Christ in 1.5; 3.14; 19.11.

Unto death: this means "until you die," not the normal end of life but death as the result of persecution and punishment. Beckwith paraphrases, "Be ready to meet the extreme penalty of death, if it should come to that." The meaning is brought out well by Mft, "Be faithful, though you have to die for it"; Brc "Prove yourself to be willing to die for your faith," and NJB "Even if you have to die, keep faithful." This phrase may also be expressed as "even if it means that you will be killed," or in languages that do not use the passive, "even if it means that they will kill you" ("they" being an unknown agent).

I will give you the crown of life: the Greek word translated **crown** means in a context like this the wreath made of laurel leaves that was given to the winner in an athletic contest (see 1 Cor 9.25; 2 Tim 2.5). The phrase **the crown of life** appears also in James 1.12; see also "the crown of righteousness" in 2 Timothy 4.8, and "the crown of glory" in 1 Peter 5.4. The genitive construction **the crown of life** means life as the crown, life as the prize, which Christ will give to those who are faithful. This is eternal life, life in the coming Kingdom. Thus Brc "I will give you life as your victor's crown," and SPCL "I will give you life as the prize."

The second and third sentences in this verse are both fairly complex, with various subordinate clauses. In the second sentence a translation must maintain a natural and easily-followed relation between the act of being thrown into prison, the purpose of the act ("to be tested"), the extent of time involved, and the fact that only some of the believers will be jailed, although this will be a test for all of them. And in the third sentence it is especially the meaning of "until death" that must be faithfully expressed, so that it means martyrdom, being put to death for being a faithful Christian. The genitive construction "the crown of life" should not appear as "the crown that belongs to life" or "the crown that life gives." Life, eternal life, is the victory prize awarded by Christ.

Alternative translation models for this verse are:

> Don't be afraid of the suffering you will most certainly undergo. Listen! The Devil is about to cause (have) your enemies to arrest some of you and put you in prison in order that they may test you. You will experience big troubles for ten days. But don't ever give up believing in me even if you are killed (must die), because I will give you eternal life as your victory prize just like a crown (garland).

Or:

Don't let your heart (liver) fall as you think of the things you are about to suffer. Beware! The Devil will have people arrest some of you in the near future and put you in prison. And God will test you. You will experience suffering for ten days. You must always be loyal to me even if it means that people kill you. I will give you real life as the prize of victory.

2.11   RSV   TEV

He who has an ear, let him hear what the Spirit says to the churches. He who conquers shall not be hurt by the second death.'	"If you have ears, then, listen to what the Spirit says to the churches! "Those who win the victory will not be hurt by the second death.

For the first sentence, **He who . . . to the churches**, see the comments at 2.7.

He who conquers shall not be hurt by the second death: the exclusively masculine "He who" can be made inclusive of men and women by using the plural "They who," "Those who," or the indefinite "Whoever" (NRSV). For **who conquers** see the comments at 2.7. If a direct object is needed in translation, something like "the forces of evil" can be said. See Jesus' statement in John 16.33.

Be hurt: here the meaning "to hurt" in connection with **the second death** seems rather mild. This verb is used with people as the object in 9.10,19 ("wound"); 11.5 ("harm"); 22.11 ("do evil"). Here the meaning is almost that of "will not be affected by," "will be spared the (evil) effects of." What it means, of course, is that such people will not experience **the second death**, which is spiritual death, eternal death, in contrast with the natural death that awaits all human beings. It is the destruction of unrepentant sinners in the lake of fire (20.6,14; 21.8). Those who conquer may be killed physically (the first death), but they will not die eternally (the second death).

If there is some trouble translating meaningfully **the second death**, an explanatory phrase may be added, "that is, eternal (or, spiritual) death," or else a footnote may direct the reader to 20.14,15; 21.8.

Alternative translation models for the second half of this verse are:

Those who defeat the forces of evil will not suffer the evil effects of the second death.

Or:

The second death will not hurt those who conquer (are victorious over) the powers of evil.

B-3. The Message to Pergamum   2.12-17

RSV	TEV
	The Message to Pergamum

12 "And to the angel of the church in Pergamum write: 'The words of him who has the sharp two-edged sword.

13 " 'I know where you dwell, where Satan's throne is; you hold fast my name and you did not deny my faith even in the days of Antipas my witness, my faithful one, who was killed among you, where Satan dwells. 14 But I have a few things against you: you have some there who hold the teaching of Balaam, who taught Balak to put a stumbling block before the sons of Israel, that they might eat food sacrificed to idols and practice immorality. 15 So you also have some who hold the teaching of the Nicolaitans. 16 Repent then. If not, I will come to you soon and war against them with the sword of my mouth. 17 He who has an ear, let him hear what the Spirit says to the churches. To him who conquers I will give some of the hidden manna, and I will give him a white stone, with a new name written on the stone which no one knows except him who receives it.'

12 "To the angel of the church in Pergamum write:

"This is the message from the one who has the sharp two-edged sword. 13 I know where you live, there where Satan has his throne. You are true to me, and you did not abandon your faith in me even during the time when Antipas, my faithful witness, was killed there where Satan lives. 14 But there are a few things I have against you: there are some among you who follow the teaching of Balaam, who taught Balak how to lead the people of Israel into sin by persuading them to eat food that had been offered to idols and to practice sexual immorality. 15 In the same way you have people among you who follow the teaching of the Nicolaitans. 16 Now turn from your sins! If you don't, I will come to you soon and fight against those people with the sword that comes out of my mouth.

17 "If you have ears, then, listen to what the Spirit says to the churches!

"To those who win the victory I will give some of the hidden manna. I will also give each of them a white stone on which is written a new name that no one knows except the one who receives it.

SECTION HEADING: TEV "The Message to Pergamum." See the suggestion at 2.1.

2.12 RSV	TEV
"And to the angel of the church in Pergamum write: 'The words of him who has the sharp two-edged sword.	"To the angel of the church in Pergamum write: "This is the message from the one who has the sharp two-edged sword.

This letter begins the same way as the previous letter (see 2.8). **Pergamum** was not as large a commercial city as Ephesus, but it was a very important religious center, with temples dedicated to Zeus and other gods, including Asclepias, the god of healing. Pergamum was also the leading center of the worship of Roman emperors, the first city in the province in which a temple had been dedicated to "the divine Augustus and the goddess Roma." When the kingdom of Pergamum became part of the Roman Empire in 133 B.C., the city of Pergamum became the capital of the province of Asia. It is not certain, however, whether it was still the capital at the end of the first century A.D. It was in Pergamum that the process of turning animal skins into parchment was developed; the word "parchment" is derived from the name **Pergamum**.

The words of: see comments at 2.1.

Him who has the sharp two-edged sword: see the comments at 1.16. So the verb **has** does not mean "carries" as such; it only indicates possession, and translators should use a verb that has this rather ambiguous meaning.

2.13   RSV   TEV

" 'I know where you dwell, where   I know where you live, there where
Satan's throne is; you hold fast my   Satan has his throne. You are true to
name and you did not deny my faith   me, and you did not abandon your faith
even in the days of Antipas my witness,   in me even during the time when Anti-
my faithful one, who was killed among   pas, my faithful witness, was killed there
you, where Satan dwells.   where Satan lives.

I know where you dwell, where Satan's throne is: in saying **where you dwell** ("where you live," "where you have your home"), Christ has in mind not only the city of Pergamum as such, but the conditions—religious, social, and moral—in which the Christians in Pergamum live, especially the emperor worship practiced there (three Roman emperors had temples dedicated to them in Pergamum). The specific feature Christ is aware of is that Satan lives in that city. The beginning of the verse, then, can be translated "I know that you live in the place (or, city) where Satan has his throne." Since the phrase **where Satan's throne is** may only indicate location, it may be better to translate "where Satan is king," "where Satan rules." It is possible that **Satan's throne** is an allusion to the giant altar to the god Zeus, placed on a cliff some 250 meters above the city. The phrase means not only that Satan rules over Pergamum, but that Pergamum is, so to speak, the capital of his worldwide empire. For **Satan** see the comments at 2.9; and for **throne** see 1.4. The word **throne** occurs some forty-five times in Revelation; in most instances it refers to God's (and the Lamb's) throne. A literal translation **where Satan's throne is** may not be as understandable as "where Satan rules as king (of the world)," "where Satan is the supreme ruler." The importance of Satan's rule is emphasized by the statement at the end of the verse, **where Satan dwells**.

You hold fast my name and you did not deny my faith: this is one compliment, stated first positively and then negatively. To "hold (fast) the name (of)" means to be true to, to be faithful and loyal to the person named. For **name** see 2.3. The statement **you did not deny my faith** means "you did not give up your faith in me," "you did not stop believing in me," or "you have always been loyal to me." The genitive phrase **my faith** is objective: "faith in me," not "the faith I have" (see the parallel statement in 3.8, "you . . . have not denied my name").

There is much speculation, but nothing for certain is known about **Antipas**.

My witness, my faithful one: it is not necessary to imitate the form of the Greek, as RSV does; "my faithful witness" is a faithful translation (so REB, TEV, SPCL, FRCL). The phrase **my witness** (see 1.5) means not "a witness who belongs to me" but "one who witnesses about me," not as a witness in court but as a faithful believer who bears witness to Christ by means of words and actions. The Greek word for **witness** is *martus*, from which comes the English "martyr." It may be that here the specialized sense of "martyr" is intended, as it most probably is meant at 17.6 (which see). It is probably better here to follow RSV and TEV, **witness**. Other ways of expressing this phrase are "who faithfully told people about me" or "who faithfully showed through his words and actions that he was my follower."

Who was killed among you: needless to say, **you** here is plural in the Greek, even though it is singular elsewhere in the letter. The translator should always keep in mind that every one of these seven letters is addressed to an individual, "the angel of the church," so that all verb forms and pronouns in Greek that apply to the angel are singular. In this context "put to death" or "executed," as a deliberate action, is better than the general expression "(was) killed." So one may also say "people executed him," "people put him to death," or ". . . killed him."

Where Satan dwells: this emphasizes the fact that Satan lives and rules permanently in Pergamum. The verb used here is the same one used at the beginning of the verse, **where you dwell**.

In many languages it will be helpful to restructure this verse as follows:

> I know that you live in the place (city) where Satan rules. You are my loyal followers, and have never stopped believing in me. You believed even during the time when they killed (executed) Antipas there where Satan rules. He (Antipas) always showed people through his words and deeds that he was my follower.

2.14	RSV	TEV
	But I have a few things against you: you have some there who hold the teaching of Balaam, who taught Balak to put a stumbling block before the sons of Israel, that they might eat food sacrificed to idols and practice immorality.	But there are a few things I have against you: there are some among you who follow the teaching of Balaam, who taught Balak how to lead the people of Israel into sin by persuading them to eat food that had been offered to idols and to practice sexual immorality.

After praise comes censure (verses 14-15).

But I have a few things against you: this is like the statement in 2.4, with the addition of **a few things**. Actually only one thing is mentioned, and that is the complaint against **some** of the believers in Pergamum.

You have some there: "there are some among you" (TEV) or "some people in your group."

Hold the teaching of Balaam: hold means to "follow" or "do according to." The reference is to Numbers 22–24 (see Deut 23.4). Balaam was the seer from Babylonia whom Balak, king of Moab, tried to get to lay a curse on the Israelites. According to one account (Num 31.16) Balaam's advice led the people of Israel to worship idols and indulge in immoral sexual practices (Num 25.1-3). So he became the first biblical example of a teacher who persuades the people to abandon God and worship idols.

Who taught Balak to put a stumbling block before the sons of Israel: the verb **taught** here does not indicate a formal course of instruction but means "told," "ordered," or else, more freely, "who showed Balak how to . . . ." "How" (TEV) may be rendered as "the way" or "the method." As elsewhere, **stumbling block** is an act or habit that makes a person fall into sin. The Greek word is *scandalon* (from which the word "scandal" is derived), which is the trigger peg in an animal trap; so NJB "who taught Balak to set a trap for the Israelites." The literal translation **the sons of Israel** may be misleading; NRSV now has "the people of Israel" (see TEV); or "the Israelites" (REB). Another way of expressing this clause is "who showed Balak how to cause the people of Israel to sin."

That they might eat food sacrificed to idols: in Greek this clause may indicate the purpose or the result of Balaam's advice. It is better to translate as result, "so that they ate." In some Hebrew sacrifices the animal was not completely consumed by the fire on the altar; only a small part of the animal was burned, and the rest was eaten by the worshipers or else sold. Because the food mentioned here had been dedicated to a pagan god, the Jews considered this meat unclean; and among Christians this became a serious problem (see especially 1 Cor 8.1-13). In some languages this clause may be restructured; for example, "He had them (persuaded them to) eat meat from animals that people had sacrificed (offered on an altar) to idols." In certain languages **idols** may be expressed as "carved representations (images) of minor (or, lesser) gods (deities)."

Practice immorality: usually this is taken quite literally to mean immoral sexual activity. Some, however, take it as a metaphor, as it often is in the Old Testament, meaning idolatry as such; but here the translation should be quite literal. The same charge is made against the Christians in Thyatira (2.20). Sexual immorality here refers to illicit sexual relations between males and females. Ways of expressing this are "having sexual relations with someone else's spouse" or "sleeping (being with) someone who is not one's own spouse" and is sometimes expressed as "acting like a dog" or some other animal that is considered promiscuous.

An alternative translation model for this verse is:

> But I must criticize you for a few things that you have done: some people in your group follow the teachings of Balaam, who showed Balak how to cause the people of Israel to sin. Balaam persuaded them to eat the meat of animals that people had sacrificed (or, offered on an altar) to worship carved images. He also caused them to sin by enticing them to commit adultery.

2.15   RSV   TEV

So you also have some who hold the teaching of the Nicolaitans.

In the same way you have people among you who follow the teaching of the Nicolaitans.

So you also: this means that the situation in the church in Pergamum was similar to the sins committed by the ancient Hebrews, and it will be appropriate in some languages to say "So, like those Israelites, you also . . . ." It seems that the **Nicolaitans** were trying to lead Christians to worship idols, that is, to pay homage to the Roman emperor as a god, and to indulge in immoral sexual conduct. See comments on the **Nicolaitans** at verse 6.

The verb **hold** is the same as the one used in verse 13, "you hold fast my name," and also in verse 14, "hold the teachings," which means "to follow the teachings."

2.16 RSV TEV

RSV	TEV
Repent then. If not, I will come to you soon and war against them with the sword of my mouth.	Now turn from your sins! If you don't, I will come to you soon and fight against those people with the sword that comes out of my mouth.

Repent: this is directed to the whole church (see comments on "repent" at 2.5).

I will come to you soon: this is a coming for judgment and punishment (see comments on the similar expression in 2.5).

And war against them with the sword of my mouth: see the comments at 1.16; 2.12. The glorified Christ will fight against those people who are following the teachings of the Nicolaitans. Instead of the literal **sword of my mouth**, the meaning may be expressed otherwise: "the sword that comes out of my mouth" (TEV, REB). This final clause may also be expressed as "and fight against them with the sword that comes (goes) out of my mouth."

2.17 RSV TEV

RSV	TEV
He who has an ear, let him hear what the Spirit says to the churches. To him who conquers I will give some of the hidden manna, and I will give him a white stone, with a new name written on the stone which no one knows except him who receives it.'	"If you have ears, then, listen to what the Spirit says to the churches! "To those who win the victory I will give some of the hidden manna. I will also give each of them a white stone on which is written a new name that no one knows except the one who receives it.

For the first sentence, **He who has an ear . . . churches**, see the comments at 2.7,11.

To him who conquers: see 2.7,11. As elsewhere, the exclusively masculine **To him** can be rendered inclusive by using the plural, "To those who conquer," or the indefinite, "Whoever conquers."

I will give him some of the hidden manna: this simple promise reflects a popular belief concerning the jar full of manna (the food the Hebrews ate during their forty years in the wilderness) that had been stored in the Covenant Box (Exo 16.32-34; see Heb 9.4). It was believed to be the jar that had been hidden by Jeremiah in a cave on Mount Nebo after the destruction of the Temple in 586 B.C. (2 Maccabees 2.4-8), where it would remain until the Messianic age, when God would once more feed the people with it. It is impossible to incorporate all this information in the text itself, and a cultural footnote may be added, or else the word can be explained in a word list. However, in languages that cannot use a passive form for **hidden**, translators may employ a general agent and say "the manna that someone (or, they) hid."

A white stone, with a new name written on the stone: there are several explanations of this white stone. It may have been a charm, an amulet, which was believed to protect the wearer against evil forces, or else something like an invitation card, authorizing the bearer to take part in the (Messianic) banquet. Some take it to have been the stone on which was written the judge's verdict of acquittal. White was the color of victory (see 19.11,14). Again, in some languages translators will need to use an indefinite agent with an active verb; for example, "on which they have written a new name."

It is impossible to decide whether the **new name** engraved on the white stone was the name of Christ himself, the name of God, or else, which is more likely, the new name the victorious person received, which was known by no one else and enabled that person to take part in the Messianic banquet. Whatever the interpretation, a translation should say nothing more than "a new name," without indicating whose it was. The final sentence of this verse may be restructured as follows: "Only the person who receives this stone will know this name."

B-4. The Message to Thyatira   2.18-29

RSV

18 "And to the angel of the church in Thyatira write: 'The words of the Son of God, who has eyes like a flame of fire, and whose feet are like burnished bronze.

19 " 'I know your works, your love and faith and service and patient endurance, and that your latter works exceed the first. 20 But I have this against you, that you tolerate the woman Jezebel, who calls herself a prophetess and is teaching and beguiling my servants to practice immorality and to eat food sacrificed to idols. 21 I gave her time to repent, but she refuses to repent of her immorality. 22 Behold, I will throw her on a sickbed, and those who commit adultery with her I will throw into great tribulation, unless they repent of her doings; 23 and I will strike her children dead. And all the churches shall know that I am he who searches mind and heart, and I will give to each of you as your works deserve. 24 But to the rest of you in Thyatira, who do not hold this teaching, who have not learned what some call the deep things of Satan, to you I say, I do not lay upon you any other burden; 25 only hold fast what you have, until I come. 26 He who conquers and who keeps my works until the end, I will give him power over the nations, 27 and he shall rule them with a rod of iron, as when earthen pots are broken in pieces, even as I myself have received power from my Father; 28 and I will give him the morning star. 29

TEV

The Message to Thyatira

18 "To the angel of the church in Thyatira write:

"This is the message from the Son of God, whose eyes blaze like fire, whose feet shine like polished brass. 19 I know what you do. I know your love, your faithfulness, your service, and your patience. I know that you are doing more now than you did at first. 20 But this is what I have against you: you tolerate that woman Jezebel, who calls herself a messenger of God. By her teaching she misleads my servants into practicing sexual immorality and eating food that has been offered to idols. 21 I have given her time to repent of her sins, but she does not want to turn from her immorality. 22 And so I will throw her on a bed where she and those who committed adultery with her will suffer terribly. I will do this now unless they repent of the wicked things they did with her. 23 I will also kill her followers, and then all the churches will know that I am the one who knows everyone's thoughts and wishes. I will repay each one of you according to what he has done.

24 "But the rest of you in Thyatira have not followed this evil teaching; you have not learned what the others call 'the deep secrets of Satan.' I say to you that I will not put any other burden on you. 25 But until I come, you must hold firmly to what you have. 26-28 To those who win the victory, who continue to the end to do what I

He who has an ear, let him hear what the Spirit says to the churches.'

want, I will give the same authority that I received from my Father: I will give them authority over the nations, to rule them with an iron rod and to break them to pieces like clay pots. I will also give them the morning star.

29 "If you have ears, then, listen to what the Spirit says to the churches!

SECTION HEADING: TEV "The Message to Thyatira." See 2.1,8.

2.18   RSV   TEV

"And to the angel of the church in Thyatira write: 'The words of the Son of God, who has eyes like a flame of fire, and whose feet are like burnished bronze.

"To the angel of the church in Thyatira write:

"This is the message from the Son of God, whose eyes blaze like fire, whose feet shine like polished brass.

See the similar opening statements at 2.1,8,12. **Thyatira** was, according to one commentator, the least important of the seven cities. It was southeast of Pergamum, halfway between it and Sardis. It was an industrial center, and one of the main industries was that of dyeing and manufacturing woolen goods (see Acts 16.14). The city had many trade guilds, which were usually somewhat religious in nature.

The words of: see 2.1,8,12.

The Son of God: this title appears only here in this book. Some languages have a general term for male or female children, and add "male" when a distinction has to be made between sons and daughters. See *A Handbook on the Gospel of Matthew*, page 487, for a more detailed discussion of this problem.

Who has eyes like a flame of fire, and whose feet are like burnished bronze: this description is taken from 1.14-15, which see. There is one slight difference in Greek: in 1.14 the word for "flame" is singular; here it is plural. As RSV shows, there is no difference in meaning. The symbolism is clear: with such eyes the Son of God can see into the most distant and darkest places, and with such feet he can stamp out all opposition to his rule.

2.19   RSV   TEV

" 'I know your works, your love and faith and service and patient endurance, and that your latter works exceed the first.

I know what you do. I know your love, your faithfulness, your service, and your patience. I know that you are doing more now than you did at first.

I know your works: see the comments at 2.2.

Your love and faith and service and patient endurance: in Greek the singular possessive adjective **your** comes after the five nouns, thereby describing them all. As in 2.4, **love** may be for Christ or for one another, but it is better taken to mean for one another; **faith** is either their faithfulness or loyalty as Christians

(TEV, REB, FRCL, BRCL, Brc, AT, Mft, Phps) or their personal faith (SPCL, NJB), whether in God or in Jesus Christ; the former seems preferable; **service** is their activity as followers of Christ, especially in their service to fellow Christians (see the same noun in Acts 11.29 ["relief"]; 1 Cor 16.15); and for **patient endurance** see 1.9.

Your latter works exceed the first: the RSV formal equivalence of the Greek is meant to say "you are now doing more than you did at first" (AT; similarly Phps, TEV, FRCL, SPCL). The meaning of "at first" can be brought out more clearly: "when you became Christians," "when you first believed in me," or "when you first became my followers" (see 2.4). This refers to their activity in Christian service, and "more" probably indicates quantity.

An alternate translation model for this verse is:

> I know how you have lived your lives. I know that you love one another and are loyal to me. I know the way you have helped one another, and your ability to endure. I know that you are now doing more than when you first believed in me (became my followers).

2.20

RSV	TEV
But I have this against you, that you tolerate the woman Jezebel, who calls herself a prophetess and is teaching and beguiling my servants to practice immorality and to eat food sacrificed to idols.	But this is what I have against you: you tolerate that woman Jezebel, who calls herself a messenger of God. By her teaching she misleads my servants into practicing sexual immorality and eating food that has been offered to idols.

After the praise comes censure.

I have this against you: see 2.4.

You tolerate the woman Jezebel: the Greek verb translated **tolerate** is different from the verb used in 2.2 "(cannot) bear." The meaning can be expressed positively, "you allow," "you permit," or negatively, "you do not forbid," "you do not put a stop to," "you do not prevent." Jezebel in the Old Testament was the Sidonian princess who was the wife of King Ahab of Israel, and who tried to impose Baal worship on the Israelites (1 Kgs 16.29-31; 18.4,19; 2 Kgs 9.22). Although it is possible that Jezebel was a woman in the church at Thyatira, it seems more probable that the name is used symbolically of this woman leader who was trying to replace the true worship of God by pagan rites and beliefs. Some translations in English indicate that this is a symbolic name by translating "that Jezebel of a woman" (Mft, AT, Brc), a rather unusual idiom in English, but in context quite understandable to native readers. It is recommended, however, that the translation be quite literal, **the woman Jezebel**.

Calls herself a prophetess: as in the case of the false apostles (2.2), who were not what they claimed to be, this woman claimed that her teaching was an authentic message from God—but it was not. So the translation can say "who falsely says she is a prophet," "who lies when she says that her message comes from God." The feminine form of the Greek word "prophet" is used here and in Luke 2.36 (Anna). In English it is becoming the practice to use the same word, where possible, for both men and women; so NRSV "who calls herself a prophet." There were Christian leaders in the early Church who were called "prophets." In translation the same word should be used of them as is used of Old Testament prophets.

Is teaching and beguiling my servants: to "beguile" is to mislead, deceive, lead astray, seduce. In certain languages it will be expressed as "cause to stray from the path" or "lead away from the true path." The participle of the verb is used as a title, "the deceiver," which is applied to Satan and his subordinates (12.9; 13.14; 19.20; 20.3,8,10). Here **my servants** means all believers, or it may be expressed as "all those who believe in me" or "all my followers" (see 1.1). The two verbs **teaching** and **beguiling** may be joined, "by means of her teaching she deceives (or, misleads) my servants."

To practice immorality and to eat food sacrificed to idols: the same evil conduct was being promoted by the Nicolaitans (see 2.14-15).

2.21   RSV   TEV

I gave her time to repent, but she refus-   I have given her time to repent of her
es to repent of her immorality.   sins, but she does not want to turn from
                                               her immorality.

I gave her time to repent: this indicates that in some way Christ's judgment had been revealed to her, but she had ignored it and insisted in continuing her evil ways. Had she repented, she would not have been punished. For **repent** see comments on 2.5.

She refuses to repent: she chooses not to abandon her evil ways, and so she will be punished.

Her immorality: the Greek noun, used also in 9.21; 14.8 and 18.3 (*"impure passion"*; 17.2,4 and 19.2 ("fornication"), is always applied to females. Female immorality in certain languages is expressed as "having an easy heart," meaning a woman who is free with her affections, or it may be expressed as "acting like a woman who sells her body," or even "acting like a female dog (bitch)." Translators should look for appropriate idioms in the receptor languages.

2.22   RSV   TEV

Behold, I will throw her on a sickbed,   And so I will throw her on a bed where
and those who commit adultery with her   she and those who committed adultery
I will throw into great tribulation, un-   with her will suffer terribly. I will do
less they repent of her doings;   this now unless they repent of the wick-
                                             ed things they did with her.

Behold: see 1.7. NRSV now has "Beware, I am throwing her on a bed," which is a rather strange use of the verb "Beware." Probably "Look now" or "Pay attention" would be better. However, in English and many other languages, it will be stylistically more natural to omit an attention-getting word or phrase in this context and say something like TEV, "And so," "Therefore," or something similar.

I will throw her on a sickbed: the Greek text says only "I throw her on a bed," but this is obviously a punishment in the form of an illness; REB translates "a bed of pain." The Greek present tense of the verb "to throw" indicates that this will happen soon. It may be better to translate "I will punish her with an illness" or "I will make her sick."

And those who commit adultery with her I will throw into great tribulation: in the Greek text the verb "to throw" is not repeated but is clearly implied. As the RSV literal equivalence shows, the text may be read as two separate actions: "I will throw her on a bed and (I will throw) into great suffering those who commit adultery with her." But it is possible that the text means that Christ will inflict the same punishment on Jezebel and on those who commit adultery with her. So TOB "Look, I throw her on a bed of sharp distress, as well as her partners in adultery" (so also TEV, Phps). In other languages this will be expressed as "I will make her sick, and I will cause the ones who commit adultery with her to suffer terribly" or "I will throw both her and those who sleep with her onto a sleeping mat where they will suffer terribly."

Again, it is possible that **commit adultery** here is worship of idols (as the related Greek word translated "practice sexual immorality" in 2.14 can mean; but the translation must be "commit adultery." For the word translated **tribulation** see 1.9; it means suffering or distress.

Unless they repent of her doings: for **repent** see 2.5. The text, strictly speaking, refers only to Jezebel's lovers, and they are told to repent of *her* evil doings. It is impossible for one person to repent of another's sin. **Her doings** here refers to what they, at her bidding, are doing with her. So Brc translates "unless they realize how wrong her conduct is, and stop participating in it."

Alternate translation models for this verse are:

> Look! I will throw her on a bed (sleeping mat) where she will become ill. And I will cause those who commit adultery with her to suffer terribly, unless they are willing to stop (repent of) the evil things they are doing (with her).

Or:

> Therefore, I will cause her to become ill, and those who sleep with her to suffer terribly unless they repent of the evil things . . . .

2.23   RSV   TEV

RSV	TEV
and I will strike her children dead. And all the churches shall know that I am he who searches mind and heart, and I will give to each of you as your works deserve.	I will also kill her followers, and then all the churches will know that I am the one who knows everyone's thoughts and wishes. I will repay each one of you according to what he has done.

And I will strike her children dead: here it seems quite clear that **her children** is not meant literally but refers to those who were following her teachings, while her lovers were her associates and colleagues. A translator may choose to say **her children** or "her followers," as TEV does. The Greek compound phrase translated **I will strike . . . dead** is very strong, implying swift and ruthless action: "I will slay" (thus Mft "I will exterminate"). In 6.8 the phrase means "to kill by means of a pestilence." "Kill" is expressed idiomatically in many languages; for example, "snuff a person's breath out," or even "wipe (a person) from the ground."

Churches: see the comments on 1.4.

I am he who searches mind and heart: because of the punishment he is going to bring upon Jezebel, her lovers, and her children (or, followers), all the believers will know that the glorified Christ is judge of all, who knows the hearts and minds of all. The Hebrew biblical phrase "to search kidneys and hearts" (see Psa 7.9) means to probe the most secret thoughts and desires. Jeremiah 17.10 is a close parallel to the last half of the verse (see also Rom 8.27). **He** can be rendered as "the one who" (TEV). The phrase **searches mind and heart** may also be expressed as "sees into the thoughts (minds) and knows what people want (the desires)."

I will give to each of you as your works deserve: it is obvious that in this statement **you** and **your** are plural. No one in Thyatira will escape Christ's punishment, and each one's punishment will be in accordance with the sin that person has committed (see also Psa 62.12). Although the language can be taken to apply both to punishment and to reward, the context seems to make it clear that here punishment is meant. So it will be possible in some languages to say "I will punish each one of you according to the sin that you [singular] have done."

An alternative translation model for this verse is:

> I will kill those who follow her teachings, and all the groups of God's people will know that I am the one who looks into the thoughts of people and knows what they really want. I will punish each one of them according to the sin that he has done.

2.24-25   RSV   TEV

24 But to the rest of you in Thyatira, who do not hold this teaching, who have not learned what some call the deep things of Satan, to you I say, I do not lay upon you any other burden; 25 only hold fast what you have, until I come.

24 "But the rest of you in Thyatira have not followed this evil teaching; you have not learned what the others call 'the deep secrets of Satan.' I say to you that I will not put any other burden on you. 25 But until I come, you must hold firmly to what you have.

Now the glorified Christ addresses the church members who have remained faithful, **the rest of you . . . who do not hold this teaching**. Reference has already been made to the teaching of Balaam (2.14) and the teaching of the Nicolaitans (2.15), and here the teaching of Jezebel is spoken of (see verse 20). The word **teaching** refers to what she teaches, not to her manner of teaching. It may be helpful in translation to specify the nature of this teaching: "evil teaching" or "false teaching." **Not hold** means "do not follow."

Who have not learned what some call the deep things of Satan: it is possible that here the Greek verb translated **have . . . learned** means "have experienced," "have had . . . experience of," as REB translates it. It appears that the followers of Jezebel called her teachings "the deep truths (or, secrets) of Satan"; see the parallel "the depths of God" (1 Cor 2.10). The adjective **deep** means "profound," "very important" (as opposed to "simple" or "elementary"). It seems strange that the followers of Jezebel themselves (or at least some of them) would call her teachings "the deep truths of Satan"; yet this is one way the text can be understood. But the qualifying phrase in Greek is literally "as they call it." This may be impersonal, meaning that others call it that. It seems best to take the subject of "as they call it" to be the followers of Jezebel. RNAB "the so-called deep secrets of Satan" is a way of avoiding being specific (as the Greek text itself is not specific). It is probable that **of Satan** is the subjective genitive, "truths (or, secrets) that Satan reveals," and not the objective genitive, "truths (or, secrets) about Satan." The use of **deep** (or, "secret") indicates that these are truths known only by a select group. For **Satan** see 2.9. With these comments in mind, this clause may also be expressed as "you have not experienced what her followers (the others) call 'the deep truths that Satan reveals.' "

To you I say, I do not lay upon you any other burden: Christ is still speaking to these Christians who have not accepted the evil doctrines and practices taught by Jezebel. The Greek word for **burden** generally means something disagreeable or painful, a heavy load to carry (Matt 20.12; Gal 6.2); in a less negative sense it may be used of a command or order that is given to someone. Taking it in this sense—a command, an order—what are the orders implied by "any other orders"? Are they the general commands inherent in the Christian faith regarding Christian conduct? Or are they specific commands issued on a certain occasion? Some commentators point to the similar language used in Acts 15.26-29 and conclude that the commands in that passage are being referred to; but this seems most unlikely. The Greek word may also mean "weighty" in the sense of "important" (see Matt 23.23; 2 Cor 10.10). The meaning here may be "I impose on you no other important command (or, duty)."

It seems very likely that what follows in verse 25 is precisely what is implied by **other**, that is, "no other command beside (or, other than) this: Hold firmly to what you have." Therefore, instead of placing a stop at the end of verse 24, as done by RSV and TEV (and most other translations), the sentence should continue without a stop, as done by TNT: "I lay upon you no other burden but to hold fast what you have until I come"; so also RNAB "on you I will place no further burden, except that you must hold fast to what you have until I come" (similarly Brc, Phps).

There is the possibility, however, that the Greek word translated **only** by RSV and "But" by TEV is used here as a conjunction, "but, otherwise," and not as an improper preposition (which normally is followed by the genitive). Considering everything, however, it seems best to follow the example of TNT and RNAB in the preceding paragraph.

Hold fast what you have: for the verb see 2.13. They are to maintain firmly their Christian faith and commitment, not to waver in their faithfulness to Christ. So this clause may also be phrased as "You must continue to believe strongly in me" or "You must remain loyal to me."

Until I come: this is the coming at the end of the age. In translation it should be clear that **until I come** modifies **hold fast**, not **what you have**. RSV is ambiguous as it is; NRSV, by eliminating the comma after **have**, is quite unambiguous in the wrong sense: "hold fast to what you have until I come." Something like TOB is quite clear: "This, only: what you have, hold it firmly until I come."

An alternative translation model for these two verses is:

> But the rest of you in Thyatira have not followed her (Jezebel's) evil teaching. You have not participated in what her followers call "the deep truths that Satan reveals." I say to you that I will not impose on you any other important (weighty) command, except that you must continue to believe strongly in me until I come.

2.26-28   RSV   TEV

26 He who conquers and who keeps my works until the end, I will give him power over the nations, 27 and he shall rule them with a rod of iron, as when earthen pots are broken in pieces, even as I myself have received power from my Father; 28 and I will give him the morning star.

26-28 To those who win the victory, who continue to the end to do what I want, I will give the same authority that I received from my Father: I will give them authority over the nations, to rule them with an iron rod and to break them to pieces like clay pots. I will also give them the morning star.

A comparison between RSV and TEV shows how TEV has restructured the material in verses 26-28. It should be noticed that in RSV verse 28 consists of **and I will give him the morning star**. In the Greek text translated by TEV, however, verse 28 begins where RSV has **even as I myself have received power from my Father**. For this reason TEV includes verse 28 in the restructuring. NRSV now has verse 28 begin with "even as I also received authority . . . ."

He who conquers: see 2.7. As elsewhere, the exclusively masculine can be eliminated by using the plural "Those who conquer," or "To everyone who conquers" (NRSV), or the impersonal "Whoever conquers."

Who keeps my works until the end: this means "who will continue until the end to do faithfully what I command," "who . . . keeps working for me until the end" (NJB); note REB "who perseveres in doing my will to the end." The verb "to keep" in 1.3 means to "obey"; here it means "to do." And here **my works** does not mean the things that Christ does but the things he orders his followers to do. And **until the end** means "until the end of the age" or "until the end of the world" (see "until I come" in verse 25).

The whole passage, from **I will give** to **broken in pieces**, is a loose citation or paraphrase of Psalm 2.8-9, a passage in which God promises to give the king of Israel dominion over the world.

I will give him power over the nations: the word translated **power** appears in this book twenty times; it may mean "power," "authority," or "right," depending on the context. Here "authority" or "authority to rule" is better in English than "power." In certain languages translators may need to use a phrase to express this

63

concept; for example, "able to" or "strong enough to." The word translated **nations** means in the Old Testament "Gentiles," "pagans," or even "non-Jews." This clause may be rendered in many languages as "I will cause (let) him to have the authority to rule over the people of other nations" or "I will cause him to be able to (to be strong enough to) rule over . . . ."

He shall rule them with a rod of iron: this means to rule completely, ruthlessly, crushing all opposition; in 12.5 and 19.15 the same language is used of the victorious Christ. The Greek verb is related to the noun "shepherd" and means "to rule as a shepherd" (see 7.17). The passage here follows the Greek Septuagint translation of the Psalm passage, and it appears that the Septuagint translators derived the Hebrew verb from the verb "to shepherd" (*ra'ah*) instead of the verb "to break" (*ra'a'*). In translation the word for "to rule" or "to govern" should be used. The "iron rod" was probably a heavy wooden club capped with iron, not a club made of iron. In translating, some cultural adjustment may have to be made. If there is no local equivalent to **a rod of iron**, the translation may say "rule them without pity," "govern them ruthlessly."

As when earthen pots are broken in pieces: this is the way the rule will be exercised. RSV does not make the connection clear; REB has "and he will rule them with a rod of iron, smashing them to pieces like earthenware" (similarly TEV, FRCL, SPCL). Clay pots are fragile objects, at best, and are easily smashed. For the verb translated **broken in pieces**, see its use in Mark 14.3. Another way of phrasing this is "as when they smash into pieces pots made from clay."

Even as I myself have received power from my Father: he transmits to his victorious followers the same authority he had received from God. Nothing is said as to when or how he received this God-given authority. Perhaps the words in Psalm 2.6-7 are in the background. This passive clause may be expressed in many languages as "even as my Father has given me power" or "even as my Father has caused (let) me to have the power to rule."

And I will give him the morning star: the morning star is probably the planet Venus, a symbol of victory and domination. Victorious Roman generals built temples in honor of Venus, and the sign of Venus was on the standards of Caesar's legions. In 22.16 Christ himself is the morning star, but it is hardly likely that the meaning here is that Christ will give himself to those who conquer. A translation of "the morning star" may be "the star that appears (or, shines) at sunrise." And in order to make some sense of this statement, a cultural footnote may be necessary, or else a note in a word list, or the translator may include the meaning here, as follows: "and to show that they are victorious, I will give them the morning star."

Verses 26-28a are one very complex sentence. TEV has restructured the material in order to make the text more intelligible, and translators are urged to do the same. FRCL has:

> To those who shall have won the victory and who shall have continued to practice to the end what I want, I will give the power that I myself received from my Father: I will give them power over the nations, they will govern them with an iron authority and will shatter them to pieces like clay pots.

Another translation model for verses 26-28 is:

> I will let those people who are victorious (who conquer), who
> continue to obey my commands until the end of time (or, the world),
> have the same power to rule that my Father has given to me: I will
> let them have the authority to rule over all the nations (or, tribes).
> They will rule over them without mercy, and will shatter them into
> pieces just like people break pots made from clay. I will also give
> them the morning star to show (or, demonstrate) their victory.

2.29   RSV   TEV

He who has an ear, let him hear what   **"If you have ears, then, listen to**
the Spirit says to the churches.'   **what the Spirit says to the churches!**

See comments on the identical statement in verses 7, 11, and 17.

B-5. The Message to Sardis   3.1-6
RSV   TEV
The Message to Sardis

1 "And to the angel of the church in Sardis write: 'The words of him who has the seven spirits of God and the seven stars.

"'I know your works; you have the name of being alive, and you are dead. 2 Awake, and strengthen what remains and is on the point of death, for I have not found your works perfect in the sight of my God. 3 Remember then what you received and heard; keep that, and repent. If you will not awake, I will come like a thief, and you will not know at what hour I will come upon you. 4 Yet you have still a few names in Sardis, people who have not soiled their garments; and they shall walk with me in white, for they are worthy. 5 He who conquers shall be clad thus in white garments, and I will not blot his name out of the book of life; I will confess his name before my Father and before his angels. 6 He who has an ear, let him hear what the Spirit says to the churches.'

1 "To the angel of the church in Sardis write:

"This is the message from the one who has the seven spirits of God and the seven stars. I know what you are doing; I know that you have the reputation of being alive, even though you are dead! 2 So wake up, and strengthen what you still have before it dies completely. For I find that what you have done is not yet perfect in the sight of my God. 3 Remember, then, what you were taught and what you heard; obey it and turn from your sins. If you do not wake up, I will come upon you like a thief, and you will not even know the time when I will come. 4 But a few of you there in Sardis have kept your clothes clean. You will walk with me, clothed in white, because you are worthy to do so. 5 Those who win the victory will be clothed like this in white, and I will not remove their names from the book of the living. In the presence of my Father and of his angels I will declare openly that they belong to me.

6 "If you have ears, then, listen to what the Spirit says to the churches!

SECTION HEADING: TEV "The Message to Sardis." See 2.1.

"And to the angel of the church in Sardis write: 'The words of him who has the seven spirits of God and the seven stars.	"To the angel of the church in Sardis write:
" 'I know your works; you have the name of being alive, and you are dead.	"This is the message from the one who has the seven spirits of God and the seven stars. I know what you are doing; I know that you have the reputation of being alive, even though you are dead!

For the opening statement see 2.1,8. **Sardis**, south of Thyatira, was the ancient capital of the kingdom of Lydia. It was a wealthy city, an important industrial center that included the manufacture of woolen and dyed goods.

The words of him: see the comments at 2.1.

Who has the seven spirits of God and the seven stars: see the comments at 1.4,16. In some languages it may not be possible to use the same verb **has** with both **the seven spirits** and **the seven stars**. According to 1.16 Christ held the seven stars in his right hand; as for the seven spirits, however, it may be better to use a verb that denotes control or authority, such as ". . . who rules the seven spirits." No verb should be used that may imply that he was possessed of the seven spirits, or that he had seven spirits in him. See also 4.5; 5.6. The phrase **of God** means that the seven spirits belong to God or else serve God. So this whole clause may also be expressed as "who rules over the seven spirits that serve God, and who holds the seven stars."

I know your works: see the comments at 2.2.

You have the name of being alive, and you are dead: here **name** means reputation, fame (thus TEV, FRCL, SPCL). Or the meaning may be expressed this way: "You seem (or, appear) to be alive . . . ." Both **alive** and **dead** refer to their spiritual condition. So this sentence may be expressed as "You appear to be faithful believers in me; but actually you do not follow me anymore." Instead of the RSV conjunction **and**, it is better to say "but."

Alternative translation models for this verse are:

> The one who rules the seven spirits that serve God, and who holds the seven stars, sends this message: I know all the things that you have done; I know that you seem to be alive, but are really dead.

Or:

> . . . I know all the things that you have done. I know that you seem to be faithful believers in me; but in reality you do not follow me anymore.

3.2   RSV   TEV

Awake, and strengthen what remains
and is on the point of death, for I have
not found your works perfect in the
sight of my God.

So wake up, and strengthen what you
still have before it dies completely. For
I find that what you have done is not
yet perfect in the sight of my God.

Awake: someone who is "dead" in verse 1 cannot logically be told to **awake**,
but this is part of the author's style. See Ephesians 5.4 for similar use of these
figures. This word should not be understood to mean "awake from sleep"; on the
contrary, it means "Become alive again," "Wake up from death," or "Begin living as
Christians (or, followers of me) again."

And strengthen what remains and is on the point of death: the verb "to
strengthen" means, in this context, to restore to strength, to renew, to invigorate, to
put strength (vigor) back into." NJB translates "put some resolve into what little
vigour you have left." And **what remains** refers to their Christian virtues or activities
that had been neglected and were about to die, that is, about to disappear
completely.

For I have not found your works perfect in the sight of my God: Christ has
investigated what the Christians at Sardis have done, and he has discovered that their
works do not measure up to the standards set by God (for **your works** see 2.2,19).
The word **perfect** here translates the perfect passive participle of a verb that means
to complete, fulfill, bring to perfection. Mft translates "nothing you have done is
complete"; REB has "brought to completion." The implication seems to be that the
Christians at Sardis had begun to do things as Christians but had lost their
enthusiasm and not finished what they had begun. Another translation model for this
clause is "For I have discovered (found out) that in God's opinion you have not
completed anything that you have done."

The phrase **in the sight of my God** means from God's point of view, or the
way God looks at things. God's standards have not been met. For this use of the
Greek adverb "before," here translated **in the sight of**, see 1 Timothy 2.3; 5.4. The
possessive **my God** means "the God I serve (or, worship)," not "the God I possess."

An alternate translation model for this verse is:

> I have found that your lives as Christians do not meet the standards
> that my God has set. So wake up from your spiritual sleep, and
> renew (or, restore) the strength of the Christian qualities you still
> have, before they die (or, disappear) completely.

3.3   RSV   TEV

Remember then what you received and
heard; keep that, and repent. If you will
not awake, I will come like a thief, and
you will not know at what hour I will
come upon you.

Remember, then, what you were taught
and what you heard; obey it and turn
from your sins. If you do not wake up,
I will come upon you like a thief, and
you will not even know the time when I
will come.

Remember then what you received and heard: the two verbs **received** and **heard** do not necessarily refer to two separate actions but to the one action of their having been taught the lessons of the Christian faith. "Remember the truths (or, lessons) you were taught." NJB translates "remember how you first heard the message." Brc has two separate events: "keep remembering the faith you have received, and the instructions you were given." Another possible way of translating is provided by FRCL: "Remember then the teaching you have received, and remember how you heard it." In languages that do not use the passive, one may say "Remember, then, the Christian truths that they taught you," where "they" is an unknown agent.

Keep that, and repent: the verb "to keep" here means not only to preserve but to put into practice, to obey, to follow. So another way of expressing this clause is "You must follow (obey) these truths." For **repent** see comments at 2.5. In some cases it may be better to reverse the order of the two verbs: "turn from your sins and obey their teachings."

If you will not awake: this points back to the command in verse 2.

I will come like a thief: this is a coming to punish them, not the final coming. This coming will be unexpected, without any warning, as explained in the following **and you will not know at what hour I will come upon you**. These words recall Jesus' warning in Matthew 24.43-44; Luke 12.29-30 (see also 1 Thes 5.2,4). One may also translate this final clause as "I will come unexpectedly as a thief comes, and you will not even know . . . ."

Alternative translation models for this verse are the following:

> Call to mind (Remember) the Christian truths that they taught you and which you heard; you must stop sinning and obey these truths. If you do not wake up, I will come unexpectedly, just as a thief comes (at night), and you will not even know the time when I will come to punish you.

Or:

> . . . If you are not awake, you will not know the time when I will come to punish you, because I will come unexpectedly like . . . .

3.4   RSV   TEV

Yet you have still a few names in Sardis, people who have not soiled their garments; and they shall walk with me in white, for they are worthy.

But a few of you there in Sardis have kept your clothes clean. You will walk with me, clothed in white, because you are worthy to do so.

Yet you have still a few names in Sardis: it should be noticed that the words are addressed to "the angel" of the church in Sardis, who is told "You still have a few people in Sardis who . . . ." If a translation follows this form, care should be taken to avoid giving the impression that the angel owns or controls these people—and this may be difficult to avoid. The text means that they belong to "your" church, the church of which you are "the angel." So it may be better to imitate TEV, "But a

few of you there in Sardis . . ."; note NJB "There are a few in Sardis, it is true, who
. . . ." In 2.1 we suggested that "angel" may be better expressed as "representative."
So in this verse one may say "In the church in Sardis, which you represent, there are
a few people . . . ." Here **names** means "people" (see 2.3), referring specifically to
Christians.

Who have not soiled their garments: to keep one's clothes clean is a figure
for pure behavior, Christian conduct. If there is danger that the figure of speech be
taken literally, the translation may abandon it and say "who have not been defiled
(or, corrupted) by sin," "who have kept themselves spiritually pure," "who have lived
pure lives as Christians." Or it may be possible to retain the figure but state it
positively, as TEV has done, "who have kept their clothes clean." In English "to soil
one's clothes" refers to a specific and unfortunate action.

And they shall walk with me in white: the color white may be symbolic of
victory, or immortality, or purity. Purity is indicated by what precedes, and victory by
what follows. But the translator must avoid the temptation to explicitly build into the
figure the meaning it is supposed to have, unless a literal rendering conveys the
wrong meaning. In that case it will be helpful to have a footnote explaining what
white refers to. The verb "to walk with" means to accompany, either as a disciple
(see John 6.66) or as a friend and companion, in the Messianic kingdom. Translators
should try to maintain the symbol of "walking" if at all possible.

For they are worthy: they deserve it, they have a right to do so, for they have
lived as Christ, or God, would have them live.

An alternative translation model for this verse is:

> But there are a few people whom you represent in Sardis who have
> lived pure lives as Christians. They will walk with me wearing pure
> white garments, because they have the right to do this.

3.5	RSV	TEV
	He who conquers shall be clad thus in white garments, and I will not blot his name out of the book of life; I will confess his name before my Father and before his angels.	Those who win the victory will be clothed like this in white, and I will not remove their names from the book of the living. In the presence of my Father and of his angels I will declare openly that they belong to me.

He who conquers: see the comments at 2.7. To avoid the exclusively
masculine sense, the translation can use a plural form, "Those who conquer," or the
indefinite "Whoever conquers." REB has "Anyone who is victorious."

Shall be clad thus in white garments: the meaning is "will wear white
clothes like this" or "like them," that is, as they do. "They will be dressed in white
like them." The passive form of the verb may indicate that God or Christ will dress
them. It seems better, though, to understand it as the Greek middle voice: "they will
dress themselves."

I will not blot his name out of the book of life: the verb **blot . . . out** means
to delete, to erase, to wipe out, to remove—whatever verb is most naturally applied

to the process of removing someone's name from a list or a book. See REB "I shall never strike his name off the roll of the living." The figure **the book of life** is a familiar one in the Bible and in scriptures of other religions (see also 13.8; 17.8; 20.12,15; 21.27). It implies that God keeps a (written) record of those who will enjoy the bliss of eternal life. In 17.8 the additional information is given, that those names were entered into the book of life before the creation of the world. For other references to **the book of life**, see Exodus 32.32-33; Psalm 69.28; Daniel 12.1; Malachi 3.16; Philippians 4.3. Instead of the abstract phrase **of life**, a translator may choose to say "of the living (ones)" (TEV, REB). **The book of life** may be expressed as "the book in which the names of those who really have life (life from God) are written down" or "the book in which God has written down the names of those who will have eternal life."

I will confess his name before my Father and before his angels: to "confess the name" means to recognize, acknowledge, proclaim a certain relationship with a person. Here the meaning is that at the final Judgment Christ will declare that these people are his, they are his followers, they belong to him (see Matt 10.32; Luke 12.8; 1 John 2.23). AT and Brc translate "I will acknowledge him as mine"; FRCL has "I will declare before my Father and before his angels that they belong to me." The literal translation **before my Father *and* before his angels** appears to imply two separate events, whereas only one is meant: "before my Father and his angels" Christ will make this declaration. The phrase **before my Father and before his angels** may also be rendered as "when I stand before my Father and . . . ," or in certain languages "as I am before the face of my Father and . . . ."

For **angel** see comments at 1.20.

An alternative translation model for this verse is:

> The person who conquers the forces of evil will wear white clothes like these do. I will not erase that person's name from the book in which the names of those who have true life are written down. As I stand before my Father and the beings (angels) who serve him, I will declare that I know this person.

3.6

RSV	TEV
He who has an ear, let him hear what the Spirit says to the churches.'	"If you have ears, then, listen to what the Spirit says to the churches!

For translating this verse see 2.7.

B-6. The Message to Philadelphia 3.7-13

RSV	TEV
	The Message to Philadelphia
7 "And to the angel of the church in Philadelphia write: 'The words of the holy one, the true one, who has the key of David, who opens and no one shall shut, who shuts and no one opens.	7 "To the angel of the church in Philadelphia write: "This is the message from the one who is holy and true. He has the key that belonged to

8 " 'I know your works. Behold, I have set before you an open door, which no one is able to shut; I know that you have but little power, and yet you have kept my word and have not denied my name. 9 Behold, I will make those of the synagogue of Satan who say that they are Jews and are not, but lie—behold, I will make them come and bow down before your feet, and learn that I have loved you. 10 Because you have kept my word of patient endurance, I will keep you from the hour of trial which is coming on the whole world, to try those who dwell upon the earth. 11 I am coming soon; hold fast what you have, so that no one may seize your crown. 12 He who conquers, I will make him a pillar in the temple of my God; never shall he go out of it, and I will write on him the name of my God, and the name of the city of my God, the new Jerusalem which comes down from my God out of heaven, and my own new name. 13 He who has an ear, let him hear what the Spirit says to the churches.'

David, and when he opens a door, no one can close it, and when he closes it, no one can open it. 8 I know what you do; I know that you have a little power; you have followed my teaching and have been faithful to me. I have opened a door in front of you, which no one can close. 9 Listen! As for that group that belongs to Satan, those liars who claim that they are Jews but are not, I will make them come and bow down at your feet. They will all know that I love you. 10 Because you have kept my command to endure, I will also keep you safe from the time of trouble which is coming upon the world to test all the people on earth. 11 I am coming soon. Keep safe what you have, so that no one will rob you of your victory prize. 12 I will make him who is victorious a pillar in the temple of my God, and he will never leave it. I will write on him the name of my God and the name of the city of my God, the new Jerusalem, which will come down out of heaven from my God. I will also write on him my new name.

13 "If you have ears, then, listen to what the Spirit says to the churches!

SECTION HEADING: TEV "The Message to Philadelphia." See 2.1.

3.7 RSV	TEV
"And to the angel of the church in Philadelphia write: 'The words of the holy one, the true one, who has the key of David, who opens and no one shall shut, who shuts and no one opens.	"To the angel of the church in Philadelphia write: "This is the message from the one who is holy and true. He has the key that belonged to David, and when he opens a door, no one can close it, and when he closes it, no one can open it.

For the opening statement see 2.1,8. **Philadelphia**, not a very large city, was a busy commercial center. It was the meeting point of roads from Sardis, from the coast, and from regions in the northeast and southeast.

For **The words of** see 2.1.

The holy one, the true one: these are divine titles. "The Holy One" is God (4.8; 6.10). In the Bible "holiness" is the very essence of God, the quality that makes God what he is, different and set apart from human beings. It carries a sense of separateness from sin, of exclusiveness, of uniqueness. And this divine quality applies to objects or people who are set apart, dedicated to the service and worship of God. The people of God are called "the holy ones" or "the saints" (5.8; see also "the holy city" in 11.2; 21.2, and "the holy angels" in 14.10). "The Holy One of God" was a Messianic title (Mark 1.24; Luke 4.34; John 6.69), meaning one who was God's servant and did God's will. In this verse translators should avoid using words for **holy** that mean "taboo," or words that refer to "purity" or "cleanness," unless these can be used in an extended sense to refer to moral purity. Another way of translating **the**

71

holy one, then, is "the one who faithfully serves God." The Greek for **the true one** occurs also in 3.14 ("true witness"); 19.11 ("called . . . True"), and elsewhere. In this context it seems to mean "the true Messiah" (so Beckwith and Caird). But **true** here may have the meaning of "faithful" (see Psa 31.5; Isa 65.16, where "God of truth" means "a faithful God"), and so here it may mean "the faithful (or, trustworthy) one" in his service to God.

Who has the key of David: this is a statement of authority; the figure is used in Isaiah 22.22 of the king's representative, Eliakim, who had the authority to rule the palace in the king's name. The keys he carried were the sign of his authority. It is probable that **of David** means "of David's kingdom," that is, of the Messianic kingdom. Here the translator is urged not to imitate TEV, inasmuch as "the key that belonged to David" implies that there was an actual key that once belonged to King David. All translations consulted have simply **the key of David**. Perhaps a footnote or an entry in the glossary can help the reader understand the meaning of this figure, or else the text itself can be translated "the key of authority" or "the key that shows he has authority." It will be helpful in certain languages to put the word "King" or "High Chief" in front of the name David to identify this person for the reader; for example, "King David's key of authority" or "The key of High Chief David."

Who opens and no one shall shut, who shuts and no one opens: this states more explicitly the supreme authority he has in God's kingdom. In Matthew 16.19 the keys represent the authority to enforce the laws of the kingdom. RSV follows literally the Greek text in translating **shall shut** and **opens**; but it is better to translate both by future tenses, or else to imitate TEV, "can close . . . can open." One may also say "When he takes the key and opens a door, no one can close it, and when . . . ."

3.8	RSV	TEV

" 'I know your works. Behold, I have set before you an open door, which no one is able to shut; I know that you have but little power, and yet you have kept my word and have not denied my name.	I know what you do; I know that you have a little power; you have followed my teaching and have been faithful to me. I have opened a door in front of you, which no one can close.

I know your works: see the comments at 2.2.

Behold: see 1.7.

The Greek text, as punctuated in the United Bible Societies' (UBS) *Greek New Testament*, sets off within dashes the clause "Look, I have set before you an open door, which no one is able to shut" (NRSV; American Standard Version [ASV] and RNAB use parentheses), because the sense of the sentence is **I know your works . . . , that you have but little power . . . .** In order to make this connection, RSV and others repeat "I know" (so REB, TNT, NJB, NIV); TEV, on the other hand, restructures the sentence, placing the statement about "the door" at the end (also FRCL, GECL, BRCL), inasmuch as the open door comes as a result of the people's faithfulness. Translators will decide which model is better for their languages.

I have set before you an open door, which no one is able to shut: the door is a figure for an opportunity for service or for preaching the gospel (see 1 Cor 16.9; 2 Cor 2.12; Col 4.3), and many see that as its meaning here. But here it can indicate free entrance into the Messianic kingdom, which no one will be able to block. Again the translator is to avoid the temptation to make the meaning of the figure explicit, unless it is likely to be misunderstood. In that case one may say "a door of opportunity."

Instead of the literal "I have set an open door in front of you," it may be better to say "I have opened a door in front of you" (TEV; FRCL); GECL has "I have opened a door for you." The word in Greek translated **open** is not an adjective as such but the perfect passive participle of the verb "to open": "an opened door," "a door that has been opened and remains open" (opened either by God or by the glorified Christ).

I know that you have but little power: here the **(little) power** the Christians at Philadelphia have is their influence in the community. The church is small, and few members, if any, have any prestige in their hometown. (In 2.26 RSV "power" translates a different Greek word.) So one may render this clause as "I know that you do not have much prestige," or idiomatically as ". . . do not have much face."

And yet you have kept my word and have not denied my name: RSV has translated the initial Greek *kai* **and yet** (also NIV, RNAB, FRCL), which agrees with the context. This should be included in the translation. Despite their lack of power the Christians in Philadelphia have been faithful to Christ. The verbal phrase **have kept my word** means "have followed my teaching," "have obeyed my commands." Phps translates "have been faithful to my message," and Brc "have been obedient to my instructions."

And have not denied my name: see the similar "did not deny my faith" in 2.13; for **my name** see 2.3. This means "you have not disowned me," "you have not renounced your faith in me," "you have not said that you do not believe in me," or "you have not said, 'I don't believe in Jesus (Christ),'" that is, "you have not apostatized." For the same verb "deny" see Matthew 10.33; Luke 12.9; 2 Peter 2.1; Jude 4.

Alternative translation models for this verse are:

> I know the life you live. I know that you have only a little prestige. You have obeyed (or, followed) my commands and have not said that you do not know me. Look, I have opened a door in front of you which no one is able to shut.

Or:

> I know the things that you do. I know that you do not have much face. You have followed my teaching and have never said, "I don't know Jesus." I have opened a door in front of you which no one is able to shut.

3.9 RSV	TEV
Behold, I will make those of the synagogue of Satan who say that they are Jews and are not, but lie—behold, I will make them come and bow down before your feet, and learn that I have loved you.	Listen! As for that group that belongs to Satan, those liars who claim that they are Jews but are not, I will make them come and bow down at your feet. They will all know that I love you.

Behold: see the comments at 1.7.

Those of the synagogue of Satan who say that they are Jews and are not, but lie: for this description of their enemies, see 2.9. Here, somewhat redundantly, the text adds "but they lie."

After identifying these opponents, the text repeats: **behold, I will make them** (RSV). A translator may prefer to imitate TEV and have a less complex sentence (so also SPCL, REB), without the repetition of the main verb.

The form of the Greek phrase translated **those of** allows the meaning "some who belong to" (as in 2.10, "some of you"): so AT, TNT. This is because the Greek preposition for **of** (RSV) can mean either "from" or "out of." But it is rather strange that only some of their enemies will be punished, and the majority of translations do not take the Greek preposition to have this restrictive sense, but take "(those) from" to mean these Jews, as distinct from all other people: "those people who belong to the synagogue of Satan" or, as was suggested in the comments on 2.9, "members of a group that belongs to Satan."

I will make them come and bow down before your feet: this is a figure of submission, ordinarily taken to mean that they will have been defeated. But this gesture can be an indication of their desire to join the Christians (see similar language in Isa 45.14; 60.14). In certain languages **bow down before your feet** will be rendered as "prostrate themselves (or, lie face down) before your feet." However, if the phrase **before your feet** sounds strange in other languages, it may be translated as "in front of you."

And learn that I have loved you: instead of **learn**, which usually implies a process of learning, the translation should be "discover, find out, know, recognize, understand." In RSV **learn** is governed by **I will make them**; it is better to follow NRSV, "and they will learn," a separate event. For the verb "to love" see 1.5. The perfect tense **I have loved** may give the impression that he no longer loves; so it is better to translate "I love you."

An alternative translation model for this verse is:

> Look! I will cause those people who are members of a group who belong to Satan, who say, "We are God's chosen people," but are really lying, to come (or, go) and lie face down at your feet and understand (or, discover) that I love you.

Because you have kept my word of patient endurance, I will keep you from the hour of trial which is coming on the whole world, to try those who dwell upon the earth.	Because you have kept my command to endure, I will also keep you safe from the time of trouble which is coming upon the world to test all the people on earth.

Because you have kept my word of patient endurance: this means little if anything in English (NRSV is the same). Here **word** means "command, instruction, order, teaching," and the genitive phrase **of patient endurance** means "to endure patiently." For the verb "to keep" see 3.8, "kept"; and for **patient endurance** see 1.9. NIV has "Since you have kept my command to endure patiently"; REB is the same, except that it uses "to stand firm." One may also say "Because you have endured patiently as I commanded you" or ". . . been patient and endured, as I commanded you."

I will keep you from the hour of trial: this is a promise that the believers in Philadelphia will not be defeated by the suffering that will soon come upon all people in the world. This **hour of trial** is the time of distress and suffering which, in apocalyptic theology, will precede the end of the age, before the Messianic coming. The promise here is not that they alone, of all the world's population, will be exempt from these sufferings; rather the promise is that God will keep them firm during this period of hardship and calamity (see the similar thought in John 17.15). So it may be better to translate "I will keep you safe (protect you) in the time of distress that is coming on the world." NJB translates "I will keep you safe in the time of trial," and Beckwith comments: "The Philadelphians . . . are promised that they shall be carried in safety through the great trial, they shall not fall."

Which is coming on the whole world may be rendered as "that the people of the world will undergo" or "during the time when the people of the world suffer terribly."

The rest of the sentence—**which is coming on the whole world, to try those who dwell upon the earth**—shows that this **hour of trial** will affect everyone (see 7.14; 13.10; 14.12; Matt 24.7-13,22). Should **hour** give the idea of only sixty minutes, it is better to say "period," "time." And for **trial**, something like "suffering," "distress" is better than TEV "trouble." REB has "the ordeal that is to fall upon the whole world." The related verb "to try" means "to put to the test" (as in 2.10).

In this book **those who dwell on earth** is often used of the followers of Satan, the enemies of the people of God (6.10; 8.13; 11.10; 13.8,12,14; 17.2,8). Here it means all people, as the preceding clause makes clear.

An alternative translation model for this verse is:

> You have endured patiently as I commanded you. So I will protect you during the time when I test all the people of the world by causing them to endure great suffering.

3.11 RSV	TEV
I am coming soon; hold fast what you have, so that no one may seize your crown.	I am coming soon. Keep safe what you have, so that no one will rob you of your victory prize.

I am coming soon: this is the final coming, to judge and to inaugurate the Messianic kingdom. The time of distress and suffering is followed by the second coming of Christ (see 1.7; 22.7,12,20).

Hold fast what you have: see the comments at 2.25.

So that no one may seize your crown: see the comments at 2.10. The crown that Christ gives to his followers as the prize for their faithfulness must be kept safe from all who would, by some means, take it from them. What is meant is that they are to remain faithful so as not to lose their ultimate reward: life with Christ in the Messianic kingdom. Other ways of expressing this clause are "so that no person may take away (steal) your victory prize by force" or "so that no one may be able to use force and steal your prize that shows that you have conquered."

3.12 RSV	TEV
He who conquers, I will make him a pillar in the temple of my God; never shall he go out of it, and I will write on him the name of my God, and the name of the city of my God, the new Jerusalem which comes down from my God out of heaven, and my own new name.	I will make him who is victorious a pillar in the temple of my God, and he will never leave it. I will write on him the name of my God and the name of the city of my God, the new Jerusalem, which will come down out of heaven from my God. I will also write on him my new name.

He who conquers: see the comments at 2.7. Here, unlike the translation of this phrase in the other letters, TEV has the singular because of the actions that follow. The plural can be used, with the addition of "each one of them" to the verb phrase **I will write on**. NRSV uses the second person singular, "If you conquer . . ."; but this can be taken to mean the angel of the church instead of the members of the church. It is more likely that the third person is intended here. Other ways of rendering this are "the one (person) who conquers," "whoever conquers," and so on.

I will make him a pillar in the temple of my God: the common meaning of **pillar** is a stone or wooden post that supports a building. Here, however, as the following clause makes clear, the meaning is that this is an important part of the building, one that is put solidly in place and will last as long as **the temple of my God**, which is the eternal kingdom of God. The word used to translate **temple** should be quite generic, indicating a building used for worship; nothing so specific as "church," or "cathedral," or "synagogue" should be used. For the possessive **my God** see the comment at 3.2. In this context **God** does not belong to the speaker, Christ, but Christ serves God.

Never shall he go out of it: the pillar is solidly, permanently, eternally, a part of the temple of God. Nothing, no one, can remove it. The meaning may be expressed in a positive manner, "and he will always remain there," or else retain the negative, "he will never have to leave it."

In what follows, the Greek text can be understood to mean that the pillar is the object of the action of writing: "I will write on the pillar" (so NJB). But it seems more likely that it is the person, or persons, who is referred to as a pillar (so most translations).

For the names written on "those who conquer," see the similar statements in 14.1; 22.4. Here **the name of my God** indicates that this person belongs to the God of the glorified Christ; **the name of the city of my God** means that person is a citizen of the eternal city, **the new Jerusalem which comes down from my God out of heaven** (see 21.2,10). Instead of **comes down** it is better to translate "will (soon) come down." Some languages, like English, have two words, "sky" and "heaven," to translate the one Greek noun that covers both. In a passage like this, "sky" would not be a faithful translation of the Greek, inasmuch as the emphasis on the passage is that the new Jerusalem owes its existence to God, who dwells in heaven (see also 4.1). The last name, **my own new name,** is not easy to identify. Perhaps it refers to the name "The Word of God" (19.12-13), or the name "King of kings and Lord of lords" (19.16), or "the Lamb" (5.6), which appears fifty times in this book.

An alternative translation model for this verse is:

> I will make the person who conquers the powers of evil an important post in the big house for worshiping God whom I serve. This person will never have to leave there. I will write on him the name of my God and the name New Jerusalem, which is the name of the city of my God, which will come down from God out of heaven. I will also write on him my own new name.

3.13	RSV	TEV

He who has an ear, let him hear what the Spirit says to the churches.'

"If you have ears, then, listen to what the Spirit says to the churches!

For the translation of this verse, see 2.7.

B-7. The Message to Laodicea   3.14-22

RSV	TEV
	The Message to Laodicea

14 "And to the angel of the church in Laodicea write: 'The words of the Amen, the faithful and true witness, the beginning of God's creation.

15 "'I know your works: you are neither cold nor hot. Would that you were cold or hot! 16 So, because you are lukewarm, and neither cold nor hot, I will spew you out of my mouth! 17 For you say, I am rich, I have prospered, and I need

14 "To the angel of the church in Laodicea write:

"This is the message from the Amen, the faithful and true witness, who is the origin of all that God has created. 15 I know what you have done; I know that you are neither cold nor hot. How I wish you were either one or the other! 16 But because you are lukewarm, neither hot nor cold, I am going to spit you out of my mouth!

nothing; not knowing that you are wretched, pitiable, poor, blind, and naked. 18 Therefore I counsel you to buy from me gold refined by fire, that you may be rich, and white garments to clothe you and to keep the shame of your nakedness from being seen, and salve to anoint your eyes, that you may see. 19 Those whom I love, I reprove and chasten; so be zealous and repent. 20 Behold, I stand at the door and knock; if any one hears my voice and opens the door, I will come in to him and eat with him, and he with me. 21 He who conquers, I will grant him to sit with me on my throne, as I myself conquered and sat down with my Father on his throne. 22 He who has an ear, let him hear what the Spirit says to the churches.'"

17 You say, 'I am rich and well off; I have all I need.' But you do not know how miserable and pitiful you are! You are poor, naked, and blind. 18 I advise you, then, to buy gold from me, pure gold, in order to be rich. Buy also white clothing to dress yourself and cover up your shameful nakedness. Buy also some ointment to put on your eyes, so that you may see. 19 I rebuke and punish all whom I love. Be in earnest, then, and turn from your sins. 20 Listen! I stand at the door and knock; if anyone hears my voice and opens the door, I will come into his house and eat with him, and he will eat with me. 21 To those who win the victory I will give the right to sit beside me on my throne, just as I have been victorious and now sit by my Father on his throne.

22 "If you have ears, then, listen to what the Spirit says to the churches!"

SECTION HEADING: TEV "The Message to Laodicea." See 2.1.

3.14   RSV   TEV

"And to the angel of the church in Laodicea write: 'The words of the Amen, the faithful and true witness, the beginning of God's creation.

"To the angel of the church in Laodicea write:

"This is the message from the Amen, the faithful and true witness, who is the origin[a] of all that God has created.

[a] origin; *or* ruler.

For the opening statement see 2.1,8. **Laodicea**, south of Philadelphia, was a wealthy and flourishing commercial city, the home of manufacturers of articles made from native wool famous for its glossy black; it was also the center of banking operations, and of the worship of Asclepius, the god of healing. The church there had a close relationship to the neighboring churches in Hierapolis and Colossae (see Col 2.1; 4.13,15-16).

The words of: see comments at 2.1.

The Amen: the word itself is an affirmation, "It is so" (see 1.6), or a wish, "So be it." Here its meaning is that Christ is the guarantee, the confirmation, of all God's promises and plans (see also 2 Cor 1.20). In languages that already have a term used by churches that expresses the meaning of **Amen**, that term may be used in this context.

The faithful and true witness: see the comments at 1.5 for **the faithful . . . witness**. Here **faithful**, applied to Christ, refers to his reliability as a witness of God's message, and **true** to the content of his testimony. So this phrase may also be rendered as "the one who reveals the truth about God faithfully."

The beginning of God's creation: in English this could be understood to mean that Christ is the first being created by God; this, however, is not what the text means. As translated by TEV, "the origin of all that God has created" (note REB "the source of God's creation"), the meaning is that Christ is the one by means of whom God created all things, and in many languages it will be translated this way (see John 1.3; Col 1.16; Heb 1.2). The same Greek word for **beginning** is used also in Colossians 1.18 in the sense of "source." As the TEV footnote indicates, the word may mean "ruler" (so NIV), but the other meaning is preferred by the large majority of commentaries and translations. Most translations use "origin"; a few use "source." The phrase **God's creation** means "what God has created"; in this context it includes everything that God has created.

An alternative translation model for this verse, beginning with the quotation, is:

> The one who is called the Amen gives this message (says all these things). He faithfully reveals the truth about God, and is the one through whom God created all things.

3.15-16 RSV	TEV
15 " 'I know your works: you are neither cold nor hot. Would that you were cold or hot! 16 So, because you are lukewarm, and neither cold nor hot, I will spew you out of my mouth.	15 I know what you have done; I know that you are neither cold nor hot. How I wish you were either one or the other! 16 But because you are lukewarm, neither hot nor cold, I am going to spit you out of my mouth!

I know your works: see comments at 2.2.

You are neither cold nor hot: this is a judgment on their spiritual condition. Three times the phrase **cold nor hot** appears in these two verses. In certain languages it will be necessary to dispense with the figurative language and say something like "You are neither unresponsive nor enthusiastic toward me."

Would that: a wish can be expressed by "How I wish (that)" (TEV, REB), "I wish that" (NRSV), or "I want you to be . . . ."

You are lukewarm: in matters of spirit and Christian life, they are indifferent, ineffective, impotent. The symptoms of their spiritual indifference are given in verses 17-18. In some languages these metaphors of heat, cold, and lukewarmness may not make sense, and an appropriate figure must be used, or else the figurative language must be abandoned altogether; for example, "You are totally ineffective" or "You are only half-hearted in your faith."

I will spew you out of my mouth: this is a figure of disgust and rejection. The glorified Christ will no longer tolerate such lukewarm, ineffective believers. They are like salt that has lost its saltness, which will be thrown out as useless (Matt 5.13). Again, in some languages it will be necessary to abandon the metaphors or figurative language and say, for example, "I will reject you."

In the verbal phrase **I will spew**, **will** represents a Greek verb that adds a note of urgency and divine authority (see 1.19).

An alternative translation model for these verses is:

79

15 I know all the things that you have done. In your lives you are neither unresponsive nor enthusiastic toward me. I wish you were either of these. 16 But, because you are only half-hearted in your belief in me, I will reject you.

3.17   RSV   TEV

For you say, I am rich, I have pros-   You say, 'I am rich and well off; I have
pered, and I need nothing; not knowing   all I need.' But you do not know how
that you are wretched, pitiable, poor,   miserable and pitiful you are! You are
blind, and naked.   poor, naked, and blind.

There is no praise for the Christians of Laodicea. Christ confronts their false claims with the truth about their spiritual condition. They boast: **I am rich, I have prospered, and I need nothing.** They are the opposite of the believers at Smyrna, who thought they were poor but who, Christ said, were really rich. **Rich** may also be rendered as "have many possessions" (see also 2.9 for other ways to express this word). **Prospered** in this context is simply a synonym for **rich.** For **I need nothing** one may say "I don't need any more possessions."

This verse has typical repetition and redundancy for emphasis. Unless the redundancy carries the wrong message, as sometimes it does, the translator should avoid the temptation to reduce it. Often redundancy is common and effective in religious services. The verbal phrases are quite general in scope, and appropriate equivalents should not be hard to find.

Not knowing that you are wretched, pitiable, poor, blind, and naked: again there is an accumulation, this time of adjectives, to indicate the spiritual poverty of the Laodicean Christians. The adjective translated **wretched** (TEV "miserable") appears elsewhere in the New Testament only at Romans 7.24. It also means "unhappy, unfortunate, or pathetic." The word translated **pitiable** means "deserving pity" (it appears also in 1 Cor 15.19). In certain languages this word will be translated as "have much shame" or "have no face." The noun **poor** appears once more in Revelation (13.16); see also 2.9 on the translation of "poverty." **Blind** appears only here in Revelation, and **naked** appears also in 16.15; 17.16. The Greek word translated **naked** sometimes means only "poorly clothed," but here the idea of being completely unclothed is required.

The translator will notice that TEV reverses the last two adjectives: "naked, and blind." It is impossible now to explain why this was done, except that "naked and blind" seems to finish the sentence better than "blind and naked." In any case, a translator should follow the order of the Greek text as in RSV, unless it is more natural in the receptor language to reverse the order of these adjectives.

Instead of making this a dependent clause, as RSV does, it is better to put a full stop at **nothing** and begin a new sentence, as TEV and others do. In some languages this second sentence can be in the form of a rhetorical question: "Don't you know that . . . ?" "Can't you see that . . . ?"

3.18 RSV TEV

Therefore I counsel you to buy from me gold refined by fire, that you may be rich, and white garments to clothe you and to keep the shame of your nakedness from being seen, and salve to anoint your eyes, that you may see.	I advise you, then, to buy gold from me, pure gold, in order to be rich. Buy also white clothing to dress yourself and cover up your shameful nakedness. Buy also some ointment to put on your eyes, so that you may see.

Therefore I counsel you to buy from me gold refined by fire: the introductory **Therefore** introduces Christ's reaction to the beginning of verse 17, "Because you say . . . ." One may also say "For this reason . . . ." The verb translated **counsel** means to advise, recommend, instruct. It does not carry the idea of force, so that "I command" or its equivalent would be wrong (see the related noun "counselor" in Rom 11.34).

The figurative language that follows the advice that Christ gives to the people of Laodicea is intended to show them how they can gain spiritual wealth, holiness, and insight. The three things they are advised to buy will meet their pitiable condition of poverty, blindness, and nakedness. The phrase **gold refined by fire** means "the finest gold," "the purest gold" (for comments on **refined** see 1.15).

That you may be rich: this is a figure for spiritual wealth, but the translator is to express the literal meaning of material riches, unless strict adherence to the literal symbol will cause people in certain cultures to think that Christians will become materially rich. In such cases it will be helpful to translate **that you may be rich** as "in order that you may become spiritually rich" or "that you may become rich in God's sight."

And white garments to clothe you: the color **white** here probably symbolizes purity, as indicated by the following phrase, **to keep the shame of your nakedness from being seen**. To be seen naked was considered a shameful thing; **the shame of your nakedness** means "your shameful nakedness." Of course the abstract quality **nakedness** can feel neither shame nor pride, so that the phrase may need to be expanded somewhat: "so that you will avoid the shame (or, disgrace) of being seen naked" or "so that you will not lose face (have shame) by having people see you naked."

And salve to anoint your eyes, that you may see: the salve was some sort of remedy for the eyes, in the form of a paste or powder. Commentators refer to the Phrygian eye powder, used by physicians in the temple of Asclepius. The generic "eye medicine" may be used, if the equivalent of the specific **salve**, or "ointment," or "paste" is not available. The compound verb translated "to anoint" is formed of the preposition *en* with the simple verb *chriō*, "to anoint," the verb that is the origin of the title *christos*, "the anointed one" (see Luke 4.18; Acts 4.27). (Another compound verb, *epichriō*, is used in John 9.6,11.) **See** in this context will be rendered in many languages by the equivalent of "look and see" or "see and recognize."

This verse is one rather long sentence, with the verb **to buy** followed by three direct objects, each of which includes a purpose clause. It may be better to follow the example of TEV and have a complete sentence for each of the three objects that are to be bought, with the repetition of the verb **to buy**.

An alternative translation model for this verse is:

For this reason, I advise you to buy from me gold that has been refined (or melted down to get rid of impurities) in order that you may become rich. You must also buy white clothes to put on yourself so that you may avoid the shame of people seeing you naked. You must also buy some salve (eye medicine) to put on (in) your eyes, so that you may be able to see.

3.19

RSV	TEV
Those whom I love, I reprove and chasten; so be zealous and repent.	I rebuke and punish all whom I love. Be in earnest, then, and turn from your sins.

Christ assures the Laodiceans that he loves them, which is precisely the reason why he disciplines them.

Those whom will often be rendered as "The people whom."

I love: the personal pronoun **I** is emphatic in the Greek text. The Greek verb *phileō* carries a warm emotional content; it can also mean "to kiss" (see Mark 14.44). With the meaning "to love" it is not, nor can it be, used in the imperative mode. For the similar verb *agapaō* see 1.5b; 3.9.

I reprove and chasten: the language is very much like that of Proverbs 3.12 and Hebrews 12.6. The first verb occurs in Revelation only here; it means "to rebuke," "to reprimand," "to scold," or "to censure." It means to tell someone what they have done wrong. The second verb can have the milder sense of "to train" (NJB), or else "to discipline," "to correct" (so TOB, SPCL, NRSV, REB, TNT, Brc, NIV, Mft, AT, Phps); it can also have the stronger meaning "to punish," "to chastise physically" (as in Luke 23.16,22; 2 Cor 6.9): so TEV, FRCL, BRCL, RNAB. One cannot be dogmatic about which is the preferable meaning here, but on the whole it seems that "to punish" fits the context best.

So be zealous and repent: the conjunction **so** connects this clause to the reason why the Christians of Laodicea must **be zealous and repent**, and that is to avoid the punishment they will otherwise suffer. The verb **be zealous** (only here in Revelation) is the opposite of lukewarmness (described in 3.16); it denotes enthusiasm, eagerness. The Greek verb is in the present tense, indicating a continuing attitude; the following **repent** is in the aorist tense, denoting a once-for-all change of mind (see 2.5). Some translators will wish to follow RSV's model and begin this final clause with the equivalent of **so** or "therefore."

3.20

RSV	TEV
Behold, I stand at the door and knock; if any one hears my voice and opens the door, I will come in to him and eat with him, and he with me.	Listen! I stand at the door and knock; if anyone hears my voice and opens the door, I will come into his house and eat with him, and he will eat with me.

Behold: see 1.7. NRSV has "Listen!"

I stand at the door and knock: the figure is of Christ's standing outside the house and seeking (not demanding) admission by knocking at the front door. Ways of seeking admission to a house vary, and the proper cultural equivalent must be used here to avoid a wrong implication. One may say, for example, "I clear my throat." Or the visitor claps his hands or uses a particular word or phrase that indicates to the people in the house that someone is outside wishing to enter. In cases where houses do not have doors, one may say "I stand outside your house asking you to let me enter." But nothing so modern as "I ring the front doorbell" should be used. If a specific way of requesting admission is unsuitable, the generic "I stand at the door of the house and ask to be allowed in" or its equivalent may be used. It is interesting to notice that what follows is "if anyone hears my voice and opens the door" (TEV), which may be the reason why SPCL translates here "I am at the door, calling." Commentators are divided as to whether this figure is of Christ's seeking admission to the heart of every individual believer, or represents the final coming of Christ. It seems more in keeping with the context to follow the first option.

If any one hears my voice and opens the door: the words imply that, not only does Christ knock at the door, but he also calls out, requesting admission. **Opens the door** may be rendered in certain cultures as "invites me into the house."

I will come in to him and eat with him, and he with me: NRSV avoids the exclusively masculine **him** and **he** by changing to the second person singular, "if you hear my voice . . . ." RSV's literal **come in to him** is not only unnatural English but may carry a sexual connotation; it is unfortunate that NRSV has not changed this wording. TEV's rendering "come into his house" is more natural.

The matter of direction in the use of the verb **come in** as opposed to "go in" may be of vital importance: "come" represents the point of view of the host; "go" represents the point of view of the guest. Of all English translations consulted, only Phps has "go." See 1.1-2, page 15, on the use of modal verbs indicating direction.

It is not necessary to repeat the literal **I will . . . eat with him, and he** (will eat) **with me**; something like "we will eat together" or "we will have a meal together" is sufficient. It seems somewhat fanciful to imagine that the words mean that at the meal Christ will first be the guest and then play the part of the host, which a literal translation may imply.

An alternative translation model for this verse is:

> Pay attention! I am standing in front of the house and clearing my throat (clapping my hands). If anyone hears me and invites me into the house, I will come (go) in and eat a meal with him.

3.21	RSV	TEV
	He who conquers, I will grant him to sit with me on my throne, as I myself conquered and sat down with my Father on his throne.	To those who win the victory I will give the right to sit beside me on my throne, just as I have been victorious and now sit by my Father on his throne.

He who conquers: see 2.7.

I will grant him to sit with me on my throne: if there is something strange about two people sitting together on the same throne, an alternative like the following can be said: "I will give him (or, them) the right to sit on a throne (or, on thrones) beside my throne" (see Luke 22.29-30). The meaning of the verb translated **grant** may be expressed by "I will give the privilege" (Brc); "the honour" (Phps); or "the right" (TEV, TNT, NIV, BRCL, FRCL). On the translation of **throne** see 1.4.

As I myself conquered and sat down: the parallelism between the experience of the believers who conquer their enemies and the conquering Christ is exact and complete. The past tense in English, **I . . . sat down** (translating the Greek aorist tense), may carry the implication that no longer does Christ sit on the throne with the Father (see 22.1,3); so something like "I have taken my seat" (AT, Phps, NJB), as a permanent, actual reality, may be preferable. Or else TEV and RNAB's use of the present tense "sit" may be better.

An alternative translation model for this verse is:

> I will give the person who is victorious over the forces of evil the right to sit on a throne beside my throne. This will be just like me, who have conquered the forces of evil and have taken my seat beside my Father.

3.22   RSV   TEV

He who has an ear, let him hear what the Spirit says to the churches.' "   **"If you have ears, then, listen to what the Spirit says to the churches!"**

See comments on the same sentence at 2.7.

C. Visions of Things to Come

(4.1–22.5)

C-1. The Scene in Heaven
(4.1–5.14)

4.1-11

RSV

1 After this I looked, and lo, in heaven an open door! And the first voice, which I had heard speaking to me like a trumpet, said, "Come up hither, and I will show you what must take place after this." 2 At once I was in the Spirit, and lo, a throne stood in heaven, with one seated on the throne! 3 And he who sat there appeared like jasper and carnelian, and round the throne was a rainbow that looked like an emerald.· 4 Round the throne were twenty-four thrones, and seated on the thrones were twenty-four elders, clad in white garments, with golden crowns upon their heads. 5 From the throne issue flashes of lightning, and voices and peals of thunder, and before the throne burn seven torches of fire, which are the seven spirits of God; 6 and before the throne there is as it were a sea of glass, like crystal.

And round the throne, on each side of the throne, are four living creatures, full of eyes in front and behind: 7 the first living creature like a lion, the second living creature like an ox, the third living creature with the face of a man, and the fourth living creature like a flying eagle. 8 And the four living creatures, each of them with six wings, are full of eyes all round and within, and day and night they never cease to sing,

"Holy, holy, holy, is the Lord God Almighty,

who was and is and is to come!"
9 And whenever the living creatures give glory and honor and thanks to him who is seated on the throne, who lives for ever and ever, 10 the twenty-four elders fall down before him who is seated on the throne and worship him who lives for ever and ever; they cast their crowns before the throne, singing,

TEV

Worship in Heaven

1 At this point I had another vision and saw an open door in heaven.

And the voice that sounded like a trumpet, which I had heard speaking to me before, said, "Come up here, and I will show you what must happen after this." 2 At once the Spirit took control of me. There in heaven was a throne with someone sitting on it. 3 His face gleamed like such precious stones as jasper and carnelian, and all around the throne there was a rainbow the color of an emerald. 4 In a circle around the throne were twenty-four other thrones, on which were seated twenty-four elders dressed in white and wearing crowns of gold. 5 From the throne came flashes of lightning, rumblings, and peals of thunder. In front of the throne seven lighted torches were burning, which are the seven spirits of God. 6 Also in front of the throne there was what looked like a sea of glass, clear as crystal.

Surrounding the throne on each of its sides, were four living creatures covered with eyes in front and behind. 7 The first one looked like a lion; the second looked like a bull; the third had a face like a man's face; and the fourth looked like an eagle in flight. 8 Each one of the four living creatures had six wings, and they were covered with eyes, inside and out. Day and night they never stop singing:

"Holy, holy, holy, is the Lord God Almighty,

who was, who is, and who is to come."

9 The four living creatures sing songs of glory and honor and thanks to the one who sits on the throne, who lives forever and ever. When they do so, 10 the twenty-four elders fall down before the one who sits on the throne, and worship him

11   "Worthy art thou, our Lord and God,
     to receive glory and honor and power,
     for thou didst create all things,
     and by thy will they existed and were
       created."
	who lives forever and ever. They throw their
	crowns down in front of the throne and say,
	11 "Our Lord and God! You are worthy
	     to receive glory, honor, and power.
	     For you created all things,
	       and by your will they were given exis-
	       tence and life."

SECTION HEADING: TEV "Worship in Heaven." Other possible headings include: "A vision of God on his throne in heaven," "A vision of God being worshiped in heaven," "John sees God on his throne in heaven," or "John sees God sitting on his high chief chair in heaven."

This vision opens with a description of God in heaven being worshiped by twenty-four elders and four living creatures. God's appearance is described, as is that of the living creatures. The vision provides the setting for the scroll that God holds in his right hand, a scroll sealed with seven seals. The Lamb takes the scroll from God and proceeds to break the seals one by one (6.1). As each seal is broken, a new vision takes place. After the vision following the breaking of the sixth seal (6.12-17), there are two other visions (7.1-17). The breaking of the seventh seal (8.1) introduces another series: the seven trumpets that are blown by seven angels. Chapter 4, then, is the beginning of a longer section which goes to 8.1.

4.1   RSV   TEV

RSV	TEV
After this I looked, and lo, in heaven an open door! And the first voice, which I had heard speaking to me like a trumpet, said, "Come up hither, and I will show you what must take place after this."	At this point I had another vision and saw an open door in heaven. And the voice that sounded like a trumpet, which I had heard speaking to me before, said, "Come up here, and I will show you what must happen after this."

After this I looked, and lo, in heaven an open door! The opening phrase **After this** formally closes one event and begins another one (see 7.1,9; 15.5; 18.1). One may also translate "After all these events (these things) had happened," or even "After I had seen all these things." **I looked** indicates that John is having a vision: REB "I had a vision"; TEV "I had another vision" (after the first one that begins at 1.12); similar are AT, Brc, FRCL. In languages that do not distinguish between dreams and visions, one may render **I looked** as "I again saw as in a dream" or "I dreamed again and saw."

Lo: see comments on "Behold" in 1.7. NRSV reads "and there in heaven." Many translators may wish to follow this model.

As noticed in 3.12, the same Greek word can mean "sky" or "heaven" (in Matt 16.1 it means "heaven"; in 16.2, "sky"). Here "sky" is not an appropriate translation; God dwells in heaven, which is not regarded as a physical place.

An open door: this translates the perfect passive participle of the verb "to open"; "a door that had been opened." The emphasis, however, is not on who opened it or when it was opened, but on the fact that it was open when John looked at it. In those cultures where doors are not used or known, one may say, for example, "An opening into heaven."

The first voice, which I had heard speaking to me like a trumpet: the voice issues out of heaven, through the open door. It is the same voice that John had heard before (1.10), the voice of Christ. It is not necessary to translate literally **the first voice**; it is more natural to say "the voice I had heard before" or "the voice that had spoken to me earlier."

Said: the Greek has the masculine participle, which does not agree either with **voice** or with **trumpet**, both of which are feminine. But John is referring to the one who spoke, that is, Christ, not to a disembodied voice. In certain languages it will be more natural to render this clause as "And the person who had a voice like a trumpet spoke to me again and said . . . ."

Come up hither: NRSV has, more appropriately, "Come up here." The command does not indicate how John will get there; this is a vision, not a physical or metaphysical experience.

I will show you what must take place after this: for the whole phrase see 1.19; for **must** see 1.1. The phrase **after this** is rather vague: it means simply "in the future" but does not specify whether it will be soon or much later. In light of 1.1, however, it is reasonable to suppose that the time for these things to happen will be soon. Another way of expressing this clause is "I will cause you to see (or, let you see) the things that will happen after this."

An alternative translation model for this verse is:

> After I had seen all these things, I dreamed again and saw that there was an opening (door) into heaven. And the person who had a voice like a trumpet spoke to me again and said, "Come up here and I will let you see the things that will happen after this."

4.2

RSV	TEV
At once I was in the Spirit, and lo, a throne stood in heaven, with one seated on the throne!	At once the Spirit took control of me. There in heaven was a throne with someone sitting on it.

At once I was in the Spirit: see the comments at 1.10. NRSV has "At once I was in the spirit," by which an ecstatic experience is meant, although this is a very unusual way in English of saying that (note AT "I found myself in a trance"; Brc "I fell into a trance"; NJB "I fell into ecstasy"). The main justification for translating this way is the fact that in Greek the word "spirit" does not have the definite article; this, however, does not prove that the writer is talking about an ecstatic experience that has nothing to do with God's Spirit. On the supposition that God's Spirit is meant, there are several ways to translate: "The Spirit came upon me" (TNT); "I knew myself to be inspired by the Spirit" (Phps); "I fell under the power of the Spirit" (SPCL); "I was overpowered by the Spirit" (BRCL). It is preferable to refer specifically to the presence and action of God's Spirit. So "God's Spirit took control of me" is also a justifiable rendering.

Lo: see "Behold" in 1.7. In many languages the equivalent of **lo** in this context will be "I saw . . . ."

A throne stood in heaven, with one seated on the throne: for **throne** see 1.4; 2.13. The verb translated **stood** is better represented in English by "was" or "was placed"; it denotes simply location, without any indication as to how it got there. RNAB has "A throne was there in heaven." The one sitting on it is described in verses 4-5 but never identified by name. If possible, a translation should avoid saying specifically that God is the one who is sitting there. In later visions John does identify God by name (7.10,15; 12.5; 19.4).

An alternative translation model for this verse is:

> At once God's Spirit took control of me, and I saw there in heaven
> a throne on which someone was sitting.

4.3   RSV   TEV

And he who sat there appeared like jasper and carnelian, and round the throne was a rainbow that looked like an emerald.	His face gleamed like such precious stones as jasper and carnelian, and all around the throne there was a rainbow the color of an emerald.

This verse continues without a stop from verse 2. The portrayal of the invisible God is in terms of similarity with light and colors, without any attempt at a physical description.

He who sat there appeared like jasper and carnelian: the important thing about the semiprecious stones **jasper** and **carnelian** is their color, not their consistency, shape, or size. Beckwith comments: "the language is meant to express merely the splendor of the light in which the prophet beholds God manifested and encircled." The Greek "had the appearance of jasper and carnelian" means "(he who sat there) shone with a light the color of jasper and carnelian." So RNAB "whose appearance sparkled like"; Phps "His appearance blazed like"; FRCL "he had the resplendent brilliance of." TEV "His face (gleamed)" is too specific and should not be imitated by translators, since in biblical literature no mortal sees the face of God.

There is no complete certainty about all the stones that appear in Revelation. The semiprecious jasper may be yellow, brown, red, or green; it is actually somewhat dull and opaque. Some commentators suggest that the writer had in mind an opal; others, a diamond. The same holds true for the carnelian, which is usually red. NJB translates "a diamond and a ruby." If the specific names for the stones are not available, a translation can say "a green and red light, like the colors of some precious stones." But in areas where semiprecious stones are unknown, one may simply say "He shone (or, glowed) with a beautiful green and red light" or "His appearance shone (or, glowed) . . . ."

And round the throne was a rainbow that looked like an emerald: the language seems to indicate that the rainbow formed a complete horizontal circle around the throne, something like a halo (which AT and Phps say). Less probable is the possibility that the rainbow formed an arch over the throne. The important thing in the comparison with the emerald, a green-colored precious stone, is not the color (a green rainbow would be a strange sight indeed, even in a vision) but its brilliance. So a translation will do well to translate "that shone like an emerald" (FRCL, BRCL), "gleaming like an emerald" (Brc), or "bright as an emerald" (REB). Again, as in the case of jaspers and carnelians above, if precious stones are unknown, a translator may say, for example, "there was a rainbow that gleamed brightly."

4.4	RSV	TEV
	Round the throne were twenty-four thrones, and seated on the thrones were twenty-four elders, clad in white garments, with golden crowns upon their heads.	In a circle around the throne were twenty-four other thrones, on which were seated twenty-four elders dressed in white and wearing crowns of gold.

Round the throne were twenty-four thrones: normal English usage requires ". . . twenty-four *other* thrones" (TEV, NIV; also FRCL, SPCL, BRCL). See 1.4 for comments on the translation of **throne**.

Twenty-four elders: the Greek word means, generally, "older (person)." In a specific sense the word indicates not only advanced age but also the authority and prestige that such a person has. The problem in translation is that of finding a term that fits this context; in English **elders** are usually certain church officers. A further complication is that the specific "(older) men" or "(older) people" should not be used; these are not human but angelic beings. In many languages it will be natural to translate **elders** as "important elderly leaders" or "elderly leaders with great prestige." In languages such as these a distinction can also be made between the thrones that these elders sat on and the other throne in the middle. There is no general agreement on the significance of the number twenty-four. One may say "In a circle around the high chief's chair were twenty-four lesser chiefs' chairs."

White garments: these may indicate purity, or victory, or immortality (see 3.5).

Golden crowns: these are not wreaths of victory, as in 2.10, but the kind of crowns that kings wear. In certain languages **crowns** in this context will be rendered as "king's hat" or "high chief's hat."

An alternative translation model for this verse is:

> In a circle around that throne (or, high chief's chair) stood twenty-four other thrones (or, lesser chiefs' chairs). Twenty-four important elderly leaders were sitting on these chairs. They wore white clothes and chiefs' hats (crowns) on their heads.

4.5-6a	RSV	TEV
	5 From the throne issue flashes of lightning, and voices and peals of thunder, and before the throne burn seven torches of fire, which are the seven spirits of God; 6 and before the throne there is as	5 From the throne came flashes of lightning, rumblings, and peals of thunder. In front of the throne seven lighted torches were burning, which are the seven spirits of God. 6 Also in front of

it were a sea of glass, like crystal.   **the throne there was what looked like a sea of glass, clear as crystal.**

In verses 5-8 the main verbs are all in the present tense (see RSV). The translator must determine what will be the effect of switching from the past tense of the previous verses to the present tense in these verses, before deciding whether or not to imitate RSV.

From the throne . . . issue flashes of lightning, and voices and peals of thunder: all three things appear, together with an earthquake, in 8.5; 11.19; 16.18. They come from God's throne; it seems that the lightning flashes down to the earth. It is possible that the Greek, literally "voices and thunders," means "peals of thunder," "the roar of thunderclaps," as one event, not two. Most translations, however, have two different things: "voices (or, noises) and thunders." The word translated **voices** usually means human voices; it can mean "sounds" or "noises" (see John 3.8; 1 Cor 14.7,8; Rev 9.9; 18.22). If a choice must be made, perhaps "sounds" or "noises" is better. The trouble with **voices** is that it is undefined; it refers most likely not to God's voice but to the voices of angels. The translator should be willing to translate "peals of thunder," "the sound of thunders" (see 6.1; 10.3; 14.2; 19.6). In certain languages **thunder** is described as "the sky roars" or "the sound of the sky roaring." In such cases the first part of this verse may be rendered as "And lightning was flashing out of the throne, along with loud rumbling noises" or ". . . and the sound of the sky roaring."

Before the throne: NRSV is better: "in front of the throne."

Burn seven torches of fire: TNT is more natural: "seven torches were burning." A torch usually consisted of a stick or club, one end of which was wrapped with some material that burned a long time, such as a tightly wound cloth soaked with pitch or resin (see 8.10; John 18.3).

Which are the seven spirits of God: for **the seven spirits** see 1.4; **of God** means "that belong to God" or "that serve God" (see 3.1). A translation should say quite literally *are* **the seven spirits** and not "represent" or "symbolize (the seven spirits of God)."

And before the throne: this repeats what is said in the previous verse. What follows is a description of the pavement of the great throne room (see Exo 24.10).

There is as it were a sea of glass like crystal: this very literal translation of the Greek is not normal English style. NRSV is better: "there is something like a sea of glass, like crystal." This is not easy to visualize, and translations differ. The words **glass** and **crystal**, like "jasper and carnelian" in verse 3, may not necessarily indicate that the water was solid as glass or crystal, but that it was as clear, or as bright, as glass or crystal. So FRCL "there was what seemed to be a glass sea, as clear as crystal"; SPCL ". . . as transparent as crystal"; REB "what looked like a sea of glass or a sheet of ice." (The Greek word translated "crystal" may mean "ice.") NJB combines the two, "a sea as transparent as crystal." Everything considered, it seems best to imitate TEV and FRCL. In some languages the equivalent of **sea** indicates too large a body of water. In such a case the equivalent of a "small lake" will be more natural.

An alternative translation model for 4.5-6a is:

Lightning flashed out of the throne, and the sky roared (thundered). In front of the throne seven torches were burning; these are the seven spirits that serve God. Also, in front of the throne there was what looked like a lake (sea) made out of clear (transparent) glass just like ice.

4.6b-7   RSV   TEV

6b And round the throne, on each side of the throne, are four living creatures, full of eyes in front and behind: 7 the first living creature like a lion, the second living creature like an ox, the third living creature with the face of a man, and the fourth living creature like a flying eagle.

6b Surrounding the throne on each of its sides, were four living creatures covered with eyes in front and behind. 7 The first one looked like a lion; the second looked like a bull; the third had a face like a man's face; and the fourth looked like an eagle in flight.

And round the throne, on each side of the throne: this is a difficult passage to understand; the Greek text says literally "in the middle of the throne and around the throne." This is usually understood as RSV and TEV have translated it. Beckwith states: "One at the middle of each of the four sides of the throne." Another possibility is presented by REB: "In the center, round the throne itself" (also NIV). What seems to be indicated is that the four living creatures stood immediately next to the throne, one on each of its four sides, and around them were the twenty-four elders on their thrones. A recent study by R.G. Hall (*New Testament Studies,* October 1990) explains this strange passage as follows: "The living creatures are part of the throne; like carved legs on a chair, they surround the seat and support it" (page 610). The writer of the book "conceives the four living creatures as an integral part of the throne. They are 'within the space taken up by the throne,' as the back, arms or legs of a chair are within the space taken up by the chair. They are around the throne as the legs, arms, and back surround a chair" (page 612). This may be correct, but it may be extremely difficult to express in an understandable manner; a footnote would certainly be required. It is recommended that the translator follow the example of TEV.

Are four living creatures, full of eyes in front and behind: the word translated **creatures** means, in most contexts, "animals," but that specific meaning should not be used here. They are simply living beings, not classified either as animals or humans. They appear frequently in chapters 4–6; see also 7.11; 14.3; 15.7; 19.4. They seem modeled after the living beings in Ezekiel 1.5-14. They are "covered with eyes in front and behind" (TEV), that is, over their whole body, not just in their heads. In many cultures where there is a long Christian tradition employing a transliteration of "cherub" or "seraph" as the equivalent of **living creature**, and if translators feel that this term should continue to be employed, a footnote or a note in the glossary describing these creatures should be provided.

In the description that follows it appears that **like a lion . . . like an ox** is meant to describe only the head, not the whole creature. (In Ezek 1.6; 10.14, it is stated that each creature had four faces.) In areas where lions are unknown and there is no word for this animal, it will be helpful to say, for example, "wild animal named 'lion,'" or employ a generic term in the language meaning "predator (flesh eating animal)" and append the name "lion." See also *Fauna and Flora of the Bible,* pages 50-51, for a further discussion on lions. Most translations here are quite literal, and it is probably better to translate "was like a lion . . . was like an ox." The word translated **ox** may mean a calf (TNT, RNAB, Phps), a bull (TEV, NJB, SPCL, BRCL), an ox (RSV, NRSV, REB, NIV, AT, Brc), a young bull (TOB), or a young calf (FRCL). It is recommended that the translation use a term for a young male animal, or simply "bull."

With the face of a man: in the case of the third creature, it is specifically stated that it had a face that looked like a human face. It is better to translate as TEV has done, "a face like a man's face," or NRSV "a face like a human face." The word "like" should not be disregarded.

Like a flying eagle: it seems probable that this indicates the appearance of the creature's head, and not the whole body. But it is better to translate quite literally, "looked like an eagle in flight" (TEV). In languages where the eagle is unknown, some other bird that soars high in the sky may be named.

4.8	RSV	TEV

And the four living creatures, each of them with six wings, are full of eyes all round and within, and day and night they never cease to sing,
    "Holy, holy, holy, is the Lord
        God Almighty,
    who was and is and is to come!"
	Each one of the four living creatures had six wings, and they were covered with eyes, inside and out. Day and night they never stop singing:
	    "Holy, holy, holy, is the Lord
	        God Almighty,
	    who was, who is, and who is to
	        come."

And the four living creatures . . . are full of eyes all round and within: the main problem here is the meaning of **within**; it seems that what is meant is that they had eyes all over the body (verse 6b), including the underside of the wings.

Each of them with six wings: like the seraphim of Isaiah 6.2.

And day and night they never cease to sing: the Greek is quite vivid: "and they have no rest, day and night, saying." TNT does an effective job of representing this: "Day and night, without resting, they sing." Where a dynamic equivalent of **day and night** does not exist, something like "they sing all the time" or "without stopping" may be said. The Greek has "saying," but in this liturgical context something like "singing" or "chanting" is quite appropriate. Certain languages will employ idiomatic expressions for continuous singing or talking; for example, "they sing without letting their mouths stop."

Holy, holy, holy, is the Lord God Almighty: this is like the song of the seraphim in Isaiah 6.3. For **holy** see 3.7. Here it represents the separateness, the apartness, of God from all created things, with probable emphasis on the purity of God, without the flaws or sins that characterize human beings. It is recommended that the song appear in poetic style (see Section F of the introduction, "Translating the Revelation to John," pages 6 and following).

For the translation of the phrase **Lord God Almighty**, see 1.8.

Who was and is and is to come: see 1.4, where the same expressions occur but in a different order.

4.9   RSV   TEV

And whenever the living creatures give glory and honor and thanks to him who is seated on the throne, who lives for ever and ever,	The four living creatures sing songs of glory and honor and thanks to the one who sits on the throne, who lives forever and ever. When they do so,

And whenever the living creatures: this is how the Greek text begins the sentence that runs through verse 11. The word **whenever** seems to contradict the preceding statement that they never stop their praise. Verses 9-10 show that their praise is done repeatedly, but not continuously. Each time the living creatures sing praise to God, the twenty-four elders prostrate themselves and worship him.

Give glory and honor and thanks: in ritual language individual words do not retain their precise distinctive meanings but mingle with other words for the total effect. What matters is the impact of the statement as a whole, not the separate meaning of each individual word or phrase.

To **give glory** to God means to proclaim that God is "glorious," that is, majestic and wonderful. To **give . . . honor** to God is to proclaim that God is great, famous, worthy of praise. To **give . . . thanks** is to thank, to declare one's gratitude for benefits received. For **glory** see 1.6; the word translated **honor** appears also in 4.11; 5.12,13; 7.12; 21.26, always associated with **glory**. The noun translated **thanks** appears elsewhere in Revelation only at 7.12.

To him who is seated on the throne: it may be necessary to introduce the name "God": "to God, who sits on his throne" (see 4.2).

Who lives for ever and ever: this is an expression used of God (see Dan 4.34; 6.26; 12.7). It may be necessary to say "who never dies" or "whose life will never end." The word "immortality" is used in 1 Timothy 6.16.

An alternative translation model for this verse is:

> The four living creatures sing songs to the one who sits on the throne, who lives forever. They sing, saying that he is powerful, with great honor, and they thank him for what he has done for them.

4.10   RSV   TEV

the twenty-four elders fall down before him who is seated on the throne and worship him who lives for ever and ever; they cast their crowns before the throne, singing,	the twenty-four elders fall down before the one who sits on the throne, and worship him who lives forever and ever. They throw their crowns down in front of the throne and say,

The twenty-four elders fall down: as in 1.17, to **fall down** means to kneel down or to lie prostrate on the ground.

Before him who is seated on the throne and worship him who lives for ever and ever: this repeats from the previous verse the two phrases that describe God. This repetition is very much a part of the style of the author, and a translation should not try to abbreviate the text by omitting what seems to be unnecessary repetition.

Worship: to worship is to acknowledge the unique status and worth of the one being worshiped, and the relationship of that one to the worshiper. Louw and Nida, *Greek-English Lexicon* (volume 1, page 540), define as follows: "to express by attitude and possibly by position one's allegiance to and regard for deity." The Greek verb used here may mean "to kneel before" (see its use in this sense in 3.9, "bow down"). However, the elders are already lying prostrate before the throne, so "kneel before" is an unlikely meaning here. A possible alternative rendering for **worship** is "and acknowledge his greatness."

They cast their crowns before the throne, singing: this action acknowledges that God is the supreme King, who rules over them. **Crowns** represent their power, authority to rule as kings, and so here they surrender their power to God. The verb has the forceful meaning of "throw," and it seems better to represent this meaning than to say something like "lay" (REB) or "lay down" (TNT). The Greek verb translated **singing** by RSV is "saying" (TEV). In many languages this clause will be rendered as "they throw their chiefs' hats down in front of the high chief's chair."

4.11   RSV   TEV

"Worthy art thou, our Lord and   "Our Lord and God! You are
    God,   worthy
to receive glory and honor and   to receive glory, honor, and
    power,   power.
for thou didst create all things,   For you created all things,
and by thy will they existed and   and by your will they were
    were created."   given existence and life."

The translator should try to present this verse as poetry (see Section F of the introduction, "Translating the Revelation to John," pages 6 and following).

Worthy art thou, our Lord and God: NRSV has "You are worthy." The adjective **Worthy** means, in this context, "You deserve . . . ," "You have the right (to receive)." The phrase **our Lord and God** means "the Lord and God we worship (or, serve)."

To receive glory and honor and power: the implied actor and the receiver can be reversed, "for people to give you . . . ," or else the verb phrase can be made a simple passive, "to be given (by people)." For **glory and honor** see verse 9. **To receive . . . power** in this context means "to receive (or, be given) praise for your power"; it does not mean to be given power. An alternative translation model for this clause is "for people to tell you how great you are, honor you, and praise you for your power."

Thou didst create all things: the verb translated **create** always has God or Christ as subject in the New Testament. The verb itself does not specify whether God created all things out of nothing (see Hebrews 11.3, where a different verb is used). Many languages will express this idea as "you caused all things to come into being," while others will use the equivalent of "make" and will say "you made all things."

By thy will they existed and were created: this is a compound sentence that repeats the thought of the previous line. The two verbs do not express two separate events but the one event expressed in two different ways. TNT translates "They owe their existence and their creation to your will"; REB "by your will they were created and have their being," and TOB "You willed that they exist, and they were created." BRCL reverses the two: "by your will they were created and exist." In languages that do not use the passive, this sentence will need to be restructured; for example, "You willed that they exist and so created them."

The final two lines of the poem may also be expressed as "you made all things, and you willed that they exist, and so they received life."

5.1-14

RSV

1 And I saw in the right hand of him who was seated on the throne a scroll written within and on the back, sealed with seven seals; 2 and I saw a strong angel proclaiming with a loud voice, "Who is worthy to open the scroll and break its seals?" 3 And no one in heaven or on earth or under the earth was able to open the scroll or to look into it, 4 and I wept much that no one was found worthy to open the scroll or to look into it. 5 Then one of the elders said to me, "Weep not; lo, the Lion of the tribe of Judah, the Root of David, has conquered, so that he can open the scroll and its seven seals."

6 And between the throne and the four living creatures and among the elders, I saw a Lamb standing, as though it had been slain, with seven horns and with seven eyes, which are the seven spirits of God sent out into all the earth; 7 and he went and took the scroll from the right hand of him who was seated on the throne. 8 And when he had taken the scroll, the four living creatures and the twenty-four elders fell down before the Lamb, each holding a harp, and with golden bowls full of incense, which are the prayers of the saints; 9 and they sang a new song, saying,

"Worthy art thou to take the scroll and
   to open its seals,
for thou wast slain and by thy blood didst
   ransom men for God
from every tribe and tongue and people
   and nation,
10   and hast made them a kingdom and
      priests to our God,

TEV
The Scroll and the Lamb

1 I saw a scroll in the right hand of the one who sits on the throne; it was covered with writing on both sides and was sealed with seven seals. 2 And I saw a mighty angel, who announced in a loud voice, "Who is worthy to break the seals and open the scroll?" 3 But there was no one in heaven or on earth or in the world below who could open the scroll and look inside it. 4 I cried bitterly because no one could be found who was worthy to open the scroll or look inside it. 5 Then one of the elders said to me, "Don't cry. Look! The Lion from Judah's tribe, the great descendant of David, has won the victory, and he can break the seven seals and open the scroll."

6 Then I saw a Lamb standing in the center of the throne, surrounded by the four living creatures and the elders. The Lamb appeared to have been killed. It had seven horns and seven eyes, which are the seven spirits of God that have been sent through the whole earth. 7 The Lamb went and took the scroll from the right hand of the one who sits on the throne. 8 As he did so, the four living creatures and the twenty-four elders fell down before the Lamb. Each had a harp and gold bowls filled with incense, which are the prayers of God's people. 9 They sang a new song:

"You are worthy to take the scroll
   and to break open its seals.
For you were killed, and by your sacrificial death you bought for God
people from every tribe, language, nation, and race.
10   You have made them a kingdom of

95

and they shall reign on earth."

11 Then I looked, and I heard around the throne and the living creatures and the elders the voice of many angels, numbering myriads of myriads and thousands of thousands, 12 saying with a loud voice, "Worthy is the Lamb who was slain, to receive power and wealth and wisdom and might and honor and glory and blessing!" 13 And I heard every creature in heaven and on earth and under the earth and in the sea, and all therein, saying, "To him who sits upon the throne and to the Lamb be blessing and honor and glory and might for ever and ever!" 14 And the four living creatures said, "Amen!" and the elders fell down and worshiped.

priests to serve our God,
and they shall rule on earth."

11 Again I looked, and I heard angels, thousands and millions of them! They stood around the throne, the four living creatures, and the elders, 12 and sang in a loud voice:

"The Lamb who was killed is worthy
to receive power, wealth, wisdom, and
strength,
honor, glory, and praise!"

13 And I heard every creature in heaven, on earth, in the world below, and in the sea—all living beings in the universe—and they were singing:

"To him who sits on the throne and to
the Lamb,
be praise and honor, glory and might,
forever and ever!"

14 The four living creatures answered, "Amen!" And the elders fell down and worshiped.

SECTION HEADING: TEV "The Scroll and the Lamb." Other possibilities are "The Lamb takes the scroll from God"; "The sealed scroll," or merely "The Lamb appears in heaven."

The scene continues from the last chapter. God is seated on his throne and holds in his right hand a sealed scroll. John then sees a lamb that goes and takes the scroll from God. This is an event that provokes praise and worship from the four living creatures, the twenty-four elders, countless millions of angelic beings, and all living creatures in the universe.

5.1   RSV   TEV

And I saw in the right hand of him who was seated on the throne a scroll written within and on the back, sealed with seven seals;

I saw a scroll in the right hand of the one who sits on the throne; it was covered with writing on both sides and was sealed with seven seals.

And I saw: this introductory statement is repeated frequently (5.2,6,11; 6.1,12). It generally marks the beginning of a new scene in the unfolding drama. This phrase can also be rendered as "The next thing I saw in my dream was . . . ." Such a rendering helps to connect these following events to those in the previous chapter; one should remember that the original Greek document wasn't broken up into chapters.

In the right hand of him who was seated on the throne: in his description of God (4.2-3) John has not spoken of physical attributes, but the nature of this scene requires God's **right hand**, in which he holds the scroll. John still avoids identifying God by name. **Him** is often rendered as "the one" or "the person." For the translation of **throne** see 1.4b and elsewhere.

A scroll written within and on the back: a scroll was a document made of sheets of parchment or papyrus that were pasted together in one long strip and then rolled up like a tube, and usually tied, or else sealed, as this scroll was. Ordinarily there was writing on only one side of the sheets; but this scroll had writing on both sides. It is useless to ask how John knew that it had writing on both sides, since it was rolled up and tightly sealed (by contrast, see Ezek 2.9-10). Instead of RSV **within and on the back**, NRSV has the more natural "on the inside and on the back"; REB is better: "with writing on both sides."

It may be impossible in a given language to use the equivalent of **scroll**; something like "a written document" may be adequate, but the main problem is to have a document that can have writing on both sides of the sheets and be sealed. Perhaps one can say "a rolled up paper document," with a footnote describing this scroll in more detail.

Sealed with seven seals: this means that the scroll was completely sealed, so that no one could unroll it. The **seals** were usually small bits of wax that were applied to the outside edge of the rolled-up scroll in order to keep it closed. They also identified the owner, or writer, of the scroll, and could not be broken except by someone who had the authority to do so. Where **seals** are unknown, this clause may be expressed as "the rolled up document was firmly closed with seven bits of wax." Again, a footnote or a description in a glossary item will be helpful.

In this setting the scroll has a description of the things that will soon take place (see 4.1), the events that mark the future of the world and of humankind, according to God's purpose and will.

Alternative translation models for this verse are:

> The next thing I saw in my dream was a scroll held in the right hand of the one (person) sitting on the throne. The scroll was covered with writing on both sides, and it was firmly closed with seven bits of wax.

Or:

> In the dream I saw that the one who was sitting on the throne was holding a rolled up scroll in his right hand. There was writing on both sides of it, and God had closed it firmly with seven seals.

5.2   RSV   TEV

and I saw a strong angel proclaiming with a loud voice, "Who is worthy to open the scroll and break its seals?"

And I saw a mighty angel, who announced in a loud voice, "Who is worthy to break the seals and open the scroll?"

A strong angel: this is the angel's first appearance (see 1.1, where it was mentioned but did not appear). Angels are God's heavenly servants and messengers. In English the word **strong** is too narrowly limited to physical strength, and something like "mighty" (NRSV, REB, TEV), or "powerful" (SPCL), or "having great authority" is better.

Proclaiming with a loud voice: the angel's message will be heard throughout the universe. What the angel proclaims is a question, and in some languages something like "asking" will be more appropriate. The Greek verb (appearing only here in Revelation) was used of a herald's task of making public announcements about important matters affecting all the people of the community.

Who is worthy to open the scroll and break its seals? The adjective **worthy** occurs in 3.4; 4.11; in this context it means to have the right, or the authority, according to God's judgment, to open the scroll and reveal its contents. "Who is qualified . . . ?" "Who has the right . . . ?" The natural order, "break the seals and open the scroll," is reversed in the Greek text. A translation need not follow the Greek, especially if it will appear ridiculous to the reader (see the logical order in TEV, REB). Here **open** means "unroll."

An alternative translation model for this verse is:

> And I saw one of God's messengers (angel), a powerful one, who asked in a loud voice, "Who has the right to break open the seven pieces of wax on the scroll (document) and unroll it?"

5.3   RSV   TEV

And no one in heaven or on earth or under the earth was able to open the scroll or to look into it,	But there was no one in heaven or on earth or in the world below[b] who could open the scroll and look inside it.

[b] WORLD BELOW: *The world of the dead (see 1.18).*

And no one in heaven or on earth or under the earth: this is a way of talking about the universe as it was conceived of at that time. It was thought to have three parts: the world of heavenly beings, the world of earthly beings, and the world of the dead (Phil 2.10). The world of the dead (**under the earth**) was called Sheol (in Hebrew) or Hades (in Greek); see comments on "Hades" in 1.18. TEV's rendering "the world below" will be misleading in some languages. It may suggest that there is an actual world or earth beneath this earth. To avoid this confusion one may say "in the space beneath the earth," or even "in the area (region) under the ground."

Was able to open the scroll or look into it: the verb translated **was able** can have the weakened sense of "could." In this context it really means that no one was "worthy" (see next verse); it does not mean that no one was strong or skilled enough to break the seals. The two verbs **open** (or "unroll") and **look** describe two parts of one action and should not be presented as two separate actions (as **or** seems to imply). This applies to verses 3 and 4. And **look** means, in this context, to read the contents of the scroll.

An alternative translation model for this verse is:

> But no one in heaven or on the earth (in the world) or under the ground had the right to open the rolled up document and read it.

5.4   RSV   TEV

and I wept much that no one was found   I cried bitterly because no one could be
worthy to open the scroll or to look into   found who was worthy to open the scroll
it.   or look inside it.

I wept much: something like "I began to weep (or, cry) bitterly" (Phps, BRCL, NRSV) better translates the imperfect tense of the Greek verb. Other ways of translating this sentence are "weep sorrowfully" or "weep a great deal."

That no one was found: it is better to translate "because no one" (TEV, NRSV, REB, TNT), stating the reason why John was weeping so much. The verb phrase "was not found" may have the more general sense of "there was no one" (BRCL), or else it may mean "no one was found who was worthy," as RSV, NRSV, and others have it, implying that a search had been made to find someone who was worthy. But the idea of a search should be left implicit and not stated explicitly. In some languages "no one was found worthy" will be restructured as "they could find no one who was worthy." On the translation of **open the scroll or look into it**, see the previous verse.

5.5   RSV   TEV

Then one of the elders said to me,   Then one of the elders said to me,
"Weep not; lo, the Lion of the tribe of   "Don't cry. Look! The Lion from Ju-
Judah, the Root of David, has con-   dah's tribe, the great descendant of
quered, so that he can open the scroll   David, has won the victory, and he can
and its seven seals."   break the seven seals and open the
                                               scroll."

Then one of the elders: for **elders** see 4.4.

Weep not: better, "Stop crying," as a translation of the present imperative of the verb.

Lo: see comments on "Behold" in 1.7.

The Lion of the tribe of Judah: this is a messianic title (see Gen 49.9). The fact that it is a title may be made clear by translating "the one who is called 'The Lion of the tribe of Judah.'" The lion was a symbol of power and dominion, and if in a given culture the lion is not considered "the king of beasts," some other animal with that reputation should be chosen. Or else the figurative language may have to be partially discarded, and something like "The Lion, that mighty ruler from the tribe of Judah, . . ." may be said. The word translated **tribe** has already been used (in 1.7) in the general sense of an ethnic group; here it is specifically one of the twelve tribes of Israel (see 7.4-8). Instead of **of the tribe of Judah**, it may be better to say "from the tribe of Judah" or "who belongs to the tribe of Judah."

The Root of David: this is another messianic title (also 22.16). It means "a famous descendant of David," the one whose coming was prophesied (see Isa 11.1,10, where the family line is traced to David's father, Jesse). In the Gospels the title "the Son of David" has the same meaning (see Mark 10.47; 12.35). In very few languages will **root** or "shoot" make much sense in a title like this, so something like "the one who is a ruling (or, powerful) descendant of King David" may have to be said. In certain languages this phrase will be expressed as "The famous one whose great ancestor (big grandfather) was King David."

Has conquered: this implies a battle or struggle of some sort against his enemies (see 3.21); but nothing definite is said. If the verb "to conquer" requires a definite object, "his enemies" should be added.

So that he can open the scroll and its seven seals: REB has translated the whole verbal clause ". . . has won the right to open the scroll . . . ." But it is better to assign a separate meaning to **has conquered** which gives the reason why this one can open the scroll. The one verb in Greek, "to open," is applied both to the scroll and to its seven seals; in some languages it may be necessary to say "to break (or, unstick) the seven seals and open (or, unroll) the scroll."

An alternative translation model for this verse is:

> Then one of the important leaders said to me, "Stop crying! Look! The Lion, that mighty ruler from the tribe of Judah, the famous one whose big ancestor was King David, has won the victory (is victorious). Therefore he can break the seven pieces of wax and unroll the paper document (scroll).

5.6

RSV	TEV
And between the throne and the four living creatures and among the elders, I saw a Lamb standing, as though it had been slain, with seven horns and with seven eyes, which are the seven spirits of God sent out into all the earth;	Then I saw a Lamb standing in the center of the throne, surrounded by the four living creatures and the elders. The Lamb appeared to have been killed. It had seven horns and seven eyes, which are the seven spirits of God that have been sent through the whole earth.

This is a complex sentence, and the precise meaning of some of the phrases is in doubt.

And between the throne and the four living creatures and among the elders: this is difficult to understand. But as previously described, the throne is in the center, the four living creatures are standing at the four sides of the throne (4.6), and the twenty-four elders are sitting on their thrones in a circle around the throne (4.4). The Greek says quite literally "in the middle of (or, among) the throne and the four living creatures, and in the middle of (or, among) the elders." TEV and others translate "(standing) in the center (or, middle) of the throne." This is what the Greek seems to require, especially in light of 7.17. But it is possible that the text means "in the center of the four living creatures around the throne." The picture is of the throne, with the living creatures close to it, and the elders in a larger circle around the living creatures and the throne. The Lamb is right in the center, either on or near the throne. TEV "standing in the center of the throne" does not seem very likely and will even appear comical in some languages. The following verse states that the Lamb went and took the scroll from the right hand of the person sitting on the throne. This indicates that John sees the Lamb standing close by the throne rather than in it or on it. So in most languages it will give a less confusing picture to say that the Lamb "was standing near the throne."

I saw a Lamb standing as though it had been slain: RSV, TEV, and others capitalize **Lamb**, indicating thereby that it is a title; but it may be better to say "a lamb." In languages that have two different terms for male and female lambs, here and elsewhere in Revelation the male form should be used; and in certain languages "lamb" will be translated as "male child of a sheep." In cultures where sheep exist but do not have the economic and religious significance that they had in Palestine, it will be helpful to give a detailed description of sheep in a glossary item for the reader. The description **as though it had been slain** does not modify the participle **standing**; rather it applies to the lamb, which is obviously a figure of Christ. The Greek word translated **Lamb** is used only in Revelation as a title of Christ; elsewhere in the New Testament it appears only (in the plural) in John 21.15, with quite a different sense. In John 1.29,36; Acts 8.32; and 1 Peter 1.19 a different Greek word for "lamb" is used, but this makes no significant difference for translators, since both terms refer to the same kind of animal. The passive participle **slain** ultimately refers to the death of Christ (verse 9; see 13.8). What is meant is that the lamb, though alive, had marks on its body that showed it had been killed. If a passive form of the verb is not available, care must be taken in the use of an active form, with the subject specified. And, as applied to a lamb, the verb "to slay" has the specific sense of "to sacrifice"; so REB "a Lamb with the marks of sacrifice on him"; NJB "a Lamb that seemed to have been sacrificed." The best translation may be "The lamb looked like someone (or, people) had killed (or, sacrificed) it." And, as TEV and others have done, **standing** should be separated from **as though it had been slain** (or, sacrificed).

With seven horns and with seven eyes, which are the seven spirits of God sent out into all the earth: the clause **which are the seven spirits . . .** applies only to **seven eyes**, not to both **seven horns and . . . seven eyes**. But, as elsewhere, the Greek here is ambiguous. In the Bible a horn is a symbol of strength and power; the eyes represent the ability of God to see and know everything. For **the seven spirits** see 1.4; 4.5. The passive **sent out** implies that God is the agent; it is God who sent the seven spirits throughout the whole world (so NJB).

An alternative translation model for this verse is:

> I saw a male sheep standing near the king's seat. He was surrounded
> by the four living creatures and the important old leaders. He looked
> like people had killed (sacrificed) him.

5.7	RSV	TEV
	and he went and took the scroll from the right hand of him who was seated on the throne.	The Lamb went and took the scroll from the right hand of the one who sits on the throne.

He went and took the scroll: in Greek the direct object **the scroll** does not appear until verse 8, "and when he took the scroll . . . ." Care must be taken in translating the verb **went** so as to maintain the proper perspective. Some translations have "came" (Phps, AT, TNT, RNAB), which reflects the point of view of God, on the throne; **went** reflects the point of view of the seer. The verb "approached" avoids the problem. The verb translated **took** does not imply force. Some translate "received" (see the same verb in 3.3), implying that God offered it to the lamb; but it is better to translate "took," unless there is a problem. In some languages "took" will imply rudeness on the part of the taker. In this case one may say "received the scroll." Translators should not be concerned as to how a sheep—an animal with hoofs, not hands—could take the scroll from God's hand. The language is symbolic and figurative, occurring in a vision.

5.8	RSV	TEV

RSV	TEV
And when he had taken the scroll, the four living creatures and the twenty-four elders fell down before the Lamb, each holding a harp, and with golden bowls full of incense, which are the prayers of the saints;	As he did so, the four living creatures and the twenty-four elders fell down before the Lamb. Each had a harp and gold bowls filled with incense, which are the prayers of God's people.

And when he had taken the scroll: it is not necessary to repeat the exact phrase of the previous verse; something more general like "And when he had done this" or "As soon as he did this" is satisfactory.

Fell down: an act of worship, as in 1.17; 4.10.

Each holding a harp, and with golden bowls full of incense: this seems to say that every one of the four living creatures and the twenty-four elders had a harp and golden bowls filled with incense, although some would restrict it to the twenty-four elders. Appropriate terms

HARPS

AN INCENSE BURNER

must be found to translate **harp, bowls**, and **incense**. The harp is a stringed musical instrument; the biblical harp was smaller than a modern harp. See *A Handbook on the Book of Psalms,* page 311, for a detailed description of the harp. In languages that have only a one-stringed instrument, that may be used here. However, in cultures where stringed instruments are unknown, one may say, for example, "a musical instrument with strings" or "a musical instrument with strings, named 'harp.'" In this case a picture will be very helpful to the reader. The bowls were either made of gold or else were ceramic bowls plated with gold leaf. Both bowls and cups are mentioned frequently in Revelation, and if the local language uses only one term for both ideas, this will be no problem for dealing with the terms in this book. A bowl is usually a wide dish deep enough to contain solid or liquid foods for several people, while a cup is smaller, is normally is used for holding liquids, and is used by only one person at a time. Incense is usually a combination of aromatic spices, gums, and resins, which is used in public worship; there it is burned so that it produces smoke with a pleasant smell (see Exo 30.34-36). The offering of incense in sacrifice is associated with prayer (see Psa 141.2). In certain languages **incense** is called "sweet smelling herbs" or "sweet smelling stuff."

Which are the prayers of the saints: the Greek says that the bowls (filled with incense) are the prayers (see 8.3). In effect the four living creatures and the twenty-four elders offer to God the prayers of the saints. In the Bible **saints** is a word used of the people of God, people who serve and worship God to the exclusion of all other deities. It is better to translate "the people who belong to God," "the people who serve God." The Greek word is the same as the adjective translated "holy" (see the comments at 3.7; 4.8).

An alternative translation model for this verse is:

> As the Lamb did this, the four living creatures and the twenty-four important leaders prostrated themselves before him. Each of the leaders held a harp and a bowl made of gold. The bowl was filled with sweet-smelling herbs that represent the prayers of people who belong to (serve) God.

5.9-10 RSV	TEV
9 and they sang a new song, saying, "Worthy art thou to take the scroll and to open its seals, for thou wast slain and by thy blood didst ransom men for God from every tribe and tongue and people and nation, 10 and hast made them a kingdom and priests to our God, and they shall reign on earth."	9 They sang a new song: "You are worthy to take the scroll and to break open its seals. For you were killed, and by your sacrificial death you bought for God people from every tribe, language, nation, and race. 10 You have made them a kingdom of priests to serve our God, and they shall rule on earth."

The translator should consider presenting the song of verses 9-10 as poetry (see Section F of the introduction, "Translating the Revelation to John," pages 6 and following).

And they sang a new song, saying: it may be helpful to reintroduce the subject of the verb, "The four living creatures and the twenty-four elders sang a new song." This is a song that has never been sung before. They sing it in honor of the Lamb, and this may be said specifically, either here or at the beginning of the song: "Lamb, you are worthy . . ." or "You, the Lamb, you are worthy . . . ." The participle **saying** is equivalent to opening quotation marks and need not be represented verbally (thus TEV, NIV, NJB, RNAB, REB). The verb **sang** in Greek is in the present tense; so NRSV has "they sing," but this makes for an odd shift in the narrative.

Worthy art thou: for **Worthy** see 4.11.

To take the scroll and to open its seals: or ". . . to break its seals." This answers the question in verse 2.

For thou wast slain and by thy blood didst ransom men for God: NRSV is in today's English, "You are worthy to take the scroll and to open its seals, for you were slaughtered and by your blood you ransomed for God (saints) . . . ." The same verb "to kill" is used here that is used in verse 6; here, as there, NJB has "sacrificed." In languages that do not use the passive, this second sentence may be expressed as "they (or, people) slaughtered (sacrificed) you, but by means of your blood you bought (ransomed) for God people from every . . . ."

The phrase **by thy blood** means "by means of your blood," "by means of your death," referring to the verb "you were slain." As in 1.5, **blood** stands for violent death, or else sacrifice. FRCL translates "For you have been put to death and, by your death, you have ransomed"; TNT "you were slaughtered and by your death you purchased for God." The phrase **by thy blood** means either the price that is paid, "at the cost of your life-blood" (Brc) or the means by which freedom was obtained (most translations).

Ransom: the Greek verb "to buy" in this context means that Christ's death was the price that was paid so that people may belong to God (which is what **for God** means). The verb is also translated sometimes as "redeem," as in 14.3. Here and in similar passages in the New Testament concerning the death of Christ, nothing is said about whom the price was paid to, and a translation should not imply that there was a seller to whom God paid this price.

Men . . . from every tribe and tongue and people and nation: the four nouns include all human groupings in the world—by common ancestry, common language, common nationality, and common race. The same four nouns appear also in 7.9; 11.9; 13.7; 14.6, but no two passages follow the same order. It is not necessary to use four different groupings, if such a list appears forced or artificial; something like "people from every country, every tribe, every language, and every race" may be satisfactory; or, more simply, "from every country and every race," or even "people from all over the world," or "people of all races." The word **men**, of course, should not be used; "people" (TEV, REB, NJB) includes everyone; NRSV "saints" is too restricted, since the term should apply to people in their condition before they were redeemed.

And hast made them a kingdom and priests to our God: see 1.6, where the same language is used. FRCL has "you have made of them a kingdom of priests to serve our God." Here **our God** is inclusive, since it is addressed to the Lamb, who also belongs to God. "The God whom we worship (or, serve)" can be said.

And they shall reign on earth: some Greek manuscripts have the present tense, but the better text has the future tense, which should appear in translation.

The verb "to reign" is properly used of kings and queens, and here implies complete power over the world and its inhabitants. So another way of expressing this is "and they shall rule over the world and its inhabitants" or "they shall have power over . . . ."

An alternative translation model for this verse is:

> The four living creatures and the twenty-four respected leaders sang a song that had never been sung before. They sang it in honor of the Lamb, saying,
> "You are worthy to take the scroll (rolled up document) and break open the seals (seven pieces of wax). For people slaughtered (sacrificed) you, and your life-blood is the means through which you purchased people from all over the world (every country and every race), and now they belong to God.
> "You have caused them to become a family (tribe, nation) of priests who serve our [inclusive] God. And they shall rule on earth."

5.11   RSV   TEV

Then I looked, and I heard around the throne and the living creatures and the elders the voice of many angels, numbering myriads of myriads and thousands of thousands,	Again I looked, and I heard angels, thousands and millions of them! They stood around the throne, the four living creatures, and the elders,

Then I looked, and I heard: it is not necessary to suppose that in saying "I looked" John means that he actually saw all the countless millions of angels. This marks the first appearance of these participants in the drama.

John describes the precise order: first the innermost throne, then the four living creatures, then the twenty-four elders, and now the millions of angels. The word **around** is better translated by NJB "gathered around"; TEV and TNT "They stood around" is too specific. A verb like "surrounded" (NRSV, RNAB) or "encircled" (NIV) is better.

Numbering myriads of myriads and thousands of thousands: the Greek word translated "myriad" means ten thousand. The whole expression means "millions and millions of them" (SPCL), "countless thousands" (RNAB "they were countless in number"); or else "too many to count" (see a similar expression in 9.16).

An alternative translation model for this verse is:

> Again I looked, and I heard the voices of countless numbers of angels standing around the throne, the four living creatures, and the elders.

5.12   RSV   TEV

saying with a loud voice, "Worthy is the Lamb who was slain, to receive power and wealth and wisdom and might and honor and glory and blessing!"	and sang in a loud voice:
	    "The Lamb who was killed is
	        worthy
	    to receive power, wealth, wis-
	        dom, and strength,
	    honor, glory, and praise!"

Saying with a loud voice: the song they sing in praise of the Lamb is like the song to God in 4.11. The rest of the verse should appear as poetry, as well as the song in the next verse (see Section F of the introduction, "Translating the Revelation to John," pages 6 and following).

Worthy is the Lamb who was slain, to receive: it should be noticed that RSV places a comma after **slain** in an attempt to prevent the reader from reading "who was slain to receive power." For **Worthy** see 5.2; for **to receive** see 4.11. As there, the meaning is "The Lamb is worthy to be praised for his power . . ." or "It is right that we praise the Lamb's power . . . ."

The seven nouns that follow the verb are all qualities or attributes of Christ, and these qualities are praised, with the exception of the last one (RSV **blessing**), which is itself praise or thanksgiving that is offered to him.

For **power** see 3.8. **Wealth** appears also in 18.17. **Wisdom** appears also in 7.12; 13.18; 17.9; it is variously rendered in some languages as "great understanding (knowledge)," "great insight," or even idiomatically, for example, "bright spirit (innermost)" (Palauan). **Might** (or "power") is used also in 7.12. For **honor** see 4.9. For **glory** see 1.6. And **blessing** (also in 5.13; 7.12) means "thanksgiving" or "praise" (TEV, FRCL, BRCL, SPCL, TNT, REB).

An alternative translation model for this verse is:

> and the multitude in heaven sang in a loud voice: "Worthy is the Lamb who was killed. We should praise him because of his great power, wealth, wisdom, and strength. He should receive great honor."

5.13   RSV   TEV

And I heard every creature in heaven and on earth and under the earth and in the sea, and all therein, saying, "To him who sits upon the throne and to the Lamb be blessing and honor and glory and might for ever and ever!"	And I heard every creature in heaven, on earth, in the world below, and in the sea—all living beings in the universe—and they were singing:
	    "To him who sits on the throne
	        and to the Lamb,
	    be praise and honor, glory and
	        might,
	    forever and ever!"

All living beings in the whole universe join in the praise offered to the Lamb and to God.

Every creature: this includes all living creatures, human beings and animals as well.

In heaven and on earth and under the earth and in the sea: here **the sea** is added to the other three (see verse 3) in order to include all living creatures. **The sea** includes all bodies of water, and in some languages the plural form may have to be used.

And all therein: this is added for emphasis; it provides no new information. This is a normal feature of the writer's style, and a translation should reflect it if possible.

Saying: as in other instances, a translation may choose to say "singing."

In this short song the imperative **be** means that what follows should be offered, or given, to God and the Lamb as praise they deserve to receive.

Blessing and honor and glory and might: this is like the list in verse 12; but **might** here translates a different Greek word from the word translated "might" in verse 12. However, in this context there is no essential difference of meaning between the two. TEV suggests a difference in meaning by using the words "strength" (verse 12) and "might" (verse 13).

For ever and ever: or, "for all time to come," "throughout all eternity."

5.14	RSV	TEV

And the four living creatures said, "Amen!" and the elders fell down and worshiped.

The four living creatures answered, "Amen!" And the elders fell down and worshiped.

Amen! "So be it!" or "It is so!" (see 1.6). In this way the four living creatures join in the song of praise by affirming that their thoughts are the same as those of the singers.

Fell down: see 1.17; 4.10.

Worshiped: see 4.10. It may be necessary to add a direct object, "worshiped God and the Lamb." REB avoids this need by translating "the elders prostrated themselves in worship."

C-2. The Seven Seals
(6.1–8.1)

6.1-17

RSV

TEV

The Seals

1 Now I saw when the Lamb opened one of the seven seals, and I heard one of the four living creatures say, as with a voice of thunder, "Come!" 2 And I saw, and behold, a white horse, and its rider had a bow; and a crown was given to him, and he went out conquering and to conquer.

1 Then I saw the Lamb break open the first of the seven seals, and I heard one of the four living creatures say in a voice that sounded like thunder, "Come!" 2 I looked, and there was a white horse. Its rider held a bow, and he was given a crown. He rode out as a conqueror to conquer.

3 When he opened the second seal, I heard the second living creature say, "Come!" 4 And out came another horse, bright red; its rider was permitted to take peace from the earth, so that men should slay one another; and he was given a great sword.

5 When he opened the third seal, I heard the third living creature say, "Come!" And I saw, and behold, a black horse, and its rider had a balance in his hand; 6 and I heard what seemed to be a voice in the midst of the four living creatures saying, "A quart of wheat for a denarius, and three quarts of barley for a denarius; but do not harm oil and wine!"

7 When he opened the fourth seal, I heard the voice of the fourth living creature say, "Come!" 8 And I saw, and behold, a pale horse, and its rider's name was Death, and Hades followed him; and they were given power over a fourth of the earth, to kill with sword and with famine and with pestilence and by wild beasts of the earth.

9 When he opened the fifth seal, I saw under the altar the souls of those who had been slain for the word of God and for the witness they had borne; 10 they cried out with a loud voice, "O Sovereign Lord, holy and true, how long before thou wilt judge and avenge our blood on those who dwell upon the earth?" 11 Then they were each given a white robe and told to rest a little longer, until the number of their fellow servants and their brethren should be complete, who were to be killed as they themselves had been.

12 When he opened the sixth seal, I looked, and behold, there was a great earthquake; and the sun became black as sackcloth, the full moon became like blood, 13 and the stars of the sky fell to the earth as the fig tree sheds its winter fruit when shaken by a gale; 14 the sky vanished like a scroll that is rolled up, and every mountain and island was removed from its place. 15 Then the kings of the earth and the great men and the generals and the rich and the strong, and every one, slave and free, hid in the caves and among the rocks of the mountains, 16 calling to the mountains and rocks, "Fall on us and hide us from the face of him who is seated on the throne, and from the wrath of the Lamb; 17 for the great day of their wrath has come, and who can stand before it?"

3 Then the Lamb broke open the second seal; and I heard the second living creature say, "Come!" 4 Another horse came out, a red one. Its rider was given the power to bring war on the earth, so that men should kill each other. He was given a large sword.

5 Then the Lamb broke open the third seal; and I heard the third living creature say, "Come!" I looked, and there was a black horse. Its rider held a pair of scales in his hand. 6 I heard what sounded like a voice coming from among the four living creatures, which said, "A quart of wheat for a day's wages, and three quarts of barley for a day's wages. But do not damage the olive trees and the vineyards!"

7 Then the Lamb broke open the fourth seal; and I heard the fourth living creature say, "Come!" 8 I looked, and there was a pale-colored horse. Its rider was named Death, and Hades followed close behind. They were given authority over one fourth of the earth, to kill by means of war, famine, disease, and wild animals.

9 Then the Lamb broke open the fifth seal. I saw underneath the altar the souls of those who had been killed because they had proclaimed God's word and had been faithful in their witnessing. 10 They shouted in a loud voice, "Almighty Lord, holy and true! How long will it be until you judge the people on earth and punish them for killing us?" 11 Each of them was given a white robe, and they were told to rest a little while longer, until the complete number of their fellow servants and brothers were killed, as they had been.

12 And I saw the Lamb break open the sixth seal. There was a violent earthquake, and the sun became black like coarse black cloth, and the moon turned completely red like blood. 13 The stars fell down to the earth, like unripe figs falling from the tree when a strong wind shakes it. 14 The sky disappeared like a scroll being rolled up, and every mountain and island was moved from its place. 15 Then the kings of the earth, the rulers and the military chiefs, the rich and the powerful, and all other men, slave and free, hid themselves in caves and under rocks on the mountains. 16 They called out to the mountains and to the rocks, "Fall on us and hide us from the eyes of the one who sits on the throne and from the anger of the Lamb! 17 The terrible day of their anger is here, and who can stand up against it?"

SECTION HEADING: TEV "The Seals." Since only six seals are mentioned in this chapter, it is also possible to use a heading such as "The first six seals" or "The things that happened as each one of the first six seals was broken open."

6.1   RSV   TEV

Now I saw when the Lamb opened one of the seven seals, and I heard one of the four living creatures say, as with a voice of thunder, "Come!"	Then I saw the Lamb break open the first of the seven seals, and I heard one of the four living creatures say in a voice that sounded like thunder, "Come!"

Now I saw when the Lamb opened one of the seven seals: instead of **opened** the translation can be "broke" (NJB, REB) or "broke open" (TEV, RNAB). In light of the breaking of the other seals (verses 3,5,7,9,12), it is possible to translate here as TEV has done, "(break open) the first of the seven seals" (also REB, AT, Brc, NIV, RNAB, FRCL, SPCL, BRCL).

Say, as with a voice of thunder: this is better said "say in a (loud) voice that sounded like thunder." The comparison has to do with the volume of sound, not the timbre of the voice. Perhaps "like the roar of thunder" or "as loud as a clap of thunder."

Come! John himself seems to be near the open door in heaven, or in heaven itself (4.1-2), and he hears one of the living creature, who are near the throne, call out **"Come!"** The command (second person singular) is addressed to someone riding a horse, who appears immediately.

In some Greek manuscripts and ancient versions the command is "Come and see" (also in verses 3,5,7), which is addressed to John himself. But the original text is only "Come," which is directed at the horseman. The translation should not imply that the horseman is told to go to heaven, but that he should come forth from wherever he is. The four horsemen ride out over the earth. It is not said where they start from, but presumably it is from somewhere in heaven, since they are God's messengers. The Greek verb can be understood to mean "Go," and some believe that this is what it means here. Given the fact that in the following verse the horseman **went out** or "rode out" (TEV), translators in many languages may find it helpful to use the word "Go" in this verse.

6.2   RSV   TEV

And I saw, and behold, a white horse, and its rider had a bow; and a crown was given to him, and he went out conquering and to conquer.	I looked, and there was a white horse. Its rider held a bow, and he was given a crown. He rode out as a conqueror to conquer.

And I saw, and behold: see 4.1. NRSV is better: "I looked, and there was" (see TNT, TEV, RNAB).

A white horse, and its rider had a bow: in all four instances the horse is referred to first, after which comes a description of the rider (see verses 4,5,8). It seems more natural to say "I saw a man with a bow, riding on a white horse," but it is better to follow the order of the Greek text and refer first to the horse. The white horse symbolizes conquest and victory. In cultures where horses are unknown, a translator should not try to find an equivalent animal from that culture. The picture in this context is of a horse, but a mule, camel, or some other animal that can be ridden may be used as long as it is commonly ridden. However, since the colors of the horses are important, an animal such as a zebra should not be employed. So a picture of a horse, along with a description of it in a footnote or glossary item, will be helpful to readers.

Its rider: in some languages there may not be a general word like **rider** to refer to someone who is riding an animal, and so it may be necessary to say "and the one who was riding it," or "the one who was mounted on it." If possible it is better to avoid something like "person," or "man," or "angel." It may be necessary to say "something that looked like a person (human)." The problem may be especially difficult in verse 8, where the rider's name is given.

A bow: this weapon requires arrows, and it may be necessary to say "a bow and arrows." Where bow and arrows are unknown, it may be necessary to say "a weapon" or "a weapon that shoots darts (missiles)," without specifying what kind of weapon it is, while carefully avoiding the implication that it is a firearm, that is, a gun that shoots bullets. The weapon should be recognized as useful in battle.

A crown was given to him: as in 4.4,10, the crown is a sign of equal authority and power; the rider is crowned a king. The passive **was given** implies that God, or an angel, gave him the crown of a king. However, since it is not certain who the agent is, in languages that do not have the passive it will be possible to say "he received a crown" or ". . . a chief's hat."

Went out: that is, out of heaven, over the earth, in order to do battle. In some languages it will be necessary to translate "went out of heaven over the earth to . . . ."

Conquering and to conquer: TNT translates "a victor searching for victory"; FRCL "as a conqueror and to conquer again," or it can be "as one who has already conquered, and will conquer again." In languages where the verb **conquer** requires an object, one may say "conquer others" or "conquer his enemies."

6.3-4   RSV   TEV

3 When he opened the second seal, I heard the second living creature say, "Come!" 4 And out came another horse, bright red; its rider was permitted to take peace from the earth, so that men should slay one another; and he was given a great sword.

3 Then the Lamb broke open the second seal; and I heard the second living creature say, "Come!" 4 Another horse came out, a red one. Its rider was given the power to bring war on the earth, so that men should kill each other. He was given a large sword.

Verse 3 is like the first part of verse 1. RSV **he opened** means "the Lamb opened" (TEV, REB, TNT, NIV, FRCL, BRCL, SPCL).

Come! See verse 1 for translation suggestions. It seems best to use the same expression for all four times it appears (verses 1,3,5,7).

Out came: only here is this said. The text does not say where the horse came from; perhaps from near the throne or behind it. In languages that must have an object indicating the place of origin, one can say "came out from the place where the throne stood (or, was)." The riders are obviously God's servants, carrying out his will.

Bright red: the color of fire, indicating not only combat but slaughter in combat. In certain languages translators will need to restructure this sentence in order to avoid RSV's apposition; for example, "A red horse came out."

Its rider was permitted to take peace from the earth: the passive **was permitted** is to be understood as referring to God; God gave this rider permission to bring war on earth. The verbal phrase **was permitted to** translates "it was given to him to"; the "it" represents something like "power" (TEV, RNAB, REB, Phps, TOB, FRCL, SPCL, BRCL), or "permission" (TNT), or "duty" (NJB), or "right." For the phrase **to take peace from the earth**, see Matthew 10.14. The meaning may be expressed by "to bring war on earth" (TEV).

So that men should slay one another: instead of **men** NRSV has "people," which is better. It may be helpful to specify this slaughter as "slay (or, kill) one another in war." The verb used here is the one used in 5.6, but in that context it seems to imply "sacrifice."

And he was given a great sword: again the passive refers to God or to an angel. Some languages can avoid this ambiguity by using the equivalent of "receive" and say, for example, "The one sitting on this horse (rider) received a large sword." However, in the case of languages that must use an agent, translators may be ambiguous and say "and some one gave him a large sword." In yet other languages a translator will have to choose between God or an angel. The former is the more likely. **A great sword**: something like "large," "huge," "long," or even "heavy" is better in English than "great" when applied to a sword.

Alternative translation models for verse 4 are:

> And a flame colored (bright red) horse came out. The one riding on it received the power to cause people to fight each other on the earth, so that they should kill (slaughter) one another in war. The rider received a large sword (war knife).

Or:

> And a bright red horse came out of the place where the throne stood (or, was). God gave the one riding on it the power to cause people to fight each other on earth, so that they should kill each other in war. For this purpose God also gave this rider a large war knife.

6.5	RSV	TEV
	When he opened the third seal, I heard the third living creature say, "Come!" And I saw, and behold, a black horse, and its rider had a balance in his hand;	Then the Lamb broke open the third seal; and I heard the third living creature say, "Come!" I looked, and there was a black horse. Its rider held a pair of scales in his hand.

The first part of this verse follows the same pattern found in verses 1 and 3.

Behold: see 1.7 for ways to translate this word. In the context of this verse, however, TEV's rendering "and there" is a good one. Another possible rendering is "and there appeared."

A black horse: this is the symbol of famine, that is, death caused by famine.

A balance: a pair of scales, on which the scarce food is weighed; see the expression "eat bread by weight" in Ezekiel 4.16 (see also Lev 26.26). This was probably a weighing device consisting of two round metal plates hanging by strings or ropes to a short wooden or metal pole held in the rider's hand. Translators should keep this picture in mind and not use words describing modern weighing systems. It is possible, then, to translate this sentence as follows: "A pair of scales was hanging from the rider's hand," or in other languages "a scale was hanging . . . ."

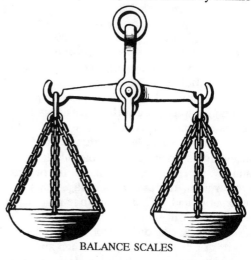

BALANCE SCALES

6.6   RSV   TEV

RSV	TEV
and I heard what seemed to be a voice in the midst of the four living creatures saying, "A quart of wheat for a denarius,[a] and three quarts of barley for a denarius;[a] but do not harm oil and wine!"	I heard what sounded like a voice coming from among the four living creatures, which said, "A quart of wheat for a day's wages, and three quarts of barley for a day's wages. But do not damage the olive trees and the vineyards!"

[a] The denarius was a day's wage for a laborer

What seemed to be a voice: as in 4.6a, "as it were," here **what seemed to be** is said in order to indicate that it was a sound like that produced by a human voice, "what sounded like a (human) voice."

In the midst of the four living creatures: this implies quite specifically that the speaker was not one of the four living creatures but was in their midst—possibly on the throne itself.

A quart of wheat: the Greek dry measure translated **quart** is equivalent to about a quart in the English system, and a little over a liter in the metric system. Where flour is measured by weight, the translation can be "two pounds" or "one kilogram" (to be precise, a liter of wheat flour weighs 570 grams). However, translators may use a suitable local equivalent, if that is considered natural and is less anachronistic than pounds or kilograms. Both wheat and barley in this verse refer to flour, not to the grain itself. Barley was cheaper than wheat and was eaten not only by the poor but also by domestic work animals.

A denarius: as the RSV footnote and the TEV text indicate, the denarius was the standard daily wage for a rural worker (see Matt 20.2). This was a very high price for a quart of wheat or three quarts of barley, perhaps as much as ten times the normal price, and indicates a severe shortage as a result of war. This can be indicated by translating "A whole day's wages for only a quart (or, two pounds) of wheat" or "It takes the wages of a hard day's work to buy only a quart of wheat."

Do not harm oil and wine: the command is addressed to the horseman, and its effect is to limit the severity of the famine. Although some commentators suggest that oil and wine were really luxury items, it seems more probable to take them as staples, needed for a normal diet at that time (see Deut 7.13; 11.14). It is not easy to determine the precise meaning of the verb "(not) to harm," which is also used of plants in 7.3; 9.4. The problem here is to determine whether **oil and wine** are the products themselves, in which case something like "do not diminish the supply of oil and wine" is meant, or else it may mean "do not adulterate the oil and wine" (that is, lower their quality by adding water to them). But **oil and wine** may refer to olive trees and grapevines (TEV), in which case the meaning is "spare the olive trees and the grapevines." Swete comments: "The oliveyards and vineyards are not to suffer to such an extent as seriously to interfere with the supply." The first possibility is preferred by SPCL, "do not cause a scarcity of oil and wine"; also NJB "do not tamper with the oil or the wine"; the second possibility is the choice of REB, "do not damage the olive and the vine" (also Brc). No one can be dogmatic, but perhaps the second possibility is the better one.

6.7-8   RSV   TEV

7 When he opened the fourth seal, I heard the voice of the fourth living creature say, "Come!" 8 And I saw, and behold, a pale horse, and its rider's name was Death, and Hades followed him; and they were given power over a fourth of the earth, to kill with sword and with famine and with pestilence and by wild beasts of the earth.

7 Then the Lamb broke open the fourth seal; and I heard the fourth living creature say, "Come!" 8 I looked, and there was a pale-colored horse. Its rider was named Death, and Hades[c] followed close behind. They were given authority over one fourth of the earth, to kill by means of war, famine, disease, and wild animals.

[c] HADES: *The world of the dead (see 1.18).*

For verse 7 see verses 1,3,5.

And I saw, and behold: see verse 2.

A pale horse: the Greek word can be taken to mean "green" or "yellowish green"; NRSV translates "pale green"; NJB "deathly pale"; REB "sickly pale." At least one language translates this as "a light dusty color."

Its rider's name was Death, and Hades followed him: this is the only horse whose rider is given a name. It is not certain whether the verb **followed** means that Hades also was riding a horse; it does not mean that Hades was on the same horse that Death rode. So translators need to use a very general word for **followed**. For **Death** and **Hades** see 1.18.

And they were given power over a fourth of the earth: the passive **they were given** means that God gave them this power. Since the focus of this clause is really not on the agent, in many languages one may say "they received power over one quarter . . ." and thus avoid a passive construction. In 2.26 the word for **power** (or, authority) meant to "rule over"; here in this verse it means "to have the power to hurt (or, kill) people." So in languages where one must state the domain of the authority, this clause may be rendered "they received the authority to hurt (or, kill) one quarter of the people in the world." The phrase **a fourth of the earth** is not used in a spatial sense, that is, one fourth of the surface of the globe, but in a numerical sense, one fourth of the world's population.

To kill with sword and with famine and with pestilence: here **sword** (translating the Greek word used in 1.16; 2.12,16) translates a different Greek word from the one used in verse 4; in translation, however, the same word may be used. **Sword** stands for battle; death by **famine** is starvation caused by shortage of food; and **pestilence** translates the Greek word "death" (as the same Greek word translates the Hebrew word for "pestilence" in the Septuagint of Lev 26.25; Jer 14.12; 24.10; and elsewhere), meaning "disease" or "epidemic."

And by wild beasts of the earth: here the Greek preposition *hupo* is used, indicating subordinate agency (living creatures as agents); in the case of **sword**, **famine**, and **pestilence**, the preposition *en* is used, indicating means (as with tools). The phrase **of the earth** indicates these are wild land animals. Many languages will express agency and means in exactly the same manner.

Alternative translation models for verse 8 are:

> I looked and saw there a pale-colored horse. Its rider had the name Death, and another being named World of the Dead was following close behind the first one. They received the power to kill one quarter of the people on earth by means of war, lack of food (starvation), sickness of all kinds, and wild animals.

Or:

> . . . God gave them the power to use war, famine, epidemics, and wild animals to kill one quarter of the people on the earth.

6.9	RSV	TEV

When he opened the fifth seal, I saw under the altar the souls of those who had been slain for the word of God and for the witness they had borne;	Then the Lamb broke open the fifth seal. I saw underneath the altar the souls of those who had been killed because they had proclaimed God's

> word and had been faithful in their
> witnessing.

When he opened the fifth seal, I saw: in the other cases (verses 1,3,5,7) the author writes "I heard." Again it will be helpful to identify who **he** is by saying "the Lamb."

Under the altar: this appears to be the heavenly counterpart of the altar in front of the Temple, on which sacrifices were burned; the animal's blood (that is, its life; see Lev 17.11) was poured out at the base of the altar (Lev 4.7). This is the first time **the altar** is mentioned in this book; however, it is referred to as if both it and its location are already well known. This kind of reference should be retained, even though readers of the translation may not yet be acquainted with it. The location of the souls **under the altar** seems a bit strange; some translate "at the base of the altar" or "at the foot of the altar" (see also 14.18). The whole picture seems to indicate a place of safety. The **altar** in the Temple was made of bronze, a metal structure on which animals were sacrificed or food was offered to God. Other Hebrew altars were sometimes made of wood (for incense) or constructed of stones. Many modern cultures have similar elevated structures for sacrificing animals or for offering gifts to a deity. Sometimes this is a stone or wood platform or table. Such terms may be used here if it is clear that this altar is dedicated to God.

The souls: this is the equivalent of "the spirits," that is, the immaterial part of a person that lives on after death. Care must be taken not to use a word that means "ghosts." The Greek word appears a good number of times in Revelation, but only at 20.4 does it have the same meaning that it has here.

Who had been slain for the word of God and for the witness they had borne: in some languages the passive clause **who had been slain** may be avoided by using an expression such as "who had suffered (received) death." But in certain other languages one must identify the agent of "kill" and say, for example, "the souls of those people whom their enemies had killed." For **word of God and for the witness which they had borne**, see the comments on "word" and "testimony" in 1.2,9. Here the second Greek phrase is literally "the witness that they had"; it can mean "the witness they had received," that is, received from Jesus Christ. Or else, as Sweet explains, "the witness of Jesus that they maintained." But the absence of the possessive phrase "of Jesus" makes this unlikely. It seems likely that the two phrases describe one activity. As often happens in this book, the **and** does not mean "in addition to" but "that is" (what is called "epexegetical and," as explained in "Translating the Revelation to John," page 5). As Beckwith explains, "the word of God, i.e., the testimony borne by Jesus." So SPCL translates "because they had proclaimed the message of God," and RNAB "because of the witness they bore to the Word of God." NJB has "on account of the Word of God, for witnessing to it." The death of these faithful martyrs is seen as a sacrifice offered to God on the altar of the heavenly temple (thus Sweet). Perhaps both ideas can be combined as follows: "because they proclaimed God's message faithfully."

An alternative translation model for this verse is:

> I saw at the base (foot) of the platform for offerings to God the
> spirits of some people. These were people who had been killed

because they proclaimed God's message faithfully (as good witnesses).

6.10   RSV   TEV

they cried out with a loud voice, "O Sovereign Lord, holy and true, how long before thou wilt judge and avenge our blood on those who dwell upon the earth?"	They shouted in a loud voice, "Almighty Lord, holy and true! How long will it be until you judge the people on earth and punish them for killing us?"

They cried out: that is, they shouted, not wept.

O Sovereign Lord: this Greek word was generally used to refer to an owner of slaves, but in this context it is used as a title meaning "Powerful Master" or "Powerful (Almighty) God." Elsewhere it appears in Luke 2.29 (RSV "Lord"); Acts 4.24; 2 Peter 2.1; Jude 4, where it has been translated as either "Lord," "Sovereign Lord," or "Master." In the Luke and Acts references it refers to God, and in 2 Peter to Christ. Here in Revelation it is a title for God.

Holy and true: see 3.7, where these qualities are ascribed to Christ. But in this verse God is described as holy or pure, and is true or trustworthy.

How long: this cry of the persecuted people of God is a request, or demand, that God act at once: "Why do you delay . . . ?" or "Don't wait any longer . . . !" or "Why do you wait so long?" (see similar cries in Psa 6.3; 13.1-2; 35.17; Isa 6.11; Zech 1.12). In many languages this idea will be expressed as "Please don't wait any longer."

Judge and avenge our blood on those who dwell upon the earth: judge may also be expressed as "decide the guilt of," "decide whether a person is guilty or innocent," or idiomatically, for example, as "untie the words of" (Yapese), or "sing a (court) case against" (Chewa). In heaven the martyrs ask that God declare the guilt of the murderers and punish them. To **avenge** means to do what is needed to get even with the guilty ones; in this context it is some form of punishment, if not death. **Our blood** here means "our death," "our murder" (see 1.5). And **those who dwell upon the earth**, although a phrase that seems to include all the people in the world, is here a reference to those who had executed these Christians.

An alternative translation model for this verse is:

> These spirits shouted in a loud voice saying, "Almighty God, you are pure and trustworthy! Please don't wait any longer to condemn and punish those people on earth who killed us."

6.11   RSV   TEV

Then they were each given a white robe and told to rest a little longer, until the number of their fellow servants and their brethren should be complete, who	Each of them was given a white robe, and they were told to rest a little while longer, until the complete number of their fellow servants and brothers were

were to be killed as they themselves had been.   killed, as they had been.

Then they were each given a white robe: either God or an angel gives each of them a white robe, a symbol of purity or victory (see 3.4-5). Of course it is difficult to imagine how a soul puts on a robe; but this is figurative language describing things seen in a vision, and the figurative language should be maintained rather literally.

And told: again the passive form is a way of referring to God or to an angel. In languages that do not use the passive, one may render these first two clauses as "God gave each of them a white robe and instructed them (told them) . . . ."

To rest a little longer, until: here **rest** means not only not having to work or strive, but also to be free of anxiety and distress over the punishment of their killers. They must be patient. God's vengeance will not be immediate but will come soon. In some languages the concept of **rest** is described idiomatically; for example, "relax (rest) the heart" or "let the heart sit down" (Chewa). **A little while longer** may also be expressed as "only a short time more."

The number . . . should be complete: this statement implies that God has decided that there will be more persecution, and that a certain number of Christians will be put to death. Once that number has been reached, God will take appropriate action. In certain languages this phrase will be placed at the end of the verse; for example, ". . . until their fellow servants and brothers will be killed to complete a number (amount)" or ". . . to bring a number to completion."

Their fellow servants and their brethren: again, this does not mean two different groups, but the same people identified in two different ways. So REB "all their brothers in Christ's service." In many languages this phrase will be expressed as "all their elders and youngers who serve Christ with them."

Who were to be killed as they themselves had been: the Greek verb form translated as the future in English (**were to be**) may be used to indicate the working of God's will (see 2.10), or else may mean that the action will take place soon (so NRSV "who were soon to be killed"). In languages that do not use the passive, one may say, for example, "whom those enemies will also kill."

Alternative translation models for this verse are:

> God gave each of them (the spirits) a white robe and told them not to worry (to rest their hearts) for a little while longer. They should do this until the complete number of their fellow servants and brothers (or, elders and youngers) were killed as they had been.

Or:

> . . . until those enemies killed more of their brothers (elders and youngers) that he (God) has allowed to be killed.

6.12   RSV   TEV

When he opened the sixth seal, I looked, and behold, there was a great earthquake; and the sun became black

And I saw the Lamb break open the sixth seal. There was a violent earthquake, and the sun became black

117

as sackcloth, the full moon became like blood,	like coarse black cloth, and the moon turned completely red like blood.

The opening of the sixth seal sets off a series of eschatological events (6.12-17); after an interlude (7.1-17) the seventh seal is broken (8.1).

When he opened: it is well to make the subject explicit, "When the Lamb opened."

I looked, and behold: see 4.1. RSV translates a Greek text that has **behold** (or "lo," as in 4.1); this word is lacking in most manuscripts, and most modern translations do not include it. NRSV has "When he opened the sixth seal, I looked . . . ."

There was a great earthquake: earthquakes are frequently one of the great events marking the end of the age (see Isa 29.6; Joel 2.10; Hag 2.6; Mark 13.8). They are caused by God as a prelude to the Last Judgment. In languages that have no specific word for earthquakes, something like "a violent shaking of the earth (ground)" may be said.

The sun became black as sackcloth: this means that the sun stopped shining (see Isa 13.10; Ezek 32.7-8; Joel 2.10; Amos 8.9; Mark 13.24). Sackcloth is a coarse black cloth that was worn in times of mourning (see Isa 50.3). FRCL, SPCL, and BRCL translate here "a mourning garment," "mourning clothes." In certain languages the figure of **sackcloth** will be unnatural. In such cases one may say, for example, "the sun stopped shining and there was complete darkness" or "the sun became dark as night."

The full moon became like blood: the moon turned completely red, as red as blood (see the quotation of Joel 2.31 in Acts 2.20). The translation should not say, or imply, that the moon became a liquid solution, like blood. The color chosen by translators should if possible be a dark red bordering on red purple. Translators in languages that have terms like "blood red" or "blood color" should use those. One may also translate **became like blood** as "turn red like blood."

6.13   RSV   TEV

and the stars of the sky fell to the earth as the fig tree sheds its winter fruit when shaken by a gale;	The stars fell down to the earth, like unripe figs falling from the tree when a strong wind shakes it.

The stars of the sky fell to the earth as the fig tree sheds its winter fruit when shaken by a gale: stars falling to earth is another of the great events marking the end (Mark 13.25). The sky is violently shaken, and the stars fall out of the sky. In some languages one must indicate where the stars fall from; for example, "the stars fell down from the sky to the earth like . . . ." The stars fall like unripe figs fall from the tree when it is shaken by a strong wind. The figure John uses to explain this great event is that of unripe figs, which grow in the winter and usually fall off in the spring. Instead of **winter fruit** (RSV), "unripe figs" or "green figs" may be said (FRCL, SPCL, BRCL, TEV, TNT, AT, and others), or else, simply "figs" (REB, NJB), or even "fresh figs." However, the important element in this figure is unripe fruit, not one particular kind of fruit. So in cultures where **figs** are unknown, one may say, for example, "green fruit" or "unripe fruit." In other languages there is specific vocabulary for the falling of leaves off a tree. In such cases this verb can be used to describe the falling of the stars, to heighten the effect of the figurative language.

Gale: this translates the Greek "a strong wind." In small island cultures the equivalent of a **gale** is "hurricane" or "typhoon."

An alternative translation model for this verse is:

> The stars fell down from the sky to the earth just like unripe figs
> (fruit) falling from the tree when a violent wind (typhoon) shakes it.

6.14   RSV   TEV

the sky vanished like a scroll that is   The sky disappeared like a scroll being
rolled up, and every mountain and is-   rolled up, and every mountain and island was removed from its place.   land was moved from its place.

The sky vanished like a scroll that is rolled up: the sky, in the creation account (Gen 1.6-8), was portrayed as a dome. In John's vision it rolls back on itself, like an immense sheet of parchment or papyrus that is rolled up like a scroll (5.1); see Isaiah 34.4. For **scroll** see 5.1. In at least one language where scrolls are unknown, this figure is translated as "like a sleeping mat that is rolled up and taken away."

Every mountain and island was removed from its place: God is in charge; these things happen as a manifestation of God's anger (verse 16). So the passive form of the verb is a way of speaking about God. The whole universe is shaken so violently that all the mountains and islands are thrown out of their places. Even though the passive form in this clause can be thought of as the so-called divine passive, yet to translate "and God moved every mountain . . ." in this context will sound a little strange. In many languages that do not use the passive, there are other ways to avoid a passive expression without making the agent explicit. Some languages use special verbs to describe the movement of land masses, such as mountains, after an earthquake. In yet other languages collocations such as "suffer move" can be employed.

6.15   RSV   TEV

Then the kings of the earth and the   Then the kings of the earth, the rulers
great men and the generals and the rich   and the military chiefs, the rich and the
and the strong, and every one, slave and   powerful, and all other men, slave and
free, hid in the caves and among the   free, hid themselves in caves and under
rocks of the mountains,   rocks on the mountains.

All people on earth try to hide from the punishment God and the Lamb are sending on them. The language is typically male-oriented: "the kings, the important men, the generals, the rich, the powerful, and every slave and free man." Prominence is given to the powerful and the wealthy.

The kings of the earth: see comments on "kings on earth" in 1.5.

The great men: these are powerful and influential people in government and commerce (see Mark 6.21, TEV "top government officials"). In certain cultures these will be called "the chiefs," "the headmen," "the honchos," or "the big men."

The generals refers to high military officers. A "general" may also be referred to as "the chief leader of an army."

The strong: this can be translated "important people," "influential leaders."

Slave and free: a "slave" is a person who is the property of someone else. He or she has no rights and must show complete obedience and loyalty to the owner. A possible alternative translation of this word in cultures where **slave** is unknown is "a person who belongs to (or, is the property of) another." In at least two languages the phrase **slaves and free** is translated as "those who are bound to a master and those who are not (bound to a master)."

Hid in the caves and among the rocks of the mountains: distinct from caves, as a good hiding place, are tall crags, or "high rocky projections or overhangs," or "tall big rocks in the mountains," which afford protection; RNAB has "among mountain crags," REB "under mountain crags." For the whole picture see Isaiah 2.19. **Caves** are often referred to as "big holes in the rocks."

An alternative translation model for this verse is:

> Then all the kings (high chiefs) of the world, the lesser chiefs, the leaders of armies, the rich, the important people, and all other people, whether they are slaves (the property of others) or are free, tried to hide themselves in caves or in the shelter of tall rocks in the mountains.

6.16   RSV   TEV

RSV	TEV
calling to the mountains and rocks, "Fall on us and hide us from the face of him who is seated on the throne, and from the wrath of the Lamb;	They called out to the mountains and to the rocks, "Fall on us and hide us from the eyes of the one who sits on the throne and from the anger of the Lamb!

Calling to the mountains and rocks, "Fall on us and hide us . . .": this reflects the language of Hosea 10.8 (see also Luke 23.30). They ask the mountains and rocks to fall on them, not because they want them to hurt or kill them, but in order to protect them from God's wrath. **Fall on us and hide us** may be also expressed as "Fall on us and cover (protect) us" or "Fall down on us and hide us."

From the face of him who is seated on the throne: here God's face is either a way of speaking of his presence as a whole or of his eyes in particular. REB translates "from the One who sits on the throne"; FRCL "from the sight of . . ."; SPCL "from the presence of . . . ." Another way of expressing this phrase is "so that the one who is sitting on the throne can't see us." For the description of God as the one who sits on the throne, see 4.2.

The wrath of the Lamb: here **wrath** is used in the sense, not of an intense emotion of anger as such, but of the expression of that anger in the form of punishment. As the phrase "the great day of their wrath" in verse 17 shows, it means the Final Judgment and the punishment that will fall on sinners. So the translation may say "from the punishment (or, vengeance) of the Lamb."

For the translation of **Lamb** see 5.6.

An alternative translation model for this verse is:

> They called out to the mountains and to the rocks, saying, "Please fall down and hide us so that the one who is sitting on the throne can't see us, and the Lamb won't be able to punish us."

6.17   RSV   TEV

for the great day of their wrath has come, and who can stand before it?"	The terrible day of their anger is here, and who can stand up against it?"

The great day of their wrath: here **great** has the negative sense of "terrible." This is the Day of Judgment, the final punishment. God and the Lamb act together to punish all the people on earth. Translators in some languages will need to retain a word like **for** in order to show the logical relationship between this verse and the former one. But in others the cry of despair may be prefaced by an expression similar to "Oh no! The terrible day . . ." or "Indeed, the terrible day . . . ."

Who can stand before it? That is, no one can survive the wrath that is coming (see Nahum 1.6).

An alternative translation model for this verse is:

> Indeed the Day when God and the Lamb will punish everyone has come, and no one will be able to survive this punishment.

7.1-8

RSV

TEV

The 144,000 People of Israel

1 After this I saw four angels standing at the four corners of the earth, holding back the four winds of the earth, that no wind might blow on earth or sea or against any tree. 2 Then I saw another angel ascend from the rising of the sun, with the seal of the living God, and he called with a loud voice to the four angels who had been given power to harm earth and sea, 3 saying, "Do not harm the earth or the sea or the trees, till we have sealed the servants of our God upon their foreheads." 4 And I heard the number of the sealed, a hundred and forty-four thousand sealed, out of every tribe of the sons of Israel, 5 twelve thousand sealed out of the tribe of Judah, twelve thousand of the tribe of Reuben, twelve thousand of the tribe of Gad, 6 twelve thousand of the tribe of Asher, twelve thousand of the tribe of Naphtali, twelve thousand of the tribe of Manasseh, 7 twelve thousand of the tribe of Simeon, twelve thousand

1 After this I saw four angels standing at the four corners of the earth, holding back the four winds so that no wind should blow on the earth or the sea or against any tree. 2 And I saw another angel coming up from the east with the seal of the living God. He called out in a loud voice to the four angels to whom God had given the power to damage the earth and the sea. 3 The angel said, "Do not harm the earth, the sea, or the trees, until we mark the servants of our God with a seal on their foreheads." 4 And I was told that the number of those who were marked with God's seal on their foreheads was 144,000. They were from the twelve tribes of Israel, 5-8 twelve thousand from each tribe: Judah, Reuben, Gad, Asher, Naphtali, Manasseh, Simeon, Levi, Issachar, Zebulun, Joseph, and Benjamin.

of the tribe of Levi, twelve thousand of the tribe
of Issachar, 8 twelve thousand of the tribe of
Zebulun, twelve thousand of the tribe of Joseph,
twelve thousand sealed out of the tribe of Benjamin.

SECTION HEADING: TEV "The 144,000 People of Israel." Other possible
headings are "The 144,000 of God's people, who are marked with God's seal"; "The
144,000 members of the people of Israel" (FRCL); "God's servants will be preserved"
(NJB). It seems quite certain that "the twelve tribes of Israel" (verse 4) is not meant
in a racial sense but stands for all the people of God, Jewish and Gentile; therefore
in a section heading it may be well to say "God's people" or "God's servants" in the
Heading, and not "Israelites" or "people of Israel."

This chapter reports two visions that take place between the breaking open of
the sixth and seventh seals. The first vision (verses 1-8) is that of the 144,000 servants
of God whom four angels mark with the seal of God, as a guarantee that they will
survive the terrible distress that is coming soon (see 9.4). In the second vision (verses
9-17) John sees in heaven the numberless thousands of the redeemed from every
race and nation, serving as priests of God and the Lamb.

It appears that two different groups are meant, and there are those who so
understand the text; most scholars, however, believe that both visions represent the
Christian believers, the people of God, in two different ways. Regardless of what is
meant, the translation must represent the plain meaning of the text, without any
interpretation.

7.1   RSV   TEV

After this I saw four angels stand-   After this I saw four angels standing at the four corners of the earth,   ing at the four corners of the earth,
holding back the four winds of the   holding back the four winds so that no
earth, that no wind might blow on earth   wind should blow on the earth or the
or sea or against any tree.   sea or against any tree.

After this I saw: as in 4.1. This is a separate vision, and everything takes place
on earth. Since this is the beginning of a new chapter, it will be equally natural in
most languages to say "The next thing that I saw . . . ."

Four angels standing at the four corners of the earth: the earth is regarded
as a vast, square surface, with four distinct corners, from each of which one wind
blows.

Holding back the four winds of the earth: the four winds blow from heaven
(Jer 49.36; Dan 7.2; Zech 6.5); here they are called **the four winds of the earth**,
blowing from north, south, east, and west. The angels keep them from blowing **on
earth or sea**, which includes all the earth's surface—the **earth**, of course, meaning
"the dry land," and the **sea** referring to large bodies of water everywhere. The
addition of **or against any tree** seems to be a detail meant to make the figure more
vivid, since trees are particularly affected by strong winds.

7.2   RSV   TEV

Then I saw another angel ascend from the rising of the sun, with the seal of the living God, and he called with a loud voice to the four angels who had been given power to harm earth and sea,	And I saw another angel coming up from the east with the seal of the living God. He called out in a loud voice to the four angels to whom God had given the power to damage the earth and the sea.

Another angel: this angel is not identified by name or function.

Ascend from the rising of the sun: this angel appears on the horizon, coming from the east. In some languages it will be necessary to state where the angel is ascending to. The following verses indicate that it is heaven. So one may say "coming up to heaven from the east."

With the seal of the living God: this is not the same as the seals used to close up the scroll in chapters 5 and 6. The seal referred to here is an instrument that marks or stamps a figure, symbol, number, or name upon an object or person. Kings and other important people had such seals, sometimes attached to a ring, called "a signet ring" (see Gen 41.42; Est 3.10; Dan 6.17). The normal purpose of the seal was to identify a document as authentic; the kind of seal spoken of in 5.1 and 20.3 was used to prevent the thing sealed from being opened (see Matt 27.66, the sealing of Jesus' tomb). In this case the seal is a mark that shows that those who have it on their foreheads are God's people (see the use of the verb "to seal" in 2 Cor 1.22; Eph 1.13; 4.30). Where an instrument like a stamp or a brand is not known, a descriptive phrase may be used, "an instrument to mark people," "an instrument to write a sign on people."

The phrase **the seal of . . . God** means the seal that God uses, or the seal that puts God's mark on people. It is not said whether the identifying mark is a number, a symbol, or a name; 14.1 speaks of 144,000 who have the names of God and of the Lamb on their foreheads (see also 22.4), and it may be assumed that this is true here (see verse 3).

For **the living God** see the similar divine name "the living one" in 1.18.

Power to harm earth and sea: the passive **who had been given** means that God had given them this power. The four angels who restrain the winds have the power to turn them loose and cause damage to the earth and the sea. For **harm** see also 6.6. By "harming the sea" the writer may have had in mind the damage done to islands in the sea; a translation, however, must say simply "the sea" here and in the next verse. The Hebrews thought of seas as having either fresh or salt water, and for the most part were only acquainted with the Mediterranean Sea, the Sea of Galilee, and the Dead Sea. However, **sea** here in Revelation is referring to all large bodies of water, whether oceans (seas) and lakes, but not rivers. In cultures where such masses of water, whether salty or fresh, are unknown, perhaps one must translate **sea** here and elsewhere as "large expanses of water." **Earth** here refers to "dry land" in contrast with the waters.

7.3   RSV   TEV

saying, "Do not harm the earth or the sea or the trees, till we have sealed the servants of our God upon their foreheads."

The angel said, "Do not harm the earth, the sea, or the trees, until we mark the servants of our God with a seal on their foreheads."

Saying: in many languages it will be better style to begin this verse in a way similar to that of TEV: "The angel said" or "God's messenger commanded, saying . . . ."

Do not harm the earth or the sea or the trees: the angel in charge is ordering the four angels not to turn loose the four destructive winds. It will be helpful in certain languages to make this explicit and say "Do not let the winds harm . . . ."

Till we have sealed the servants of our God upon their foreheads: the angel and his helpers, who are also angels (**we**), will mark God's servants. The four angels spoken to do not join in the task of marking, so the **we** is exclusive. Instead of the verb **sealed** it may be better to have "mark with a seal" (TEV, NRSV, and others) or "put a sign upon . . . with God's instrument for marking people." In contrast with **we**, the **our** in **our God** includes the four angels addressed.

An alternative translation model for this verse is:

> The angel said, "Do not let the winds harm the land, the seas (large bodies of water), or the trees, until we put a sign on the foreheads of the servants of our [inclusive] God with his instrument to mark people.

7.4-8   RSV   TEV

4 And I heard the number of the sealed, a hundred and forty-four thousand sealed, out of every tribe of the sons of Israel, 5 twelve thousand sealed out of the tribe of Judah, twelve thousand of the tribe of Reuben, twelve thousand of the tribe of Gad, 6 twelve thousand of the tribe of Asher, twelve thousand of the tribe of Naphtali, twelve thousand of the tribe of Manasseh, 7 twelve thousand of the tribe of Simeon, twelve thousand of the tribe of Levi, twelve thousand of the tribe of Issachar, 8 twelve thousand of the tribe of Zebulun, twelve thousand of the tribe of Joseph, twelve thousand sealed out of the tribe of Benjamin.

4 And I was told that the number of those who were marked with God's seal on their foreheads was 144,000. They were from the twelve tribes of Israel, 5-8 twelve thousand from each tribe: Judah, Reuben, Gad, Asher, Naphtali, Manasseh, Simeon, Levi, Issachar, Zebulun, Joseph, and Benjamin.

And I heard the number: presumably the angel in charge, or some other angel, told John. It may be better to translate "I was told" (TEV, FRCL, SPCL, BRCL), or "someone told me."

Of the sealed: it is much better to use a descriptive phrase, "of all those who had been marked on their foreheads with God's seal" or "all those whom the angels had marked on their foreheads with God's seal." For **seal** see the previous verse.

A hundred and forty-four thousand: the number is symbolic, 12,000 from each of the twelve tribes, indicating the totality of all of God's people. As is true of other numbers and symbols in this book, this is not meant literally.

Every tribe of the sons of Israel: it is better to translate "every one of the tribes of Israel" or "all the Israelite tribes."

Alternative translation models for verse 4 are:

> Someone told me that the number of those people whom the angels had marked with God's seal on their forehead was 144,000. These people were from all twelve tribes of Israel.

Or:

> Someone told me that the angels had marked 144,000 people on their foreheads with God's seal. These people were from . . . .

There is no generally accepted explanation of the twelve tribes that are named. In the Old Testament the tribes are named for ten of Jacob's twelve sons (Reuben, Simeon, Judah, Issachar, Zebulun, Dan, Benjamin, Naphtali, Gad, and Asher) and the two sons of Joseph (Manasseh and Ephraim). Two of Jacob's sons, Levi and Joseph, do not have tribes named after them. In this list Levi and Joseph are named as tribes; Dan and Ephraim are not listed. There is also no explanation for the order of the names; it is generally assumed that Judah is named first because it was the tribe to which Jesus belonged.

For verses 5-8 some translators may find it helpful to imitate TEV in giving the information, while others may wish to reproduce the style of the Greek text, as RSV does, if that is the way that lists of names and numbers are handled in the receptor-language culture.

7.9-17

RSV

9 After this I looked, and behold, a great multitude which no man could number, from every nation, from all tribes and peoples and tongues, standing before the throne and before the Lamb, clothed in white robes, with palm branches in their hands, 10 and crying out with a loud voice, "Salvation belongs to our God who sits upon the throne, and to the Lamb!" 11 And all the angels stood round the throne and round the elders and the four living creatures, and they fell on their faces

TEV
The Enormous Crowd

9 After this I looked, and there was an enormous crowd—no one could count all the people! They were from every race, tribe, nation, and language, and they stood in front of the throne and of the Lamb, dressed in white robes and holding palm branches in their hands. 10 They called out in a loud voice: "Salvation comes from our God, who sits on the throne, and from the Lamb!" 11 All the angels stood around the throne, the elders, and the four living creatures. Then they

before the throne and worshiped God, 12 saying, "Amen! Blessing and glory and wisdom and thanksgiving and honor and power and might be to our God for ever and ever! Amen."

13 Then one of the elders addressed me, saying, "Who are these, clothed in white robes, and whence have they come?" 14 I said to him, "Sir, you know." And he said to me, "These are they who have come out of the great tribulation; they have washed their robes and made them white in the blood of the Lamb.

15   Therefore are they before the throne of God,
     and serve him day and night within his temple;
     and he who sits upon the throne will shelter them with his presence.

16   They shall hunger no more, neither thirst any more;
     the sun shall not strike them, nor any scorching heat.

17   For the Lamb in the midst of the throne will be their shepherd,
     and he will guide them to springs of living water;
     and God will wipe away every tear from their eyes."

threw themselves face downward in front of the throne and worshiped God, 12 saying, "Amen! Praise, glory, wisdom, thanksgiving, honor, power, and might belong to our God forever and ever! Amen!"

13 One of the elders asked me, "Who are these people dressed in white robes, and where do they come from?"

14 "I don't know, sir. You do," I answered.

He said to me, "These are the people who have come safely through the terrible persecution. They have washed their robes and made them white with the blood of the Lamb. 15 That is why they stand before God's throne and serve him day and night in his temple. He who sits on the throne will protect them with his presence. 16 Never again will they hunger or thirst; neither sun nor any scorching heat will burn them, 17 because the Lamb, who is in the center of the throne, will be their shepherd, and he will guide them to springs of life-giving water. And God will wipe away every tear from their eyes."

SECTION HEADING: TEV "The Enormous Crowd." Other possibilities are "The immense multitude in heaven," "A huge crowd of people standing in heaven," or "The rewarding of the saints" (so NJB) or ". . . of God's people."

All the action in this vision takes place in heaven.

7.9   RSV   TEV

After this I looked, and behold, a great multitude which no man could number, from every nation, from all tribes and peoples and tongues, standing before the throne and before the Lamb, clothed in white robes, with palm branches in their hands,

After this I looked, and there was an enormous crowd—no one could count all the people! They were from every race, tribe, nation, and language, and they stood in front of the throne and of the Lamb, dressed in white robes and holding palm branches in their hands.

After this I looked, and behold: a new vision (see 4.1).

A great multitude which no man could number: this can be expressed by "a crowd too large to be counted" or "a crowd so large that no one could count all the people."

From every nation, from all tribes and peoples and tongues: all four words (in different order) are used in 5.9. For emphasis the writer uses all of them, to indicate the whole human race.

Standing before the throne and before the Lamb: the language used makes it appear that the crowd stood facing the throne, not in a circle around it. For the translation of **throne** see 1.4b and elsewhere. For the translation of **Lamb** see 5.6.

White robes: see 3.4-5; 6.11.

Palm branches: this indicates joy and celebration (see John 12.13; also 1 Maccabees 13.51; 2 Maccabees 10.7). If palms are unknown in a given language group, it may be necessary to say "branches" or "branches of trees," and it may be useful, in some instances, to add the explanation "to show their happiness."

An alternative translation model for this verse is:

> After this I looked and saw there a crowd of people so large that no one could count them all. They came from every tribe in the world, and stood in front of the throne and the Lamb. They wore white robes, and each person was holding a palm branch in his hand.

7.10 RSV TEV

RSV	TEV
and crying out with a loud voice, "Salvation belongs to our God who sits upon the throne, and to the Lamb!"	They called out in a loud voice: "Salvation comes from our God, who sits on the throne, and from the Lamb!"

It may be better to end verse 9 with a full stop and begin verse 10 as a new sentence, as TEV and NRSV do.

Salvation belongs to our God: here, and in the similar passage in verse 12, there is no verb; the Greek text says "Salvation to our God," a way of confessing that God is the one who saves. So something like TEV can be said, or else a verb phrase, "We are saved by our God," or "It is our God who has saved us." The Greek noun is usually translated **salvation**; in some instances it may mean "victory," and that is how SPCL and REB translate it. One commentator says "It is not their salvation that the martyrs are celebrating, but their triumphant passage through persecution" (Caird). Most, however, translate "salvation," and this is probably the better choice. If the crowd is understood as addressing one another, then **our God** is inclusive. However, if this is a statement of praise and worship addressed to God and the Lamb, then **our God** is exclusive. Local worship practices in the receptor-language culture may help determine which form to use. In certain languages **Salvation** will need an object to indicate what it is that God saves them from. In this context it most likely refers to the time of great suffering in 6.1–7.3. So one may translate "It is our God who has brought us through the time of great suffering safely."

Who sits upon the throne: see 4.2-3.

And to the Lamb: the Lamb is associated with God in the salvation, or victory, that has been achieved.

Alternative translation models for this verse are:

> They called out in a loud voice, saying:
> "It is our God and the Lamb who have saved us, our God who sits on the throne."

Or:

> They called out in a loud voice, "It is you our God and the Lamb
> who have saved us, you our God who sits on the throne."

7.11   RSV   TEV

And all the angels stood round the throne and round the elders and the four living creatures, and they fell on their faces before the throne and worshiped God,	All the angels stood around the throne, the elders, and the four living creatures. Then they threw themselves face downward in front of the throne and worshiped God,

All the angels: the scene is the same as in 5.11, except that here the twenty-four elders are named before the four living creatures, not after.

They fell on their faces before the throne and worshiped God: see 1.17; 4.10; 5.14. Instead of the verb "to fall" it may be better to say "they prostrated themselves (lay prostrate) in front of the throne," or "they lay face downwards in front of the throne."

Worshiped God: see 4.10.

7.12   RSV   TEV

saying, "Amen! Blessing and glory and wisdom and thanksgiving and honor and power and might be to our God for ever and ever! Amen."	saying, "Amen! Praise, glory, wisdom, thanksgiving, honor, power, and might belong to our God forever and ever! Amen!"

Amen! The angels affirm the praise offered by the immense crowd in verse 10 (see 1.6).

As in verse 10, there is no verb in Greek (RSV **be to** and TEV "belong to" are adjustments for English style).

Blessing and glory: of the seven nouns used in this song of praise, six appear also in the praise offered to the Lamb in 5.12 (which see). The Greek word translated **thanksgiving** is used also in 4.9 (where it is translated "thanks"). As in 5.12,13, verbal phrases may be a more effective way to translate these nouns; for example, "We proclaim that our God is great, powerful, majestic (mighty), and wise (with complete knowledge). Let us praise him and thank him for ever and ever. So be it!" The "we" and "our" should follow the same inclusive or else exclusive pattern used in verse 10.

7.13   RSV   TEV

Then one of the elders addressed me, saying, "Who are these, clothed in	One of the elders asked me, "Who are these people dressed in white robes,

white robes, and whence have they come?" and where do they come from?"

Then one of the elders addressed me, saying: on the translation of **elders** see 4.4. The verbal phrase **addressed me, saying** represents the Greek form, which consists of the aorist of the verb "to say" (or "to answer") and the participle "saying." The Greek verb for **addressed**, which usually means "to answer," is often used in passages where there is no previous question. It then introduces a statement that is a response to, or a result of, something that has just happened. In English "spoke up" is an effective translation, as in RNAB "spoke up and said to me"; REB translates "turned to me and asked"; NJB "spoke and asked me." FRCL, SPCL, BRCL, and NIV are like TEV, "asked me."

The question, "Who are these . . . and where do they come from?" is a question used for revealing John's ignorance, leading him to ask the elder to give him the information. That is why TEV has "I don't know" in verse 14. In many languages it will be good to expand this sentence and say "Who are these people?" as in TEV.

Dressed in white robes may be expressed as "wearing white robes." For **robes** see 1.13.

7.14 RSV	TEV
I said to him, "Sir, you know." And he said to me, "These are they who have come out of the great tribulation; they have washed their robes and made them white in the blood of the Lamb.	"I don't know, sir. You do," I answered. He said to me, "These are the people who have come safely through the terrible persecution. They have washed their robes and made them white with the blood of the Lamb.

Sir, you know: the title **Sir** represents the Greek *kurios,* which may mean "master" or "lord," or "a respected elder." Here **Sir** is the appropriate equivalent in English.

They who have come out of the great tribulation: the verb "to come out (of)" has here the meaning "to survive," "to live through," or "pass through . . . safely." In 2.22 reference is made to "a great tribulation"; here, however, it is **the great tribulation**, that is, the time of distress and cruel persecution that will take place before the end of the world (see Matt 24.21). REB and NRSV translate "the great ordeal," and Brc has "the terrible time of trouble." Or it can be "the time of great (terrible) suffering."

They have washed their robes and made them white in the blood of the Lamb: this figurative language, as elsewhere, is a way of talking about purification from sin by means of the death of Christ (see 1.5b; 22.14; Heb 9.14; 1 John 1.7). For **robes** see 3.4-5; 6.11; 7.9,13; 22.14; and for **the blood of the Lamb**, see 1.5b. There may be a logical inconsistency in the statement that the robes are made white by being washed in blood. It would be very difficult, however, and quite inappropriate to attempt to avoid this inconsistency. As in 1.5b, **the blood of the Lamb** means the sacrificial death of Christ. In certain languages this sentence will be expressed as "They have used the blood of the Lamb to wash their robes and make them white. An alternative translation model for this verse is:

> I answered, "I don't know."
>   He said to me, "These are people who have passed through the time of terrible suffering safely (without dying). They have washed their robes in the blood of the Lamb to make them white.

7.15   RSV   TEV

Therefore are they before the throne of God, and serve him day and night within his temple; and he who sits upon the throne will shelter them with his presence.	That is why they stand before God's throne and serve him day and night in his temple. He who sits on the throne will protect them with his presence.

RSV prints verses 15-17 in the form of poetry. This may be effective in some languages; in others it may seem strange to have part of the elder's answer in prose and part in poetry. See Section F of the introduction, "Translating the Revelation to John," pages 6 and following.

Therefore: this refers to the fact that all of these people have made their robes white by washing them in the blood of the Lamb. Another way to render this is "For this reason."

The throne of God . . . his temple: the language does not mean to imply that heaven has a palace (or, a throne room) and a temple also; it portrays heaven as God's kingdom and God's temple. For **temple** see 3.12. **Day and night** means that they stood there "unceasingly," "unendingly," or "continually."

Serve: the verb means "to serve as a priest" (see 1.6; 5.10; Heb 8.4-5); it may mean "to worship" (as in 22.3).

He who sits upon the throne: as in 4.2,9; 5.1.

Will shelter them with his presence: literally "will tent upon them." The Greek verb, which is related to the noun "tent," is the one used in John 1.14, where it is translated "dwelt" by RSV; here it is followed by the preposition "upon," so that the idea is not just of living with but of sheltering and protecting. NJB and TNT translate "will spread his tent over them," NRSV "will shelter them," or it can be "live with them." One may also render this clause as "will be with them and protect them."

7.16   RSV   TEV

They shall hunger no more, neither thirst any more;	Never again will they hunger or thirst; neither sun nor any scorching heat will

> the sun shall not strike them,   burn them,
>   nor any scorching heat.

The language in verses 16-17 reflects Isaiah 49.10.
They shall hunger no more, neither thirst any more: this may be translated "Never again will they be hungry or thirsty" or "They will never be hungry again or ever be thirsty again."
The sun shall not strike them: this means that the hot rays of the sun will not harm them (see Psa 121.6). The Greek word translated **scorching heat** may mean "the (desert) wind," reflecting the meaning of Isaiah 49.10 (so NJB). Or else **sun** and **scorching heat** may refer only to the sun's heat: "the burning heat of the sun will not harm them" (so TNT)

7.17   RSV   TEV

> For the Lamb in the midst of the throne will be their shepherd, and he will guide them to springs of living water; and God will wipe away every tear from their eyes."

> because the Lamb, who is in the center of the throne, will be their shepherd, and he will guide them to springs of life-giving water. And God will wipe away every tear from their eyes."

For the Lamb in the midst of the throne: see 5.6.
Will be their shepherd: this is a striking figure, representing Christ as shepherd of his people (see John 10.1-16; 21.15-17). Alternative ways to translate this clause are "will take care of them like a shepherd," or in cultures where shepherds are unknown, one may say "will take care of them as a person who looks after animals (or, livestock) does," or one may need to remove the figurative language and just say "will look after them" or "will take care of them."
He will guide them to springs of living water: this recalls the language of Psalm 23.2. This is not the quiet, stagnant water of a pool but the flowing water of a spring (21.6; 22.1,17; John 4.14). Another way of phrasing this clause is "he will lead them to places where fresh, pure water is flowing."
God will wipe away every tear from their eyes: see Isaiah 25.8. The meaning is that God will remove every source of pain and sorrow; but the vivid figure of wiping away all tears should be kept, if possible (also in 21.4).

C-3. The Seven Trumpets
(8.1–11.19)

8.1-5

RSV   TEV
                                      The Seventh Seal

1 When the Lamb opened the seventh seal, there was silence in heaven for about half an hour.

1 When the Lamb broke open the seventh seal, there was silence in heaven for about half an

2 Then I saw the seven angels who stand before God, and seven trumpets were given to them. 3 And another angel came and stood at the altar with a golden censer; and he was given much incense to mingle with the prayers of all the saints upon the golden altar before the throne; 4 and the smoke of the incense rose with the prayers of the saints from the hand of the angel before God. 5 Then the angel took the censer and filled it with fire from the altar and threw it on the earth; and there were peals of thunder, voices, flashes of lightning, and an earthquake.

hour. 2 Then I saw the seven angels who stand before God, and they were given seven trumpets.

3 Another angel, who had a gold incense container, came and stood at the altar. He was given a lot of incense to add to the prayers of all God's people and to offer it on the gold altar that stands before the throne. 4 The smoke of the burning incense went up with the prayers of God's people from the hands of the angel standing before God. 5 Then the angel took the incense container, filled it with fire from the altar, and threw it on the earth. There were rumblings and peals of thunder, flashes of lightning, and an earthquake.

SECTION HEADING: TEV "The Seventh Seal." "The Lamb breaks open the seventh seal" may be a better heading for this section, or "The Lamb breaks open the seventh piece of wax."

At last the Lamb breaks open the seventh seal on the scroll. Unlike the breaking of the other seals, there is no action that follows the breaking of this last seal; instead the stage is set for a new series of seven, the seven angels blowing seven trumpets.

8.1   RSV   TEV

When the Lamb opened the seventh seal, there was silence in heaven for about half an hour.

When the Lamb broke open the seventh seal, there was silence in heaven for about half an hour.

The Lamb opened the seventh seal: the Greek text says simply "He opened," but it is recommended that RSV and TEV be imitated and the subject be made specific. This is the last seal, and so the scroll can now be opened and its message be revealed. This, however, does not happen.

For **Lamb** see 5.6.

For **seal** see 5.1.

There was silence in heaven for about half an hour: this period of silence not only emphasizes the importance of what is to follow; it may also serve to make it possible for the prayers of the people of God to be heard. All the heavenly singers (for example, those mentioned in 4.8-9; 5.9-14; 7.10-12) are quiet as the prayers of God's people ascend to heaven. **There was silence in heaven** may also be rendered as "there was no sound in heaven," "all over, heaven it was completely quiet," or "all over heaven, no one made a sound." In certain languages an ideophone meaning "complete silence" will be helpful here. Some languages will not have specific vocabulary for "minutes," "hours," and so on. In such cases a translator may say, for example, "for a short period of time." The length of time does not have any particular significance here.

8.2   RSV   TEV

Then I saw the seven angels who stand before God, and seven trumpets were given to them.

Then I saw the seven angels who stand before God, and they were given seven trumpets.

The seven angels who stand before God: these are the seven chief angels, "the Angels of the Presence," who are believed to be continually in God's presence. See Tobit 12.15, "I am Raphael, one of the seven angels who stand in the glorious presence of the Lord, ready to serve him" (TEV); and Luke 1.19, "I am Gabriel . . . I stand in the presence of God" (TEV). This is the first time they appear in Revelation (see the seven spirits in front of the throne in 1.4; 4.5).

Trumpets: see 1.10. A modern trumpet is a brass wind instrument. The biblical trumpet could be a ram's horn (1 Kgs 1.34) or a metal instrument (Num 10.2). There is no way of determining which type the writer had in mind; in the Septuagint the same Greek word translates the Hebrew names of both instruments. Trumpets were used mainly in war and for religious

TRUMPETS OF BRASS AND OF RAMS HORN

celebrations. In cultures where the horns of animals are still used for blowing, the terms in those cultures can be used here. But in cultures where **trumpets** are unknown, a picture will be helpful along with a footnote describing this musical instrument. In such cultures a loan word may have to be used for **trumpet**.

Were given to them: either by God or by an angel. In languages that do not use the passive, one may say, for example, "and they received trumpets" or "someone gave trumpets to them."

An alternative translation model for this verse is:

> Then I saw the seven chief angels (heavenly messengers) who stand before God, and they received trumpets.

8.3   RSV   TEV

And another angel came and stood at the altar with a golden censer; and he was given much incense to mingle with the prayers of all the saints upon the golden altar before the throne;

Another angel, who had a gold incense container, came and stood at the altar. He was given a lot of incense to add to the prayers of all God's people and to offer it on the gold altar that stands before the throne.

Another angel came: as in all instances of verbs of movement, the translator must decide on the point of reference. Here **came** implies that the point of reference is the altar itself, whereas "went" (Mft) makes the point of reference a spectator, such as the author of the book. The latter point of reference is to be preferred.

The altar: it is not certain whether this altar is the same one that appears in 6.9, which seems to be the altar of sacrifice, or is the gold altar of incense, which appears at the end of this verse. The normal rules of language make **the altar** different from **the golden altar before the throne** later in the verse; but normal rules of language do not always apply in this book. There are those who maintain that in this verse there are two altars, the altar of sacrifice and the altar of incense; others maintain that there is only one altar in this verse, the altar of incense; and there are others who maintain that this one altar, the altar of incense, is also the altar in 6.9 (the view especially of Charles' commentary). The translator's task is to translate quite literally **the altar** and **the golden altar before the throne**, without trying to indicate any relation between the two. "At the altar" (TEV) means "in front of the altar."

A golden censer: a censer was a small metal bowl or pan in which the incense was burned. It had a handle so that the priest could hold it and carry it to the altar. In this instance **golden** means that the censer was made of gold; 1 Kings 7.50 states that all such instruments in Solomon's Temple were made of gold. Instead of saying **with a golden censer** or "had a . . ." (TEV), many translators will need to say "held a golden censer," making it clear that the angel was holding the pan with his hand. So another way of stating the first part of this verse is "Another angel, who held a gold incense container, came . . . ."

He was given much incense: again the passive voice of the verb indicates that God or an angel gave this angel the incense, and many translators will wish to say either "Someone gave him much incense" or "He received much incense." For comments on **incense** see 5.8.

To mingle with the prayers: the Greek text says "to give with the prayers"; instead of **to mingle with** (RSV) or "to add to" (TEV), it is better to render "to offer with the prayers" (NRSV, REB). The prayers of God's people are regarded as offerings to God. The incense is added to make them acceptable to God, and they are offered on the gold altar of incense.

Saints: see 5.8.

The golden altar before the throne: this **altar** is the altar of incense (also in 9.13; see Exo 30.1; 1 Kgs 7.48), and **the throne** is the throne of God, so it may be well to say so, or to indicate by a demonstrative reference; for example, "the chief's chair where God sits."

8.4   RSV   TEV

and the smoke of the incense rose with the prayers of the saints from the hand of the angel before God.	The smoke of the burning incense went up with the prayers of God's people from the hands of the angel standing before God.

The smoke of the incense: it is better to make this quite clear: "the smoke that rose from the burning incense."

The prayers of the saints: see the previous verse.

From the hand of the angel: the angel is holding the gold censer, in which the incense is burning on coals taken from the altar, causing smoke to go up (see the process described in Lev 10.1; 16.12; Num 16.46). If readers in certain languages understand this phrase to mean that the burning incense was actually in the hands of the angel rather than in a censer, then one should render this phrase as "from the censer (pan) in the hand of the angel . . . ."

Before God: both RSV and TEV connect this phrase with the angel. This follows quite literally the order of words in the Greek text and may be defended as the meaning of the text. It seems much more likely, however, that **before God** modifies the verb **rose**, and that the meaning is that the smoke rose to God's presence. So NJB "in the presence of God"; SPCL "to the presence of God" (similarly NRSV, REB, TNT, AT, Brc, Phps, RNAB). Other possible translations are "to where God was" or "to where God could see it."

An alternative translation model for this verse is:

> The smoke from the burning incense (sweet smelling powder) in the censer that the angel was holding, and also the prayers of God's people, went up to where God was.

8.5   RSV   TEV

Then the angel took the censer and filled it with fire from the altar and threw it on the earth; and there were peals of thunder, voices, flashes of lightning, and an earthquake. | Then the angel took the incense container, filled it with fire from the altar, and threw it on the earth. There were rumblings and peals of thunder, flashes of lightning, and an earthquake.

Filled it with fire from the altar: the angel took live coals from the altar and put them in the censer, and threw the burning incense and the live coals on the earth. In many languages simply filling the censer with fire will sound strange, so it will be helpful to make certain information explicit and say "Then the angel took the incense container and filled it with burning coals from the altar."

Peals of thunder, voices, flashes of lightning: see 4.5.
Earthquake: see 6.12.

8.6-13

RSV | TEV
| **The Trumpets**

6 Now the seven angels who had the seven trumpets made ready to blow them.

7 The first angel blew his trumpet, and there followed hail and fire, mixed with blood, which fell on the earth; and a third of the earth was burnt up, and a third of the trees were burnt up, and all green grass was burnt up.

8 The second angel blew his trumpet, and something like a great mountain, burning with fire,

6 Then the seven angels with the seven trumpets prepared to blow them.

7 The first angel blew his trumpet. Hail and fire, mixed with blood, came pouring down on the earth. A third of the earth was burned up, a third of the trees, and every blade of green grass.

8 Then the second angel blew his trumpet. Something that looked like a huge mountain on fire was thrown into the sea. A third of the sea

was thrown into the sea; 9 and a third of the sea became blood, a third of the living creatures in the sea died, and a third of the ships were destroyed.

10 The third angel blew his trumpet, and a great star fell from heaven, blazing like a torch, and it fell on a third of the rivers and on the fountains of water. 11 The name of the star is Wormwood. A third of the waters became wormwood, and many men died of the water, because it was made bitter.

12 The fourth angel blew his trumpet, and a third of the sun was struck, and a third of the moon, and a third of the stars, so that a third of their light was darkened; a third of the day was kept from shining, and likewise a third of the night.

13 Then I looked, and I heard an eagle crying with a loud voice, as it flew in midheaven, "Woe, woe, woe to those who dwell on the earth, at the blasts of the other trumpets which the three angels are about to blow!"

was turned into blood, 9 a third of the living creatures in the sea died, and a third of the ships were destroyed.

10 Then the third angel blew his trumpet. A large star, burning like a torch, dropped from the sky and fell on a third of the rivers and on the springs of water. 11 (The name of the star is "Bitterness.") A third of the water turned bitter, and many people died from drinking the water, because it had turned bitter.

12 Then the fourth angel blew his trumpet. A third of the sun was struck, and a third of the moon, and a third of the stars, so that their light lost a third of its brightness; there was no light during a third of the day and a third of the night also.

13 Then I looked, and I heard an eagle that was flying high in the air say in a loud voice, "O horror! horror! How horrible it will be for all who live on earth when the sound comes from the trumpets that the other three angels must blow!"

SECTION HEADING: the TEV section (with the heading "The Trumpets") is quite long, from 8.6 to 9.21. It may be better to have smaller sections, as follows: "The first four trumpets" (8.6-13); "The fifth trumpet" (9.1-12); and "The sixth trumpet" (9.13-21). In each case, instead of a title a complete sentence can be used: "The first four angels blow their trumpets," "The fifth angel blows his trumpet," and "The sixth angel blows his trumpet."

Like the breaking of the seven seals, the first six angels blow their trumpets, one after the other. After each trumpet blast there is an event that causes destruction and suffering. There is a brief interval between the fourth and the fifth trumpets (8.13), and between the blowing of the sixth trumpet (9.13) and the seventh trumpet (11.15) there is a longer interval, in which there is another vision (10.1–11.14), and during which John himself is involved in some of the actions.

8.6-7   RSV   TEV

6 Now the seven angels who had the seven trumpets made ready to blow them.

7 The first angel blew his trumpet, and there followed hail and fire, mixed with blood, which fell on the earth; and a third of the earth was burnt up, and a third of the trees were burnt up, and all green grass was burnt up.

6 Then the seven angels with the seven trumpets prepared to blow them.

7 The first angel blew his trumpet. Hail and fire, mixed with blood, came pouring down on the earth. A third of the earth was burned up, a third of the trees, and every blade of green grass.

The angels take some action—perhaps bringing the trumpets to their lips—that signals to John that they are getting ready to blow their trumpets (verse 6). **Who had the seven trumpets**: in some languages it will be more natural to say "holding the seven trumpets."

And there followed: after the trumpet blast the following things happened. RSV is a bit awkward (**and there followed**); it is better to imitate TEV, with a full stop and a new sentence, or to translate "and the following things happened at once."

Hail and fire, mixed with blood: for **hail and fire** see the plague described in Exodus 9.23-25 (see also Psa 18.12). **Hail** is frozen rain drops; in some languages a hailstorm is called a rain of rocks or stones. The **fire** may represent lightning (as lightning was part of the plague). The **blood** may be an allusion to the first plague (Exo 7.20). Ezekiel 38.22 speaks of hail, fire, and bloodshed.

Fell on the earth: in Greek the text says "was thrown (or, hurled) to the earth" (so NRSV "and they were hurled to the earth"). The same verb occurs in verse 8. This seems to imply that God or an angel threw them down on the earth. In such a case a translator may render this whole clause as "And the angels hurled frozen rocks (hail) and fire mixed with blood down upon the earth." This may be a vivid way of saying "fell suddenly" (also in verse 8).

The destruction caused by this disaster affected one third of the earth's surface: one third of the trees was destroyed by fire, that is, the trees that grew in that one third part of the earth's surface. **All green grass** is probably a way of saying "all plants," "all vegetation" (since it would be hard to envision only the grass as such being destroyed, but not the smaller plants and shrubs). The text seems to say all the vegetation on earth was burned up, but it is quite certain that in this context the meaning is all the vegetation that grew on that same one third section of the earth's surface was destroyed. In certain languages the passive expression **was burnt up** may be avoided by saying something like "suffer burn completely."

An alternative translation model for the latter part of this verse is:

> The fire burned up a third part of the earth, destroying all the trees
> and vegetation on that part.

8.8-9	RSV	TEV

8 The second angel blew his trumpet, and something like a great mountain, burning with fire, was thrown into the sea; 9 and a third of the sea became blood, a third of the living creatures in the sea died, and a third of the ships were destroyed.		8 Then the second angel blew his trumpet. Something that looked like a huge mountain on fire was thrown into the sea. A third of the sea was turned into blood, 9 a third of the living creatures in the sea died, and a third of the ships were destroyed.

The destruction that follows the second trumpet blast affects one third of the earth's water mass.

Something like a great mountain: this describes a huge solid object, the size and shape of a mountain. John cannot identify with precision this huge burning mass. The verb **was thrown** may be used in the general sense of "fell"; but it may be that the passive is used as a way of indicating that God or an angel hurled this burning mass into the sea. Another way of rendering this clause in languages that do not use the passive is "Then they (someone) threw something that looked like a huge burning mountain into the sea (oceans)."

If it is asked which sea the text is talking about, the obvious answer is the Mediterranean Sea. In this context, however, the word stands for all bodies of salt water on earth—inasmuch as one third of all fish in the seas died, and one third of the ships were destroyed (see "the sea" in 5.13).

A third of the sea: this means that one third of the water of the oceans was changed into blood; the other two thirds were not affected.

Became blood: the Greek text says the sea water turned into blood. Some believe the meaning is that the color of the water became red, like blood (as in the case of the moon, in 6.12); but it is better to translate quite literally. This disaster is reminiscent of the plague described in Exodus 7.17-19. Translators in languages that do not use the passive may imitate RSV and say "became blood."

RSV (and NRSV) and TEV differ as to where verse 9 begins. TEV follows the numbering of the Greek text, as do all other translations. RSV seems to be a mistake, as both the King James Version and the American Standard Version begin verse 9 where TEV begins it.

Living creatures in the sea: the biblical classification of marine animals sometimes distinguished between fishes and the huge sea monsters. Here all marine life is meant. Another way of rendering this is "the things that have life in the sea" or "the things living in the sea."

A third of the ships were destroyed: these ships were on the one third of the ocean that was turned into blood. Care must be taken that the word used for **ships** does not mean modern steamships but sailing vessels. In land-bound cultures where only small boats are known, one may say, for example, "boats of all sizes" or "all kinds of boats."

An alternative rendering for verses 8b-9 is the following:

> *8b* The water in one-third of the seas was turned into blood, *9* and all the living creatures and ships (or, vessels) found in that part were destroyed.

8.10   RSV   TEV

The third angel blew his trumpet, and a great star fell from heaven, blazing like a torch, and it fell on a third of the rivers and on the fountains of water.

Then the third angel blew his trumpet. A large star, burning like a torch, dropped from the sky and fell on a third of the rivers and on the springs of water.

A great star . . . blazing like a torch: this seems to depict a huge falling star or a blazing comet. For **torch** see 4.5.

From heaven: in many languages it will be more natural to say "fell (dropped) from the sky," as in TEV.

On a third of the rivers: this destruction affects one third of the fresh water on the earth's surface, as contrasted with the oceans of verses 8-9. The Greek text says quite specifically that **it fell** (as RSV and TEV have it), and that is how a translation must render it.

And on the fountains of water: this seems to mean *all* fountains of water on the earth's surface. In light of what is said in verse 11, however, it is quite certain that what is meant is one third of the fountains of water (see the same thing with "all green grass" in verse 8). Translators are urged to translate it this way. For **fountains of water** see "springs of living water" in 7.17.

8.11	RSV	TEV

The name of the star is Wormwood. A third of the waters became wormwood, and many men died of the water, because it was made bitter.	(The name of the star is "Bitterness.") A third of the water turned bitter, and many people died from drinking the water, because it had turned bitter.

Wormwood: the name of the star derives from its effect on the water; it turned the water sour and bitter, so that it killed many of those who drank it. Wormwood itself is a bitter drug, made from an aromatic plant (*Artemisia absinthium*). See also *Fauna and Flora of the Bible,* pages 197-198. The drug is not poisonous, but passages like Jeremiah 9.15; 23.15 show that it was considered poisonous. Where a proper noun is lacking for this plant, the generic word "Bitterness" or "Bitter Drug" may be used as the name of the star (see "bitter" at the end of the verse). "Harsh-Tasting Substance" is another possible translation.

The water in one third of all rivers and fountains **became wormwood** (or, as TEV translates, "turned bitter"). In many languages it will be helpful to say "a third of the fresh water." It is somewhat strange that not all the people who drank of the water died, only **many** of them.

8.12	RSV	TEV

The fourth angel blew his trumpet, and a third of the sun was struck, and a third of the moon, and a third of the stars, so that a third of their light was darkened; a third of the day was kept from shining, and likewise a third of the night.	Then the fourth angel blew his trumpet. A third of the sun was struck, and a third of the moon, and a third of the stars, so that their light lost a third of its brightness; there was no light during a third of the day and a third of the night also.

At the blowing of the fourth trumpet, the sun, the moon, and the stars lost a third of their light. This suggests the plague of darkness in Egypt (Exo 10.21-23; see also Isa 13.10; Joel 2.31; Amos 8.9). The text seems to say that they shone only at two thirds of their normal intensity; but as the conclusion of the verse makes clear, it means that they shone only two thirds of the time. One third of the daytime was completely dark, for the sun stopped shining; likewise for one third of the night the moon and the stars stopped shining.

Was struck: only here in the New Testament is this verb used; it suggests some force that hit the sun, moon, and stars and made them stop shining for one third of the time. In certain languages that do not use the passive, this phrase may be rendered as "suffered hit (or, strike)," but in others one must say, for example, "Something struck . . . ."

And likewise a third of the night: the Greek text says simply "and the night likewise"; as the context makes clear, this means that during the night, as during the day, there was complete darkness for one third of the time. For the translation of **a third**, see verse 7 of this chapter.

Something like the following can serve as a model for this verse:

> Then the fourth angel blew his trumpet. The sun, the moon, and the stars were all damaged (or, struck), so that they did not shine for one third of the time. There was no sunlight during one third of the daytime, and during one third of the night the moon and the stars did not shine.

Or:

> And something struck and damaged one-third of the sun, the moon and the stars. The sun did not shine (give light) for one third of the daytime, and the moon and the stars did not shine for one third of the night.

8.13   RSV   TEV

Then I looked, and I heard an eagle crying with a loud voice, as it flew in midheaven, "Woe, woe, woe to those who dwell on the earth, at the blasts of the other trumpets which the three angels are about to blow!"	Then I looked, and I heard an eagle that was flying high in the air say in a loud voice, "O horror! horror! How horrible it will be for all who live on earth when the sound comes from the trumpets that the other three angels must blow!"

Then I looked, and I heard: this is a separate episode that serves as a prelude to the last three trumpet blasts. In certain languages translators may say "Then I looked up, and I heard," or idiomatically, for example, "Then I raised my face up and looked, and I heard."

An eagle crying with a loud voice: the normal verb that expresses the sound made by an eagle should not be used; here the eagle is said to speak with a human voice.

As it flew in midheaven: that is to say, it was flying high in the sky.

Woe, woe, woe: this is an exclamation of horror, and a translator should use a term that expresses dismay at the horrible suffering that is coming on the inhabitants of the world. Most English translations are like RSV. NJB has "Disaster," and TNT "Calamity"; other possibilities are "How terrible!" "How tragic!" or "Misfortune! Misfortune!"

An alternative translation model for the first part of this verse is "Then I looked and I saw an eagle flying high up in the sky, and I heard it crying out, saying, 'Misfortune! Misfortune!' "

Translators should note that the word **woe** is pronounced three times. This coordinates with the way in which the text keeps count of the "woes" as they occur, in 9.12 and 11.14. Therefore the term used should be one that can be repeated in those places.

Those who dwell on the earth: this includes all human beings, even though God's faithful people will not be destroyed. In many languages it will be necessary to specify that this refers only to people, not animals; for example, "all people (humans) on earth.' "

The three angels: it is better to say "the other three angels" or "the remaining three angels." The last three trumpet blasts will be followed by even worse disasters for the whole human race.

Are about to blow: for the auxiliary verb indicating future, **are about to**, see the same Greek term translated "is to take place" in 1.19. REB is like TEV, "must now blow."

9.1-12

RSV	TEV
1 And the fifth angel blew his trumpet, and I saw a star fallen from heaven to earth, and he was given the key of the shaft of the bottomless pit; 2 he opened the shaft of the bottomless pit, and from the shaft rose smoke like the smoke of a great furnace, and the sun and the air were darkened with the smoke from the shaft. 3 Then from the smoke came locusts on the earth, and they were given power like the power of scorpions of the earth; 4 they were told not to harm the grass of the earth or any green growth or any tree, but only those of mankind who have not the seal of God upon their foreheads; 5 they were allowed to torture them for five months, but not to kill them, and their torture was like the torture of a scorpion, when it stings a man. 6 And in those days men will seek death and will not find it; they will long to die, and death will fly from them.	1 Then the fifth angel blew his trumpet. I saw a star which had fallen down to the earth, and it was given the key to the abyss. 2 The star opened the abyss, and smoke poured out of it, like the smoke from a large furnace; the sunlight and the air were darkened by the smoke from the abyss. 3 Locusts came down out of the smoke upon the earth, and they were given the same kind of power that scorpions have. 4 They were told not to harm the grass or the trees or any other plant; they could harm only the people who did not have the mark of God's seal on their foreheads. 5 The locusts were not allowed to kill these people, but only to torture them for five months. The pain caused by the torture is like the pain caused by a scorpion's sting. 6 During those five months they will seek death, but will not find it; they will want to die, but death will flee from them.
7 In appearance the locusts were like horses arrayed for battle; on their heads were what looked like crowns of gold; their faces were like human faces, 8 their hair like women's hair, and their teeth like lions' teeth; 9 they had scales like iron breastplates, and the noise of their wings was like the noise of many chariots with horses rushing into battle. 10 They have tails like scorpions, and stings, and their power of hurting men for five months lies in their tails. 11 They have as king over them the angel of the bottomless pit; his name in Hebrew is Abaddon, and in Greek he is called Apollyon.	7 The locusts looked like horses ready for battle; on their heads they had what seemed to be crowns of gold, and their faces were like men's faces. 8 Their hair was like women's hair, their teeth were like lions' teeth. 9 Their chests were covered with what looked like iron breastplates, and the sound made by their wings was like the noise of many horse-drawn chariots rushing into battle. 10 They have tails and stings like those of a scorpion, and it is with their tails that they have the power to hurt people for five months. 11 They have a king ruling over them, who is the angel in

12 The first woe has passed; behold, two woes are still to come.

charge of the abyss. His name in Hebrew is Abaddon; in Greek the name is Apollyon (meaning "The Destroyer").

12 The first horror is over; after this there are still two more horrors to come.

SECTION HEADING: as suggested at the beginning of the TEV section (8.6), it may be helpful to begin a new section here that goes through verse 12. It may have the heading "The fifth trumpet" or "The fifth angel blows his trumpet."

9.1   RSV   TEV

And the fifth angel blew his trumpet, and I saw a star fallen from heaven to earth, and he was given the key of the shaft of the bottomless pit;

Then the fifth angel blew his trumpet. I saw a star which had fallen down to the earth, and it was given the key to the abyss.[d]

[d] ABYSS: *The place in the depths of the earth where the demons were imprisoned until their final punishment.*

I saw a star fallen from heaven to earth: in some languages it may not be necessary to say **from heaven**, since it is essentially redundant information. Care should be taken that the text says "I saw a star that had fallen . . . ." John does not say that he saw the star as it fell to earth.

He was given: the star is spoken of as a living being, either an angel or a minor deity. Such poetic passages as Judges 5.20 or Job 38.7 show that stars could be spoken of as living beings. It is clear that here the same kind of imagery is at work (see Jude 13). In 20.1 an angel appears who has the key to the abyss, but that angel is not the same being as the fallen star in this passage. If in some languages it is difficult to use a personal pronoun to refer to the star, it is possible to say here "the star was given," and at the beginning of verse 2, "The star opened . . . ." In languages that do not use the passive, one may say, for example, "someone gave it (or, him) a key" or "it (or, he) had received a key."

The shaft of the bottomless pit: this is the opening of the abyss. The Greek word translated **shaft** by RSV may be translated "opening" or "passage leading to" (which is what the English word "shaft" means). But the Greek word may mean "well" or "pool" (see Luke 14.5; John 4.11-12) as a description of the abyss itself (see Psa 55.23a; 69.15b). The picture is that of an opening with a lid or a door on it that can be closed and locked. The Greek word translated **bottomless pit** by RSV means, more simply, "deep pit" or "very deep hole." It does not mean literally an abyss that has no bottom to it. The word refers to the place in the depths of the earth where evil spirits were thought to be imprisoned (see Luke 8.31). In some places it is another word for Sheol, the world of the dead (Psa 71.20c; Rom 10.7).

An alternative translation model for the latter part of this verse is:

I saw something like a star that had fallen down to earth. Someone (They) had given it a key to open the very deep pit.

9.2   RSV   TEV

he opened the shaft of the bottomless pit, and from the shaft rose smoke like the smoke of a great furnace, and the sun and the air were darkened with the smoke from the shaft.	The star opened the abyss, and smoke poured out of it, like the smoke from a large furnace; the sunlight and the air were darkened by the smoke from the abyss.

He opened the shaft of the bottomless pit: it is often better to say, simply, "he (or, the star) opened (or, unlocked) the abyss," ". . . the entrance to the abyss," or ". . . the entrance to the very deep pit."

And from the shaft rose smoke like the smoke of a great furnace: it is not necessary to represent the literal form of the Greek text, which is quite redundant. Something like the following is satisfactory: "and smoke came pouring out, like the smoke from a large furnace." Presumably the smoke came from the fire in the abyss, the fire that burns in Gehenna. **A great furnace**: in cultures that do not have large wood- or coal-burning furnaces for baking bread, pottery, or even for smelting metals such as iron, there may be specialized vocabulary for big ovens for cooking, or pits dug in the ground for roasting pigs or other animals. Such terms may be used here. This clause may also be expressed as "and smoke came pouring out of the pit, just like smoke coming out of a pit dug in the ground to roast animals." It is important to avoid terms used for the type of stove to heat a home.

The sun and the air were darkened: there was so much smoke, and it was so thick, that it filled the air and blocked out the sunshine. The text does not mean that the sun quit shining; rather, its rays could not penetrate the smoke, and all was dark. One may also say "the smoke blocked out the rays of the sun" or "the smoke did not let the rays of the sun shine through."

9.3   RSV   TEV

Then from the smoke came locusts on the earth, and they were given power like the power of scorpions of the earth;	Locusts came down out of the smoke upon the earth, and they were given the same kind of power that scorpions have.

LOCUSTS

From the smoke that filled the air, locusts descended upon the earth. Huge swarms of locusts were not uncommon in that part of the world (see Exo 10.1-20 for the plague of locusts in Egypt), and the prophet Joel spoke of swarms of locusts as instruments of God's wrath. In cultures where **locusts** do not exist but grasshoppers are known, one may say "grasshoppers." However, in cultures where creatures like this are nonexistent, it may be necessary to borrow a word from English or some other major language and describe the creature in the glossary. A picture of a **locust** will also be helpful. In some parts of the world a cultural equivalent in jungle areas may be used; for example, "(large) leaf-eating insect." However, the insect chosen should have the tendency to appear in large numbers or swarms, as locusts do.

They were given power: these creatures are under God's control; the power they receive is the power to injure people—the kind of power that scorpions have, that is, to sting people. As in verse 10, **power** here means something more like "capacity," "capability." In languages that do not use the passive, translators may say, for example, "they received the ability" or "someone gave them the ability."

Scorpions of the earth: scorpions are small creatures with eight legs and a long tail that has a poisonous sting; they can inflict very painful wounds, which are sometimes fatal. The added phrase **of the earth** seems to mean that these are actual scorpions, unlike the locusts, which are demonic beings (verses 7-11).

SCORPIONS

For information concerning locusts and scorpions, a translator should consult a Bible dictionary or encyclopedia, or else *Fauna and Flora of the Bible,* pages 53-54 and 70-71.

An alternative translation model for this verse is:

> Locusts came down out of the smoke onto the earth, and they received the power to sting people, like that of scorpions.

9.4   RSV   TEV

they were told not to harm the grass of the earth or any green growth or any tree, but only those of mankind who have not the seal of God upon their foreheads;	They were told not to harm the grass or the trees or any other plant; they could harm only the people who did not have the mark of God's seal on their foreheads.

They were told: it must be assumed that the order comes from God or from an angel who speaks in God's name. **Told** can also be expressed as "commanded" or "ordered." In languages that do not use the passive, this phrase may be rendered as "someone commanded them."

Not to harm: the same verb appears here that is used in 2.11 ("hurt"); 6.6; 7.2,3. In certain languages this phrase must be rendered as direct speech; for example, "Do not harm."

The grass of the earth or any green growth or any tree: this is a rather full way of speaking of all vegetable life (trees, plants, weeds), which the swarms of locusts usually devour.

But only those of mankind: only people are to be harmed, not plant life.

Who have not the seal of God upon their foreheads: see 7.2-3. God's people are not to be harmed (see Ezek 9.4).

Alternative translation models for this verse are:

> Someone commanded them, "Do not harm any plants, but only people, that is, those people who do not have the seal of God on their foreheads."

Or:

> Someone commanded them, "You must harm only those people who have not been marked with the seal of God on their foreheads. But don't harm any plants."

9.5	RSV	TEV
	they were allowed to torture them for five months, but not to kill them, and their torture was like the torture of a scorpion, when it stings a man.	The locusts were not allowed to kill these people, but only to torture them for five months. The pain caused by the torture is like the pain caused by a scorpion's sting.

They were allowed to torture them for five months: the passive **they were allowed** again makes it clear that God is in control. This can be rendered "they were given permission," "they received permission," "they were given the right," or in languages that do not use the passive, one may say "God gave them permission." Here the very strong verb and noun **to torture** and **the torture** are used (the Greek noun for "torture" is used only in this book; see "torment" in 14.11; 18.7,10,15). This shows how terrible is the suffering the people will endure. Five months is the normal life span of a locust, and it stands here for a prolonged period of suffering and pain. Five months should not be thought of as a short period of time. **Torture** may also be expressed as "cause to suffer extreme pain."

Their torture was like the torture of a scorpion: a scorpion does not torture a person; it stings, wounds, hurts, harms, injures, or the like. So it is preferable to say something like TEV: "the pain they inflict is like the great pain that a person suffers when struck (or, stung) by a scorpion." The verb translated **stings** by RSV is used to speak of a sword stroke (Mark 14.47) or a blow with the hand (Matt 26.67-68).

An alternative translation model for this verse is:

God allowed them to inflict extreme pain on those people for five months, but not to kill them. The pain that they inflict is like the great pain a person suffers when a scorpion stings him.

9.6

RSV	TEV
And in those days men will seek death and will not find it; they will long to die, and death will fly from them.	During those five months they will seek death, but will not find it; they will want to die, but death will flee from them.

In those days: that is, during those five months. The verse vividly portrays the suffering caused by the locusts: the pain will be so intense that the people who are stung will want to die. See similar expressions of despair in Job 3.21; Jeremiah 8.3.

Will seek death and will not find it; they will long to die, and death will fly from them: for emphasis the same idea is expressed twice. This is a poetic way of saying that people would like to die but will live on. It is not necessary to try to represent literally the figure of death fleeing from people if it is a strange and unnatural expression in a given language.

9.7-8

RSV	TEV
7 In appearance the locusts were like horses arrayed for battle; on their heads were what looked like crowns of gold; their faces were like human faces, 8 their hair like women's hair, and their teeth like lions' teeth;	7 The locusts looked like horses ready for battle; on their heads they had what seemed to be crowns of gold, and their faces were like men's faces. 8 Their hair was like women's hair, their teeth were like lions' teeth.

RSV has one long sentence for verses 7-9. In most languages it will be preferable to have several sentences.

The description of these locusts shows that they are really demonic beings that swarm and fly like huge locusts.

In appearance the locusts were like horses arrayed for battle: see Joel 2.4. A war horse was often given protective covering, including a breast shield, and sometimes had ornaments on its bridle. The Greek verb translated **arrayed** means "prepared," "made ready." The simplest way to translate is to say something like "These locusts looked like (war) horses, ready to go into battle." **Battle** in some languages will be rendered in a similar way to the English expression "battlefield," namely, the place for fighting. An alternative translation model for this clause, then, is "These locusts looked like (war) horses ready to go where men were fighting."

Crowns of gold: see 4.4; 6.2.

Their faces were like human faces: this probably means the whole head (including the ears) and not just the face as such.

Hair like women's hair: that is, long and wavy.

Teeth like lions' teeth: big and sharp (see Joel 1.6). For **lion** see 4.7.

A traveler in 1772 reported that an Arab from the desert described the locust as follows: "He compared the head of a locust with the head of a horse, its breast with the breast of a lion, its feet with the feet of a camel, its body with the body of a snake, its tail with the tail of a scorpion, its antennae with the hair of a maiden" (cited by Beasley-Murray).

9.9	RSV	TEV
	they had scales like iron breastplates, and the noise of their wings was like the noise of many chariots with horses rushing into battle.	Their chests were covered with what looked like iron breastplates, and the sound made by their wings was like the noise of many horse-drawn chariots rushing into battle.

Scales like iron breastplates: the Greek text says "breastplates like iron breastplates" (using the same word twice). Besides this passage and 9.17, the word occurs also at Ephesians 6.14 and 1 Thessalonians 5.8. War horses sometimes wore breast shields to protect them from the enemy's spears and swords. Instead of **scales**, something like "body-armour" (NJB) is preferable. SPCL translates "their bodies were covered with a kind of iron armor," or the translation can be "their bodies were covered with what looked like pieces of metal used to protect the chests of people."

The noise of their wings: for a similar description of the noise of locusts' wings, see Joel 2.5. In some languages this phrase will be rendered as "the flapping (whirring) noise of their wings" or "the noise that their wings made as they flew."

The noise of many chariots with horses rushing into battle: a chariot was a two-wheeled vehicle pulled by one or more horses. The loud and rustling noise

HORSES PULLING A CHARIOT

made by the wings of these locusts sounded like many horse-drawn chariots rushing into battle. The noise in some languages will be described with an adjective or an ideophone. An alternative rendering is "the rattling noise" (see Nahum 3.2). **Chariots** in many languages is translated as "horse-drawn war carts" or "war carts (wagons) pulled by horses." So this clause may also be rendered as "the whirring (rattling) noise of many horse-drawn war carts racing (dashing) into the battlefield."

9.10   RSV   TEV

They have tails like scorpions, and stings, and their power of hurting men for five months lies in their tails.	They have tails and stings like those of a scorpion, and it is with their tails that they have the power to hurt people for five months.

Tails like scorpions, and stings: what is meant is that their tails were like scorpions' tails, with stings at the end.

Their power of hurting men: the word translated **power** can also mean "authority" or "capability." The final sentence may be translated as follows: "It is with the stings on their tails that they are able to hurt people for five months." See also 9.5 on hurting or torturing people.

9.11   RSV   TEV

They have as king over them the angel of the bottomless pit; his name in Hebrew is Abaddon, and in Greek he is called Apollyon.[b]	They have a king ruling over them, who is the angel in charge of the abyss. His name in Hebrew is Abaddon; in Greek the name is Apollyon (meaning "The Destroyer").

[b] Or *Destroyer*

They have as king: according to Proverbs 30.27 locusts have no king, but these demonic beings have one. Their king is **the angel of the bottomless pit**, that is, the angel in charge of, looking after or taking care of, the abyss. For the translation of **bottomless pit** or "abyss," see 9.1.

In Hebrew: in many languages this will be rendered as "in the Hebrew language."

Abaddon: this is the Hebrew word for "destruction" (or, "place of destruction") as a name for Sheol, as in Job 26.6 (parallel with Sheol); 28.22 (Abaddon and Death); Psalm 88.11b (parallel with grave); Proverbs 15.11 (Sheol and Abaddon).

The Greek word **Apollyon** means "Destroyer." It appears only here in the New Testament. **In Greek**: see the comment on **Hebrew** above. Translators are urged to imitate TEV, which gives in the text itself the meaning of the Greek word.

9.12   RSV   TEV

> The first woe has passed; behold, two woes are still to come.

> The first horror is over; after this there are still two more horrors to come.

With this verse John separates the fifth trumpet blast from the two more still to come. For **woe** see 8.13; for **behold** see 1.7.

An alternative translation model for this verse is:

> The first terrible (horrible) punishment is over. After this there are still two more terrible punishments coming.

9.13-21

RSV   TEV

13 Then the sixth angel blew his trumpet, and I heard a voice from the four horns of the golden altar before God, 14 saying to the sixth angel who had the trumpet, "Release the four angels who are bound at the great river Euphrates." 15 So the four angels were released, who had been held ready for the hour, the day, the month, and the year, to kill a third of mankind. 16 The number of the troops of cavalry was twice ten thousand times ten thousand; I heard their number. 17 And this was how I saw the horses in my vision: the riders wore breastplates the color of fire and of sapphire and of sulphur, and the heads of the horses were like lions' heads, and fire and smoke and sulphur issued from their mouths. 18 By these three plagues a third of mankind was killed, by the fire and smoke and sulphur issuing from their mouths. 19 For the power of the horses is in their mouths and in their tails; their tails are like serpents, with heads, and by means of them they wound.

20 The rest of mankind, who were not killed by these plagues, did not repent of the works of their hands nor give up worshiping demons and idols of gold and silver and bronze and stone and wood, which cannot either see or hear or walk; 21 nor did they repent of their murders or their sorceries or their immorality or their thefts.

13 Then the sixth angel blew his trumpet. I heard a voice coming from the four corners of the gold altar standing before God. 14 The voice said to the sixth angel, "Release the four angels who are bound at the great Euphrates River!" 15 The four angels were released; for this very hour of this very day of this very month and year they had been kept ready to kill a third of all mankind. 16 I was told the number of the mounted troops: it was two hundred million. 17 And in my vision I saw the horses and their riders: they had breastplates red as fire, blue as sapphire, and yellow as sulfur. The horses' heads were like lions' heads, and from their mouths came out fire, smoke, and sulfur. 18 A third of mankind was killed by those three plagues: the fire, the smoke, and the sulfur coming out of the horses' mouths. 19 For the power of the horses is in their mouths and also in their tails. Their tails are like snakes with heads, and they use them to hurt people.

20 The rest of mankind, all those who had not been killed by these plagues, did not turn away from what they themselves had made. They did not stop worshiping demons, nor the idols of gold, silver, bronze, stone, and wood, which cannot see, hear, or walk. 21 Nor did they repent of their murders, their magic, their sexual immorality, or their stealing.

SECTION HEADING: "The sixth trumpet" or "The sixth angel blows his trumpet."

9.13   RSV   TEV

Then the sixth angel blew his trumpet, and I heard a voice from the four horns of the golden altar before God,	Then the sixth angel blew his trumpet. I heard a voice coming from the four corners of the gold altar standing before God.

Now comes the answer to the prayer of God's people (8.3-4).

A voice from the four horns of the golden altar: this is like 6.6, in that the location of the speaker is given, but the speaker is not identified. This is the gold altar of incense (8.3). The four corners were four projections in the shape of horns, one on each end of the four top corners of the altar (see Exo 30.1-3). Some ancient manuscripts do not have **four** (so AT, Brc, REB, FRCL, TOB); in any case the number is quite redundant. If a translator wishes to keep the figurative language found in the Greek, and it seems natural in the receptor language, the following is a possible translation model that avoids redundancy: "a voice coming from the projections shaped like horns on the corners of the altar."

9.14   RSV   TEV

saying to the sixth angel who had the trumpet, "Release the four angels who are bound at the great river Euphrates."	The voice said to the sixth angel, "Release the four angels who are bound at the great Euphrates River!"

"The voice said" (TEV) may also be rendered as "The voice ordered (or, commanded)."

The sixth angel who had the trumpet: the Greek text is again somewhat redundant, and a translator may feel free to omit **who had the trumpet**, since in verse 13 he is identified as having a trumpet. If a translator wishes to keep this clause, one may also say "who was holding the trumpet."

The four angels who are bound at the great river Euphrates: like the four winds (7.1), these angels have been bound. In Old Testament times the Euphrates was the great river of the empires of Babylonia and Assyria, the enemies of Israel (see Isa 7.20; 8.7). At the time of Revelation it marked the eastern boundary of the Roman Empire. Beyond it lay the lands of the dreaded Parthians. The passive form **are bound** emphasizes anew that God is in charge. The four angels will be released only when God chooses to do so. The preposition **at** does not indicate where along the length of the river the angels were bound. The preposition **at** is also vague as to whether the angels were "in" the river or "beside" it. Translators should keep their translations equally vague. In languages that do not use the passive, one may render this sentence as "who suffer bound (or, tied up)," or introduce an agent and say "whom God had them bind" or "whom God had them tie up."

An alternative translation model for this verse is:

The voice said to the sixth angel who was holding the trumpet, "Release the four angels whom God had them tie up at the great Euphrates River!"

9.15   RSV   TEV

So the four angels were released, who had been held ready for the hour, the day, the month, and the year, to kill a third of mankind.	The four angels were released; for this very hour of this very day of this very month and year they had been kept ready to kill a third of all mankind.

The four angels were released: the translation can be "The sixth angel released those four angels."

Had been held ready: the form of this expression shows that it was God who had determined the exact time when these angels would be released to do the work that God had for them. For comments on the Greek verb translated **held ready**, see "arrayed" in verse 7.

The hour, the day, the month, and the year: it may be more natural to have something like TEV, or else "the moment of that day of that very month and year." NJB has "this hour of this day of this month of this year"; REB translates "this very year, month, day, and hour." God had fixed the precise time of their release. However, in languages that do not have vocabulary for such precise time divisions, one may say "at this exact time."

To kill a third of mankind: unlike RSV and TEV, it seems best to connect this purpose clause to the verb **released** (and not to **had been held ready**); so AT, Brc, Phps, TNT, SPCL, NIV. On the translation of **third** see 8.7.

An alternative translation model for languages that do not have the passive is:

The sixth angel released those four angels to kill a third of all humans (or, people on the earth). God had kept them ready for this exact time.

9.16   RSV   TEV

The number of the troops of cavalry was twice ten thousand times ten thousand; I heard their number.	I was told the number of the mounted troops: it was two hundred million.

The four angels disappear from the vision; in their place appear two hundred million cavalry troops. It seems implied that the four angels were in charge of these troops, but the text does not specifically say so. For **the troops of cavalry** something like "cavalry troops" (RNAB) or "mounted troops" (NJB), or even "soldiers who ride on horses" may be better. Those who ride these war horses are not identified; if possible, a neutral term such as **troops** should be used, which avoids saying they are human beings. But this may not be possible.

In some languages it may be difficult, if not impossible, to speak precisely of two hundred million mounted horses. Where such is the case, some superlative such as "a very large number" or "too many to count" may be used (as in 5.11; see also 7.9).

I heard their number: see 7.4. Another way of saying this is "Someone told me . . . ."

9.17   RSV   TEV

And this was how I saw the horses in my vision: the riders wore breastplates the color of fire and of sapphire[c] and of sulphur, and the heads of the horses were like lions' heads, and fire and smoke and sulphur issued from their mouths.

And in my vision I saw the horses and their riders: they had breastplates red as fire, blue as sapphire, and yellow as sulfur. The horses' heads were like lions' heads, and from their mouths came out fire, smoke, and sulfur.

[c] Greek *hyacinth*

The Greek text says literally "And thus I saw the horses in the vision and the riders on them having fiery breastplates." The Greek manuscripts have no punctuation marks; all such marks are inserted by editors of the printed Greek text. It is possible therefore that the Greek text means what RSV has, that is, only the riders wore the breastplates (also NRSV, SPCL, Brc, NJB, FRCL); but it is also possible that the text means what TEV says, that is, that both riders and horses had breastplates (so REB, BRCL, TNT, NIV); see verse 9. On the whole it appears that the form of the Greek text favors TEV, but a translator should feel free to follow the RSV rendering. **Breastplates** in this context may also be expressed as "armor protecting their chests" or "metal plates protecting their chests."

In my vision: this is the only place in the book where the noun **vision** is used; the meaning is elsewhere always expressed by the verb "I saw." **Vision** in many languages will be translated as "dream."

The riders: as in the case of the riders of the four horses in 6.2,4,5,8, the text does not say whether they are human or angelic (or demonic) beings; if in translation a specific term must be used, it seems better not to identify them as human beings. If possible the translation should say "those who were riding them."

The color of fire and of sapphire and of sulphur: that is, red, blue, and yellow (see TEV). The sapphire is a precious stone, usually dark blue. Sulfur is a yellow substance that burns with great heat and produces an unpleasant smell. If specific terms for sapphire and sulfur are not readily available, the translation can say simply "blue and yellow." But sulfur appears later in this verse and also in the next verse. It will be helpful in the case of **sulphur** to include an explanatory note in the glossary. See also *A Handbook on the Book of Psalms,* page 114.

Alternative translation models for this clause are:

> They had armor protecting their chests, which was red like fire, blue like sapphires, and yellow like sulphur.

Or:

> The metal plates protecting their chests were red like the color of
> fire, blue like a sky-colored precious stone, and yellow like sulphur.

Like lions' heads: as in 4.7, these horses had heads like those of lions.

Fire and smoke and sulphur issued from their mouths: the picture is
something like that of a dragon belching flames.

9.18	RSV	TEV
	By these three plagues a third of mankind was killed, by the fire and smoke and sulphur issuing from their mouths.	A third of mankind was killed by those three plagues: the fire, the smoke, and the sulfur coming out of the horses' mouths.

These three plagues: a plague is a very great disaster that injures and kills
many people. In the Bible, plagues are seen as God's punishment (as in the case of
the ten plagues sent upon the Egyptians). The word means simply "a blow" and is
used of the strike of a sword (13.14). If a specific word for **plagues** is not available,
something like "calamities" or "disasters" may be used. In languages that have a
general word which covers all kinds of trouble, one may say "terrible (or, fearful)
trouble."

A third of mankind: as specified in verse 15.

The fire and smoke and sulphur: it is understood, of course, that the sulfur
is coming from the horses' mouths (or nostrils) in the form of vapor, together with
the flames and the smoke.

An alternative translation model for this verse is:

> These three plagues, which were the fire, the smoke, and the sulphur
> coming out of the horses' mouths, killed one third of all humans.

9.19	RSV	TEV
	For the power of the horses is in their mouths and in their tails; their tails are like serpents, with heads, and by means of them they wound.	For the power of the horses is in their mouths and also in their tails. Their tails are like snakes with heads, and they use them to hurt people.

The horses kill, not only with what pours out of their mouths, but also with
their tails, which are like snakes with heads. The picture is of a snake connected by
its tail to the horse's rear, the snake's head being the other end of the horse's tail.
It is the head that strikes at people and wounds them (the same verb is used in verse
10; see 2.11).

In English the use of the word **serpents** (RSV, NRSV, REB, TNT, Phps, Mft,
RNAB) evokes images of dragons rather than of snakes. (The *American Heritage*

Dictionary does not list "snake" as one of the meanings of "serpent.") It appears that a contemporary translation should use the word "snake"; but this is of no great importance.

An alternative translation model for this verse is:

> For it is the mouths and tails of the horses that have the power (or, ability) to hurt people. Their tails are like snakes with heads. They use these to hurt people.

9.20

RSV	TEV
The rest of mankind, who were not killed by these plagues, did not repent of the works of their hands nor give up worshiping demons and idols of gold and silver and bronze and stone and wood, which cannot either see or hear or walk;	The rest of mankind, all those who had not been killed by these plagues, did not turn away from what they themselves had made. They did not stop worshiping demons, nor the idols of gold, silver, bronze, stone, and wood, which cannot see, hear, or walk.

The rest of mankind, who were not killed by these plagues: the two thirds of the human race that remained alive are the subject of what follows. They are all portrayed as wicked and unrepentant, deserving God's punishment. For **repent** see 2.5. In languages that do not use the passive, another way to translate this is "The humans who did not suffer death by means of these plagues."

The works of their hands: these are idols, which these people worship—a common way in the Old Testament to refer to idols and images (see Deut 4.28; Psa 115.4-7; 135.15-17). Instead of **did not repent of the works of their hands** (RSV), it may be better to say something like "did not give up the idols (or, images) they had made."

Nor give up worshiping demons and idols: as is often the case in this book, it does not seem that this is something in addition to their not having **repent**[ed] **of the works of their hands** (RSV). Rather, this is an elaboration on that theme, a fuller explanation of it. A translator is encouraged to imitate TEV here.

Demons: they were thought of as evil spiritual beings ("evil spirits") or "dirty spirits" under the control of the Devil, who inflicted physical and psychological damage on people. They appear also in 16.14; 18.2. See 2.10 for further help on the translation of "Devil" or "cvil spirits."

The description of the idols of gold, silver, bronze, stone, and wood reflects the two passages in Psalms cited above. **Bronze** is a metal made from a mixture of copper and tin. Even if cultures do not have these metals, they are so important throughout the Bible that translators should use terms such as "metal named 'gold,'" and so on, and also have descriptions of these metals in the glossary. See the glossary in TEV as an example.

9.21   RSV   TEV

nor did they repent of their murders or   Nor did they repent of their murders,
their sorceries or their immorality or   their magic, their sexual immorality, or
their thefts.   their stealing.

Sorceries: this can be called "black magic," "evil spells," "witchcraft." The
word refers to mysterious words and actions that are presumed to involve evil
spiritual forces, and which are usually practiced to harm or kill others, or to cause
curses to come on others (see 18.23; 21.8; 22.15; Gal 5.20).

The sins of murder, witchcraft, and sexual immorality were commonly
associated with the practice of idolatry. For **immorality** (TEV "sexual immorality")
see 2.14.

An alternative translation model for this verse is:

These people did not repent of their murdering each other, or
practicing black magic, or having sexual relations with someone else's
spouse, or stealing.

10.1-11

              RSV   TEV
                                              The Angel and the Little Scroll

1 Then I saw another mighty angel coming   1 Then I saw another mighty angel coming
down from heaven, wrapped in a cloud, with a   down out of heaven. He was wrapped in a cloud
rainbow over his head, and his face was like the and had a rainbow around his head; his face was
sun, and his legs like pillars of fire. 2 He had a like the sun, and his legs were like columns of fire.
little scroll open in his hand. And he set his right 2 He had a small scroll open in his hand. He put
foot on the sea, and his left foot on the land, his right foot on the sea and his left foot on the
3 and called out with a loud voice, like a lion roar- land, 3 and called out in a loud voice that sounded
ing; when he called out, the seven thunders sound- like the roar of lions. After he had called out, the
ed. 4 And when the seven thunders had sounded, seven thunders answered with a roar. 4 As soon as
I was about to write, but I heard a voice from   they spoke, I was about to write. But I heard a
heaven saying, "Seal up what the seven thunders voice speak from heaven, "Keep secret what the
have said, and do not write it down." 5 And the seven thunders have said; do not write it down!"
angel whom I saw standing on sea and land lifted   5 Then the angel that I saw standing on the
up his right hand to heaven 6 and swore by him   sea and on the land raised his right hand to heav-
who lives for ever and ever, who created heaven en 6 and took a vow in the name of God, who
and what is in it, the earth and what is in it, and lives forever and ever, who created heaven, earth,
the sea and what is in it, that there should be no and the sea, and everything in them. The angel
more delay, 7 but that in the days of the trumpet said, "There will be no more delay! 7 But when
call to be sounded by the seventh angel, the   the seventh angel blows his trumpet, then God will
mystery of God, as he announced to his servants accomplish his secret plan, as he announced to his
the prophets, should be fulfilled.   servants, the prophets."

8 Then the voice which I had heard from   8 Then the voice that I had heard speaking
heaven spoke to me again, saying, "Go, take the from heaven spoke to me again, saying, "Go and
scroll which is open in the hand of the angel who take the open scroll which is in the hand of the
is standing on the sea and on the land." 9 So I angel standing on the sea and on the land."
went to the angel and told him to give me the   9 I went to the angel and asked him to give
little scroll; and he said to me, "Take it and eat; it me the little scroll. He said to me, "Take it and
will be bitter to your stomach, but sweet as honey eat it; it will turn sour in your stomach, but in
in your mouth." 10 And I took the little scroll your mouth it will be sweet as honey."

from the hand of the angel and ate it; it was sweet as honey in my mouth, but when I had eaten it my stomach was made bitter. 11 And I was told, "You must again prophesy about many peoples and nations and tongues and kings."

10 I took the little scroll from his hand and ate it, and it tasted sweet as honey in my mouth. But after I swallowed it, it turned sour in my stomach. 11 Then I was told, "Once again you must proclaim God's message about many nations, races, languages, and kings."

SECTION HEADING: TEV "The Angel and the Little Scroll"; or "A vision of an angel with a little scroll," or "The dream about the heavenly messenger and the little scroll."

This vision is the first part of two events that come between the blowing of the sixth trumpet (9.13) and the blowing of the seventh trumpet (11.15). This interval emphasizes the importance of what will happen when the seventh trumpet is blown (see 10.7).

John had been in heaven (4.1), but now he is on earth (verse 1), and it is on earth that he goes to the angel and asks for the scroll the angel is holding (verses 8-9).

10.1   RSV   TEV

Then I saw another mighty angel coming down from heaven, wrapped in a cloud, with a rainbow over his head, and his face was like the sun, and his legs like pillars of fire.

Then I saw another mighty angel coming down out of heaven. He was wrapped in a cloud and had a rainbow around his head; his face was like the sun, and his legs were like columns of fire.

I saw: this is a new vision. One may also say "I dreamed again and saw."

Another mighty angel coming down from heaven: perhaps this is the angel of 5.2, who is also described as "a strong angel." **Heaven**, or God's dwelling place, is in focus here, not the sky.

Wrapped in a cloud: the verb "to wrap around" is used in the sense of "to clothe" (see 3.5,18; 4.4; 7.9,13), and this is how it should be translated here (as TNT, AT, and Phps do). The cloud was the garment, or robe, the angel was wearing. So in some languages this may be rendered as "the angel wore a cloud like clothes," "the angel's clothes were a cloud," "the angel had a cloud around him as if he were wearing clothes," or "the angel was clothed with a cloud."

A rainbow over his head: for **rainbow** see 4.3. It is not certain what the Greek preposition (literally "on") is meant to portray here, whether the rainbow forms a complete circle "around" the angel's head, like a halo (TEV, FRCL), or is a semicircle "over" his head (RSV). Some translations have simply "on" or "upon."

His face was like the sun: his face shone like the sun (see 1.16).

His legs like pillars of fire: the Greek word translated **legs** ordinarily means "feet"; but the comparison "like columns of fire" makes it obvious that the writer is describing the angel's legs. The word "pillars" appears in 3.12.

An alternative translation model for this verse is:

156

I dreamed again and saw a mighty angel coming down out of heaven. He had a cloud around him like clothes, and a rainbow was around (or, encircling) his head; his face shone like the sun, and his legs looked like columns (or, pillars) of fire.

10.2

RSV	TEV
He had a little scroll open in his hand. And he set his right foot on the sea, and his left foot on the land,	He had a small scroll open in his hand. He put his right foot on the sea and his left foot on the land,

A little scroll: this differs from the scroll in 5.1; this one is small and is not sealed, but lies **open**, that is, unrolled, in the angel's hand (see Ezek 2.10). A Greek diminutive form for "scroll" is used, hence **little scroll**. Its contents can be seen. If a translation must specify which hand of the angel is meant, probably the right hand should be chosen. So another way of expressing this clause is "He held a small unrolled scroll (or, paper document) in his hand."

His right foot on the sea, and his left foot on the land: this indicates that the angel is gigantic. It is pointless to try to identify the sea as the Mediterranean. The picture is meant to show that the message is for the inhabitants of the whole earth. So it is possible to say "He put his right foot down upon (or, on the surface of) the oceans, and his left foot on the dry land."

10.3

RSV	TEV
and called out with a loud voice, like a lion roaring; when he called out, the seven thunders sounded.	and called out in a loud voice that sounded like the roar of lions. After he had called out, the seven thunders answered with a roar.

Called out with a loud voice: the text does not say what the angel said; it may be that this shout is to get attention for the message that is about to come from heaven (verses 4-7).

Like a lion roaring: not only loud, but also frightening. God's voice is compared to the roar of a lion in Hosea 11.10 (see also Amos 3.8). On the translation of **lion** see 4.7.

The seven thunders sounded: this is a definite number, but there is no reference in biblical or Bible-related literature to seven thunders as such. As elsewhere, the number indicates completion, totality. In John 12.28-29, to some people God's voice from heaven sounds like thunder. Other instances of thunder in Revelation precede God's acts of judgment (8.5; 11.19; 16.18). In certain languages this clause will be expressed as "There was the sound of thunder answering seven times," "there was thunder seven times in reply," or "the sky roared seven times in reply."

10.4 RSV	TEV
And when the seven thunders had sounded, I was about to write, but I heard a voice from heaven saying, "Seal up what the seven thunders have said, and do not write it down."	As soon as they spoke, I was about to write. But I heard a voice speak from heaven, "Keep secret what the seven thunders have said; do not write it down!"

I was about to write: for comments on the Greek auxiliary verb indicating an immediate action, see 2.10, as well as 6.11, "were to be," and 8.13, "are about to." John was about to write down what the seven thunders had said.

A voice from heaven: this is probably God's voice, but the text avoids saying this explicitly, and so should a translation. However, certain translators will need to express this clause as "but I heard someone say from heaven," or even "but I heard words coming from heaven."

Seal up . . . and do not write it down: it is clear that John did not write anything before the command not to write. So the RSV literal translation **Seal up** may be misleading, since it implies sealing a written document. It is better to imitate TEV and others, "Keep secret . . . and do not write" (also NJB, TNT, SPCL, FRCL, BRCL), or one may say "Do not reveal to anyone . . . ." Or the two commands may be combined into one: "Do not write (down) what the thunders said."

Alternative translation models for this verse are:

> As soon as the seven thunders sounded, I was about to write down what they said. But I heard someone from heaven say, "Don't tell what they said; do not write it down."

Or:

> As soon as the sky roared seven times, I was about to write down the message that I heard. But I heard someone in heaven say, "Don't write what you heard; do not reveal (or, tell) it yet."

10.5 RSV	TEV
And the angel whom I saw standing on sea and land lifted up his right hand to heaven	Then the angel that I saw standing on the sea and on the land raised his right hand to heaven

As RSV and TEV show, the writer refers to the angel as "the one I saw standing on the sea and on the land." In some languages this redundant information may be unnatural, and it may be more effective to say simply "And then the angel raised his right hand . . . ."

Lifted his right hand to heaven: this is the gesture of one who makes a vow, or a promise, before God, as specified in the next verse (see Dan 12.7; Deut 32.40). **To heaven** may also be expressed as "towards heaven."

10.6   RSV   TEV

and swore by him who lives for ever and | and took a vow in the name of God, who
ever, who created heaven and what is in | lives forever and ever, who created
it, the earth and what is in it, and the | heaven, earth, and the sea, and every-
sea and what is in it, that there should | thing in them. The angel said, "There
be no more delay, | will be no more delay!

Swore by him who: this may be expressed by "made a solemn promise in the name of him who" or "took a vow in the name of him who," "made a strong promise in," or "stated solemnly, using God's name, that everything he would say is true." The name of God is used in order to show that what the angel is about to say is absolutely true. See *A Handbook on the Gospel of Matthew*, page 148, for a detailed discussion on the difference in English between "promise," "vow," "swear," or "oath." In this context the angel is taking an oath, making a solemn statement, with God as witness, that something is true.

Him who lives for ever and ever: see 4.10 for this way of speaking about God.

Created heaven ... the earth ... and the sea: this means the whole universe. The addition in each case of **and what is in it** (see also 12.12) is meant to emphasize that everything that exists, animate and inanimate, was all created by God (see 14.7).

That there should be no more delay: instead of using the indirect discourse, as RSV does, it is better to use direct discourse, with a colon or comma and quotation marks to begin the message of the angel (as most translations do). This avoids the ambiguity of **should** of RSV, which can be taken to mean "there ought not to be any more delay." NRSV reads "There will be no more delay, [7] but in the days when the seventh angel is to blow his trumpet, the mystery of God will be fulfilled, as he announced to his servants the prophets."

If the impersonal form "there will be no more delay" of the Greek and the English is difficult or unnatural in other languages, the translation can be "God will not wait any longer." NJB translates "The time of waiting is over"; this is a good model to imitate.

An alternative translation model for this verse is:

> And he solemnly stated, using the name of God who never dies and who created the universe, that he was speaking the truth. He said, "God will not wait any longer to do what he has planned. . . ."

10.7   RSV   TEV

but that in the days of the trumpet call | But when the seventh angel blows his
to be sounded by the seventh angel, the | trumpet, then God will accomplish his
mystery of God, as he announced to his | secret plan, as he announced to his
servants the prophets, should be ful- | servants, the prophets."
filled.

In the days of: it is more natural to say "at the time when," since it is obvious that the trumpet blast would not last several days. REB and SPCL have "when the time comes"; TNT "at the time of"; NJB "at the time when."

The mystery of God . . . should be fulfilled: here **mystery** stands for God's plan, as yet unrevealed (see 1.20). God's plan is to fulfill his purposes for humanity by means of Jesus Christ. Beckwith defines it as follows: "the purpose of God to bring his kingdom to its consummation—a purpose hidden from the world but in the end to be fully revealed in its accomplishment."

Fulfilled: to fulfill is to accomplish, to complete, to bring to intended final form. In certain languages it will be expressed as "bear fruit." So this clause may also be rendered as "Then God will let it (cause it to) happen according to his secret plan (purpose)" or "Then God will cause his secret plan to take place (be completed)."

As he announced to his servants the prophets: the verb "announce" is the same that is translated "to proclaim the Good News" (see TEV Luke 8.1). A prophet is one who proclaimed God's message (see "prophecy" in 1.3). Here the reference can be to the prophets of the Old Testament; but it seems more likely that it refers to Christian prophets (see the same phrase in 11.18). In this context, what God announced to them was the time when he intended to fulfill his plan. So it is also possible to say "at the time which he has announced to his servants . . . ." For **prophets** discussed in the context of "prophetic message," see 1.3, and for **servants** see 1.1.

The following may serve as a model for translating the angel's message in verses 6b-7:

> "God will not delay (or, wait) any longer! He will act as soon as the seventh angel blows his trumpet. He will complete his secret plan, as he announced to his servants, the prophets."

10.8   RSV   TEV

Then the voice which I had heard from heaven spoke to me again, saying, "Go, take the scroll which is open in the hand of the angel who is standing on the sea and on the land." | Then the voice that I had heard speaking from heaven spoke to me again, saying, "Go and take the open scroll which is in the hand of the angel standing on the sea and on the land."

The voice . . . from heaven spoke to me again: this refers back to verse 4. In certain languages one cannot talk about "voices" speaking, and one must identify the speaker or owner of the voice. In such cases one may also translate this clause as "The person who had spoken to me from heaven said . . ." or "I again heard the voice speaking to me."

Take the scroll: this does not imply force; as verse 9 says, John asks the angel for the scroll. Certain languages will state this clause differently by saying "Go and receive the open scroll from the hand." Here the diminutive form of **scroll** is not used, as in verse 2, but the same form that appears in 5.1.

For the rest of the verse, see verse 2.

10.9   RSV   TEV

So I went to the angel and told him to   I went to the angel and asked him
give me the little scroll; and he said to   to give me the little scroll. He said to
me, "Take it and eat; it will be bitter to   me, "Take it and eat it; it will turn sour
your stomach, but sweet as honey in   in your stomach, but in your mouth it
your mouth."   will be sweet as honey."

    Told him to give me: it may be better to translate "asked him to give me" or
"asked him, 'Please give me . . . .' "
    The little scroll: the word that is used in verse 2.
    Take it and eat: it is better to have the object with the verb **eat** as well: "Take
it and eat it."
    It will be bitter to your stomach, but sweet as honey in your mouth: for
a similar situation see Ezek 2.8–3.3. The Greek text uses the verb "to make bitter,"
"to embitter" (as in 8.11). This may be represented by "sour" or "acid." The logical
order would be "sweet as honey in your mouth but bitter in your stomach," as in the
next verse; a translation is advised to stay with the order of the Greek text. **Honey**:
this, of course, refers to the sweet product of the bodies of bees, and certain cultures
call **honey** "bee excretion" or "bee water." In cultures where bees are unknown, one
may say, for example, "The sweet excretion from an insect named 'bee,' " "the sweet
food made by . . . ," or "the sweet juice from bees." Here a picture of a bee and a
description of this insect in an item in the glossary will be helpful. (See *Fauna and
Flora*, pages 10-11.)

10.10   RSV   TEV

And I took the little scroll from the   I took the little scroll from his
hand of the angel and ate it; it was   hand and ate it, and it tasted sweet as
sweet as honey in my mouth, but when   honey in my mouth. But after I swal-
I had eaten it my stomach was made   lowed it, it turned sour in my stomach.
bitter.

    For **my stomach was made bitter** the translation can say "it turned sour in
my stomach" or "my stomach turned sour." In English this condition is normally
called "a heartburn." Whatever is the normal term in a language for when one
experiences "acid stomach" or "heartburn" should be used here.
    All the words and phrases of this verse are used previously and require no
further comment.

10.11   RSV   TEV

And I was told, "You must again proph-   Then I was told, "Once again you must
esy about many peoples and nations and   proclaim God's message about many
tongues and kings."   nations, races, languages, and kings."

I was told: this translates the impersonal third plural active, "They say to me." This probably refers to an angel, but it can refer to God.

Must: see 1.1.

Again prophesy: this is in addition to what John has already revealed in the earlier part of the book. To **prophesy** is to proclaim God's message (see 1.3; 10.7).

About: most translations give the Greek preposition this meaning (see similar construction in John 12.16, "written of [about] him"). NJB translates "against," but no other translation consulted does this. GECL provides a good model: "You must now proclaim again what God has planned for . . . ."

Peoples and nations and tongues: see 5.9; here **kings** is added, for emphasis. **Tongues**: it will not be natural in many languages to say "proclaim God's message about many . . . languages." Rather, those translators will render this something like the following: "people speaking all sorts of languages."

An alternative translation model for this verse is:

> Then they ordered me, "You must now proclaim (announce) again what God has planned for the people of many nations and races, who speak all sorts of languages, and with all the kings (high chiefs)."

11.1-14

RSV	TEV
	The Two Witnesses
1 Then I was given a measuring rod like a staff, and I was told: "Rise and measure the temple of God and the altar and those who worship there, 2 but do not measure the court outside the temple; leave that out, for it is given over to the nations, and they will trample over the holy city for forty-two months. 3 And I will grant my two witnesses power to prophesy for one thousand two hundred and sixty days, clothed in sackcloth."	1 I was then given a stick that looked like a measuring-rod, and was told, "Go and measure the temple of God and the altar, and count those who are worshiping in the temple. 2 But do not measure the outer courts, because they have been given to the heathen, who will trample on the Holy City for forty-two months. 3 I will send my two witnesses dressed in sackcloth, and they will proclaim God's message during those 1,260 days."
4 These are the two olive trees and the two lampstands which stand before the Lord of the earth. 5 And if any one would harm them, fire pours from their mouth and consumes their foes; if any one would harm them, thus he is doomed to be killed. 6 They have power to shut the sky, that no rain may fall during the days of their prophesying, and they have power over the waters to turn them into blood, and to smite the earth with every plague, as often as they desire. 7 And when they have finished their testimony, the beast that ascends from the bottomless pit will make war upon them and conquer them and kill them, 8 and their dead bodies will lie in the street of the great city which is allegorically called Sodom and Egypt, where their Lord was crucified. 9 For three days and a half men from the peoples and tribes and tongues and nations gaze at their dead bodies and refuse to let them be placed in a tomb, 10 and	4 The two witnesses are the two olive trees and the two lamps that stand before the Lord of the earth. 5 If anyone tries to harm them, fire comes out of their mouths and destroys their enemies; and in this way whoever tries to harm them will be killed. 6 They have authority to shut up the sky so that there will be no rain during the time they proclaim God's message. They have authority also over the springs of water, to turn them into blood; they have authority also to strike the earth with every kind of plague as often as they wish. 7 When they finish proclaiming their message, the beast that comes up out of the abyss will fight against them. He will defeat them and kill them, 8 and their bodies will lie in the street of the great city, where their Lord was crucified. The symbolic name of that city is Sodom, or Egypt. 9 People from all nations, tribes, languages, and

162

those who dwell on the earth will rejoice over them and make merry and exchange presents, because these two prophets had been a torment to those who dwell on the earth. 11 But after the three and a half days a breath of life from God entered them, and they stood up on their feet, and great fear fell on those who saw them. 12 Then they heard a loud voice from heaven saying to them, "Come up hither!" And in the sight of their foes they went up to heaven in a cloud. 13 And at that hour there was a great earthquake, and a tenth of the city fell; seven thousand people were killed in the earthquake, and the rest were terrified and gave glory to the God of heaven.

14 The second woe has passed; behold, the third woe is soon to come.

races will look at their bodies for three and a half days and will not allow them to be buried. 10 The people of the earth will be happy because of the death of these two. They will celebrate and send presents to each other, because those two prophets brought much suffering upon mankind. 11 After three and a half days a life-giving breath came from God and entered them, and they stood up; and all who saw them were terrified. 12 Then the two prophets heard a loud voice say to them from heaven, "Come up here!" As their enemies watched, they went up into heaven in a cloud. 13 At that very moment there was a violent earthquake; a tenth of the city was destroyed, and seven thousand people were killed. The rest of the people were terrified and praised the greatness of the God of heaven.

14 The second horror is over, but the third horror will come soon!

SECTION HEADING: TEV "The Two Witnesses." Or else "God's two witnesses" or "The two witnesses sent by God." There may be some difficulty in speaking of "witnesses" in a short title, and the phrase "God's witnesses" may be ambiguous. In verse 3 it is said that they will prophesy, and in verse 10 they are called "prophets"; so it may be better to say "The two prophets," or "God's two prophets," or "The two prophets sent by God," or "God sends two prophets."

This is the second episode in the interval between the blowing of the sixth trumpet (9.13) and the blowing of the seventh trumpet (11.15). John is told to measure the Temple and the worshipers, but the narrative does not actually say that he did so. From verse 3 onward, attention is paid to the two witnesses, or prophets, sent by God. They are like Elijah, who announced a drought that lasted three and a half years (verse 6; see 1 Kgs 17.1), and like Moses, who brought the plagues upon Egypt (verse 6; see Exo 7.14-21). After their death, resurrection, and ascension into heaven, an earthquake destroys one tenth of Jerusalem and kills seven thousand of its citizens. This is the end of the second horror, that is, the destruction and suffering that follow the blast of the sixth trumpet (verse 14; see 9.12).

11.1	RSV	TEV

Then I was given a measuring rod like a staff, and I was told: "Rise and measure the temple of God and the altar and those who worship there,		I was then given a stick that looked like a measuring-rod, and was told, "Go and measure the temple of God and the altar, and count those who are worshiping in the temple.

I was given: either by God or by an angel. One may also translate "Someone gave me . . ." or "God gave me . . . ," but the former rendering is probably more accurate, as we do not know the actual agent; we can only guess.

A measuring rod like a staff: the meaning of the Greek is better expressed by NJB "a long cane like a measuring rod"; note REB "a long cane to use as a measuring rod," NIV "a reed like a measuring rod"; Chewa has "a reed for measuring with (that looked) like a walking stick." The first word, *kalamos,* designates a reed, or a cane (see its use in 21.15: TEV "measuring stick"); the second word, *rabdos,* is a staff, or a rod. Elsewhere in Revelation it refers to the "iron rod" (or, scepter) used by Jesus Christ (12.5; 19.15) and his followers (2.27). It is better to follow TEV or NJB in translating the passage here.

I was told: this translates the masculine singular participle "saying"; the speaker is God (see "my two witnesses" in verse 3). So in languages that do not use the passive, one must say "God told me" or "God commanded me."

Rise and measure: the Greek verb translated **Rise** by RSV functions as an auxiliary when used in connection with a verb of action; it does not imply that the one addressed is sitting or lying down. Something like FRCL is better, "Go measure," or REB, NIV "Go and measure." NRSV and RNAB "Come and measure" changes the point of reference and seems to imply that the temple to be measured is in heaven. But since this temple is on earth, it is better to translate "Go and measure." The purpose of this measuring is to measure off the area and the people, that is, to isolate them, to put them under divine protection, in order to keep them from being affected by the disasters that are coming. **Measure** means to gauge the size of something or survey something to determine its size or boundaries.

The temple of God and the altar and those who worship there: this temple is on earth, the Jerusalem Temple (as verse 2 makes clear); here it is a symbol of the Church, the people of God. The translation can be "the Temple, which belongs to God" or "the Temple, where God is worshiped," or "The temple where they worship God." The Greek word translated **temple** usually means the central sanctuary, not the whole Temple complex, and a translator may use the specific word for sanctuary, if two different words exist in the language.

The altar: this is either the altar for burning incense (as in 8.3,5; 9.13; see also 6.9) or the altar for offering sacrifices, which was not in the sanctuary but outside, in the priests' court. In the Jerusalem Temple the altar for burning incense was in the Holy Place, near the entrance to the Most Holy Place. (See Exo 38.1-7 for a description of the altar for offering sacrifice in front of the Tent of the Presence.) It is more probable that here the altar of sacrifice is meant; but the translation will say simply **the altar**, without further identifying it.

AN ANCIENT STONE ALTAR

THE ALTAR FOR BURNING INCENSE

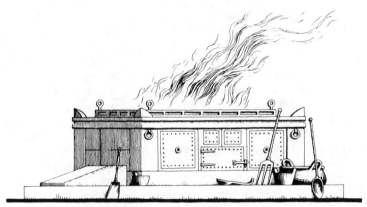

THE ALTAR FOR OFFERING SACRIFICES

And those who worship there: in Greek the imperative verb **measure** has the worshipers as direct object also. It is strange to speak of "measuring" people, so it seems better to say either "count" or "number" them. The demonstrative pronoun **there** refers to the Temple, not specifically to the altar.

An alternative translation model for this verse is:

> Someone gave me a stick (piece of wood) that looked like what people use for measuring things, and God commanded me, "Go and measure my temple and the altar, and count those people who are worshiping me there.

11.2   RSV   TEV

but do not measure the court outside | But do not measure the outer courts,
the temple; leave that out, for it is given | because they have been given to the
over to the nations, and they will tram- | heathen, who will trample on the Holy
ple over the holy city for forty-two | City for forty-two months.
months.

The order of the Greek text for the first part of this verse is "The court outside the temple—exclude it and do not measure it." Most translations invert the order of the two verbal commands in order to make the text easier to understand. In the Jerusalem Temple this court, outside the inner sanctuary, was known as the court of the Gentiles, for that is where they could assemble. They could get no nearer the inner sanctuary, however. In this passage this court and its people stand for the unbelievers, who will not be spared the disasters to come. Another way of expressing this initial clause is "But do not measure the open spaces with walls around them outside the temple."

It is given over to the nations: again the passive form of the verb shows that God is in charge. **The nations** are the Gentiles, here a symbol of non-Christians. In languages that do not use the passive, one must say, for example, "I (God) have given these to those who are not my people" or "I have let those who do not believe in me occupy these." See the previous verse, where God is the speaker.

They will trample over the holy city for forty-two months: the verb **trample** implies that the Gentiles will walk all over Jerusalem, the Holy City, as haughty conquerors of a defeated city (see the same verb translated "trodden down" in the similar passage in Luke 21.24). The period of time, **forty-two months** (also 13.5-7), is equal to 1,260 days (verse 3; see 12.6) and is equal also to three and a half years, the conventional period in apocalyptic literature for the temporary triumph of evil before the end of the age (see 12.14; also Dan 7.25; 12.7; see also the similar "three days and a half," 11.9). Its meaning is that these outsiders will "dominate" or "rule over," not that they will walk around for forty-two months, trampling on everything. So in some languages it will be more meaningful to say "who will rule over the Holy City . . . ." **Holy city** may also be rendered as "God's city," or simply "Jerusalem."

It may be desirable to establish the relation between **forty-two months** of verse 2 and "one thousand two hundred and sixty days" of verse 3. This can be done by translating verse 2b ". . . and the Gentiles will trample all over the Holy City for forty-two months, that is, for 1,260 days." And verse 3 can begin "During all that time" or "During those 1,260 days."

An alternative translation model for this verse is:

> But you must not measure the open areas (courts) outside the temple, because I (God) have given those to the people who do not believe in me. They will rule over my city for forty-two months (or 1,260 days).

11.3 RSV TEV

And I will grant my two witnesses power to prophesy for one thousand two hundred and sixty days, clothed in sackcloth."

I will send my two witnesses dressed in sackcloth, and they will proclaim God's message during those 1,260 days."

I will grant my two witnesses power to prophesy: the Greek text says "I will give to my two witnesses, and they will prophesy." Some translations say "give authority" (TNT, REB, NRSV); RNAB has "I will commission (my two witnesses)"; others have "I will send" (TEV, SPCL, FRCL, BRCL, NJB). Any of these is a satisfactory translation of the text. **To prophesy** means to proclaim God's message. Since God is the speaker, here the translation can say "to proclaim my message." So this clause may also be translated as "I will send two witnesses to proclaim my message" or "I will give my two witnesses the authority to proclaim my message."

My two witnesses: this can be translated "the two who will speak the truth about me." Since they are the same as the prophets in verse 10, it is possible to translate "the two men who will proclaim my message."

For one thousand two hundred and sixty days: see verse 2. FRCL translates "during those one thousand two hundred and sixty days," to identify the time span with the forty-two months of the preceding verse. In many societies a figure expressed in words rather than numbers will be preferable. See the alternative translation model below.

Clothed in sackcloth: see 6.12. The sackcloth was coarse cloth, usually made of goat's hair, which was worn as a sign of mourning, and which shows that the message of the two witnesses, or prophets, is to be one of doom and destruction, and a call for people to repent while there is still time. In cultures where sackcloth is unknown, it will be more natural to say "They wore clothes that showed that they were mourning (or distressed)."

An alternative translation model for this verse is:

I will send my two men who will proclaim my true message. They will wear mourning clothes and will proclaim my message during those one thousand two hundred and sixty days.

11.4 RSV TEV

These are the two olive trees and the two lampstands which stand before the Lord of the earth.

The two witnesses are the two olive trees and the two lamps that stand before the Lord of the earth.

The two olive trees: the way in which this is stated makes it clear that it refers to Zechariah 4.1-14, where the two olive trees, on either side of the lampstand, are the two men chosen and anointed by God to serve him, the Lord of the whole earth. Where olive trees are unknown, some decision must be made about how to represent olive trees, olives, and olive oil, all of which appear frequently in the Bible. Because of the importance of the olive tree in the Palestinian cultures, it will be well for translators in cultures where these trees are unknown to say something like "tree named olive" and introduce a picture, and also have a description in a glossary item. For additional help on olive trees, see *Fauna and Flora,* pages 156-158.

The two lampstands: see 1.12. Translators should use the same word as was employed in 1.12, and not imitate TEV's translation "lamp" in this verse.

Which stand: in the Greek the gender of the participle "standing" is masculine, so that it refers not to the olive trees or the lampstands, but to the two witnesses themselves. So the translation should be "who stand" or "and they stand." In order to convey this idea in many languages, one must say, for example, "The two witnesses stand before the Lord of the earth, and they are the two olive trees and the two lampstands," or "The two witnesses are the two olive trees and two lampstands. These two men stand before the Lord of the earth."

Before the Lord of the earth: this means "in the presence of God, the Lord of the whole world." The verb **stand** shows that they are God's servants, ready to do what God commands. The phrase **the Lord of the earth** may also be expressed as "the one who rules over the whole world."

An alternative translation model for this verse is:

> The two men who proclaim God's message stand in the presence of the Lord who rules over the whole world. They are those two olive trees and the two lampstands.

11.5   RSV   TEV

And if any one would harm them, fire   If anyone tries to harm them, fire comes
pours from their mouth and consumes   out of their mouths and destroys their
their foes; if any one would harm them,   enemies; and in this way whoever tries
thus he is doomed to be killed.   to harm them will be killed.

If any one would harm them: the same verb is used in 2.11; 7.2; 9.4, 10 ("hurting"), 19 ("wound"). Other ways of expressing this are "Whoever tries to hurt them" or "If any person attempts to injure them."

Fire pours from their mouth: this is like the fire that pours out of the horses' mouths in 9.17-18. Elijah called down fire from heaven to destroy his enemies (2 Kgs 1.10,12).

And consumes their foes: one should avoid leaving the reader with the impression that the **foes** and **any one** in the first part of the verse are two different sets of people. Perhaps one may translate the first part of the verse as "If any person tries to hurt these two men, fire shoots out of their mouths and destroys these enemies." **Their foes**: in certain languages this will be expressed as "the people who hate them."

Consumes: this translates the Greek verb "eats up"; so something like "kills," or "destroys," or any other verb that goes with fire, is a satisfactory translation.

If any one would harm them: this clause is repeated from the beginning of the verse, although in Greek the verb form is different. The literal repetition of this clause may not be effective in some languages, and something like TEV may be preferable.

Thus: that is, by means of the fire. TEV "in this way."

He is doomed: this translates the impersonal verb "it is necessary," "it must be," or "it is proper," which is generally used of the divine judgment and will (see 1.1). So the final clause may be rendered as "and in this way God will kill whoever tries to hurt them."

11.6 RSV	TEV
They have power to shut the sky, that no rain may fall during the days of their prophesying, and they have power over the waters to turn them into blood, and to smite the earth with every plague, as often as they desire.	They have authority to shut up the sky so that there will be no rain during the time they proclaim God's message. They have authority also over the springs of water, to turn them into blood; they have authority also to strike the earth with every kind of plague as often as they wish.

Power: or "authority" (TEV), or "the right." This is given them by God, and it may be that in some languages it will be better to translate "God has given them the authority (or, power)."

To shut the sky: where this figure of speech makes no sense or makes the wrong sense, it may be necessary to say simply "to stop the rain from falling"; in English the normal way to say this is "to keep it from raining." This is the power that the prophet Elijah had (see 1 Kgs 17.1; 18.1; Luke 4.25; James 5.17).

During the days of their prophesying: the drought caused by Elijah lasted into the third year (1 Kgs 18.1,43-45), that is, it lasted not quite three years. But Luke 4.25 and James 5.17 show that it had become three and a half years. **Days of their prophesying** may also be rendered as "the time when they proclaimed God's message."

Power over the waters to turn them into blood: this is the power that Moses exercised (Exo 7.14-21). Instead of "the springs of water" (TEV), the meaning of the Greek **the waters** may be better expressed by "all bodies of water" or "to turn water into blood."

To smite the earth with every plague: this is the power that Moses had to bring the plagues down on Egypt (see 9.18). The verb **to smite** is used also in 19.15; it means "to strike," "to hit," "to injure," "to wound." For **plague** see 9.18. Translators in some languages will express this sentence as "to cause every kind of calamity (terrible trouble) to injure those living on the earth."

An alternative translation model for this verse is:

> God has given them authority to stop the rain from falling during the time they proclaim his message. They have also received the authority to turn water into blood, and to cause all kinds of terrible calamities to hurt (strike) the earth. They can do this as often as they want to.

11.7   RSV   TEV

And when they have finished their testimony, the beast that ascends from the bottomless pit will make war upon them and conquer them and kill them,	When they finish proclaiming their message, the beast that comes up out of the abyss will fight against them. He will defeat them and kill them,

They have finished their testimony: this refers to their witness, the message given by God for them to proclaim.

The beast that ascends from the bottomless pit: for **bottomless pit** see 9.1. In chapters 13–20 two or perhaps three different beasts appear (mentioned some thirty-seven times), and in some passages it is difficult to tell which one is meant. Besides these various beasts there is also the dragon, who first appears in 12.3. The word translated **beast** means simply "animal" (see 6.8), and AT and Phps translate here "the animal," which is a bit strange in English. A translator must find, if possible, a distinctive word for these creatures. Perhaps use can be made of words taken from legends or fairy tales, where fantastic animals are fairly common. Here something like "monster" or "wild beast," or even "ogre," may be appropriate. It is probable that this beast is the same one that appears in 13.1.

Will make war upon them and conquer them and kill them: in this context to **make war** is not quite natural; something like "will attack them" or "will fight them" is better. And for **conquer** the verb "defeat" is more natural here.

11.8   RSV   TEV

and their dead bodies will lie in the street of the great city which is allegorically[d] called Sodom and Egypt, where their Lord was crucified.	and their bodies will lie in the street of the great city, where their Lord was crucified. The symbolic name of that city is Sodom, or Egypt.

[d] Greek *spiritually*

Their dead bodies will lie in the street of the great city: it was a shameful thing for corpses not to be buried. To translate the Greek literally **the street**, as RSV and TEV do, may make it appear that this was a city that had only one street. So it may be preferable to translate "the main street" or "the public square," or "the open places where people gathered." For **great city** the translation can be "the famous city" or "the important city." The writer clearly identifies the city as Jerusalem (**where their Lord was crucified**). But, as in all other such matters, what the writer has in mind is not a specific geographical location as such but the general role played in sacred history by such places. For the translation of **city** compare 11.2.

Allegorically called Sodom and Egypt: the adverb **allegorically** may be represented by "symbolically" (TEV "the symbolic name"); or else, "in figurative language." Instead of **Sodom and Egypt** a translation may choose to say "Sodom or Egypt" (TEV, TNT, FRCL, REB), to avoid giving the impression that the city was called by a double name.

Where their Lord was crucified: this is a reference to Jesus, the Lord of the two prophets. In languages that do not use the passive, one may translate, for example, "where people crucified (hung on a cross) the Lord of these two (prophets)."

It is better not to follow slavishly the order of the Greek text, as RSV does. A careless reader may understand that it was Sodom and Egypt where their Lord was crucified. TEV offers another way of ordering the various items of information.

An alternative translation model for this verse is:

> Their dead bodies (corpses) will lie in the main street of that important city where people crucified their Lord. People have given that city the symbolic name of Sodom or Egypt.

11.9 RSV	TEV
For three days and a half men from the peoples and tribes and tongues and nations gaze at their dead bodies and refuse to let them be placed in a tomb,	People from all nations, tribes, languages, and races will look at their bodies for three and a half days and will not allow them to be buried.

Men from the peoples and tribes and tongues and nations: see the same list in 5.9, in which the same four words appear, but not in the same order.

Gaze: the word means simply "look at," "see." As RSV shows, the Greek text has the verb in the present tense; this continues through verse 10a, and at "they will exchange presents" the future tense appears once more. At verse 11 the past tense is used. It is difficult to account for these changes of verb tense; the main thing for a translation to do is to use the appropriate tense in the context of the narrative as a whole.

Be placed in a tomb: a dead person was usually buried the same day that death occurred, or within twenty-four hours at the most. Where a burial does not involve a grave or a tomb, the normal way to refer to being buried should be used. If cremation is the normal way of disposing of dead bodies, it seems advisable to say something that fits better the biblical context. Another way of expressing this clause is "and will not let anyone take the corpses and bury them."

11.10 RSV	TEV
and those who dwell on the earth will rejoice over them and make merry and exchange presents, because these two prophets had been a torment to those who dwell on the earth.	The people of the earth will be happy because of the death of these two. They will celebrate and send presents to each other, because those two prophets brought much suffering upon mankind.

Those who dwell on earth: this refers to all the unrepentant sinners in the world (see the use of this expression in 3.10; 6.10; 8.13).

Will rejoice over them and make merry: the Greek text has the present tense, "they rejoice over them and celebrate," but in this context it is better to maintain the future tense. To **rejoice over** means to be happy because they have been killed. It is advised that this information be made explicit in the translation, to make it easier to understand. In certain languages one may render the first clause as "will be happy (hearts, or liver, will be cool, or sweet, or bright) because these two have died." **Make merry** (TEV "celebrate"): translators should choose an expression for this action that is most natural in the receptor language; for example, "have parties (fiestas)."

Exchange presents: a way of showing their happiness. NIV provides a good model for translators: ". . . will gloat over them and celebrate by sending each other gifts."

Those two prophets had been a torment: the verbal phrase **had been a torment** translates the Greek verb "to cause pain," "to torment" (see 9.5; 12.2 ["anguish"]; 14.10; 20.10). This refers back to verse 6. For **prophets** see 10.7.

Alternative translation models for this verse are:

> All the people of the world will gloat because these two have died. They will hold parties and send gifts to each other, because these two prophets have caused humans to suffer terribly.

Or:

> . . . They will celebrate by exchanging gifts, because these two prophets . . . .

11.11   RSV   TEV

But after the three and a half days a breath of life from God entered them, and they stood up on their feet, and great fear fell on those who saw them.	After three and a half days a life-giving breath came from God and entered them, and they stood up; and all who saw them were terrified.

A breath of life from God: for this kind of language see Ezekiel 37.5,9-10; Genesis 2.7. Even though in Greek there is no definite article with **breath**, it seems better to translate "God's life-giving breath" or "the breath of life from God" (NRSV, REB, AT, Mft, Brc). NJB has "God breathed life into them," which is a good model to imitate. However, one may also say "God caused his breath to enter them and they came back to life." Something like "God brought them back to life" can be said in languages where the figure of God breathing life into them may be difficult to express.

They stood up on their feet: TEV's model "they stood up" will be more natural in most languages.

Great fear fell on those who saw them: something like "those who saw them were terrified" (TEV) should be said, to express their great fear. In certain languages this may be expressed idiomatically; for example, "their hearts (liver) fell" or "their souls flee and bile stirs up" (Thai), or "their hearts came outside" (Chewa).

11.12   RSV   TEV

Then they heard a loud voice from heaven saying to them, "Come up hither!" And in the sight of their foes they went up to heaven in a cloud.	Then the two prophets heard a loud voice say to them from heaven, "Come up here!" As their enemies watched, they went up into heaven in a cloud.

Then they heard: to avoid any ambiguity it is better to make the subject explicit, "Then the two prophets heard." Some manuscripts have "I heard," a text preferred by some commentators and NJB (also NRSV margin); REB uses the passive, "A loud voice was heard." It seems best to have the two prophets as the subject.

A loud voice from heaven: see 10.4,8. This is either God or an angel speaking. Alternative translation models for this first sentence are: "Then the two prophets heard someone speaking to them in a loud voice from heaven" or "Then a loud voice from heaven said to the prophets."

In the sight of their foes: this is more naturally expressed by "as their enemies watched" (TEV), "while their enemies were watching them," or "while the people who hate them . . . ." For **enemies** see 11.5 ("foes").

They went up to heaven in a cloud: the Greek preposition translated **to** by RSV may mean "into" (TEV); either meaning fits the context. **A cloud** serves as their transportation to heaven (see Acts 1.9; similar is the whirlwind of 2 Kings 2.11).

11.13   RSV   TEV

And at that hour there was a great earthquake, and a tenth of the city fell; seven thousand people were killed in the earthquake, and the rest were terrified and gave glory to the God of heaven.	At that very moment there was a violent earthquake; a tenth of the city was destroyed, and seven thousand people were killed. The rest of the people were terrified and praised the greatness of the God of heaven.

At that hour: this is more naturally said "Immediately after that" or "At that very moment."

A great earthquake: see 6.12.

A tenth of the city fell: it may be easier to say "one tenth of the buildings in the city were destroyed," or "collapsed," or "came crashing down." In certain languages this will be rendered as "one in every ten houses in the city was destroyed."

Seven thousand people were killed: perhaps this means that the population of the city was set at 70,000, but this is not certain; in any case, the number is symbolic. In Greek the phrase translated **people** is "names of people"; see "names" in 3.4, and "the crowd of names" in Acts 1.15 (RSV "the company of persons").

The rest: means "those who survived" or "those who did not die."

Terrified: see "fear" in verse 11 of this chapter.

The rest . . . gave glory to the God of heaven: their action shows how great was the fear that made the survivors repent and acknowledge God's power. It may be implied that they confessed their sins (see similar language in Josh 7.19). Only here in the New Testament and in 16.11 is the phrase "the God of heaven" used (see Ezra 1.2; Dan 2.18; Jonah 1.9). Something like "the God who lives in heaven" or "God, who rules from heaven" may be said. In some languages **gave glory to** will need to be changed into direct speech; for example, "they confessed, 'You, God, who live in heaven, are very great (powerful).'"

11.14

RSV	TEV
The second woe has passed; behold, the third woe is soon to come.	The second horror is over, but the third horror will come soon!

For this verse see 8.13; 9.12. It seems that **The second woe** refers to the disasters that followed the blowing of the sixth trumpet (9.13-21); the events described in 10.1–11.13 come as an interval between the blowing of the sixth trumpet and the blowing of the seventh trumpet. Some believe that the second woe refers to the disaster described in 11.13. It is not easy to identify the third woe, which "is soon to come." No disaster falls upon humanity after the blowing of the seventh trumpet. Many believe that the disasters and sufferings that come at the outpouring of the seven bowls of God's anger (chapter 16) are the third woe; but the writer himself does not say so.

11.15-19

RSV

TEV

The Seventh Trumpet

15 Then the seventh angel blew his trumpet, and there were loud voices in heaven, saying, "The kingdom of the world has become the kingdom of our Lord and of his Christ, and he shall reign for ever and ever." 16 And the twenty-four elders who sit on their thrones before God fell on their faces and worshiped God, 17 saying,
"We give thanks to thee, Lord God Almighty, who art and who wast,
that thou hast taken thy great power
and begun to reign.
18 The nations raged, but thy wrath came,
and the time for the dead to be judged,
for rewarding thy servants, the prophets
and saints,
and those who fear thy name, both
small and great,
and for destroying the destroyers of the earth."
19 Then God's temple in heaven was opened, and the ark of his covenant was seen within his temple; and there were flashes of lightning, voices, peals of thunder, an earthquake, and heavy hail.

15 Then the seventh angel blew his trumpet, and there were loud voices in heaven, saying, "The power to rule over the world belongs now to our Lord and his Messiah, and he will rule forever and ever!" 16 Then the twenty-four elders who sit on their thrones in front of God threw themselves face downward and worshiped God, 17 saying:
"Lord God Almighty, the one who is and who was!
We thank you that you have taken your great power
and have begun to rule!
18 The heathen were filled with rage,
because the time for your anger has come,
the time for the dead to be judged.
The time has come to reward your servants, the prophets,
and all your people, all who have reverence for you,
great and small alike.
The time has come to destroy those who destroy the earth!"
19 God's temple in heaven was opened, and the Covenant Box was seen there. Then there

were flashes of lightning, rumblings and peals of
thunder, an earthquake, and heavy hail.

SECTION HEADING: TEV "The Seventh Trumpet," or "The seventh angel blows
his trumpet."

Verses 15-19 form a climax in the book, and what follows is not disaster for the
world but an acclamation of the power and goodness of God and the Messiah. The
seventh trumpet blast sets in motion a long series of events that extends to the end
of the age (see 10.7).

11.15   RSV   TEV

Then the seventh angel blew his
trumpet, and there were loud voices in
heaven, saying, "The kingdom of the
world has become the kingdom of our
Lord and of his Christ, and he shall
reign for ever and ever."

Then the seventh angel blew his
trumpet, and there were loud voices in
heaven, saying, "The power to rule over
the world belongs now to our Lord and
his Messiah, and he will rule forever
and ever!"

Then the seventh angel blew his trumpet: see 8.7,8,10,12; 9.1.13.

There were loud voices in heaven, saying: this can be expressed by "loud
voices were heard in heaven; they said" or "I heard loud voices in heaven that said."
It is assumed that these are angels speaking, but the text does not identify the
speakers. However, in languages that cannot talk about **voices** speaking, one must
say, for example, "I heard angels (or, many speakers) in heaven saying in a loud
voice . . . ." The translator should consider the possibility of presenting the rest of
the verse as poetry (see Section F of the introduction, "Translating the Revelation
to John," pages 6 and following).

The kingdom of the world: the Greek word for **kingdom** here does not mean
a region or country ruled by a king but the power to rule as king: kingship,
sovereignty, dominion. God and his Messiah have now taken complete control over
the world. The underlying thought is that they have defeated Satan and his servants,
who had been allowed to rule for a while. FRCL and BRCL translate "The power to
rule over the world," SPCL "the right to rule over the world." TNT and REB have
"Sovereignty over the world," while Brc uses a more dynamic expression, "Our Lord
and his Messiah have become the sovereigns of the world." The abstract notion of
sovereignty or kingship may be difficult to express; and it may not be enough simply
to say, as TEV does, "The power to rule over the world belongs now" to God and his
Messiah. It should be said that now they have actually begun to rule.

Has become: this implies that the power to rule now belongs to them and not
to someone else. REB has "has passed to . . . ."

Of our Lord and of his Christ: here **our Lord** means God, and **our** is
inclusive. The phrase **his Christ** (a title) may be better expressed by "his Anointed
One" or "his Chosen One," if it is clear to the reader that Jesus Christ is meant. The
possessive **his (Christ)** means "the one he chose to be the Messiah" or ". . .
Anointed Savior." An alternate translation model for this clause is "Our [inclusive]
God and the one he has chosen to be the Savior have the right now to rule over the
world."

And he shall reign for ever and ever: the singular subject here is God, and the grammar should be faithfully followed. That the Messiah will reign with God is implicit but should not be explicitly stated. For the expression **for ever and ever**, see 1.6.

An alternative translation model for this verse is:

> Then the seventh angel blew his trumpet, and I heard angels in heaven speaking loudly and saying, "Our God and his chosen Savior have the right to rule over the whole world, and God will rule for all time to come."

11.16   RSV   TEV

And the twenty-four elders who sit on their thrones before God fell on their faces and worshiped God,	Then the twenty-four elders who sit on their thrones in front of God threw themselves face downward and worshiped God,

The twenty-four elders who sit on their thrones before God: see 4.4.

Fell on their faces and worshiped God: they prostrated themselves (thus REB, NJB, TNT); for **worshiped** see 4.10.

11.17   RSV   TEV

saying,	saying:
"We give thanks to thee, Lord God Almighty, who art and who wast, that thou hast taken thy great power and begun to reign.	"Lord God Almighty, the one who is and who was! We thank you that you have taken your great power and have begun to rule!

The translator should consider rendering verses 17-18 as poetry (see Section F of the introduction, "Translating the Revelation to John," pages 6 and following).

We give thanks to thee: only here in Revelation is the verb "to give thanks" used.

Lord God Almighty: this may be expressed in various ways: "Lord, the Almighty God" or "Lord God, the Almighty One." For the title **Almighty** see 1.8.

Who art and who wast: see 1.8. Some manuscript copyists added "and who is to come" (as in 1.4,8), but this is not part of the original text here. TNT has a striking translation, "O God Almighty, Lord of the past and of the present."

That: this is more naturally expressed in English by NJB: "We give thanks to you . . . for (assuming your great power)." Another way of rendering this word is "because."

Thou hast taken thy great power and begun to reign: this means that now God is making use of his great power, God is exercising his great power. If a direct object is needed after the verb **to reign**, something like "over the (whole) world" may be said.

An alternative translation model for this verse is:

"(Lord) God who is all powerful (the strongest of all), who lives now and has always lived, we thank you that you are showing your great power and have begun to rule.

11.18 RSV	TEV
The nations raged, but thy wrath came, and the time for the dead to be judged, for rewarding thy servants, the prophets and saints, and those who fear thy name, both small and great, and for destroying the destroyers of the earth."	The heathen were filled with rage, because the time for your anger has come, the time for the dead to be judged. The time has come to reward your servants, the prophets, and all your people, all who have reverence for you, great and small alike. The time has come to destroy those who destroy the earth!"

The nations raged: this reflects the language of the Greek Septuagint version of Psalm 2.1. Here **the nations** are "the Gentiles" (or, "the heathen"), people who do not worship the God of Israel. The Greek verb translated **raged** means "became very angry (or, furious)" and appears only here in Revelation. In certain languages **raged** will be expressed idiomatically; for example, "have very hot heart (liver)."

But thy wrath came: the Greek conjunction used here usually means "and" (so NIV); TEV has "because" (a possible meaning), but most translations have **But**. The Greek noun translated **wrath** is related to the verb translated **raged**, and a translation that can use the two related words is urged to do so. Here the abstract **wrath** stands not only for the emotion but for the expression of that emotion, as the rest of the verse shows. So something like "the time has come for you to show (or, express) your anger" represents the meaning of the Greek. NJB has "and now has come the time for your retribution."

The time for the dead to be judged: it may be better to use the active voice, "the time has come for you to judge all who have died." After the dead are raised to life, they will be judged by God (see 20.11-13). Here the word translated "time" can be represented by "the right time," "the right occasion." For **judge** see 6.10. An alternative translation model for the first part of this verse is as follows:

Those who do not believe in you (or, the heathen) were having hot hearts; but the time for you to become angry has come; the right time has come for you to judge all people who have died.

For rewarding thy servants, the prophets and saints: the RSV punctuation is somewhat odd; it seems to make **the prophets and saints** an apposition to **thy servants**, that is, **the prophets and saints** are the ones to whom **thy servants** refers. (Thus also NRSV, in poetic form.) This does not seem right. It seems more reasonable that **the prophets** defines those who are **thy servants**, that is, "your servants, the prophets" (see 10.7), and that **the saints** goes with **those who fear thy name**. For **saints** see 5.8. **Rewarding** here means that God will "pay back," "recompense," "do good things to," these people for what they have done. For the translation of **servants** see 1.1.

Those who fear thy name: the biblical expression "to fear God's name" means to respect God, to honor God, to have reverence for God. TEV places "all who have reverence for you" in apposition with "all your people" (also Mft and AT); but it is possible that "all who have reverence for you" is another group, larger than "all your people." But the TEV rendering seems preferable: God's people are further defined as those who honor and worship him in prayer and obedience to him.

Both small and great: this can be translated "the weak and the powerful," "the lowly and the famous." Most languages have terms that distinguish between the powerful and the powerless (see also 13.16; 19.5,18; 20.12).

For destroying the destroyers of the earth: these are specifically the pagan rulers of the Roman Empire. Both the verb **destroying** and the noun **destroyers** may mean "for corrupting the corrupters" (see 19.2); but the sense of destroying fits the context here better (compare 8.9). A translation must not give the impression that the writer is talking about people who destroy the environment, making the earth unfit for human habitation; he is talking about those who mistreat and kill people. **Destroying** may be expressed as "killing," "wiping out," or even "wiping from the ground" (Yapese). So one may translate this final clause as "The time has come for you to wipe out (destroy) all those who kill people on earth."

11.19   RSV   TEV

Then God's temple in heaven was opened, and the ark of his covenant was seen within his temple; and there were flashes of lightning, voices, peals of thunder, an earthquake, and heavy hail.

God's temple in heaven was opened, and the Covenant Box was seen there. Then there were flashes of lightning, rumblings and peals of thunder, an earthquake, and heavy hail.

God's temple in heaven was opened: it is to be assumed that an angel opened the door of the heavenly temple. The phrase **God's temple** is used also in 11.1, but there it refers to the Jerusalem Temple; here it is the heavenly temple (see 7.15). Some languages have special words for **opened** that can be both active and passive in this clause; for example, "God's house (temple) in heaven opened up"; but in other languages one may have to say "Someone opened God's temple in heaven."

The ark of his covenant: in the Jerusalem Temple this was the wooden box that contained the two stone tablets on which were inscribed the Ten Commandments. In the Jerusalem Temple the Covenant Box was kept in the Most Holy Place (see 1 Kgs 8.1-9). The Hebrew and Greek words for **covenant** appear many times in the Bible, and a translation should have by now found the appropriate word or phrase to describe this relationship that God and Jesus Christ have established with the people of God. To avoid the passive, this clause may be expressed as "I saw the Covenant Box there."

At the crucifixion of Jesus the heavy curtain that separated the Most Holy Place from the Holy Place was torn in two (Matt 27.51), and also at that time there was an earthquake.

Flashes of lightning, voices, peals of thunder, an earthquake, and heavy hail: see 4.5; 8.5,7.

12.1-18

RSV

1 And a great portent appeared in heaven, a woman clothed with the sun, with the moon under her feet, and on her head a crown of twelve stars; 2 she was with child and she cried out in her pangs of birth, in anguish for delivery. 3 And another portent appeared in heaven; behold, a great red dragon, with seven heads and ten horns, and seven diadems upon his heads. 4 His tail swept down a third of the stars of heaven, and cast them to the earth. And the dragon stood before the woman who was about to bear a child, that he might devour her child when she brought it forth; 5 she brought forth a male child, one who is to rule all the nations with a rod of iron, but her child was caught up to God and to his throne, 6 and the woman fled into the wilderness, where she has a place prepared by God, in which to be nourished for one thousand two hundred and sixty days.

7 Now war arose in heaven, Michael and his angels fighting against the dragon; and the dragon and his angels fought, 8 but they were defeated and there was no longer any place for them in heaven. 9 And the great dragon was thrown down, that ancient serpent, who is called the Devil and Satan, the deceiver of the whole world—he was thrown down to the earth, and his angels were thrown down with him. 10 And I heard a loud voice in heaven, saying, "Now the salvation and the power and the kingdom of our God and the authority of his Christ have come, for the accuser of our brethren has been thrown down, who accuses them day and night before our God. 11 And they have conquered him by the blood of the Lamb and by the word of their testimony, for they loved not their lives even unto death. 12 Rejoice then, O heaven and you that dwell therein! But woe to you, O earth and sea, for the devil has come down to you in great wrath, because he knows that his time is short!"

13 And when the dragon saw that he had

TEV

The Woman and the Dragon

1 Then a great and mysterious sight appeared in the sky. There was a woman, whose dress was the sun and who had the moon under her feet and a crown of twelve stars on her head. 2 She was soon to give birth, and the pains and suffering of childbirth made her cry out.

3 Another mysterious sight appeared in the sky. There was a huge red dragon with seven heads and ten horns and a crown on each of his heads. 4 With his tail he dragged a third of the stars out of the sky and threw them down to the earth. He stood in front of the woman, in order to eat her child as soon as it was born. 5 Then she gave birth to a son, who will rule over all nations with an iron rod. But the child was snatched away and taken to God and his throne. 6 The woman fled to the desert, to a place God had prepared for her, where she will be taken care of for 1,260 days.

7 Then war broke out in heaven. Michael and his angels fought against the dragon, who fought back with his angels; 8 but the dragon was defeated, and he and his angels were not allowed to stay in heaven any longer. 9 The huge dragon was thrown out—that ancient serpent, named the Devil, or Satan, that deceived the whole world. He was thrown down to earth, and all his angels with him.

10 Then I heard a loud voice in heaven saying, "Now God's salvation has come! Now God has shown his power as King! Now his Messiah has shown his authority! For the one who stood before our God and accused our brothers day and night has been thrown out of heaven. 11 Our brothers won the victory over him by the blood of the Lamb and by the truth which they proclaimed; and they were willing to give up their lives and die. 12 And so be glad, you heavens, and all you that live there! But how terrible for the earth and the sea! For the Devil has come down to you, and he is filled with rage, because he knows that he has

been thrown down to the earth, he pursued the woman who had borne the male child. 14 But the woman was given the two wings of the great eagle that she might fly from the serpent into the wilderness, to the place where she is to be nourished for a time, and times, and half a time. 15 The serpent poured water like a river out of his mouth after the woman, to sweep her away with the flood. 16 But the earth came to the help of the woman, and the earth opened its mouth and swallowed the river which the dragon had poured from his mouth. 17 Then the dragon was angry with the woman, and went off to make war on the rest of her offspring, on those who keep the commandments of God and bear testimony to Jesus. And he stood on the sand of the sea.

only a little time left."

13 When the dragon realized that he had been thrown down to the earth, he began to pursue the woman who had given birth to the boy. 14 She was given the two wings of a large eagle in order to fly to her place in the desert, where she will be taken care of for three and a half years, safe from the dragon's attack. 15 And then from his mouth the dragon poured out a flood of water after the woman, so that it would carry her away. 16 But the earth helped the woman; it opened its mouth and swallowed the water that had come from the dragon's mouth. 17 The dragon was furious with the woman and went off to fight against the rest of her descendants, all those who obey God's commandments and are faithful to the truth revealed by Jesus. 18 And the dragon stood on the seashore.

SECTION HEADING: TEV "The Woman and the Dragon." This can be stated as "The vision of the woman and the dragon." In many cultures dragons or similar huge snake-like creatures are well known in the folklore and mythology. However, in cultures where dragons are unknown, since the dragon is the Devil (see verse 9), the section heading may be "The woman and the Devil (or, Satan)."

In some instances a translation may wish to have more than one section for this chapter. The chapter divides quite naturally into verses 1-6, 7-12, 13-18, with the following headings: "The woman and the dragon," "The dragon is expelled from heaven" or "They expel the dragon from heaven," and "The dragon persecutes the woman's descendants."

This vision and the one in chapter 13 do not advance the narrative as such but supply information that allows the reader to understand the part played in the drama by the dragon and the two beasts. The first vision (chapter 12) shows that the reason why Christians suffer persecution now and will suffer even more in days to come is Satan's hatred for the Messiah. Satan's initial defeat and his expulsion from heaven guarantee his ultimate defeat. These are not future events; they are portrayed as having taken place in the past. Unable to kill the woman and her son, the dragon sets out to wage war against "the rest of her descendants," that is, the Christians. They will suffer persecution until the final victory of God and his Messiah.

The second vision (chapter 13) reveals the agents through whom Satan wages war against the Messiah's followers.

The importance of these two chapters in the development of the book is stressed by commentators. G. R. Beasley-Murray has the following to say (page 191):

> These chapters . . . form the central section of the book. Not only do they come at the midpoint of the work, they provide an understanding of the nature of the conflict in which the Church is engaged, and into which John sees she is to be drawn to the limit. The struggle of the saints against the Caesars is here portrayed in the context of an age-long resistance to the God of heaven on the part of evil powers. That process is about to reach its climax in an all out warfare against the Church of Christ. The raging of the powers of

hell, however, terrible as it may be, is shown to be in vain, for in the victory of the crucified and ascended Christ they have been defeated, and their final overthrow is not far distant.

12.1 RSV   TEV

And a great portent appeared in heaven, a woman clothed with the sun, with the moon under her feet, and on her head a crown of twelve stars;

Then a great and mysterious sight appeared in the sky. There was a woman, whose dress was the sun and who had the moon under her feet and a crown of twelve stars on her head.

And a great portent appeared in heaven: the word translated **portent** usually means "sign," "symbol," that is, an object or event that has spiritual significance. As such it is a key word in the Gospel of John (see John 2.11 and throughout the Gospel, where it is translated "sign" in RSV). Here it means "an extraordinary sight," "the appearance of an unusual (or, unique) event." TEV tries to bring out the component of hidden meaning by translating "a great and mysterious sight." Brc has "a sight full of meaning." The adjective **great** here does not refer to size but to its effect, which NIV tries to bring out by translating "A great and wondrous sign." Another possible translation is "A great sign (sight) that amazes everyone."

Here and in verse 3 the writer uses **appeared**, which in Greek is a passive verb, instead of the active "I saw," which he usually employs (see the next vision, 13.1). This is significant, and if possible something like **appeared** in English and other languages should be used. A translation should not say "I saw a mysterious sight . . . ."

In languages that have two different words for heaven, as the dwelling place of God, and the sky, the translation here and in verse 3 should say "the sky" (TEV), not **heaven** (RSV).

A woman clothed with the sun: for the verb **clothed** see "wrapped" in 10.1. It may be difficult to speak of the sun as the garment worn by the woman, but the figure should be maintained: "a woman who had (or, used) the sun around her like a dress (clothes)," or "a woman whose dress was the sun."

The moon under her feet: the picture does not seem to portray the woman as standing on the moon, but that she was seated, and the moon served as a footstool on which she rested her feet. The meaning may be expressed by "and her feet were resting on the moon."

A crown of twelve stars: for **crown** see 4.4. The meaning may be expressed by "a crown made of twelve stars" or "a crown that had twelve stars in it."

12.2 RSV   TEV

she was with child and she cried out in her pangs of birth, in anguish for delivery.

She was soon to give birth, and the pains and suffering of childbirth made her cry out.

This verse is quite wordy, emphasizing the woman's intense suffering as she was giving birth to the child. NRSV is a considerable improvement over the literal rendition of RSV; it reads: "She was pregnant and was crying out in birthpangs, in the agony of giving birth." This is much the same as NJB: "She was pregnant, and in labour, crying aloud in the pangs of childbirth." Something like the following can be said: "The woman was pregnant; she was about to give birth to her child, and her intense labor pains made her cry out." The Greek verb represented by RSV **in anguish** is the one used in 9.5; 11.10, where it means "to cause suffering," "to torture." Here a term should be used that fits the context of childbirth. **Pregnant**: translators should use the most natural term in their language, but it should be one that will not offend readers.

12.3   RSV   TEV

And another portent appeared in heaven; behold, a great red dragon, with seven heads and ten horns, and seven diadems upon his heads. | Another mysterious sight appeared in the sky. There was a huge red dragon with seven heads and ten horns and a crown on each of his heads.

And another portent appeared in heaven: as in verse 1.

Behold, a great red dragon: for **behold** see 1.7. TEV has "There was." It is also possible to say "it (the strange event) was." Here **great** means "large," "huge." The **dragon** was a legendary beast, conceived of as a huge snake, or lizard, and sometimes thought of as living in the ocean depths. It appears in the Old Testament under various names; see Job 7.12 ("sea monster"); Psalm 74.14 ("Leviathan"); 89.10 ("Rahab"); Isaiah 27.1; 51.9. This monster was a figure for the forces of destruction and chaos; here it is identified as Satan (verse 9). In some cultures in Asia the dragon is a symbol of good luck.

With seven heads and ten horns: for **ten horns** (but on a single head) see Daniel 7.7,20. They must be thought of as like the horns of a bull.

Seven diadems upon his heads: this indicates the dragon's great authority. The translation should make clear that each head has one diadem. The Greek word translated **diadems** (NJB "coronet") is different from the word translated "crown" in verse 1. A diadem is a smaller, less elaborate crown. If a language lacks the two different words, it may be possible to say something like "seven small crowns" or "seven small kings' hats (high chiefs' hats)."

12.4   RSV   TEV

His tail swept down a third of the stars of heaven, and cast them to the earth. And the dragon stood before the woman who was about to bear a child, that he might devour her child when she brought it forth; | With his tail he dragged a third of the stars out of the sky and threw them down to the earth. He stood in front of the woman, in order to eat her child as soon as it was born.

His tail swept down: the tail is like that of a crocodile. The verb translated **swept (down)** is the one used in John 21.8 of the disciples dragging to shore the net full of fish. So another way of saying this is "drag down." The phrase may then be expressed as "He used his tail to drag down . . . ."

A third of the stars of heaven: as in the case of the first four trumpets (8.7-12) and the sixth trumpet (9.15,18), the destruction here affects one third of the total. Caird remarks: "The stars are angelic representatives of pagan powers." See 8.7 on the translation of **third**.

And cast them to the earth: see Daniel 8.10. These stars are thrown down from their exalted position. **Cast them** indicates an action where the tail propels the stars down to the earth violently.

The rest of the verse is, as RSV shows, quite redundant. In some languages it may be deemed unnecessary to repeat **who was about to bear a child** or to say literally **when she brought it forth**. Something like the following can be said: "The dragon stood in front of the woman in order to devour her child as soon as it was born." If in some languages there is no neuter term to refer to an unborn child, whose sex is not yet known, it is possible to say "her son," as the next verse specifies.

12.5   RSV   TEV

she brought forth a male child, one who is to rule all the nations with a rod of iron, but her child was caught up to God and to his throne,	Then she gave birth to a son, who will rule over all nations with an iron rod. But the child was snatched away and taken to God and his throne.

She brought forth a male child: the Greek text says "She gave birth to a son, a male," which is quite redundant. NRSV has "She gave birth to a son, a male child," an expression that sounds odd in English. Most translations are like TEV; NJB is able to make it fairly natural, "The woman was delivered of a boy, the son who was . . . ," and in other languages one may translate in a manner similar to TEV and say "The woman gave birth to a son who will . . . ."

One who is to rule all the nations with a rod of iron: this uses the language of Psalm 2.9 and portrays the child as the Messiah, the one who is chosen by God to rule the world (see also Rev 2.27; 19.15). The Greek auxiliary verb translated **is to** may indicate that this will happen soon, or that this is in accordance with God's will; so REB "who is destined to rule" (see comments on the verb translated "are about to" in 2.10). The expression **to rule . . . with a rod of iron** means to rule with complete authority, ruthlessly defeating all enemies. For the verb translated **to rule** see 2.27. **All the nations** may be expressed as "all the people on the earth."

But: instead of being devoured by the dragon, the newborn child was snatched up to heaven. It may be necessary to state this quite explicitly: "But the dragon did not devour the child (or, boy); instead it (or, he) was snatched up to God."

Was caught up to God: the passive is used quite deliberately. If an active form must be used, something like "an angel carried the child up . . ." or "an angel snatched up the child and took him to God . . ." may be said; or else, with God as agent, "God caused the child to go up . . . ." This same verb in the passive is used in similar contexts in Acts 8.39; 2 Corinthians 12.2-3; 1 Thessalonians 4.17.

To God and to his throne: not only is the child taken up to God, but to God as the supreme ruler of the universe, to share God's power. For **throne** see 1.4b. An alternative translation model for this verse is:

> Then she gave birth to a son, who will rule with complete authority over all the people on the earth. But an angel snatched the child (boy) up and took him to God and his throne.

12.6

RSV	TEV
and the woman fled into the wilderness, where she has a place prepared by God, in which to be nourished for one thousand two hundred and sixty days.	The woman fled to the desert, to a place God had prepared for her, where she will be taken care of for 1,260 days.

The woman fled into the wilderness: this **wilderness** or "desert" is presented as a definite place; however, as with other geographical indications, it is not to be identified with any location on earth. This desert is for her a place of refuge, of safety. A **wilderness** or "desert" in the Mideast refers to a desolate area that has no permanent human inhabitants. The only vegetation in such dry and arid places are small bushes or grassy patches where animals can graze. In areas where wildernesses are unknown, one may say, for example, "place where no people live," "the area far away from where people stay," or "rocky place with little vegetation."

Where she has a place prepared by God: the language is vague and general, and the **place** is not to be identified as a house or anything else that specific. The text says quite clearly that God had prepared this place; but it may be understood to mean "a place that God had commanded to be prepared for her." For the verb translated **prepared** see its use in 9.7 ("arrayed"), 15 ("held ready").

In which to be nourished: in Greek the verb is the third plural present of the active voice, "they nourish her." This is the same as an impersonal passive (as the verb appears in verse 14). The verb means not only to provide food, to feed, but in a more general sense "to take care of," "to sustain," "to provide for." In languages that do not use the passive, one may say "where they (unknown agents) will take care of her."

For the time period—1,260 days—see 11.2-3.

12.7

RSV	TEV
Now war arose in heaven, Michael and his angels fighting against the dragon; and the dragon and his angels fought,	Then war broke out in heaven. Michael and his angels fought against the dragon, who fought back with his angels;

Now war arose in heaven: as the context makes clear, this is the dwelling place of God, not the sky. NRSV uses more current English: "And war broke out in heaven." Instead of **war** some translations have "a battle" (FRCL, SPCL). The Greek noun translated **war** is related to the verb "to fight," used twice in this same verse. In certain languages one must express this as "They began to fight one another in heaven."

Michael and his angels: Michael is one of the archangels, who in Daniel 10.21 is identified as the special protector of Israel (and see Jude 9). Michael's angels are those under his command. They are God's heavenly messengers and servants. Another way of expressing this is "One of God's chief messengers (archangel), named Michael, along with other messengers under him, fought against (attacked) the dragon."

It may be more natural to arrange the various items in this verse as follows: "Suddenly war broke out in heaven: the chief angel Michael and his angels attacked the dragon, and the dragon and his angels fought back." If possible, the same word should be used for Michael's **angels** and the dragon's **angels**. In many languages where the term or expression for **angels** is, for example, "God's messengers" or "heavenly messengers," translators must find another expression for **angels** who serve the dragon. In such cases one may say, for example, "and the dragon and his supporters (or, messengers) fought back" or ". . . fought back against Michael."

12.8   RSV   TEV

but they were defeated and there was no   but the dragon was defeated, and he
longer any place for them in heaven.   and his angels were not allowed to stay
                                              in heaven any longer.

But they were defeated: in Greek the verb is singular, not plural: "and he (that is, the dragon) did not prevail (or, win)." Of course the dragon's angels were also defeated, as the next statement makes clear. **Defeated** in certain languages will be rendered as "did not win" or "could not overcome."

There was no longer any place for them in heaven: this is a rather indirect way of saying "they could not stay in heaven any longer." NJB uses the positive form: "they were driven out of heaven." This general statement of fact is made more specific in the verse that follows.

An alternative translation model for this verse is:

> But the dragon did not win, and they (unknown agents) would not
> allow him and his supporters to stay in heaven any longer.

12.9   RSV   TEV

And the great dragon was thrown down,   The huge dragon was thrown out—that
that ancient serpent, who is called the   ancient serpent, named the Devil, or
Devil and Satan, the deceiver of the   Satan, that deceived the whole world. He
whole world—he was thrown down to the   was thrown down to earth, and all his
earth, and his angels were thrown down   angels with him.
with him.

The great dragon: as in verse 3.

Was thrown down: the sense of the Greek verb "throw," without a following preposition, is "was overthrown," that is, from his place of power and prestige. At the end of the verse the Greek text says explicitly "he was thrown to the earth," and the following clause has "and his angels were thrown with him." In all three instances the subject of the verb in the active voice is Michael and his angels; and a language that does not use the passive voice may say this explicitly; for example, "Michael and his supporters threw that huge dragon out of heaven. He is that . . . ."

That ancient serpent: this is a reference to the Devil as the snake in the Garden of Eden (Gen 3.1-15); Wisdom of Solomon 2.24 is the first written text we have that makes this identification: "but through the devil's envy death entered the world . . ." (see also 2 Cor 11.3). The word translated **serpent** is in other contexts rendered "snake"; in Revelation it is used only to refer to the Devil (12.14,15; 20.2). The word **ancient** does not mean primarily that the devil is old, but that he goes back to ancient times, to the primeval days. So TNT and NJB translate "the primeval serpent." One may also say "that serpent (snake) from ancient times."

The Devil and Satan: these are the two titles, the first one the Greek form, meaning "slanderer," "accuser" (see 2.10), and the second one the Hebrew form, meaning "adversary," "opponent" (see 2.9). This is not a double name, as RSV **the Devil and Satan** might be understood; these are two names, "the Devil, or Satan" (TEV, REB, NJB).

The deceiver of the whole world: for the verb "to deceive" see 2.20, where it is translated "to beguile." Some languages express **deceiver** as "the one who makes . . . go astray." Here it means to lead into sin, or into rebellion against God, by means of lies. The Greek noun for **world** is here specifically "the inhabited earth." It means, of course, all the people on earth, and one may express this phrase as "that caused all the people on earth to sin."

As both RSV and TEV show, the text says twice that the dragon was expelled from heaven, he and his angels. In some languages it will not be natural to interrupt the flow of the narrative with the identification of the dragon as the Devil, or Satan, and it may be better to translate somewhat as follows:

> The dragon and his angels were expelled from heaven. That ancient serpent, known as the Devil, or Satan, who causes everyone to sin, was thrown down to earth, together with his angels.

Or:

> Michael and his angels expelled the huge dragon and his supporters from heaven. This dragon is the serpent from ancient times, known as the Devil or Satan, who causes everyone to sin. They threw him down to earth along with all his helpers.

12.10   RSV   TEV

And I heard a loud voice in heaven, saying, "Now the salvation and the

Then I heard a loud voice in heaven saying, "Now God's salvation has power and the kingdom of our God and the authority of his Christ have come, for the accuser of our brethren has been thrown down, who accuses them day and night before our God.

come! Now God has shown his power as King! Now his Messiah has shown his authority! For the one who stood before our God and accused our brothers day and night has been thrown out of heaven.

And I heard a loud voice in heaven: see 10.4; 11.12. John is on earth, the voice comes from heaven. The speaker is not identified, but the phrase **the accuser of our brethren** may lead one to infer that the speaker is one of the martyrs at the foot of the altar in heaven (6.9-11), or else one of the enormous crowd of the redeemed standing in front of the throne of God (7.9-17). But it seems more likely that the speaker is an angel; it should be noticed that in 19.10 the angel says to John "I am a fellow servant of yours and of your brothers." In any case a translation should not try to identify the speaker. However, in some languages one must say "Then I heard someone in heaven speaking with a loud voice, saying . . . ."

Now the salvation and the power and the kingdom of our God . . . have come: the adverb **Now** is quite important and should not be overlooked: "At last God . . . ." It is not very natural to use the verb "to come" with the nouns **salvation** and **power**. Many passages in the New Testament affirm that God's kingdom has come, is coming, or will come, by which is meant that God rules or will rule as king over the world (see 11.15). As for **salvation** (see 7.10), it will most often be necessary to use a verbal phrase, "God will now save his people." Some scholars believe that **salvation** here means "victory": "God has now won the victory." It seems preferable to express the idea of **salvation**. As for **power** (see 3.8), it is to be noticed that TEV connects this with the following **kingdom**: "God has shown his power as King!" Or it is possible to say "God will now use his power and rule as king over the world" (see 11.17). The verbal phrase **have come** translates the same verb used in 11.15, but here it is used in the sense "have come into existence."

In the same way **the authority of his Christ** must be translated "and his Messiah will now exercise his authority over the world." For **authority** see 2.26; for **his Christ** see 11.15. This phrase may also be rendered as "and his chosen Savior will now use his authority."

For the accuser of our brethren . . . who accuses them day and night: this describes the Devil either as a prosecuting attorney in the heavenly court, who tries to get God to condemn people (see Job 1.6-12; Zech 3.1-4), or else as one who appears in court to testify against the person on trial (accusers in court are mentioned in Acts 23.30,35; 25.16,18). **Accuses** may also be rendered as "tell what they have done wrong." In at least one language it is expressed as "break word on someone." Here **our brethren** should be made inclusive of both genders, "our fellow believers," "our brothers and sisters," since it is not restricted to males.

Day and night before our God: the phrase **day and night** may be rendered "continuously," "without ceasing"; the possessive **our** is inclusive.

A possible model for ordering the various elements in this verse may be as follows:

Then I heard someone in heaven say in a loud voice: "Now our God will save his people! (or, Now our God has won the victory!) Now he will use his power and rule as king! Now his Messiah will assert his authority over the world! For the Devil no longer stands in the presence of our God, accusing our fellow servants day and night. The Devil has been thrown out of heaven!"

12.11   RSV   TEV

And they have conquered him by the blood of the Lamb and by the word of their testimony, for they loved not their lives even unto death.	Our brothers won the victory over him by the blood of the Lamb and by the truth which they proclaimed; and they were willing to give up their lives and die.

In order to make clear who is the subject of this verse, it may be well to imitate TEV: "Our fellow servants (or, Our brothers and sisters) have defeated him (the Devil) . . . ."

They have conquered him: for the verb see 2.7. Here the defeat of the Devil is attributed to the faithful believers, the followers of Jesus Christ.

By the blood of the Lamb: see 1.5; 5.9; 7.14. By means of the sacrificial death of Jesus Christ, believers are able to defeat Satan.

By the word of their testimony: this, of course, is the gospel; "by means of the message they announced" or "by means of the truth they proclaimed" (see 1.2,9). In certain languages it will be well to reorder these clauses and say "The blood of the Lamb and the true message that they proclaimed let them (caused them to) have the victory over the Devil." In other languages **the word of their testimony** has been translated as "the word of God that they proclaim."

For they loved not their lives even unto death: this is not too clear in English; NRSV is better: "for they did not cling to life even in the face of death" (see Mark 8.35; John 12.25). The force of the statement is that they were willing to pay the price of martyrdom in order to be faithful to Jesus Christ. It may be that RSV **for** (also TNT; NJB "because") correctly interprets the Greek conjunction, which is normally understood to mean "and." But it is difficult to understand how **for** relates to what precedes. It seems better to interpret as TEV has done (also REB, RNAB, SPCL, TOB), as an additional reason, or as the underlying attitude that enabled them to defeat Satan. One may also say "and they were even willing to die if necessary," "holding their lives lightly, they were prepared to die," or "They said, 'Let them kill us (if need be).' They did not fear death."

12.12   RSV   TEV

Rejoice then, O heaven and you that dwell therein! But woe to you, O earth and sea, for the devil has come down to you in great wrath, because he knows that his time is short!"	And so be glad, you heavens, and all you that live there! But how terrible for the earth and the sea! For the Devil has come down to you, and he is filled with rage, because he knows that he has only a little time left."

Rejoice then, O heaven: the Greek verb is the same one translated "make merry" in 11.10. Even though "all you that live there" (TEV) is added, it may be impossible in some languages to address heaven as such and exhort it to be glad; so it may be necessary to say "All of you who live in heaven must rejoice" or "Be happy, all who live in heaven." Heaven's inhabitants are the angels. For the verb "to dwell" see comments on its use in 7.15, where it is translated "shelter."

Woe to you, O earth and sea: for **woe** see 8.13. Here as well, the emphasis is on the terrible fate that will befall the people of the world. In this context it is possible to translate "Those who live on earth and in the sea will suffer terribly." By **earth and sea** the writer means those who live on earth and in the sea. So it may be necessary to translate "How terrible it will be for those who live on earth and in the sea!" "The earth and the sea" is a way of speaking of the whole planet Earth. For the translation of **earth and sea**, see 7.1.

The devil has come down to you: here it is important to establish the point of reference. The voice proclaims this from heaven, and so it may be better to say "has gone down to you." Mft translates "has descended to you," and AT "has descended upon you."

In great wrath: this may be rendered "extremely angry," "furious," "has a very hot heart (liver)."

He knows that his time is short: this should not be translated in such a way as to imply that the Devil knows that he will soon die. He knows that he doesn't have much more time to carry on his work of deceiving people (verse 9). This may be translated "he knows that he doesn't have much more time to act," "he knows that he will soon be stopped."

An alternative translation model for this verse is:

> All you who live in heaven should rejoice (be very glad). But you who live on the earth and in the sea will suffer terribly. For the Devil has come (gone) down to you, and his heart is very hot because he knows that he doesn't have much more time to act.

12.13 RSV	TEV
And when the dragon saw that he had been thrown down to the earth, he pursued the woman who had borne the male child.	When the dragon realized that he had been thrown down to the earth, he began to pursue the woman who had given birth to the boy.

In verses 13-16 the writer speaks again of the dragon's attempt to kill the woman. It is not clear how this relates to the attempt described in verses 4-6, but the precise relation between the two cannot be indicated in translation. This is presented here as a later attempt.

When the dragon saw: the verb "to see" has here the meaning "to perceive," "to understand," "to become aware of," "to realize" (TEV, FRCL).

He had been thrown down to the earth: exactly as it is stated in verse 9b.

He pursued the woman who had borne the male child: here again the information **who had borne the male child** may be quite redundant in some languages and may be omitted. There is no other woman in this scene. The verb "to pursue" means to follow after or chase after, with hostile intent.

12.14   RSV   TEV

But the woman was given the two wings of the great eagle that she might fly from the serpent into the wilderness, to the place where she is to be nourished for a time, and times, and half a time.	She was given the two wings of a large eagle in order to fly to her place in the desert, where she will be taken care of for three and a half years, safe from the dragon's attack.

The woman was given: either by an angel or by God. In certain languages one may avoid the passive by saying "she received," but in other languages it will be necessary to translate as "someone gave her," or even "they gave the woman."

The two wings of the great eagle: again the RSV literal translation **the great eagle** makes it appear that the writer had a specific, large eagle in mind. So it is better to translate "the (two) wings of a large eagle." For **eagle** see 4.7. This clause may be rendered as "They gave the wings of a large eagle to the woman so that she could fly . . . ."

She might fly . . . into the wilderness: for **wilderness** see verse 6. In Greek the phrase translated **from the serpent** comes at the end of the verse; literally it reads "from the face (that is, the presence) of the serpent." Instead of connecting it with the verb "to fly," TEV takes it to mean "safe from the serpent's attack" (also FRCL, BRCL; note TNT "away from the serpent," and REB "out of reach of the serpent"). This seems preferable to RSV and others.

From the serpent: the text switches from "the dragon" in verse 13 to "the serpent" in verses 14-15, and then back to "the dragon" in verses 16-17. A translation should feel free to keep "the dragon" in all passages, if translating the text literally proves confusing to the readers.

The place where she is to be nourished: as in verse 6.

A time, and times, and half a time: this is a way of saying "a year, two years, and half a year," an expression used in Daniel 7.25; 12.7, to indicate a limited period of intense suffering. It is the same as forty-two months or 1,260 days (see 11.2-3).

An alternative translation model for this verse is:

> She received (or, they gave her) the wings of a large eagle so that she could fly to her place in the desert. There they (unknown agents) will take care of her for three and a half years, and the dragon will not be able to hurt her.

12.15   RSV   TEV

The serpent poured water like a river out of his mouth after the woman, to sweep her away with the flood.	And then from his mouth the dragon poured out a flood of water after the woman, so that it would carry her away.

The serpent: or "The dragon" (as in verses 13-14, above).

Poured water like a river out of his mouth: in English the verb "to spew" is the most natural one in such a context: "spewed a flood of water from his mouth." The verb in Greek in most contexts means simply "to throw."

To sweep her away with the flood: this translates the Greek "to make her waterborne," that is, to float her away.

Alternative translation models for this verse are:

> Then the dragon spewed water out of his mouth like a river that flowed after that woman, so that it would make her float away.

Or:

> In order to let the water carry the woman off, the snake (or, dragon) spewed a great water out of its mouth after her.

12.16   RSV   TEV

But the earth came to the help of the woman, and the earth opened its mouth and swallowed the river which the dragon had poured from his mouth.

But the earth helped the woman; it opened its mouth and swallowed the water that had come from the dragon's mouth.

The earth came to the help of the woman: it may not be natural to speak of the earth acting like a living being, but in most cultures there are stories that include fantastic events such as this one. Here it is necessary to say only "The earth helped the woman"; the Greek text does not suggest the sort of movement implied by RSV **came to the help**. The word chosen to translate **earth** here should indicate the land, or the soil, not the planet Earth.

Opened its mouth: see similar language in Genesis 4.11. If the figure of the earth opening its mouth is too strange, it may be better to say "A large opening appeared in the earth . . . ." But this diminishes the vividness of the account; it is much better to retain the mythological language of the text, or to find an idiomatic way to express the dramatic nature of these events.

At the end of the verse, RSV **had poured** translates the same verb used at the beginning of verse 15.

12.17   RSV   TEV

Then the dragon was angry with the woman, and went off to make war on the rest of her offspring, on those who keep the commandments of God and bear testimony to Jesus. [18] And he stood^e on the sand of the sea.

The dragon was furious with the woman and went off to fight against the rest of her descendants, all those who obey God's commandments and are faithful to the truth revealed by Jesus.

e Other ancient authorities read *And I
stood,* connecting the sentence with 13.1

In RSV the last verse of this chapter is numbered 17, and it includes what
appears as verse 18 in TEV. But NRSV has verse 18 also, in agreement with the
United Bible Societies' Greek New Testament.

The dragon was angry with the woman: the Greek verb "to be angry"
appears in Revelation only here and in 11.18, where it is translated "raged"; see the
related noun "anger," "wrath" in 6.16,17; 11.18.

He went off to make war: see the similar expression in verse 7.

The rest of her offspring: these "other descendants" are in addition to her
son (verses 5,13); they are the faithful Christians, as the next statement makes clear.
In certain languages **her offspring** will be expressed as "her children and grandchil-
dren" or "those who came down from her."

Keep the commandments of God and bear testimony to Jesus: here the
verb "to keep" means "to obey" (see 1.3). And for **bear testimony to Jesus**, the
Greek has "and have (or, hold) the testimony of Jesus," which may be translated as
TEV has it, "are faithful to the truth revealed by Jesus." See the discussion of
"testimony of Jesus Christ" in 1.2, where it is taken to mean "truth coming from
Jesus Christ."

12.18   RSV   TEV

[18] And he stood*e* on the sand of the   And the dragon stood*e* on the seashore.
sea.

                                                 e And the dragon stood; *some manu-*
e Other ancient authorities read *And I   scripts have* And I stood, *connecting this*
stood,* connecting the sentence with 13.1   *verse with what follows.*

And he stood on the sand of the sea: as the RSV and TEV footnotes show,
some Greek manuscripts and early versions have "I stood" and connect this with
what follows in chapter 13. But **he stood** has stronger textual evidence in its favor
and should be followed. Again **the sea** does not indicate a specific sea; so something
like TEV "the seashore" or "the beach" may be better.

13.1-18

              RSV   TEV
                                                      The Two Beasts

1 And I saw a beast rising out of the sea,   1 Then I saw a beast coming up out of the
with ten horns and seven heads, with ten diadems   sea. It had ten horns and seven heads; on each of
upon its horns and a blasphemous name upon its   its horns there was a crown, and on each of its
heads. 2 And the beast that I saw was like a   heads there was a name that was insulting to God.
leopard, its feet were like a bear's, and its mouth 2 The beast looked like a leopard, with feet like a
was like a lion's mouth. And to it the dragon gave   bear's feet and a mouth like a lion's mouth. The
his power and his throne and great authority.   dragon gave the beast his own power, his throne,
3 One of its heads seemed to have a mortal   and his vast authority. 3 One of the heads of the
wound, but its mortal wound was healed, and the   beast seemed to have been fatally wounded, but

whole earth followed the beast with wonder. 4 Men worshiped the dragon, for he had given his authority to the beast, and they worshiped the beast, saying, "Who is like the beast, and who can fight against it?"

5 And the beast was given a mouth uttering haughty and blasphemous words, and it was allowed to exercise authority for forty-two months; 6 it opened its mouth to utter blasphemies against God, blaspheming his name and his dwelling, that is, those who dwell in heaven. 7 Also it was allowed to make war on the saints and to conquer them. And authority was given it over every tribe and people and tongue and nation, 8 and all who dwell on earth will worship it, every one whose name has not been written before the foundation of the world in the book of life of the Lamb that was slain. 9 If any one has an ear, let him hear:

10   If any one is to be taken captive,
          to captivity he goes;
      if any one slays with the sword,
          with the sword must he be slain.

Here is a call for the endurance and faith of the saints.

11 Then I saw another beast which rose out of the earth; it had two horns like a lamb and it spoke like a dragon. 12 It exercises all the authority of the first beast in its presence, and makes the earth and its inhabitants worship the first beast, whose mortal wound was healed. 13 It works great signs, even making fire come down from heaven to earth in the sight of men; 14 and by the signs which it is allowed to work in the presence of the beast, it deceives those who dwell on earth, bidding them make an image for the beast which was wounded by the sword and yet lived; 15 and it was allowed to give breath to the image of the beast so that the image of the beast should even speak, and to cause those who would not worship the image of the beast to be slain. 16 Also it causes all, both small and great, both rich and poor, both free and slave, to be marked on the right hand or the forehead, 17 so that no one can buy or sell unless he has the mark, that is, the name of the beast or the number of its name. 18 This calls for wisdom: let him who has understanding reckon the number of the beast, for it is a human number, its number is six hundred and sixty-six.

the wound had healed. The whole earth was amazed and followed the beast. 4 Everyone worshiped the dragon because he had given his authority to the beast. They worshiped the beast also, saying, "Who is like the beast? Who can fight against it?"

5 The beast was allowed to make proud claims which were insulting to God, and it was permitted to have authority for forty-two months. 6 It began to curse God, his name, the place where he lives, and all those who live in heaven. 7 It was allowed to fight against God's people and to defeat them, and it was given authority over every tribe, nation, language, and race. 8 All people living on earth will worship it, except those whose names were written before the creation of the world in the book of the living which belongs to the Lamb that was killed.

9 "Listen, then, if you have ears! 10 Whoever is meant to be captured will surely be captured; whoever is meant to be killed by the sword will surely be killed by the sword. This calls for endurance and faith on the part of God's people."

11 Then I saw another beast, which came up out of the earth. It had two horns like a lamb's horns, and it spoke like a dragon. 12 It used the vast authority of the first beast in its presence. It forced the earth and all who live on it to worship the first beast, whose wound had healed. 13 This second beast performed great miracles; it made fire come down out of heaven to earth in the sight of everyone. 14 And it deceived all the people living on earth by means of the miracles which it was allowed to perform in the presence of the first beast. The beast told them to build an image in honor of the beast that had been wounded by the sword and yet lived. 15 The second beast was allowed to breathe life into the image of the first beast, so that the image could talk and put to death all those who would not worship it. 16 The beast forced all the people, small and great, rich and poor, slave and free, to have a mark placed on their right hands or on their foreheads. 17 No one could buy or sell unless he had this mark, that is, the beast's name or the number that stands for the name.

18 This calls for wisdom. Whoever is intelligent can figure out the meaning of the number of the beast, because the number stands for a man's name. Its number is 666.

SECTION HEADING: TEV "The Two Beasts." For translation suggestions on "beasts" see the first paragraph of comments on 13.1.

13.1   RSV   TEV

And I saw a beast rising out of the sea, with ten horns and seven heads, with ten diadems upon its horns and a blasphemous name upon its heads.

Then I saw a beast coming up out of the sea. It had ten horns and seven heads; on each of its horns there was a crown, and on each of its heads there was a name that was insulting to God.

A beast: see 11.7, which speaks of the beast that came out of the abyss (see also 17.8); the beast here comes out of the sea. It is possible that the two are the same beast, since "the abyss" was often used to refer to the depths of the ocean. In any case the translated text will not establish any clear relationship between the two. **Beast**, in certain languages where there are only the two categories, domesticated or wild, will need defining phrases such as "a terrible wild animal," "a huge, horrible animal," or even "a frightening, savage animal."

Rising out of the sea: as in 10.2, it is futile to try to identify this as a specific body of water (see Dan 7.3).

Ten horns . . . seven heads . . . ten diadems upon its horns: like the dragon (12.3) this marine beast has seven heads and ten horns; but unlike the dragon this beast has a diadem on each of its ten horns. These diadems indicate his royal status. For **diadems** see 12.3.

A blasphemous name upon its heads: RSV translates a Greek text that has the singular **name**; TEV translates a text that has the plural "names." The text translated by TEV is preferable, and the translation can be, like TEV, "a name on each of its heads" or "names on its heads." Here **blasphemous** means "insulting to God" (see "slander" in 2.9). The common interpretation is that these are names, or titles, that should be used only of God, such as "Lord," "God," "Almighty," "Divine," "Worthy of Worship." These seven heads represent seven rulers (see 17.9-10) who claim divine rank. If this interpretation is correct, then the meaning of **blasphemous** or "insulting" in this context means "to bring dishonor to God," "to mock God," or "be an affront to God." So an alternative translation model for this final clause is "and on each of its heads there was a name that was an affront to (or, mocked) God."

13.2   RSV   TEV

And the beast that I saw was like a leopard, its feet were like a bear's, and its mouth was like a lion's mouth. And to it the dragon gave his power and his throne and great authority.

The beast looked like a leopard, with feet like a bear's feet and a mouth like a lion's mouth. The dragon gave the beast his own power, his throne, and his vast authority.

And the beast that I saw: the relative clause **that I saw** is another example of needless redundancy in this book and may be omitted in translation in many languages.

A leopard: where this animal is unknown, it may be necessary to speak of a tiger, or a jaguar, or another of the large cats, with the exception of a lion, which also appears in this verse. See *Fauna and Flora*, pages 48–49, for a detailed description of a leopard. In cultures where such large cats are unknown, a picture for the readers will be helpful.

Its feet were like a bear's: instead of **feet**, "paws" is more naturally used of a bear (so NJB). Where the bear is unknown, the text may have to describe the beast's feet as big and hairy, with long, sharp claws. In such cultures a generic term for bear may be used; for example, "a wild animal named 'bear.' " In such a case a picture and a description in the glossary should also be used. See also *Fauna and Flora*, pages 8–9. An alternative translation of this sentence is "Its feet were big and hairy, with long, sharp claws like those of the wild animal named 'bear.' "

Its mouth was like a lion's mouth: a large, powerful mouth, with sharp teeth.

The dragon gave his power and his throne and great authority: all three describe the vast authority of the dragon, which he confers on the beast. For **power** see 3.8; **throne**, 1.4; 2.13; **authority**, 2.26, where it is translated "powers." If the statement that he **gave . . . his throne** might be taken literally, it will be necessary to express the idea of **his power and his throne** by "his royal power" or "his power as king (or, ruler)." Perhaps one may combine these three terms and say "The dragon let the beast have his own power and great authority to rule as king."

The concept of the transfer of power and authority must not be stated in such terms as to imply that from then on the dragon had no power. So in some instances it may be helpful to say "The dragon shared with the beast his royal power and his great authority," or "The dragon caused the beast to have as much royal power and great authority as he himself had," or "The dragon let the beast have as much power to rule and great authority as . . . ." From now on the beast is the dragon's deputy, his lieutenant, with authority to speak and to act in the name of the dragon.

13.3 RSV	TEV
One of its heads seemed to have a mortal wound, but its mortal wound was healed, and the whole earth followed the beast with wonder.	One of the heads of the beast seemed to have been fatally wounded, but the wound had healed. The whole earth was amazed and followed the beast.

One of its heads: it must be clear that this refers to the beast; the dragon also had seven heads.

Seemed to have a mortal wound: the meaning is, rather, "had a wound that seemed to be fatal (or, mortal)." The English adjective **mortal** translates the perfect passive participle of the verb "to kill" (see its use in TEV 5.6: "The Lamb appeared to have been killed"). Here it means that it appeared that one of the heads had been killed, but the text goes on to say that "his deadly wound had healed," implying that there was a scar that showed how severe the wound had been. Whether or not the wound had been fatal depends on how verse 14 is understood.

The whole earth followed the beast with wonder: the Greek text says "The whole earth marveled after the beast." The verb means "to wonder," "to marvel," "to be amazed." For **the whole earth** it is better to say "everyone on earth" or "all the people of the world."

Alternative translation models for the first part of this verse are:

On one of the heads of the beast was a scar that seemed to have been the result of a fatal (or, mortal) wound. But the wound had healed.

Or:

... the scar from a wound that should have killed it (or, caused it to die). But ....

13.4

RSV   TEV

Men worshiped the dragon, for he had given his authority to the beast, and they worshiped the beast, saying, "Who is like the beast, and who can fight against it?"

Everyone worshiped the dragon because he had given his authority to the beast. They worshiped the beast also, saying, "Who is like the beast? Who can fight against it?"

Men worshiped the dragon: after saying, in verse 3, "the whole earth," this verse begins "They worshiped." This should be stated inclusively, "They all" or "Everyone." For the verb "to worship" see 4.10. The full meaning of **worshiped** is intended; the people who followed the dragon worshiped him as their God, and in the same way they worshiped the beast.

Who is like the beast, and who can fight against it? This rhetorical double question is a way of saying "No one is like the beast" or "No one is as strong (or, powerful) as the beast"—since it is his power and strength that are in focus. "No one can fight against it," that is, "... fight against it and win." This is practically a psalm sung in praise of the great beast (see similar expressions of praise to God in Exo 15.11; Psa 35.10; 113.5).

An alternative translation model for this verse is:

They all showed reverence to the dragon as if he were God, because he had let the beast have authority. They also worshiped the beast, saying, "No one is as strong as the beast. No one can fight against it and win."

13.5

RSV   TEV

And the beast was given a mouth uttering haughty and blasphemous words, and it was allowed to exercise authority for forty-two months;

The beast was allowed to make proud claims which were insulting to God, and it was permitted to have authority for forty-two months.

The beast was given a mouth: here **mouth** represents the power of speech; "was allowed to speak," "received the ability (or, power) to speak." The passive verb points to God as the one who allows the beast to speak. So in those languages that do not use the passive, one may say "God allowed the beast to ...."

Uttering haughty and blasphemous words: the Greek text says "great (utterances) and blasphemies," which may be understood to mean "outrageous blasphemies." For "blasphemy" see verse 1. For the whole statement see Daniel 7.8, 20,25. As translated by TEV, the "proud claims" were themselves insults to God. The idea is that the beast was claiming rights and authority that belong only to God. One may also render this as "boast about his authority and thus insult God."

It was allowed to exercise authority: again, God is in control; "God allowed the beast to have authority."

Forty-two months: see 11.2-3.

Alternative translation models for languages that do not use the passive are:

> The beast received the right to boast about himself and thus insult God. He received authority to act for forty-two months.

Or:

> God allowed the beast to boast about his authority and thus insult him (God). God permitted him to have this authority for forty-two months.

13.6	RSV	TEV
	it opened its mouth to utter blasphemies against God, blaspheming his name and his dwelling, that is, those who dwell in heaven.	It began to curse God, his name, the place where he lives, and all those who live in heaven.

It opened its mouth: in this context **it opened its mouth** means simply "it spoke" or "it began to speak." This sentence carries on from the previous verse and specifies the outrageous blasphemies the beast began to utter. **Utter blasphemies**: in some languages this phrase will be rendered as "say bad (or, evil) things about God." In English "to insult" or "to curse" conveys adequately the meaning of the verb.

Blaspheming his name: this is an insult directed at the titles or names by which God is known.

His dwelling, that is, those who dwell in heaven: the Greek text says "to blaspheme his name and his dwelling, those who live in heaven." RSV takes **those who dwell in heaven** in apposition with **his dwelling**—a common device in this book. TEV takes it as an additional object of the verb (also NJB, NIV, FRCL, SPCL, BRCL, Phps, RNAB). REB, Mft, and AT are like RSV. In all it seems better to imitate RSV: **those who live in heaven** is an explanation of what the author means by "God's dwelling." In Greek the noun translated **dwelling** and the verb translated "to dwell" are related; for the verb see its use in making a shelter in 7.15 (see also 21.3). It is impossible to determine precisely who are included among **those who dwell in heaven**. The translation should not try to be specific. Some commentators say that the phrase stands in deliberate contrast with "those who live on earth" (a different verb is used), that is, those who are God's people as opposed to those who are not.

13.7   RSV   TEV

Also it was allowed to make war on the   It was allowed to fight against God's
saints and to conquer them.[f] And au-   people and to defeat them, and it was
thority was given it over every tribe and given authority over every tribe, nation,
people and tongue and nation,   language, and race.

[f] Other ancient authorities omit this
sentence

It was allowed: as in verse 5; God allowed it, that is, the beast.

To make war on the saints and to conquer them: for **to make war** see 2.16,
where the glorified Christ threatens to fight the Nicolaitans in the church in
Pergamum; for **saints** see 5.8; for **conquer** see 2.7. See the similar statement in
Daniel 7.21.

As the RSV footnote shows, some Greek manuscripts and early versions omit
this sentence; but the evidence for its genuineness is very strong.

Authority was given it: God gave him this authority.

Every tribe and people and tongue and nation: see 5.9; 7.9; 11.9.

13.8   RSV   TEV

and all who dwell on earth will worship   All people living on earth will worship it,
it, every one whose name has not been   except those whose names were written
written before the foundation of the   before the creation of the world in the
world in the book of life of the Lamb   book of the living which belongs to the
that was slain.   Lamb that was killed.

All who dwell on earth: the same expression is used in 3.10; 6.10; 8.13; 11.10.

Every one whose name has not been written: it may be better to imitate
TEV and refer to those whose names *had* been written: "All the people in the world
will worship him, except those whose names had been written . . . ." Or it may be
better to have two complete sentences: "Almost everyone will worship the beast. But
some will not worship him; those who have their names written . . . will not worship
him."

**Not been written before the foundation of the world in the book of life of
the Lamb that was slain**: for **the book of life** see 3.5; for **the Lamb that was
slain**, see 5.6,9.

In Greek the phrase "from the foundation of the earth" comes at the end of
the verse, immediately following **the Lamb that was slain**. Most translations, relying
in part on 17.8, connect "from the foundation of the earth" with the verbal phrase
been written. See TEV "except those whose names were written before the creation
of the world in the book of the living." Some, however, connect it with "the Lamb
that was slain": Phps, NIV, and REB (a change from NEB); and this understanding of
the verse is supported by some commentators (for example, Sweet, Caird) who point
out that such a statement is not without parallel in other New Testament passages
(see especially 1 Peter 1.19-20). A translator must decide which interpretation to

follow; it may be possible to have one in the text and the other one in a footnote. All in all, it seems preferable to go along with RSV, TEV, and others.

The various items of information should be properly related to one another in terms of the development of the narrative. Something like the following may serve as a model for this verse:

> Everyone on earth will worship him, except those whose names were written in the book of the living before the world was created. That book belongs to the Lamb who was killed.

Or:

> . . . whose names were recorded in the book in which God has written down before the world was created the names of those who really have life. That book belongs to the Lamb whom people killed.

13.9-10 RSV	TEV

9 If any one has an ear, let him hear:
10   If any one is to be taken captive,
      to captivity he goes;
   if any one slays with the sword,
      with the sword must he be
         slain.
Here is a call for the endurance and faith of the saints.
	9 "Listen, then, if you have ears!
	10 Whoever is meant to be captured will surely be captured; whoever is meant to be killed by the sword will surely be killed by the sword. This calls for endurance and faith on the part of God's people."

In these two verses the writer issues a warning to his readers. He seems to be speaking consciously as a prophet. TEV places the two verses within quotation marks in order to make clear that the two verses are directed at the readers of the book; also similar is FRCL.

If any one has an ear, let him hear: this is like the exhortation at the end of each of the letters to the seven churches in chapters 2–3 (see 2.7,11, and the others).

The translator may consider translating the next sentence as poetry, as RSV does (see Section F in the introduction, "Translating the Revelation to John," pages 6 and following).

If any one is to be taken captive, to captivity he goes: for this and the next statement, see Jeremiah 15.2; 43.11. The meaning here is that any believer who is destined by God to be imprisoned will surely be imprisoned. It is likely that this is more than an affirmation that such a person's arrest and imprisonment is inevitable; it is a way of counseling that person to submit to arrest and imprisonment, without trying to escape his or her God-given destiny. In languages that do not use the passive, one may say, for example, "Whoever must be a captive will be one" or "Whomever God has destined for them (unknown agents) to take captive will be a captive."

If any one slays with the sword, with the sword must he be slain: this translates a Greek text that is different from the text translated by TEV. The text translated by TEV (UBS Greek New Testament) is based on one very important early

Greek manuscript; the other text is supported by most Greek manuscripts and early versions. It is interesting that most modern translations are like TEV; of those consulted, only Mft, Phps, AT, and NRSV agree with RSV. But most commentaries consulted (Swete; Beckwith; Caird; Sweet; Beasley-Murray) agree with the RSV text; only Charles differs.

The internal evidence favors the text translated by TEV, because it is a parallel to the first part of the verse (and see Jer 15.2; 43.11). The RSV text expresses a thought like the one found in Matthew 26.52, a warning to Christians not to use a sword in their own defense. It is impossible to be dogmatic about which text is to be preferred; everything considered, it is recommended that the text translated by TEV be followed.

Killed by the sword is referring to people being executed for their beliefs. So it is possible to translate "Those persons whom God destines to be executed will be executed" or ". . . for people to kill (or, execute) will suffer execution."

Here is a call for the endurance and faith of the saints: see 14.12 for a similar statement. The Greek text says simply "Here is the endurance and the faith of the saints." This is not so much a statement of fact as an exhortation, "This means that the saints must endure and be faithful." Awareness of the fact that it is God's will that many of them be imprisoned and slain calls for endurance and faith on their part. For **endurance** see 1.9, and for **faith** see 2.19. It is probable that here the Greek word means "faithfulness," as NIV, BRCL, and REB translate it; RNAB translates the whole phrase "faithful endurance." For **saints** see 5.8. So one may translate "This means that God's people must endure faithfully."

13.11   RSV   TEV

Then I saw another beast which rose out of the earth; it had two horns like a lamb and it spoke like a dragon.

Then I saw another beast, which came up out of the earth. It had two horns like a lamb's horns, and it spoke like a dragon.

A translator may wish to begin a new section here that will go through verse 18 (see the beginning of this chapter). This section deals with another beast, one that **rose out of the earth**.

Two horns like a lamb: these horns are small and inoffensive and depict this beast as a gentle creature. **Lamb** in certain languages will be rendered as "young male sheep" or "a baby sheep."

It spoke like a dragon: it is not certain what this implies, whether its speech was loud and harsh or gentle and persuasive, as was the snake's in the Garden of Eden. This is the opinion of most commentators, but a dragon is rarely portrayed as a soft-spoken creature. It seems better to have the dragon speak harshly and furiously, if the translation must be explicit.

13.12

RSV	TEV
It exercises all the authority of the first beast in its presence, and makes the earth and its inhabitants worship the first beast, whose mortal wound was healed.	It used the vast authority of the first beast in its presence. It forced the earth and all who live on it to worship the first beast, whose wound had healed.

It exercises: as RSV shows, the writer switches from the past tense in verse 11 to the present tense in verses 12-18. Among major modern translations, only Mft, AT, Phps, RSV, and NRSV make this change; most continue, as does TEV, to use the past tense. A translator must decide here, as elsewhere, what effect the shift of tense will have on the reader.

It exercises all the authority of the first beast in its presence: the second beast acts as the representative, the deputy, of the first beast. It can act with all the authority of the first beast, who had received its authority from the dragon (verse 2). In the presence of the first beast, the second beast enforces the wishes of the first beast. **All the authority** can be expressed as "the wide-reaching authority." **In its presence** may be rendered as "before the eyes (or, face) of the first beast" or "while it is with the first beast."

Makes the earth and its inhabitants worship the first beast: as in the case of "heaven and you that dwell therein" in 12.12, here it may be necessary to say "it forces all the people in the world to worship the first beast." For the phrase **its inhabitants** see the similar expression "all who dwell on earth" in verse 8.

Whose mortal wound was healed: see verse 3.

13.13

RSV	TEV
It works great signs, even making fire come down from heaven to earth in the sight of men;	This second beast performed great miracles; it made fire come down out of heaven to earth in the sight of everyone.

It works great signs: it should be clear to the reader that the subject is the second beast, not the first one. Here **signs** means "amazing things," "miracles," "prodigies," "great acts of power that amaze people" (see Matt 24.24; 2 Thes 2.9). For **signs** see also "portent" in 12.1.

Even making fire come down from heaven to earth: this is reminiscent of the prophet Elijah (1 Kgs 18.36-39; see Luke 9.54).

In the sight of men: this must be made inclusive of men and women: "before the face of everyone," "in the presence of everyone," or "so that everybody saw it."

13.14

RSV	TEV
and by the signs which it is allowed to work in the presence of the beast, it deceives those who dwell on earth, bid-	And it deceived all the people living on earth by means of the miracles which it was allowed to perform in the presence

ding them make an image for the beast | of the first beast. The beast told them to
which was wounded by the sword and | build an image in honor of the beast
yet lived; | that had been wounded by the sword
| and yet lived.

By the signs . . . it deceives those who dwell on earth: for **deceives** see
2.20, where the same Greek word is translated "is beguiling," and see "deceiver" in
12.9. Care must be taken that there is no confusion on the identity of the two beasts;
if necessary the translation can say here "the second beast is allowed." Again the
phrase **those who dwell on earth** is used of those who are not God's people (see
its use in 3.10; 6.10; 8.13; 13.8,12).

It is allowed to work: the passive indicates that only by God's consent was the
second beast able to perform its miracles. So one may translate "God allowed it to
do its work."

In the presence of the beast: here **the beast** is the first beast of 13.1-8. The
picture seems to be that of the second beast performing the miracles while the first
beast looked on, much like a master magician performing in the presence of the king.

Bidding them make an image: this is the specific way in which the second
beast deceived people: it led them into idolatry. **Bidding** may be rendered as
"commanded" or "ordered." The word translated **image** may be translated "idol"
or "statue" (Mft, AT, Phps). See also 2.14.

It deceives: see comments under 2.20, where it is translated "is beguiling."

For the beast: here it is better to say "in honor of the beast"; it appears that
this was a statue of the first beast that people were to worship, as seems clear from
the information in the following verse about breathing life into this image. To make
this explicit one may also say "in honor of that first beast."

Which was wounded by the sword and yet lived: the text seems to mean,
more precisely, "that was mortally wounded (or, put to death) by the sword and came
back to life" or "that someone had killed with a sword, and it . . . ." The meaning
is not that the beast survived a serious wound, but that it came back to life after
having been killed (see a similar statement in 2.8, where the same form of the verb
"to live" is used). Of major modern translations, however, only Brc and TOB say
"came back to life," "lived again" (RNAB "revived" seems to imply that the beast had
lost consciousness). Only here is the detail **by the sword** added. There is no way of
knowing who delivered the fatal sword thrust. Many commentators see this as a
deliberate allusion to Nero, who took his own life with his sword.

Alternative translation models for this verse are:

> The second beast was allowed (by God) to perform miracles in the
> presence of the first beast. By means of these miracles he was able
> to cause all people on earth to go astray. He ordered them to build
> a statue of (or, make an image in honor of) the first beast, the one
> who had been killed by the sword but had come back to life.

Or:

> The second beast led all the people living on the earth astray
> through the marvelous deeds that God allowed it to perform while

the first beast was watching. He commanded them, saying, "You must build a statue of the first beast . . . ."

13.15 RSV TEV

and it was allowed to give breath to the image of the beast so that the image of the beast should even speak, and to cause those who would not worship the image of the beast to be slain.	The second beast was allowed to breathe life into the image of the first beast, so that the image could talk and put to death all those who would not worship it.

It was allowed: God allowed him.

To give breath to the image of the beast: that is, to make the statue of the first beast come to life. So something like "to breathe life into the statue" may be said. See 11.11 for similar language.

So that the image of the beast should even speak: it is not necessary to repeat, as RSV does, **of the beast**; this is quite redundant here. And RSV **even** does not seem warranted by the Greek text.

To cause those . . . to be slain: the subject here is not the second beast, as RSV has it, but the living statue of the first beast. NRSV is better: "so that the image of the beast could even speak and cause those who would not worship the image of the beast to be killed." Even NRSV retains the needless redundancy of the second "of the beast."

As RSV shows, the full phrase **the image of the beast** appears three times in this verse. This stylistic feature of the book need not be carried over into translation. A more natural way may be used, one that does not omit any information:

> The second beast was allowed (by God) to make the statue of the first beast come to life, so that the statue could talk and could order anyone who did not worship it to be put to death.

Or:

> God allowed the second beast to make (or, cause) the statue of the first beast to have life, so that the statue could talk and could command them (or, people) to execute anyone who did not worship it.

13.16 RSV TEV

Also it causes all, both small and great, both rich and poor, both free and slave, to be marked on the right hand or the forehead,	The beast forced all the people, small and great, rich and poor, slave and free, to have a mark placed on their right hands or on their foreheads.

It causes all: conceivably the subject could be the living statue; but it is certain that the subject is, as TEV specifically states, the second beast (also FRCL, BRCL). So some translators will wish to say "The second beast causes . . . ."

Both small and great: see 11.18. Here two further classifications are added in order to include all the people of the world: **rich and poor, both free and slave**. For **rich and poor** see 3.17. For **free and slave** see 6.15.

It causes all . . . to be marked: this causative expression may be translated "it required everyone . . . to be marked" or "it gave an order for everyone . . . to be marked." Conceivably this could mean "to mark themselves." In Greek the impersonal third person plural of the active voice is used as an impersonal passive (see similar comments in 12.6). As explained in the next verse, this mark is the beast's name, or a numerical equivalent of its name. It would be something like a seal, or a brand, that could be stamped on a person's hand or forehead. It is more likely, though, that the beast's agents did the marking.

An alternative translation model for this verse is:

> The second beast gave an order for everyone, whether they were of high or low status, had many or few possessions, were the property of another person or were free, to receive a mark on their hands or their foreheads.

13.17   RSV   TEV

so that no one can buy or sell unless he has the mark, that is, the name of the beast or the number of its name.	No one could buy or sell unless he had this mark, that is, the beast's name or the number that stands for the name.

No one can buy or sell unless he has the mark: here **buy or sell** includes business of any kind that involves exchange of money. In some languages it may be more natural to say "Only those who had this mark could buy or sell."

The name of the beast: that is, the name of the first beast.

The number of its name: in some languages, including Hebrew and Greek, numbers were represented by letters, and each letter had a numerical value. The number of a name would be the sum total of the numerical value of the letters of that name.

13.18   RSV   TEV

This calls for wisdom: let him who has understanding reckon the number of the beast, for it is a human number, its number is six hundred and sixty-six.[g]	This calls for wisdom. Whoever is intelligent can figure out the meaning of the number of the beast, because the number stands for a man's name. Its number is 666.

[g] Other ancient authorities read *six hundred and sixteen*

This calls for wisdom: here the writer is addressing his readers (see a similar statement at the end of 13.10), and the exhortation may be made more directly in translation: "You must be wise in order to understand this (or, to figure this out)." But it is possible to take this as an affirmation, "Here is wisdom," that is, the key to understanding the true meaning of the beast. Most translations, however, understand this as an exhortation. For the translation of **wisdom** see 5.12. **Calls for wisdom** may also be rendered as "One must use wisdom (or, great understanding)" or "It is necessary to have wisdom for this."

Let him who has understanding reckon: this is the way in English to express a command. Another way is "Whoever has sense (or, understanding) must figure out what the number of the beast means."

It is a human number: this is the writer's way of telling the readers that the number stands for the name of some person. TEV "stands for" means "represents."

Six hundred and sixty-six: there are many interpretations of the name represented by the number 666. The most widely accepted one is that it stands for the Roman Emperor Nero. Written in Hebrew letters, the numerical value of the letters of the (Latin) name "Neron Caesar" adds up to 666. Some commentators are of the opinion that no one specific person was in the writer's mind, but that by 666 the writer meant total imperfection. Number six is one short of the perfect seven, and three indicates completeness, so the imperfect number six given three times symbolizes "complete imperfection." But the way in which the writer states the matter makes it quite probable that he had some historical person in mind. In languages where, for example, there are only two numerals, and any amount above two is thought of as "many," translators will have to be very creative here. It may in fact in some languages be impossible to accurately represent 666.

As the RSV footnote shows, one Greek manuscript and a few ancient versions have 616, but 666 is the better attested text.

14.1-5

RSV	TEV
	The Lamb and His People
1 Then I looked, and lo, on Mount Zion stood the Lamb, and with him a hundred and forty-four thousand who had his name and his Father's name written on their foreheads. 2 And I heard a voice from heaven like the sound of many waters and like the sound of loud thunder; the voice I heard was like the sound of harpers playing on their harps, 3 and they sing a new song before the throne and before the four living creatures and before the elders. No one could learn that song except the hundred and forty-four thousand who had been redeemed from the earth. 4 It is these who have not defiled themselves with women, for they are chaste; it is these who follow the Lamb wherever he goes; these have been redeemed from mankind as first fruits for God and the Lamb, 5 and in their mouth no lie was found, for they are spotless.	1 Then I looked, and there was the Lamb standing on Mount Zion; with him were 144,000 people who have his name and his Father's name written on their foreheads. 2 And I heard a voice from heaven that sounded like a roaring waterfall, like a loud peal of thunder. It sounded like the music made by musicians playing their harps. 3 The 144,000 people stood before the throne, the four living creatures, and the elders; they were singing a new song, which only they could learn. Of all mankind they are the only ones who have been redeemed. 4 They are the men who have kept themselves pure by not having sexual relations with women; they are virgins. They follow the Lamb wherever he goes. They have been redeemed from the rest of mankind and are the first ones to be offered to God and to the Lamb. 5 They have never been known to tell lies; they are faultless.

SECTION HEADING: TEV "The Lamb and His People." Other possibilities are "The Lamb and the redeemed," "The Lamb and the people he saves," "The hymn of the redeemed."

This chapter has three distinct visions, each one beginning with "I looked" or "I saw" (verses 1,6,14). In the first vision (verses 1-5) the writer sees the redeemed with the Lamb on Mount Zion. This is a vision of the End and does not report any action leading to the End.

14.1

RSV	TEV
Then I looked, and lo, on Mount Zion stood the Lamb, and with him a hundred and forty-four thousand who had his name and his Father's name written on their foreheads.	Then I looked, and there was the Lamb standing on Mount Zion; with him were 144,000 people who have his name and his Father's name written on their foreheads.

I looked, and lo: see comments on "behold," 1.7; 4.1.

Mount Zion: this was the hill on which stood the Jebusite stronghold that was captured by King David's forces (see 2 Sam 5.6-7). The name was later extended in meaning to refer to the hill (Mount Moriah) on which Solomon built the Temple; sometimes it was used to speak of the city of Jerusalem. Here it represents the seat of the Messianic kingdom on earth, not in heaven itself.

The Lamb: see 5.6. Another translation model for this first sentence is "Then I looked and saw the Lamb standing there on Mount Zion."

A hundred and forty-four thousand: this is the same number reported in 7.4.

His name and his Father's name written on their foreheads: this may correspond to the seal of God upon the foreheads of his servants in 7.3 and 9.4. The passive **written** may indicate an angel as the one who did the writing. In many languages this final part of the verse will be rendered in a similar way to the following: "One hundred and forty-four thousand people were standing with him. These are the ones on whose foreheads they (unknown agents) have written the names of the Lamb and his Father."

14.2

RSV	TEV
And I heard a voice from heaven like the sound of many waters and like the sound of loud thunder; the voice I heard was like the sound of harpers playing on their harps,	And I heard a voice from heaven that sounded like a roaring waterfall, like a loud peal of thunder. It sounded like the music made by musicians playing their harps.

I heard a voice from heaven: the reader is not told whose voice this was (see 10.4). The answer depends on how "they sing" in verse 3 is understood.

Like the sound of many waters: see the same expression in 1.15. This can mean the sound of a waterfall (TEV) or the roar of the ocean (NJB). A translator cannot be dogmatic about which one it is, but it should be pointed out that **many**

waters is not a natural expression in English. One may also say "I heard the voice of someone from heaven which was like the roar of . . . ," or in languages that cannot refer to voices only, "I heard someone speaking in heaven. His voice was like . . . ." The two English words **voice** and **sound** translate the same Greek noun.

Loud thunder: see 6.1.

Harpers playing on their harps: for **harps** see 5.8. In standard English a person who plays a harp is called a harpist (as NRSV has it). In some languages it will be more natural for translators to say "plucking the strings of their harps (or, banjos, ukeleles)."

An alternative translation model for this verse is:

> And I heard the voice of someone in heaven as loud as the roar of a waterfall (or, the ocean), or the sky roaring. It sounded like music being made by musicians playing their harps (or, banjos).

14.3 RSV	TEV
and they sing a new song before the throne and before the four living creatures and before the elders. No one could learn that song except the hundred and forty-four thousand who had been redeemed from the earth.	The 144,000 people stood before the throne, the four living creatures, and the elders; they were singing a new song, which only they could learn. Of all mankind they are the only ones who have been redeemed.

They sing: as noticed in 13.12, RSV reproduces the present tense of the Greek verb; for purpose of narrative most translators will prefer to continue to use the past tense, as TEV and other modern translations do. Who is the subject? As it stands in Greek, and as translated by RSV and others, it can be the harpists of the previous verse. But this seems quite unlikely. Most translations reproduce the Greek form quite mechanically, but this should not be done unless the translator concludes that the harpists are the ones doing the singing. A number of commentators believe the singers are the countless angels surrounding God's throne (see 5.11-12; 7.11-12). Others, however, believe that the 144,000 are the singers, as made explicit by TEV, and FRCL "these thousands of people were in front of the throne"; also similar is BRCL. It is recommended that the singers be identified as the 144,000 redeemed. So TEV's rendering provides a good translation model.

A new song: as in 5.9.

Before the throne . . . the four living creatures and . . . the elders: see the description of the heavenly throne room in chapter 4.

No one could learn that song: to ask who would be teaching that song to the 144,000 goes beyond the writer's intention in giving this information. This is a way of saying that only these 144,000 could sing this song—it could be sung by no one else.

Who had been redeemed from the earth: here **the earth** represents the earth's inhabitants, the human race (see "redeemed from mankind" in verse 4). Of all people on earth these are the ones who had been redeemed. For **redeemed** see "ransom" in 5.9. If it is necessary to use the active voice of the verb, the translation can say "whom God has redeemed," "whom God has saved." This sentence may also be expressed as "They are the people whom God has saved."

14.4

RSV	TEV
It is these who have not defiled themselves with women, for they are chaste;[h] it is these who follow the Lamb wherever he goes; these have been redeemed from mankind as first fruits for God and the Lamb,	They are the men who have kept themselves pure by not having sexual relations with women; they are virgins. They follow the Lamb wherever he goes. They have been redeemed from the rest of mankind and are the first ones to be offered to God and to the Lamb.

[h] Greek *virgins*

Have not defiled themselves with women, for they are chaste: the literal meaning of this statement is that these 144,000 are men who have never had sexual intercourse; as the RSV footnote shows, the Greek word translated **chaste** means "virgins" (TEV). The meaning can be: (1) male virgins, in the normal sense of the word; (2) men who had committed neither fornication nor adultery, that is, who were "pure" sexually; (3) men who had kept themselves spiritually pure and undefiled by their complete devotion to God and their refusal to worship idols. Often in the Old Testament idolatry is compared to sexual immorality (and see Jezebel and her followers, in 2.20-22). Most commentators favor this spiritual understanding of the language; but a translation should faithfully reproduce the literal meaning of the Greek text. In some translations it may be helpful to present in a footnote the various interpretations of the figure. For the verb "to defile" see comment on "soiled" in 3.4; see the related noun "defilement" in 2 Corinthians 7.1. **Defile themselves with women**: translators need to find the most natural and acceptable phrase in the receptor language. In certain languages this is expressed as "sleep with," "be with," "stay and eat with," "lie on one mat and pillow with," and so on. **Chaste** will be translated in some languages as "unmarried man" or "has not been with women." However, saying this will repeat the information in the first clause and be unnecessarily redundant in many languages. In such a case one may simply say "They are the men who have never been with (or, slept with) women, and so are pure."

Follow the Lamb wherever he goes: this shows their complete devotion to Jesus Christ; they are his faithful followers, ready to follow him to death. Another way of expressing this is "Go with (or, accompany) the Lamb . . . ."

These have been redeemed may be expressed as "God has redeemed (or, saved) them from the rest of the people on earth" or "They are the people whom God has saved." See also the previous verse.

As first fruits for God and the Lamb: in Hebrew agricultural society the first part of the harvest of grain or of fruit was dedicated to God, as a symbol that the whole harvest belonged to him (see Exo 23.19). Rarely will the literal translation "as first fruits for God" make any more sense in other languages than it does in English. For the use of the word elsewhere in the New Testament, see Romans 11.16; James 1.18. If an attempt is made to preserve the figure, something like the following may be said: "these men belong to God and to the Lamb; they are like the first part of the harvest, which is offered (or, given) to God."

14.5 RSV TEV

and in their mouth no lie was found, for they are spotless.

They have never been known to tell lies; they are faultless.

In their mouth no lie was found: this translates the Greek text quite literally, but it is most unnatural English. Something like "they never lied" or TEV "They have never been known to lie" expresses the meaning in a more natural way. This may be the writer's way of saying that these people never denied they were Christians, as some may have done in an attempt to avoid persecution and martyrdom. The translation, however, must state quite precisely what the Greek text says. On the translation of **lie** see comments on "false" in 2.2. Some languages will express **lie** idiomatically; for example, "weave the mouth" (Yapese).

For they are spotless: this has to do with moral or spiritual purity. The same Greek word is used of Christ in Hebrews 9.14 and 1 Peter 1.19, and of people in Philippians 2.15, Colossians 1.22, Jude 24. Some English translations have "blameless"; RNAB has "unblemished," and Brc translates "faultless in their purity." One may also express this as "they have never done any evil things."

14.6-13

RSV TEV

The Three Angels

6 Then I saw another angel flying in mid-heaven, with an eternal gospel to proclaim to those who dwell on earth, to every nation and tribe and tongue and people; 7 and he said with a loud voice, "Fear God and give him glory, for the hour of his judgment has come; and worship him who made heaven and earth, the sea and the fountains of water."

8 Another angel, a second, followed, saying, "Fallen, fallen is Babylon the great, she who made all nations drink the wine of her impure passion."

9 And another angel, a third, followed them, saying with a loud voice, "If any one worships the beast and its image, and receives a mark on his forehead or on his hand, 10 he also shall drink the wine of God's wrath, poured unmixed into the cup of his anger, and he shall be tormented with fire and sulphur in the presence of the holy angels and in the presence of the Lamb. 11 And the smoke of their torment goes up for ever and ever; and they have no rest, day or night, these worshipers of the beast and its image, and whoever receives the mark of its name."

12 Here is a call for the endurance of the saints, those who keep the commandments of God

6 Then I saw another angel flying high in the air, with an eternal message of Good News to announce to the peoples of the earth, to every race, tribe, language, and nation. 7 He said in a loud voice, "Honor God and praise his greatness! For the time has come for him to judge mankind. Worship him who made heaven, earth, sea, and the springs of water!"

8 A second angel followed the first one, saying, "She has fallen! Great Babylon has fallen! She made all peoples drink her wine—the strong wine of her immoral lust!"

9 A third angel followed the first two, saying in a loud voice, "Whoever worships the beast and its image and receives the mark on his forehead or on his hand 10 will himself drink God's wine, the wine of his fury, which he has poured at full strength into the cup of his anger! All who do this will be tormented in fire and sulfur before the holy angels and the Lamb. 11 The smoke of the fire that torments them goes up forever and ever. There is no relief day or night for those who worship the beast and its image, for anyone who has the mark of its name."

12 This calls for endurance on the part of

and the faith of Jesus.

13 And I heard a voice from heaven saying, "Write this: Blessed are the dead who die in the Lord henceforth." "Blessed indeed," says the Spirit, "that they may rest from their labors, for their deeds follow them!"

God's people, those who obey God's commandments and are faithful to Jesus.

13 Then I heard a voice from heaven saying, "Write this: Happy are those who from now on die in the service of the Lord!"

"Yes indeed!" answers the Spirit. "They will enjoy rest from their hard work, because the results of their service go with them."

SECTION HEADING: TEV "The Three Angels." Other possibilities are "The messages of three angels" or "Three angels and their messages." NJB has "Angels Announce the Day of Judgement." Another possible rendering is "Angels (or, heavenly messengers) announce that God will judge all people."

In this vision John sees and hears three angels flying high in the air, proclaiming that God's judgment of humanity will take place soon: Babylon will be destroyed, and the followers of the beast will suffer eternal punishment. The final message, which comes from heaven, is one of hope and encouragement for the Christians (verse 13).

14.6   RSV   TEV

Then I saw another angel flying in midheaven, with an eternal gospel to proclaim to those who dwell on earth, to every nation and tribe and tongue and people;

Then I saw another angel flying high in the air, with an eternal message of Good News to announce to the peoples of the earth, to every race, tribe, language, and nation.

Another angel: several angels have already appeared (see 5.2; 10.1).

Flying in midheaven: the same expression is used in 8.13.

With an eternal gospel to proclaim: with in this context means "having," "carrying" in the sense of ready to proclaim. Here the word **gospel** is not used in the specialized sense of the good news of salvation through Jesus Christ. It means "good news" in general, or more specifically "a message from God." TNT has "a message of eternal good news." The verb translated **to proclaim** is the verb form of the noun **gospel** (see its use in 10.7 "announce"). The adjective **eternal** means that the message is valid forever, or that it refers to an eternal truth about God and his will for humankind. The angel's message is that God will soon judge humanity; for God's persecuted people this is indeed good news. An alternative translation model for the first part of this verse is "Then I saw another angel (or, heavenly messenger) flying high in the sky. He was going to announce a message . . . ."

Those who dwell on earth: see the similar expression in 3.10; 8.13. The Greek verb used here is different and usually means "to sit," but here it has the same meaning of "to live," "to inhabit."

To every nation and tribe and tongue and people: the Greek text begins this phrase with "and," which RSV and other translations rightly take to indicate that **every nation . . . and people** is in apposition to **those who dwell on earth.** For this phrase see 5.9.

210

14.7 RSV TEV

and he said with a loud voice, "Fear God and give him glory, for the hour of his judgment has come; and worship him who made heaven and earth, the sea and the fountains of water."

He said in a loud voice, "Honor God and praise his greatness! For the time has come for him to judge mankind. Worship him who made heaven, earth, sea, and the springs of water!"

Fear God: see the verb "fear" in "fear thy name" in 11.18. It means to honor, to respect, to hold in awe and reverence. One may also say "You must show respect for God."

Give him glory: this probably implies repentance and confession of sins (see 11.13), but in translation it will be better in some languages to say "You must say that he is great," and in others this clause will sound more natural in direct discourse; for example, "You must say, 'O God, you are very great (or, powerful).'"

For the hour of his judgment has come: this is the good news for the persecuted followers of the Lamb. The time (**hour**) has come for God to judge all peoples and punish the wicked. In certain languages one must use the verb "judge" and make the object explicit; for example, "judge all people on earth." For **worship** see 4.10.

And worship him who made heaven and earth: this may be more naturally expressed by "worship the Creator of . . . ." The phrase **heaven and earth, the sea and the fountains of water** means the whole universe, everything that exists (as stated in 4.11). **The sea and the fountains of water** is a way of including all bodies of water, both salt water and fresh water (compare 8.10; 16.4, where only fresh water is mentioned).

Alternative translation models for this verse are:

> You must show respect for God and tell him how great he is. For the time has come for him to judge all people on earth. Show respect for him, because he is the creator of the heavens and the earth, the oceans (or, seas) and the springs of water.

Or:

> You must show respect for God and tell him, "God, you are very great." For the time has come for him to judge all people on earth. You must show respect for him because he has created the heaven and the earth along with all the water, both salty and fresh.

14.8 RSV TEV

Another angel, a second, followed, saying, "Fallen, fallen is Babylon the great, she who made all nations drink the wine of her impure passion."

A second angel followed the first one, saying, "She has fallen! Great Babylon has fallen! She made all peoples drink her wine—the strong wine of her immoral lust!"

211

Another angel, a second, followed, saying: a more natural way of saying this in English appears in TEV, "A second angel followed the first one." The idea of **followed** here is not that the second angel pursued the first one, but that he appeared high in the air after the first one had disappeared. In some languages this will be expressed as "When the first angel left a second one appeared." **Saying** in many languages will be rendered as "called out" or "shouted."

Fallen, fallen is Babylon the great: when used of a city, the verb "to fall" means that the city no longer exists as a place where people can lead normal lives; for whatever reason—war, earthquake, fire, pestilence—it has ceased to function as a community and is abandoned by its citizens (see a more detailed description in 18.2-3). The repetition of the verb **fallen** is to emphasize the complete nature of Babylon's ruin. For some languages translators will need to find a term or phrase that carries the idea of the complete collapse of a city's government and economy. One may say something like "The great city of Babylon is finished (or, collapsed). It is completely deserted (or, no people left in it)." Babylon is called **the great** because of its power and prestige. Most commentators agree that the name is a way of referring to imperial Rome.

She: cities in some languages, mostly the Indo-European, are often spoken of as female, but in most languages they occur with pronouns that are not marked for gender.

Made all nations drink: the causative form of the verb "to drink" does not mean that Babylon necessarily forced the nations to drink her wine, but that she gave it to them, shared it with them. For this figure of drinking wine, see Jeremiah 51.7.

Wine: although the Greek word for **wine** is used, in translation a general word for "strong drink" or "strong alcoholic beverage" can be used, rather than the specific fermented beverage made from grapes. In some cultures palm wine will be the closest natural equivalent.

The Greek text says "the wine of the fury of her immorality." RSV, TEV, and other translations take "fury" here to mean "strong," "wild," "unrestrained," referring to the immorality of Babylon; RSV **(impure) passion**; NRSV "(the wine of) her licentious (passion)"; TEV "her immoral (lust)." But others take the word to refer to God's anger (as in 14.10), so that the statement combines the idea of the corrupting power of Babylon's immorality and God's anger, or punishment. It is possible therefore to translate "She made all the nations drink the wine of her immorality, the wine that brings God's anger (or, punishment) on her." TNT has "has made all nations drink the wine of her sexual vice, the wine that brings God's anger." REB translates "the wine of God's anger roused by her fornication." This understanding of the passage may well be correct, and a translator may choose to follow it. **Immorality** here refers to all kinds of sexual sins, not just sleeping with someone else's spouse. In some languages it will be expressed as "evil sexual practices."

The verdict is that Babylon, with her immorality (that is, her idolatry), has corrupted all the nations. It may be impossible to speak of "the wine of her impure passion," so it may be necessary to translate somewhat as follows:

> Babylon's immoral actions corrupted all the nations on earth. It was as though she gave them wine to drink, and this will cause God to punish them.

Or:

> Babylon's evil sexual practices have caused all the nations on earth to sin in a similar way. It was as though . . . .

14.9-10   RSV   TEV

RSV	TEV
9 And another angel, a third, followed them, saying with a loud voice, "If any one worships the beast and its image, and receives a mark on his forehead or on his hand, 10 he also shall drink the wine of God's wrath, poured unmixed into the cup of his anger, and he shall be tormented with fire and sulphur in the presence of the holy angels and in the presence of the Lamb.	9 A third angel followed the first two, saying in a loud voice, "Whoever worships the beast and its image and receives the mark on his forehead or on his hand 10 will himself drink God's wine, the wine of his fury, which he has poured at full strength into the cup of his anger! All who do this will be tormented in fire and sulfur before the holy angels and the Lamb.

Another angel, a third, followed them: the more natural way to say this is "A third angel followed them" or ". . . followed the first two," "Another angel followed the other two angels," or even "Another angel appeared after the other two angels had left."

If any one worships: the Greek uses the conditional form; in translation it is easier to imitate TEV and others, and say "Those who worship" (NRSV) or "All who worship" (NJB). For **worships** see 4.10.

The beast and its image: this is the first beast, the one that came up out of the sea (13.1), and its image, or statue (13.14-15). If in 13.14-15 the word "statue" is used, it should be used here also.

Receives a mark on his forehead or on his hand: if the translation must specify the hand, it should say the right hand (see 13.16).

The wine of God's wrath: this means "the wine that represents (or, brings) God's wrath (or, punishment)." See verse 8 for comments on the translation of **wine** and **wrath**. In that verse the same Greek word meaning "fury" is used.

Poured unmixed into the cup of his anger: here God's anger is represented as "the cup (or, bowl)" that holds the wine of his wrath. For the translation of **cup** see the comment in 5.8 contrasting "bowl" and "cup." Although the language is not logical, the figure is a forceful and dramatic way of portraying God's anger against Babylon and his punishment of those who are corrupted by her. The wine is **unmixed**, that is, it has no water in it to weaken it (as was most often the case when wine was served). For **anger** see 6.16-17, where the same term is translated "wrath." There are a number of Old Testament passages in which a cup of wine is used as a symbol of punishment. In Jeremiah 25.15-29 this figure is fully developed. Other passages where the figure is found are Psalm 75.8; Jeremiah 49.12; Obadiah 16; and Habakkuk 2.16. Since this is a very common symbol in the Bible and is related to wine, which of course is one of the central features of Palestinian culture, translators should keep the figure if at all possible. However, this may present a problem in areas where wine is unknown, or a cup or bowl has never been used with any symbolic meaning. Translators must then decide whether a new figure of speech will be acceptable and understandable to the readers. For further comments see Obadiah 16 in *A Handbook on the Books of Obadiah and Micah*. In certain languages one may say, for example, "God will be angry and will punish him severely, just as if he drank bitter wine (or, strong drink) that God had poured at full strength (or, unmixed) into a cup."

He shall be tormented with fire and sulphur: see 9.17-18; 19.20; 20.10. Sodom was destroyed by fire and sulfur (Gen 19.24; see also Psa 11.6). Here, as there, **fire and sulphur** means "burning sulfur" (so RNAB). Sulfur burns with great heat and produces an unpleasant smell. For the verb "to torment" see "torture" in 9.5. If "torment" means specifically "torture," a more general verbal phrase may be used, "will suffer," "will be made to suffer," "God will cause him to suffer," or even "God will use . . . to torment him."

In the presence of: for comments on **in the presence of**, see 13.12. The punishment of the wicked is made even greater by the fact that they can see the blessed state of the angels and the Lamb.

The holy angels: occasionally in the New Testament the adjective **holy** is used of angels (see Mark 8.38; Luke 9.26; Acts 10.22). It is a word of dignity and respect, and does not imply that some of God's angels are not holy. The basic meaning of the word, when applied to objects or people (or, as here, to angels) is that of total dedication to God (see 3.7). Other ways of translating this phrase, then, are "the respected angels (or, heavenly messengers)" or even "God's angels (or, messengers)."

RSV, following the form of the Greek, has one sentence for verses 9-10. TEV tries to simplify the material by having two sentences. But it is possible to divide the angel's announcement into even more sentences, as follows:

> All those who worship the beast and its statue, and who have the mark of the beast on their foreheads or on their (right) hands, will have to drink the wine of God's anger. This is the undiluted wine that God himself poured into the cup of his anger. These people will also be made to suffer in burning sulfur in the presence of the holy angels and of the Lamb.

Or:

> . . . will be severely punished by God. It will be as if they drink undiluted (or full strength) wine that God himself has poured into the cup that represents his anger. God will cause burning sulfur to torment these people in the sight of his angels and of the Lamb.

14.11   RSV   TEV

And the smoke of their torment goes up for ever and ever; and they have no rest, day or night, these worshipers of the

The smoke of the fire that torments them goes up forever and ever. There is no relief day or night for those who

beast and its image, and whoever re-   worship the beast and its image, for
ceives the mark of its name."   anyone who has the mark of its name."

The smoke of their torment: this means "the smoke of the fire that torments them." For **torment** see "torture" at 9.5.

Goes up for ever and ever: if it is not natural to speak simply of the smoke rising forever, it may be better to say "The fire in which they are tormented (or, are punished) will burn forever" or "The fire that is tormenting (or, punishing) them will burn forever (or, never stop burning)."

They have no rest: this means they will have no relief from their suffering (see "they never cease," 4.8). One may also translate "those who worship . . . will suffer continually (or, day and night)."

And whoever receives the mark of its name: this does not refer to another group, different from those who worship the beast and its image (or, statue); it is another way of describing them. TEV has tried to make this equivalence clear, but it may be made even clearer by saying "Those who worship the beast and its statue and have on them the mark of its name will have no relief, day or night, from their suffering." For **the mark of its name**, see 13.16-17. Here it means that they are marked with the name of the beast.

An alternative translation model for this verse is:

> The fire that torments them will burn forever. For those people who worship the beast and its statue (or, image) and have the mark of its name on them will never stop suffering.

14.12   RSV   TEV

Here is a call for the endurance of the saints, those who keep the commandments of God and the faith of Jesus.	This calls for endurance on the part of God's people, those who obey God's commandments and are faithful to Jesus.

Here is a call for: see 13.10 for comments on the translation of this phrase.

This verse is similar to 13.10b. For **saints** see 5.8; for **those who keep the commandments of God**, see 12.17; and for **keep . . . the faith of Jesus**, see 2.13. Here **faith** may have the sense of belief, "those who continue to believe in Jesus," or it may mean faithfulness, "those who are faithful followers of Jesus." The latter is to be preferred.

Alternative translation models for this verse are:

> All of this means that God's people must be patient. These are the people who obey God's commandments and follow Jesus faithfully.

Or:

All of this means that the people who obey God's commandments
and continue to believe in Jesus must be patient. They are God's
people.

14.13   RSV   TEV

And I heard a voice from heaven saying, "Write this: Blessed are the dead who die in the Lord henceforth." "Blessed indeed," says the Spirit, "that they may rest from their labors, for their deeds follow them!"	Then I heard a voice from heaven saying, "Write this: Happy are those who from now on die in the service of the Lord!" "Yes indeed!" answers the Spirit. "They will enjoy rest from their hard work, because the results of their service go with them."

A voice from heaven: see 14.2.

Saying: that is, "saying to me." The voice is speaking to John, as the second
person imperative **Write** makes clear.

Write this may also be expressed as "You must write the following (things)."

Blessed are the dead who die in the Lord henceforth: for **Blessed** see 1.3.
Instead of the literal **the dead who die**, it is better to say something like "those who
die." The phrase **in the Lord** means "united with the Lord," "in union with the
Lord." This is a way of referring to faithful followers of Jesus Christ. In the context
of persecution and possible martyrdom, it seems likely that the words refer
specifically to those who do not abandon their faith but persevere to the end. One
may also translate "those who from now on die as followers of the Lord (or, Jesus
Christ)" or "those people who after this time die because they faithfully follow the
Lord."

Henceforth (TEV "from now on"): this adverb makes it even more probable
that martyrdom is meant.

"Blessed indeed," says the Spirit: for the first time in this book the Spirit
of God speaks. So it is quite certain that **a voice from heaven** at the beginning of
this verse is not the Spirit speaking, but God or an angel. Nothing is said about
where the Spirit is speaking from. **Indeed** may also be rendered as "That's true!" or
"Yes, it's true!"

That they may rest from their labors: this is not a very satisfactory rendering
of the meaning of the Greek text. NRSV has done better: " 'Yes,' says the Spirit, 'they
will rest from their labors.' " This describes the "blessedness" or happiness of these
people. Here **their labors** refers to their difficulties and persecutions as followers
of Jesus (see 2.2.). Other ways of expressing this clause are "They will not have to
labor hard anymore" or "They will not have to go through any more troubles."

Their deeds follow them: this means that the record or the result of their
service as followers of Jesus Christ accompanies them, and in the heavenly court
serves as evidence of their faithful work. A good translation is "the record of what
they did goes with them," or "their deeds go with them and speak for them," or even
"the record of what they did will be recognized."

14.14-20

RSV	TEV
	The Harvest of the Earth

14 Then I looked, and lo, a white cloud, and seated on the cloud one like a son of man, with a golden crown on his head, and a sharp sickle in his hand. 15 And another angel came out of the temple, calling with a loud voice to him who sat upon the cloud, "Put in your sickle, and reap, for the hour to reap has come, for the harvest of the earth is fully ripe." 16 So he who sat upon the cloud swung his sickle on the earth, and the earth was reaped.

17 And another angel came out of the temple in heaven, and he too had a sharp sickle. 18 Then another angel came out from the altar, the angel who has power over fire, and he called with a loud voice to him who had the sharp sickle, "Put in your sickle, and gather the clusters of the vine of the earth, for its grapes are ripe." 19 So the angel swung his sickle on the earth and gathered the vintage of the earth, and threw it into the great wine press of the wrath of God; 20 and the wine press was trodden outside the city, and blood flowed from the wine press, as high as a horse's bridle, for one thousand six hundred stadia.

14 Then I looked, and there was a white cloud, and sitting on the cloud was what looked like a human being, with a crown of gold on his head and a sharp sickle in his hand. 15 Then another angel came out from the temple and cried out in a loud voice to the one who was sitting on the cloud, "Use your sickle and reap the harvest, because the time has come; the earth is ripe for the harvest!" 16 Then the one who sat on the cloud swung his sickle on the earth, and the earth's harvest was reaped.

17 Then I saw another angel come out of the temple in heaven, and he also had a sharp sickle.

18 Then another angel, who is in charge of the fire, came from the altar. He shouted in a loud voice to the angel who had the sharp sickle, "Use your sickle, and cut the grapes from the vineyard of the earth, because the grapes are ripe!" 19 So the angel swung his sickle on the earth, cut the grapes from the vine, and threw them into the wine press of God's furious anger. 20 The grapes were squeezed out in the wine press outside the city, and blood came out of the wine press in a flood two hundred miles long and about five feet deep.

SECTION HEADING: TEV "The Harvest of the Earth." Another possibility is "A vision of the final judgment" or "A dream where God judges people for the last time."

This vision is also of the End, not of events preceding the End. God's final judgment of humanity is in places portrayed as a harvest (Joel 3.13; Matt 13.30, 39-43).

14.14 RSV TEV

Then I looked, and lo, a white cloud, and seated on the cloud one like a son of man, with a golden crown on his head, and a sharp sickle in his hand.

Then I looked, and there was a white cloud, and sitting on the cloud was what looked like a human being, with a crown of gold on his head and a sharp sickle in his hand.

I looked, and lo: see 4.1.

One like a son of man: see 1.13. This is the language of Daniel 7.13 and is a way of referring to the Messiah.

A golden crown on his head: see 4.10. This shows he is a king.

A sharp sickle: a sickle is a blade, with a handle, that is usually curved and is used to cut grain plants or grass. In some cultures the appropriate term is "a reaping knife" or "a reaping hook," or "machete for reaping."

An alternative translation model for this verse is:

> Then I looked, and saw a white cloud. Someone who looked like a human being was sitting on the cloud. He had a gold crown (or, king's hat) on his head and held a sharp sickle (or, reaping knife, machete) in his hand.

14.15   RSV   TEV

And another angel came out of the temple, calling with a loud voice to him who sat upon the cloud, "Put in your sickle, and reap, for the hour to reap has come, for the harvest of the earth is fully ripe."	Then another angel came out from the temple and cried out in a loud voice to the one who was sitting on the cloud, "Use your sickle and reap the harvest, because the time has come; the earth is ripe for the harvest!"

Another angel: this one is in addition to the three angels of verses 6,8,9. It should be quite clear in translation that the phrase **another angel** does not imply that "the one like a son of man" is also an angel.

The temple: this is the temple in heaven, as in verse 17, below. It will be helpful in many languages to make this information explicit and say "the temple in heaven," as this is the first mention of this temple since 11.19.

Calling with a loud voice: this angel is announcing God's command to the Messiah. As the New Testament makes clear, only God knows the time of the final Judgment (see Mark 13.32). In certain languages translators will prefer to say "and shouted" or similar language.

Put in your sickle, and reap: the most natural way of saying this may be "Start working with your sickle and reap," "Start reaping with your sickle," or "Take your sickle and begin to cut."

The harvest of the earth is fully ripe: there may be some trouble in making the meaning of this clear. Here **the earth** stands for humanity, so that "the earth" itself is the harvest. The translation should try to keep the figure of reaping the harvest with a sickle. However, if the word for **reap** in a language means literally to "cut and collect" or "gather" crops, alternative ways of translating the command would be "Get to work with your sickle! The harvest on earth is now completely ripe, and the time has come to reap the harvest" or "Start cutting with your sickle (or, knife, or machete for reaping). What is to be gathered on the earth is now ripe (or, ready), and it is now the time to gather them."

14.16   RSV   TEV

So he who sat upon the cloud swung his sickle on the earth, and the earth was reaped.	Then the one who sat on the cloud swung his sickle on the earth, and the earth's harvest was reaped.

He who sat upon the cloud: the text does not say whether he got off the cloud in order to reap. A translation should not say or imply that he did.

Swung his sickle on the earth: this is a natural way in English to speak of working with a sickle. In some languages it may be more natural to say "cut with his sickle," or "reaped with his sickle," or "worked with his sickle."

The earth was reaped: that is, the harvest on earth was reaped; the harvest is the human race. However, translators should not say this explicitly. An alternative translation model is "collected (or, gathered) the harvest."

14.17 RSV	TEV
And another angel came out of the temple in heaven, and he too had a sharp sickle.	Then I saw another angel come out of the temple in heaven, and he also had a sharp sickle.

Another angel: the second one in this vision.

The temple in heaven: as in verse 15.

He too had a sharp sickle: the Greek word for **sickle** is the same as in verses 14-16, but this sickle is for harvesting grapes. In some cultures the tool for harvesting grapes is different from the one used for harvesting grain. In such cases it will be helpful to say, for example, "a knife (or, machete) for harvesting grapes." For the figure of harvesting grapes as the final Judgment, see Joel 3.13b.

14.18 RSV	TEV
Then another angel came out from the altar, the angel who has power over fire, and he called with a loud voice to him who had the sharp sickle, "Put in your sickle, and gather the clusters of the vine of the earth, for its grapes are ripe."	Then another angel, who is in charge of the fire, came from the altar. He shouted in a loud voice to the angel who had the sharp sickle, "Use your sickle, and cut the grapes from the vineyard of the earth, because the grapes are ripe!"

Came out from the altar: this is the altar of incense in heaven (see 6.9). It is possible that the Greek text means that the angel emerged from inside the altar, but this does not seem very likely. Rather, he came from the area near the altar. So one may also translate "came from near (or, by) the altar."

Who has power over fire: this probably identifies him as the angel in charge of the fire on the altar (see 8.3-5). But it is possible that the phrase means this is the angel in charge of fire, like the one in charge of water in 16.5 (see also the ones in charge of the winds in 7.1). But it is more probable that he is in charge of the fire on the altar. This angel's action answers the cries of the martyrs in 6.10. **Has power over** may also be rendered as "looks after," "takes care of," or "is responsible for."

To him who had the sharp sickle: this is the angel of verse 17.

Gather the clusters of the vine of the earth: this is the action of cutting the clusters of grapes off the vine (see the verb in Luke 6.44). So it may be better to say "cut the grapes from the vineyard of the earth" (TEV). Here **the vine of the earth** is used in the same way as "the harvest of the earth" in verse 15. This is a vision of the punishment of the wicked, who are represented as clusters of ripe grapes. In cultures where grapes are unknown, translators should not substitute some other fruit that grows on a vine. One way to translate this clause is to use a generic term for fruit and say "gather the bunches of fruit named grape from the vine that is the earth." It will also be helpful for translators to include a picture of a grape vine with bunches of grapes hanging from it.

A VINE WITH CLUSTERS OF GRAPES

14.19 RSV	TEV
So the angel swung his sickle on the earth and gathered the vintage of the earth, and threw it into the great wine press of the wrath of God;	So the angel swung his sickle on the earth, cut the grapes from the vine, and threw them into the wine press of God's furious anger.

Swung his sickle on the earth: as in verse 16.

Gathered the vintage of the earth: this means "cut off the clusters of grapes from the vine (or, vineyard) of the earth." The Greek word translated **the vintage** by RSV is the same one that is translated "the vine" in verse 18. The English word "vintage" means the yield, or harvest, of grapes from a vineyard or a given wine district. An alternative way to translate this in cultures where grapes are unknown is "gathered all the fruit named grape from the vine of the earth."

Threw it into the great wine press of the wrath of God: here, in another change of figures, it is the wine press that represents God's anger. The wine press at that time was usually a pit cut into stone in which the grapes were placed. People would them trample on the grapes, in this way causing the grape juice to flow out. By means of a channel cut into the wine press, the juice ran into a bucket, or vat, placed lower than the press itself. One may also translate "the place where the juice is squeezed out of grapes" or "the place where they trample grapes and squeeze the juice out of them."

A WINE PRESS

In Greek the adjective **great** is masculine, whereas **wine press** is feminine. Commentators and translations take this to be an error in concordance; of the translations consulted only TEV takes the adjective to modify **wrath**, which is feminine. It is recommended that the adjective be made to modify **wine press**. So one may say "the great wine press" or "the large place to trample grapes."

If there is some difficulty in representing "the great wine press of the wrath of God," it may be better to translate "The angel threw the grapes into the place where they are to be squeezed out (or, trampled). This represents God's punishment of the wicked." But it is better, if possible, simply to maintain the figurative language of the Greek text, without any additional information.

14.20 RSV TEV

and the wine press was trodden outside the city, and blood flowed from the wine press, as high as a horse's bridle, for one thousand six hundred stadia.[i]

The grapes were squeezed out in the wine press outside the city, and blood came out of the wine press in a flood two hundred miles long and about five feet deep.

[i] About two hundred miles

The wine press was trodden: this means, of course, that the grapes in the wine press were trampled on. Again the passive form of the verb is used. Given the fact that this is a figure of the punishment of the wicked, it would be very difficult to try to identify the ones who were treading on the grapes. But if a subject is required, one may use an unknown subject (agent) and say "They trod on the grapes and squeezed the juice out." However, in languages that must identify the subject, one may say "God's angels trod . . . ."

Outside the city: the location of the winepress is new information, but it is given in such a way as to allow the reader to think that the wine press was taken outside the city for the grapes to be trampled on. NJB tries to incorporate this information in the discourse in a normal way by placing it at the very beginning of the verse, as follows: ". . . and put it into a huge winepress, the winepress of God's anger, outside the city." The city here is Jerusalem.

Blood flowed from the wine press: instead of grape juice it is blood that flows out.

As high as a horse's bridle: some take the Greek text to mean "as high as the bridles of the horses," by which it is implied that warriors on war horses were riding through this flood of blood. But it seems better to take the Greek to mean the depth of the flow of blood, as RSV and TEV interpret it. If the expression makes sense, it can be retained; otherwise it will be better to imitate TEV and say "about five feet deep" or "about a meter and a half deep."

One thousand six hundred stadia: it is not certain whether the figure 1600 has a symbolic meaning, so it is better to give the distance in modern terms. A stade was a Greek measure of distance, 607 feet or 185 meters long; the total distance comes to 184 miles or 296 kilometers. NRSV has now "for a distance of about two hundred miles."

C-5. The Seven Bowls
(15.1–16.21)

15.1-8

RSV

TEV

The Angels with the Last Plagues

1 Then I saw another portent in heaven, great and wonderful, seven angels with seven plagues, which are the last, for with them the wrath of God is ended. 2 And I saw what appeared to be a sea of glass mingled with fire, and those who had conquered the beast and its image and the number of its name, standing beside the sea of glass with harps of God in their hands. 3 And they sing the song of Moses, the servant of God, and the song of the Lamb, saying,
"Great and wonderful are thy deeds,
O Lord God the Almighty!
Just and true are thy ways,
O King of the ages!
4 Who shall not fear and glorify thy name,
O Lord?
For thou alone art holy.
All nations shall come and worship thee,
for thy judgments have been revealed."
5 After this I looked, and the temple of the tent of witness in heaven was opened, 6 and out of

1 Then I saw in the sky another mysterious sight, great and amazing. There were seven angels with seven plagues, which are the last ones, because they are the final expression of God's anger. 2 Then I saw what looked like a sea of glass mixed with fire. I also saw those who had won the victory over the beast and its image and over the one whose name is represented by a number. They were standing by the sea of glass, holding harps that God had given them 3 and singing the song of Moses, the servant of God, and the song of the Lamb:
"Lord God Almighty,
how great and wonderful are your deeds!
King of the nations,
how right and true are your ways!
4 Who will not stand in awe of you, Lord?
Who will refuse to declare your greatness?
You alone are holy.
All the nations will come

the temple came the seven angels with the seven plagues, robed in pure bright linen, and their breasts girded with golden girdles. 7 And one of the four living creatures gave the seven angels seven golden bowls full of the wrath of God who lives for ever and ever; 8 and the temple was filled with smoke from the glory of God and from his power, and no one could enter the temple until the seven plagues of the seven angels were ended.

and worship you,
because your just actions are seen by all."

5 After this I saw the temple in heaven open, with the Covenant Tent in it. 6 The seven angels who had the seven plagues came out of the temple, dressed in clean shining linen and with gold bands tied around their chests. 7 Then one of the four living creatures gave the seven angels seven gold bowls full of the anger of God, who lives forever and ever. 8 The temple was filled with smoke from the glory and power of God, and no one could go into the temple until the seven plagues brought by the seven angels had come to an end.

SECTION HEADING: TEV "The Angels with the Last Plagues." A possible alternative is "Preparation for the last seven plagues," or simply "The seven final punishments."

This section introduces the seven last punishments that are to come upon the earth, as described in detail in chapter 16. Here once again the narrative picks up the events that precede the End. Since the blowing of the seventh trumpet (11.15-19), there has been an interruption in the sequence of events leading to the End. Some commentators interpret these seven last plagues to be the third horror, predicted in 11.14; but the writer himself does not make this identification.

15.1   RSV   TEV

Then I saw another portent in heaven, great and wonderful, seven angels with seven plagues, which are the last, for with them the wrath of God is ended.

Then I saw in the sky another mysterious sight, great and amazing. There were seven angels with seven plagues, which are the last ones, because they are the final expression of God's anger.

Another portent in heaven: see 12.1. Here, however, John explicitly says **I saw**. What he sees takes place in heaven itself, not high in the air, nor in "the sky" as in TEV.

Great and wonderful: the two adjectives are used together in verse 3 also. **Great** does not mean "large" or "powerful" in this context, but rather "incredible" or "important." **Wonderful** can be understood to mean "impressive," "amazing," "astonishing." The related verb is used in 13.3, translated there as "with wonder."

Seven plagues: for **plagues** see 9.18. Care should be taken in translating **seven angels with seven plagues** to avoid giving the impression that these seven angels are suffering from some incurable disease. So it may be better to say "seven angels who had the responsibility of inflicting the seven last plagues on the world" or ". . . of causing the people of the world to receive the seven final punishments."

With them the wrath of God is ended: for **wrath** see 12.12. The Greek verb translated **ended** means not only to cease but also to complete. In this context the seven plagues express fully and completely God's anger at sinners. So NJB translates "they exhaust the anger of God"; REB "was completed"; RNAB "is accomplished"; TNT "is consummated"; Brc, rather wordily, "reached its climax and consummation." Some languages, however, cannot speak about **wrath** (or, "anger") being accomplished or ended. In such cases translators may say "when these punishments are finished God will stop being angry," or "when God finishes punishing people these seven times, he will stop being angry," or ". . . his hot heart will cool down."

15.2   RSV   TEV

And I saw what appeared to be a sea of glass mingled with fire, and those who had conquered the beast and its image and the number of its name, standing beside the sea of glass with harps of God in their hands.	Then I saw what looked like a sea of glass mixed with fire. I also saw those who had won the victory over the beast and its image and over the one whose name is represented by a number. They were standing by the sea of glass, holding harps that God had given them

What appeared to be a sea of glass: see 4.6.

Mingled with fire: it is impossible to know precisely what the writer is describing. Perhaps flashes of light, like lightning, were being reflected on the surface of what seemed to be a sea of glass, or crystal. Or it may have been that the sea was red in color.

Conquered the beast and its image and the number of its name: for **conquered** see 2.7; 6.2. The construction of the Greek text makes it appear that the conquerors had conquered three things: (1) the beast, (2) its image (or, statue), and (3) the number of its name. But all three refer to the same one, that is, the first beast, who came up out of the sea (13.1), in whose honor a statue was built, which people were ordered to worship (13.14-15), and whose name was represented by a number (13.16-17). To avoid giving the idea of three different things, perhaps something like the following can be said: "I also saw those who had defeated the beast and its statue, that beast whose name is represented by a number." This may be better than saying they had conquered a number. FRCL has "they had won the victory over the beast, over its image, and over the number that corresponds to his name." The meaning of the statement is the same as what is said of the redeemed in 14.4-5: they had remained faithful to Jesus Christ and had not worshiped the beast.

Harps of God: that is, harps given to them by God. For **harps** see 5.8.

15.3   RSV   TEV

And they sing the song of Moses, the servant of God, and the song of the Lamb, saying, 　　"Great and wonderful are thy 　　　　deeds, 　　O Lord God the Almighty!	and singing the song of Moses, the servant of God, and the song of the Lamb: 　　"Lord God Almighty, 　　　how great and wonderful are 　　　your deeds!

Just and true are thy ways,	**King of the nations,**[f]
O King of the ages![j]	**how right and true are your**
	ways!

[j] Other ancient authorities read *the nations*

[f] nations; *some manuscripts have* ages.

They sing: as in 14.3. Here the song is identified as **the song of Moses**, which probably means the song that Moses sang (or, the song that Moses composed); see Exodus 15.1-18. Some believe that this is an allusion to the song of Moses in Deuteronomy 32.1-44. The translation can say "the song that Moses, the servant of God, sang (or, composed)." For **servant** see 1.1. As for **the song of the Lamb**, the context requires the same meaning: "the song that the Lamb sang (or, composed)." The song (verses 3-4) may be rendered in poetic form (see Section F of the introduction, "Translating the Revelation to John," pages 6 and following).

Great and wonderful are thy deeds: these are the same two adjectives used in verse 1.

Lord God the Almighty: as in 1.8; 4.8.

Just and true are thy ways: the Greek word translated **ways** means literally "roads," "paths." In a figurative sense God's **ways** are the things that he does, or the motives that make him do what he does. Very specifically, God's **ways** are his actions on behalf of his people (see Psa 145.17). The two adjectives **just and true** are not to be sharply distinguished in meaning; with reference to actions they mean "correct," "right," "fair." For **true** see 3.7. The same two adjectives are used to modify God's "judgments" in 16.7; 19.2.

King of the ages: this means "King forever and ever." This Greek text speaks of God as ruler for all time, from beginning to end. The Greek text translated by TEV says "King of the nations," that is, king of all the world. The textual evidence is fairly evenly divided, and translations differ. Most translations, including NRSV, prefer "nations"; AT, NIV, and REB translate "ages." One may also translate "You who rule over the nations" or ". . . over all the people of the world."

In many languages the vocative **O King of the ages** should be placed at the beginning of the statement, as in TEV, not at the end.

An alternative translation model for this verse is:

> And they sang the song that Moses the servant of God sang (or, composed) and the song that the Lamb sang (or, composed), saying,
>> You, God who are all-powerful,
>>> you do incredible and amazing deeds.
>> You rule over all the nations.
>> Everything you do is correct and fair.

15.4 RSV	TEV

Who shall not fear and glorify
    thy name, O Lord?
For thou alone art holy.
All nations shall come and wor-
	Who will not stand in awe of you,
	    Lord?
	Who will refuse to declare your
	    greatness?

ship thee,
for thy judgments have been re-
vealed."

You alone are holy.
All the nations will come
and worship you,
because your just actions are
seen by all."

Who shall not fear and glorify thy name, O Lord? This is a rhetorical way of saying "Everyone will fear and glorify your name," and in some languages it may be better to use the positive statement instead of the negative rhetorical question. For **fear . . . thy name** see 11.18; for **glorify thy name** see 11.13; 14.7. TEV divides the one question into two, and some translators may wish to do the same. The following is an alternative translation model for the first part of this verse: "Everyone will have reverence for you, O Lord! All people will confess, 'You are very great and powerful.'"

Thou alone art holy: the Greek word translated **holy** (which appears also in 16.5) is different from the one used in 3.7, but the meaning is the same. It is what characterizes the essence of God as God, that is, God's divinity, his separateness from humanity. Beckwith defines it: "his unapproachable majesty and power." Certain translators will find it helpful to render this as "You alone are truly God!"

All nations shall come and worship thee: this may be rendered "People from all nations," "All the people in the world." As for the verb **come**, the translator must be aware of the point of reference and decide whether "go" or "come" is more appropriate. Since those who sing this song are in heaven, "come" seems appropriate. For **worship** see 4.10.

Thy judgments have been revealed: the Greek word translated **judgments** appears here and in 19.8, and means either "righteous (or, just) decrees" (so REB) or "righteous (or, just) actions" (TEV, TNT, FRCL, NIV, RNAB). The latter seems more appropriate in this context. The word parallels "deeds" at the beginning of the song, in verse 3. God's righteousness, God's justice, is shown by what he does. The passive **have been revealed** may be rendered "have been seen by all" or "everyone has seen your righteous acts."

15.5-6	RSV	TEV

5 After this I looked, and the temple of the tent of witness in heaven was opened, 6 and out of the temple came the seven angels with the seven plagues, robed in pure bright linen, and their breasts girded with golden girdles.

5 After this I saw the temple in heaven open, with the Covenant Tent in it. 6 The seven angels who had the seven plagues came out of the temple, dressed in clean shining linen and with gold bands tied around their chests.

The temple of the tent of witness: there is some uncertainty as to what this compound genitive phrase means. A literal rendering, such as RSV and NRSV, is quite ambiguous, but the average reader probably understands that it means that in the tent of witness there is a temple. There are three possibilities: (1) **the tent of witness** is in apposition to **the temple**: "the temple, that is, the Witness Tent" (AT, NJB, SPCL, NIV, RNAB); (2) "the Witness Tent in the Temple" (TEV, FRCL, BRCL); (3)

"the sanctuary of the Witness Tent" (TNT, REB, Brc, Phps). In favor of the last interpretation—which is the one that is recommended—is the fact that the word translated **temple** (*naos*) is used in a specialized sense of the inner sanctuary of the Temple, as contrasted with the large worship area (*hieron*). The inner sanctuary (in which the Covenant Box was kept) was separated by a heavy curtain from the worship area, in which were located the altar of incense and the table on which were placed daily the loaves offered to God. This was also the arrangement of the Covenant Tent, the "Tent of Meeting" (see Exo 40.1-33). It seems best, then, to translate here "the sanctuary (or, most Holy Place) that was in the Witness Tent." The name "Witness Tent" (also Acts 7.44) was sometimes applied to the Tent of Meeting, or Covenant Tent, that the Hebrews carried with them in their forty years of wandering through the wilderness. A translation should use here the name most often used in the Old Testament and in Acts 7.44.

Was opened: as in 11.19. An alternative translation model for verse 5 is:

> After these people finished singing, I looked and saw that they (unknown agents) had opened the Most Holy Place inside the Witness Tent (or, Tent of Meeting).

The seven angels with the seven plagues: as in verse 1.

Robed in pure white linen: robed translates a participle of the same verb rendered "clothed" in 1.13. For a description of the flax plant, from which **linen** is made, the translator should consult a Bible dictionary or *Fauna and Flora,* pages 119–121. Where linen is unknown the translation can say "wearing white shining clothes" or "wearing a white shining robe."

Their breasts girded with golden girdles: as in 1.13. The Greek word for "breasts (or, chests)" in 1.13 is different from the one used here, but the meaning is the same. NRSV is much better than RSV: "golden sashes across their chests"; note NIV and RNAB "gold sashes around their chests."

An alternative translation model for verse 6 is:

> The seven angels (or, heavenly messengers) who had the seven punishments came out of the Witness Tent. Each one was wearing a white shining robe, and had a gold colored band (or, sash) across his chest.

15.7   RSV   TEV

And one of the four living creatures gave the seven angels seven golden bowls full of the wrath of God who lives for ever and ever;

Then one of the four living creatures gave the seven angels seven gold bowls full of the anger of God, who lives forever and ever.

One of the four living creatures: see 4.6-8.

Seven golden bowls full of the wrath of God: it may be assumed that the liquid in the bowls is wine, "the wine of God's wrath" (14.10; see the language of chapter 16). So it may be well to express the meaning here by saying "seven gold bowls full of the wine that represents the anger of God" or ". . . the wine of God's anger." In a more elaborate way the translation may say "And one of the four living creatures gave to each angel a gold bowl filled with a terrible punishment that God, who lives for ever and ever, will pour out on the world."

Who lives for ever and ever: see 4.9.

15.8

RSV	TEV
and the temple was filled with smoke from the glory of God and from his power, and no one could enter the temple until the seven plagues of the seven angels were ended.	The temple was filled with smoke from the glory and power of God, and no one could go into the temple until the seven plagues brought by the seven angels had come to an end.

The temple was filled with smoke from the glory of God: if the translation has "sanctuary" or its equivalent in verse 5, the same word should be used here. For a similar statement of God's presence in the Tent and the Temple, see Exodus 40.34; 1 Kings 8.10-11; 2 Chronicles 5.13-14; Isaiah 6.4. God's **glory** (see 1.6) is the visible manifestation of his presence in the form of a brilliant light. The double phrase **the glory of God and . . . his power** may mean "God's greatness (or, majesty) and power" or "God's majestic power." For **power** see 2.26; 3.8.

No one could enter: this is like the instances in the Old Testament referred to above, in which God's glory made it impossible for priests or worshipers to enter the Tent or the Temple.

Were ended: this is the same verb used in verse 1.

An alternative translation model for this verse is:

> The Witness Tent was filled with smoke that came from God's greatness and power. No one could go into the Tent until the seven punishments that the seven angels had brought were finished.

16.1-21

RSV

TEV

The Bowls of God's Anger

1 Then I heard a loud voice from the temple telling the seven angels, "Go and pour out on the earth the seven bowls of the wrath of God."

2 So the first angel went and poured his bowl on the earth, and foul and evil sores came upon the men who bore the mark of the beast and worshiped its image.

3 The second angel poured his bowl into the sea, and it became like the blood of a dead man, and every living thing died that was in the sea.

4 The third angel poured his bowl into the rivers and the fountains of water, and they became

1 Then I heard a loud voice speaking from the temple to the seven angels: "Go and pour out the seven bowls of God's anger on the earth!"

2 The first angel went and poured out his bowl on the earth. Terrible and painful sores appeared on those who had the mark of the beast and on those who had worshiped its image.

3 Then the second angel poured out his bowl on the sea. The water became like the blood of a dead person, and every living creature in the sea died.

4 Then the third angel poured out his bowl on the rivers and the springs of water, and they turned into blood. 5 I heard the angel in charge of

blood. 5 And I heard the angel of water say,
"Just art thou in these thy judgments,
thou who art and wast, O Holy One.
6   For men have shed the blood of saints
        and prophets,
    and thou hast given them blood to drink.
    It is their due!"
7 And I heard the altar cry,
"Yea, Lord God the Almighty,
    true and just are thy judgments!"
8 The fourth angel poured his bowl on the
sun, and it was allowed to scorch men with fire;
9 men were scorched by the fierce heat, and they
cursed the name of God who had power over
these plagues, and they did not repent and give
him glory.

10 The fifth angel poured his bowl on the
throne of the beast, and its kingdom was in darkness; men gnawed their tongues in anguish 11 and
cursed the God of heaven for their pain and sores,
and did not repent of their deeds.

12 The sixth angel poured his bowl on the
great river Euphrates, and its water was dried up,
to prepare the way for the kings from the east.
13 And I saw, issuing from the mouth of the
dragon and from the mouth of the beast and from
the mouth of the false prophet, three foul spirits
like frogs; 14 for they are demonic spirits, performing signs, who go abroad to the kings of the
whole world, to assemble them for battle on the
great day of God the Almighty. 15 ("Lo, I am
coming like a thief! Blessed is he who is awake,
keeping his garments that he may not go naked
and be seen exposed!") 16 And they assembled
them at the place which is called in Hebrew
Armageddon.

17 The seventh angel poured his bowl into
the air, and a loud voice came out of the temple,
from the throne, saying, "It is done!" 18 And
there were flashes of lightning, voices, peals of
thunder, and a great earthquake such as had never
been since men were on the earth, so great was
that earthquake. 19 The great city was split into
three parts, and the cities of the nations fell, and
God remembered great Babylon, to make her
drain the cup of the fury of his wrath. 20 And
every island fled away, and no mountains were to
be found; 21 and great hailstones, heavy as a
hundred-weight, dropped on men from heaven, till
men cursed God for the plague of the hail, so
fearful was that plague.

the waters say, "The judgments you have made are
just, O Holy One, you who are and who were!
6 They poured out the blood of God's people and
of the prophets, and so you have given them blood
to drink. They are getting what they deserve!"
7 Then I heard a voice from the altar saying,
"Lord God Almighty! True and just indeed are
your judgments!"

8 Then the fourth angel poured out his
bowl on the sun, and it was allowed to burn
people with its fiery heat. 9 They were burned by
the fierce heat, and they cursed the name of God,
who has authority over these plagues. But they
would not turn from their sins and praise his
greatness.

10 Then the fifth angel poured out his bowl
on the throne of the beast. Darkness fell over the
beast's kingdom, and people bit their tongues
because of their pain, 11 and they cursed the God
of heaven for their pains and sores. But they did
not turn from their evil ways.

12 Then the sixth angel poured out his bowl
on the great Euphrates River. The river dried up,
to provide a way for the kings who come from the
east. 13 Then I saw three unclean spirits that
looked like frogs. They were coming out of the
mouth of the dragon, the mouth of the beast, and
the mouth of the false prophet. 14 They are the
spirits of demons that perform miracles. These
three spirits go out to all the kings of the world, to
bring them together for the battle on the great
Day of Almighty God.

15 "Listen! I am coming like a thief! Happy
is he who stays awake and guards his clothes, so
that he will not walk around naked and be
ashamed in public!"

16 Then the spirits brought the kings
together in the place that in Hebrew is called
Armageddon.

17 Then the seventh angel poured out his
bowl in the air. A loud voice came from the
throne in the temple, saying, "It is done!"
18 There were flashes of lightning, rumblings and
peals of thunder, and a terrible earthquake. There
has never been such an earthquake since the
creation of man; this was the worst earthquake of
all! 19 The great city was split into three parts,
and the cities of all countries were destroyed. God
remembered great Babylon and made her drink
the wine from his cup—the wine of his furious
anger. 20 All the islands disappeared, all the
mountains vanished. 21 Huge hailstones, each
weighing as much as a hundred pounds, fell from
the sky on people, who cursed God on account of
the plague of hail, because it was such a terrible
plague.

SECTION HEADING: TEV "The Bowls of God's Anger." Other possibilities are "The seven last manifestations of God's anger," "The seven last punishments."

After the preparation described in chapter 15, seven angels pour out on humankind the seven last punishments ("plagues") sent by God before the Final Judgment.

16.1   RSV   TEV

Then I heard a loud voice from the temple telling the seven angels, "Go and pour out on the earth the seven bowls of the wrath of God."

Then I heard a loud voice speaking from the temple to the seven angels: "Go and pour out the seven bowls of God's anger on the earth!"

A loud voice from the temple: the voice comes from the temple, or sanctuary, in heaven. Since 15.8 says that there was no one in the temple now, this command comes from God (10.4). See 14.15 on other ways to translate **loud voice**.

Go and pour: the angels are in heaven (15.1), and they must go out in order to pour out on the earth the contents of their bowls. So **go** is the right verb to use in this context.

Pour out . . . the seven bowls: this can be stated "empty out . . . the seven bowls." In some languages it may be necessary to specify what is to be poured out; if so, something like the following can be said: "Go and pour out on the earth the wine of God's anger that is in the (seven) bowls" (see 14.10).

16.2   RSV   TEV

So the first angel went and poured his bowl on the earth, and foul and evil sores came upon the men who bore the mark of the beast and worshiped its image.

The first angel went and poured out his bowl on the earth. Terrible and painful sores appeared on those who had the mark of the beast and on those who had worshiped its image.

Poured his bowl on the earth: if necessary the translation can say "poured out on the earth what was in his bowl."

Foul and evil sores: the two adjectives in English, **foul and evil**, have moral content and hardly apply to sores. (The two Greek adjectives normally mean "bad and evil.") Something like "terrible and awful" or "awful and painful" applies more naturally to sores. These are like the plague of boils that struck the Egyptians (see Exo 9.9-10). For **sores** see Luke 16.21. In many languages translators may use terms that refer to open sores such as "ulcers."

The men who bore the mark of the beast and worshiped its image: instead of **the men** the more inclusive "the people" or "those who . . ." will be better. For **the mark of the beast**, see 13.16,17; 14.9; for **worshiped its image** see 13.15; 14.9,11. On the translation of **worshiped** see 4.10. If a translation has preferred "statue" to **image**, the same must be done here.

An alternative translation model for this verse is:

So the first angel (or, heavenly messenger) poured the contents of the bowl (or, what was in his bowl) on the earth. Terrible (or, horrible, dreadful) and painful sores appeared on those on whom the beast had put his mark, and on those people who had worshiped (or, acknowledged the greatness of) its statue.

16.3   RSV   TEV

The second angel poured his bowl   Then the second angel poured out
into the sea, and it became like the   his bowl on the sea. The water became
blood of a dead man, and every living   like the blood of a dead person, and
thing died that was in the sea.   every living creature in the sea died.

Into the sea: as in 8.8-9 this represents all bodies of salt water.

It became like the blood of a dead man: it may be better to speak of the water in the sea becoming like the blood of a dead person. This refers not simply to the color of the water but to its consistency; it became like the coagulated, dark blood of a corpse. This is like the plague on Egypt described in Exodus 7.20-21.

Every living thing . . . in the sea: see 5.13.

16.4   RSV   TEV

The third angel poured his bowl   Then the third angel poured out
into the rivers and the fountains of   his bowl on the rivers and the springs of
water, and they became blood.   water, and they turned into blood.

The rivers and the fountains of water: as in 8.10, all bodies of fresh water.

Became blood: as in 8.9.

16.5   RSV   TEV

And I heard the angel of water say,   I heard the angel in charge of the wa-
    "Just art thou in these thy judg-   ters say, "The judgments you have made
        ments,   are just, O Holy One, you who are and
    thou who art and wast, O Holy   who were!
        One.

The angel of water: nowhere else in Revelation is this angel referred to; presumably he is in charge of all water on earth (see 14.18 for the angel in charge of fire). It is appropriate that he speak here, since the second and third bowls of God's anger were poured out on all bodies of water.

Say: the angel speaks to God, so it may be well to say explicitly "say to God."

Just art thou in these thy judgments: for **Just** see 15.3. The noun phrase **these thy judgments** translates a verbal phrase in Greek, "that you judged these (things)." For the verb "to judge" see 6.10. In many languages it will be natural to imitate RSV and TEV and use a noun phrase. Since in this context **judgments** refers to the plagues that are being sent on the world, it is possible to translate "these punishments."

Thou who art and wast: these verb forms in modern English appear as in TEV. See comments on "who is and who was" in 1.4.

O Holy One: see 15.4.

In some languages it may be more satisfactory to change the order of the various clauses and phrases as follows:

"You are the Holy God (or, "You are truly God); you are the God who lives now and have always lived! These punishments you send on the world are just.

16.6

RSV	TEV
For men have shed the blood of saints and prophets, and thou hast given them blood to drink. It is their due!"	They poured out the blood of God's people and of the prophets, and so you have given them blood to drink. They are getting what they deserve!"

Men have shed the blood of saints and prophets: in Greek there is no subject of the active verb **have shed** (TEV "poured out"); something like "people" or "evil people" is better than **men**. "They" of TEV has no clear antecedent and should not be imitated. In Greek the verb translated **shed** by RSV is the same verb, "poured out," used of the angels emptying their bowls. But if "to pour out (or, shed) blood" is not a normal way of speaking of killing, it will be necessary to say "people killed" or "people slaughtered." So this clause may also be rendered as "Evil people have killed God's people and his prophets." However, since **blood to drink** is the due punishment for **shed the blood**, it will be good to retain somehow the figure of blood in this first line, if possible.

For **saints** see 5.8; for **prophets** see 10.7. The two are paired also in 11.18; 18.24.

Thou hast given them blood to drink: this is a vivid way of describing the punishment that God sends on them; instead of water to drink from the rivers and springs of water, they will have only blood to drink.

It is their due! This translates the adjective "(they are) worthy," a way of saying "they deserve it" (see "worthy" in 3.4; 4.11). NJB and NRSV have "It is what they deserve."

16.7

RSV	TEV
And I heard the altar cry, "Yea, Lord God the Almighty, true and just are thy judgments!"	Then I heard a voice from the altar saying, "Lord God Almighty! True and just indeed are your judgments!"

I heard the altar cry: in some languages it may be impossible to speak of an altar crying out or saying something; in these cases it may be necessary to imitate TEV, "I heard a voice from the altar" (see in 6.9 the souls of the martyrs near the altar). In 8.3-5 the prayers of God's people are offered on the altar of incense, and here it is probably this altar that is meant. In languages that cannot speak of voices crying, one may need to say, for example, "I heard someone crying out from the altar, saying . . . ."

Yea: something like "Indeed" or "Truly" is better in English. NRSV has "Yes."

Lord God the Almighty: see comments on 1.8; 11.17.

True and just: see 15.3. Since **judgments** here, as in verse 5, refers specifically to the punishments, the translation can say "your punishments (or, the punishments you send) are fair and well deserved." Or it is possible to translate "You have judged them fairly and justly."

16.8	RSV	TEV
	The fourth angel poured his bowl on the sun, and it was allowed to scorch men with fire;	Then the fourth angel poured out his bowl on the sun, and it was allowed to burn people with its fiery heat.

On the sun: unlike the first three angels, who pour out the contents of their bowls on earth, this one pours his out on the sun. As a result the sun becomes much hotter than usual.

It was allowed: the sun is spoken of as God's instrument, or servant. God authorizes it, or permits it, to burn people with its terrible heat. The same passive construction "it was given to him (or, them)" is used in the same sense of divine authorization in 6.4a; 7.2; 9.5; 13.7a,15. FRCL has "it was authorized," and NIV "the sun was given power to scorch." The verb **to scorch** here and in verse 9 means "to burn" people, but not badly enough to cause their death. The **fire** is the heat from the sun. In languages that do not use the passive, one may say "and God allowed the sun to burn people with its fiery heat."

16.9	RSV	TEV
	men were scorched by the fierce heat, and they cursed the name of God who had power over these plagues, and they did not repent and give him glory.	They were burned by the fierce heat, and they cursed the name of God, who has authority over these plagues. But they would not turn from their sins and praise his greatness.

Men were scorched by the fierce heat: something like "people received severe burns" can be said. The verb chosen to translate **scorched** (TEV "burned") should not mean "destroyed by fire." One may also translate "The sun caused people to receive severe (or, painful) burns with its terrible heat."

They cursed the name of God: see 13.6, "blaspheming the name," where the same Greek verb is used.

Had power over these plagues: the use of the past tense of the verb, **had**, may wrongly imply that God no longer has this authority. For **power** see 2.26. For comments on **plagues** see 9.18.

They did not repent and give him glory: for **repent** see 2.5; for **give him glory** see 11.13. Something like "praise his greatness" or "acknowledge his power" expresses the meaning of the phrase. Alternative translation models for this final sentence are "They did not stop sinning and would not praise God's greatness" or ". . . and would not say, 'God, you are very great (or, powerful).'"

16.10-11   RSV   TEV

10 The fifth angel poured his bowl on the throne of the beast, and its kingdom was in darkness; men gnawed their tongues in anguish 11 and cursed the God of heaven for their pain and sores, and did not repent of their deeds.	10 Then the fifth angel poured out his bowl on the throne of the beast. Darkness fell over the beast's kingdom, and people bit their tongues because of their pain, 11 and they cursed the God of heaven for their pains and sores. But they did not turn from their evil ways.

The throne of the beast: this is the first beast (see 13.2; see also "Satan's throne" in 2.13).

Its kingdom was in darkness: the beast is a king, and the "country" it rules is a **kingdom**. Something like "darkness covered its kingdom" or "its kingdom was plunged into darkness" can be said (see the plague of darkness in Egypt, Exo 10.21-22). For the verb "to become dark," see 9.2. In the symbolism of this book the beast's kingdom was the Roman Empire. One may also express this as "The place where he ruled as king (or, high chief) became completely dark," or even "All light disappeared from the place where . . . ."

Men gnawed their tongues in anguish: instead of **men** the gender-inclusive "people" should be used. And instead of **gnawed** something like "bit" may be more appropriate. The word translated **anguish** means "pain," "suffering" (it is used also in 21.4, where it is translated "pain"). The pain, or suffering, of these people was not caused by the darkness as such; it seems that the confusion caused by the darkness intensified the pain of the sores they had received when the first bowl was poured out (verse 2).

Cursed: as in verse 9. For **God of heaven** see 11.13.

For their pain and sores: this can be taken to mean "because of the pain of their sores," that is, "because their sores were so painful."

Did not repent of their deeds: as in 9.20,21, the meaning here is that they did not cease from their evil actions.

An alternative translation model for verse 11 is:

> And they said bad (or, evil) things about God, who lives in heaven, because their sores (or, ulcers) were so painful. But they did not stop doing evil things.

16.12 RSV TEV

The sixth angel poured his bowl on the great river Euphrates, and its water was dried up, to prepare the way for the kings from the east.

Then the sixth angel poured out his bowl on the great Euphrates River. The river dried up, to provide a way for the kings who come from the east.

The great river Euphrates: see 9.14.

Its water was dried up: this can be stated "its water stopped flowing." The language recalls Isaiah 11.15-16; and see Joshua 3.13-17.

To prepare the way for the kings from the east: by drying up the river Euphrates, the angel made it possible for the kings who ruled in the east to advance with their armies and attack the kingdom of the beast. It is generally agreed that **the east** refers to the region then known as Parthia (now in north central Iraq). The noun **east** translates the Greek phrase "rising of the sun" (also in 7.2), and in certain languages this will be a more natural translation.

16.13 RSV TEV

And I saw, issuing from the mouth of the dragon and from the mouth of the beast and from the mouth of the false prophet, three foul spirits like frogs;

Then I saw three unclean spirits that looked like frogs. They were coming out of the mouth of the dragon, the mouth of the beast, and the mouth of the false prophet.

Issuing from the mouth: instead of following the order of the Greek text, as RSV does, it may be better to restructure the verse in order to avoid having the long participial clause **issuing from . . . false prophet** separating the main verb **I saw** from its object **three foul spirits**. TEV provides a useful model.

The dragon . . . the beast . . . the false prophet: from now on the second beast, the one that came up out of the earth (13.11-15), is called **the false prophet** (see 19.20; 20.10). This defines his role as the spokesman of the first beast, with the task of misleading people with his message. In this case one may also express this as "the second beast, the one who gave a false message."

Foul spirits: the adjective is the same one in the Gospels and Acts that is translated "unclean (spirits)." These are evil spirits, or demons, that possessed people and made them ritually unclean and so unable to participate in ordinary religious and social affairs until they were made ritually pure once more. Here the adjective may not have that specialized sense and may mean more generally "terrible" or "evil." See 2.10 for further discussion on the translation of "demons," "devil," or "evil spirits."

Like frogs: that is, they had the shape of frogs. In languages where frogs are unknown, other loathsome-looking creatures should be used. However, a picture of frogs may also be helpful. See *Fauna and Flora,* pages 32-33.

An alternative translation model for this verse is:

Then I saw three disgusting-looking spirits (or, demons) that looked like frogs. They were coming out of the mouth of the dragon, the mouth of the first beast, and the mouth of the second beast, the one who gave a false message.

16.14   RSV   TEV

for they are demonic spirits, performing signs, who go abroad to the kings of the whole world, to assemble them for battle on the great day of God the Almighty.	They are the spirits of demons that perform miracles. These three spirits go out to all the kings of the world, to bring them together for the battle on the great Day of Almighty God.

Demonic spirits: this translates "spirits of demons" (see the similar "the spirit of an unclean demon" in Luke 4.33). In translation it may not be advisable to say literally, as TEV does, "the spirits of demons"; it will be better to say "demons" or "evil spirits," or **demonic spirits**, as RSV does.

Performing signs: for **signs** see 13.13-14.

Go abroad means "go out everywhere." These spirits do not enter people and possess them, but they "go out to all the kings of the world, to bring them together for the battle" (TEV). For **the whole world** the Greek phrase is "the whole inhabited earth" (as in 3.10). On the translation of **kings** see 1.5.

To assemble them for battle: the evil spirits bring together all the kings of the world for the battle of the End. For **battle** see 9.7. This phrase may also be rendered as "to bring together all the kings of the world to the place where they will fight" (or, battlefield).

The great day of God the Almighty: this is Judgment Day, when God will condemn and punish all evildoers. The battle will be between the forces of evil and the heavenly forces of God (see 19.11-15). For **God the Almighty** see similar language in 1.8; 4.8; 11.17; 16.7. This phrase may also be rendered as "The Day when God, who is all powerful, will judge people."

16.15   RSV   TEV

("Lo, I am coming like a thief! Blessed is he who is awake, keeping his garments that he may not go naked and be seen exposed!")	"Listen! I am coming like a thief! Happy is he who stays awake and guards his clothes, so that he will not walk around naked and be ashamed in public!"

Both RSV and TEV indicate that this verse is not part of the narrative as such but is a word from the Lord Jesus Christ. RSV does this by means of quotation marks and parentheses, TEV by quotation marks and a paragraph. It will be appropriate to say specifically, as FRCL does, "The Lord says . . . ."

Lo: as in "Behold" in 1.7.

I am coming like a thief: suddenly and undetected (see 3.3).

Blessed: see 1.3.

Who is awake: that is, who stays awake; who doesn't fall asleep; who keeps watch. The verb is used in the sense of "wake up" in 3.2,3.

Keeping his garments that he may not go naked: this can mean "keeping his clothes on" (NJB, TNT, NRSV ["is clothed"]); but it may also mean "keeps his clothes ready (to put on)," as REB, RNAB, Phps, Brc translate. This seems to be preferable. It is possible that the Greek phrase (which says, simply, "keeping his clothes") means "keeping his clothes clean" (as is said clearly in 3.4), but this is rather unlikely.

Be seen exposed: this translates the Greek "they see his shame," where "shame" is regarded by many as a euphemism for "private parts" of the body. The third plural active of the verb "to see" is an impersonal plural, meaning simply "and be seen," as RSV has it. The noun translated **exposed** occurs in the New Testament only here and in Romans 1.27, "shameless" (see in 3.18 the more complete phrase "the shame of your nakedness").

An alternative translation model for this verse is:

The Lord says, "Pay attention! I am coming just like a thief comes (at night). How fortunate is the person who stays awake, keeping his clothes ready so that he will not walk around naked and be ashamed (or, lose face) when people look at him."

16.16　　　RSV　　　　　　　　　　　　TEV

And they assembled them at the place which is called in Hebrew Armageddon.

Then the spirits brought the kings together in the place that in Hebrew is called Armageddon.

And they assembled them: the same verb is used in verse 14. It is helpful to specify both the subject and the object of the verb, as TEV has done.

Armageddon: this is the transliteration (in Greek) of the Hebrew *harmegiddo* "the hill of Megiddo." The name itself does not appear in the Old Testament. The Plain of Megiddo in northern Palestine was the scene of some important battles in Israelite history (see Judges 5.19; 2 Kgs 23.29-30; 2 Chr 35.22). **Armageddon** is the most commonly used English form of the word; but NRSV has "Harmagedon"; REB "Harmageddon"; TNT "Har-Magedon." **Is called** may also be rendered "they call in the Hebrew language" or "has the name Armageddon in Hebrew."

16.17　　　RSV　　　　　　　　　　　　TEV

The seventh angel poured his bowl into the air, and a loud voice came out of the temple, from the throne, saying, "It is done!"

Then the seventh angel poured out his bowl in the air. A loud voice came from the throne in the temple, saying, "It is done!"

Into the air: the direction is downward; the angel is in heaven, and from there he empties the contents of the bowl in the air, between heaven and earth.

A loud voice came out of the temple: the temple in heaven, as in 16.1. For **loud voice** see 14.15 and elsewhere.

From the throne: this is God's throne (see 1.4), indicating that the speaker is God. There are several ways of combining **out of the temple, from the throne**: "a voice was heard from the temple; it came from the throne" (FRCL); "out of the sanctuary came a voice that came from the throne" (SPCL); or "from the throne in the temple" (TEV).

"It is done!" This translates the perfect tense of "to become"; in this context the meaning can be "the End has come" (NJB, Phps) or "It is over" (REB), as indicated in the statement about "the wrath of God" in 15.1 (see also "fulfilled," 10.6-7; "has become," 11.15).

An alternative translation model for this verse is:

> Then the seventh angel poured out the contents from his bowl down into the sky. God spoke with a loud voice from the throne in the temple, saying, "Everything is done" (or, "I have completed everything").

16.18	RSV	TEV

And there were flashes of lightning, voices, peals of thunder, and a great earthquake such as had never been since men were on the earth, so great was that earthquake.	There were flashes of lightning, rumblings and peals of thunder, and a terrible earthquake. There has never been such an earthquake since the creation of man; this was the worst earthquake of all!

Flashes of lightning, voices, peals of thunder, and a great earthquake: see 4.5; 8.5; 11.19. This great earthquake is described as the most destructive of all earthquakes in history. In certain languages this will be expressed as "and the earth shook frighteningly (or, in a frightening way)."

Since men were on the earth: this can be said, more naturally, "ever since the creation of humankind," "ever since the human race has existed," or "ever since humans have existed in the world."

An alternative translation model for the final sentence of this verse is:

> Since humans have lived in the world, the earth has never shaken in such a destructive way.

16.19	RSV	TEV

The great city was split into three parts, and the cities of the nations fell, and God remembered great Babylon, to	The great city was split into three parts, and the cities of all countries were destroyed. God remembered great Babylon

make her drain the cup of the fury of his wrath.	and made her drink the wine from his cup—the wine of his furious anger.

The great city: that is, Babylon (see 14.8). Some commentators take it to be Jerusalem.

Split into three parts: the picture here is of an earthquake that causes large cracks in the earth, thus dividing the city into three separate sections. In certain languages it will be helpful to begin this verse in the following way: "The earthquake split the city . . ." or "When the ground shook, the city split (or, divided) into three parts."

The cities of the nations fell: this refers to all the cities in the world. For the verb **fell** see 14.8. One may also translate "and all the other cities in the world were destroyed" or "the earthquake . . . also destroyed all the other cities in the world."

God remembered great Babylon: the Greek text avoids naming God as subject by the use of the passive form of the verb: "Babylon . . . was remembered before God." The meaning here is that God now fixes his attention on Babylon and punishes her. In some languages it may be better to say "God did not forget Babylon; he made her drink . . . ."

To make her drain the cup of the fury of his wrath: the Greek text says "to give her the cup of the wine of the fury of his wrath." Here the verb "to give" does not mean that God simply offered Babylon this cup. So instead of NRSV "to give her," it is better to translate "to make her drink." RSV omits "the wine"; NRSV has "the wine-cup of the fury of his wrath." Again it seems better to say that God "forced Babylon to drink the wine of his furious wrath that was in the cup" or ". . . the wine that represents (or, brings) his wrath (or, punishment)." The phrase "of his furious wrath" modifies "the wine" and not "the cup." It is the wine that stands for God's wrath. See 14.10 for "the wine of God's wrath" and "the cup of his anger."

16.20-21 RSV	TEV
20 And every island fled away, and no mountains were to be found; 21 and great hailstones, heavy as a hundred-weight, dropped on men from heaven, till men cursed God for the plague of the hail, so fearful was that plague.	20 All the islands disappeared, all the mountains vanished. 21 Huge hailstones, each weighing as much as a hundred pounds, fell from the sky on people, who cursed God on account of the plague of hail, because it was such a terrible plague.

Every island fled away, and no mountains were to be found: this is a vivid way of saying that all the islands and mountains disappeared from sight. This is the result of the terrible earthquake; the islands sank into the sea, and the mountains were all leveled (see 6.14). Some translators will find it helpful to connect this verse to verse 18 by saying "The earthquake shook all the islands . . ." or "When the earth shook, all the islands . . . ."

Great hailstones: see comments on 8.7. In some languages these will be described as "frozen rocks."

239

Heavy as a hundredweight: in the American system a hundredweight equals one hundred pounds; in the British system, one hundred and twelve pounds. The Greek word is "(the weight) of a talent," which may be a way of saying "an enormous weight"; so RNAB "like huge weights," and Phps "like heavy weights." But the writer may have had in mind the actual weight of a talent (which was a unit of weight). Estimates vary between eighty and one hundred and twenty pounds. NRSV and NIV both have "about one hundred pounds." The metric equivalent of one hundred pounds is forty-five kilograms. SPCL translates "more than thirty kilograms," and FRCL "up to forty kilograms." In languages that have a limited group of numbers, or where objects have to be counted by a limited number of body parts such as fingers and toes, it will be better to say "Huge hailstones of tremendous weight (or, weighing as much as an adult person)."

Dropped on men from heaven, till men cursed God: instead of the exclusively male **men**, the inclusive "people" should be used. In languages that distinguish between heaven as the abode of God, and the sky, it is preferable to use "sky" here. For **cursed God** see verses 9 and 11.

The plague of the hail: this is like the plague that struck Egypt (see Exo 9.23-25); for **plague** see 9.18; 15.1.

So fearful was that plague: this translates the Greek "that plague was exceedingly great"; something like "terrible" or "awful" can be said.

An alternative translation model for these two verses is:

> When the earth shook violently, all the islands and mountains disappeared. Huge hailstones (or, frozen rocks), each weighing around one hundred pounds, fell from the sky on people. But because God punished them so severely (or, terribly) by sending hail like this, they cursed (or, said evil things against) him.

C-6. The Destruction of Babylon, and the Defeat of the Beast, the False Prophet, and the Devil
(17.1–20.10)

17.1-18

RSV

1 Then one of the seven angels who had the seven bowls came and said to me, "Come, I will show you the judgment of the great harlot who is seated upon many waters, 2 with whom the kings of the earth have committed fornication, and with the wine of whose fornication the dwellers on earth have become drunk." 3 And he carried me away in the Spirit into a wilderness, and I saw a woman sitting on a scarlet beast which was full of blasphemous names, and it had seven heads and ten horns. 4 The woman was arrayed in purple and scarlet, and bedecked with gold and jewels and pearls, holding in her hand a golden cup full of abominations and the impurities of her fornication; 5 and on her forehead was written a name of

TEV

The Famous Prostitute

1 Then one of the seven angels who had the seven bowls came to me and said, "Come, and I will show you how the famous prostitute is to be punished, that great city that is built near many rivers. 2 The kings of the earth practiced sexual immorality with her, and the people of the world became drunk from drinking the wine of her immorality."

3 The Spirit took control of me, and the angel carried me to a desert. There I saw a woman sitting on a red beast that had names insulting to God written all over it; the beast had seven heads and ten horns. 4 The woman was dressed in purple and scarlet, and covered with gold ornaments, precious stones, and pearls. In her hand she held

mystery: "Babylon the great, mother of harlots and of earth's abominations." 6 And I saw the woman, drunk with the blood of the saints and the blood of the martyrs of Jesus.

When I saw her I marveled greatly. 7 But the angel said to me, "Why marvel? I will tell you the mystery of the woman, and of the beast with seven heads and ten horns that carries her. 8 The beast that you saw was, and is not, and is to ascend from the bottomless pit and go to perdition; and the dwellers on earth whose names have not been written in the book of life from the foundation of the world, will marvel to behold the beast, because it was and is not and is to come. 9 This calls for a mind with wisdom: the seven heads are seven mountains on which the woman is seated; 10 they are also seven kings, five of whom have fallen, one is, the other has not yet come, and when he comes he must remain only a little while. 11 As for the beast that was and is not, it is an eighth but it belongs to the seven, and it goes to perdition. 12 And the ten horns that you saw are ten kings who have not yet received royal power, but they are to receive authority as kings for one hour, together with the beast. 13 These are of one mind and give over their power and authority to the beast; 14 they will make war on the Lamb, and the Lamb will conquer them, for he is Lord of lords and King of kings, and those with him are called and chosen and faithful."

15 And he said to me, "The waters that you saw, where the harlot is seated, are peoples and multitudes and nations and tongues. 16 And the ten horns that you saw, they and the beast will hate the harlot; they will make her desolate and naked, and devour her flesh and burn her up with fire, 17 for God has put it into their hearts to carry out his purpose by being of one mind and giving over their royal power to the beast, until the words of God shall be fulfilled. 18 And the woman that you saw is the great city which has dominion over the kings of the earth."

a gold cup full of obscene and filthy things, the result of her immorality. 5 On her forehead was written a name that has a secret meaning: "Great Babylon, the mother of all prostitutes and perverts in the world." 6 And I saw that the woman was drunk with the blood of God's people and the blood of those who were killed because they had been loyal to Jesus.

When I saw her, I was completely amazed. 7 "Why are you amazed?" the angel asked me. "I will tell you the secret meaning of the woman and of the beast that carries her, the beast with seven heads and ten horns. 8 That beast was once alive, but lives no longer; it is about to come up from the abyss and will go off to be destroyed. The people living on earth whose names have not been written before the creation of the world in the book of the living, will all be amazed as they look at the beast. It was once alive; now it no longer lives, but it will reappear.

9 "This calls for wisdom and understanding. The seven heads are seven hills, on which the woman sits. They are also seven kings: 10 five of them have fallen, one still rules, and the other one has not yet come; when he comes, he must rule only a little while. 11 And the beast that was once alive, but lives no longer, is itself an eighth king who is one of the seven and is going off to be destroyed.

12 "The ten horns you saw are ten kings who have not yet begun to rule, but who will be given authority to rule as kings for one hour with the beast. 13 These ten all have the same purpose, and they give their power and authority to the beast. 14 They will fight against the Lamb; but the Lamb, together with his called, chosen, and faithful followers, will defeat them, because he is Lord of lords and King of kings."

15 The angel also said to me, "The waters you saw, on which the prostitute sits, are nations, peoples, races, and languages. 16 The ten horns you saw and the beast will hate the prostitute; they will take away everything she has and leave her naked; they will eat her flesh and destroy her with fire. 17 For God has placed in their hearts the will to carry out his purpose by acting together and giving to the beast their power to rule until God's words come true.

18 "The woman you saw is the great city that rules over the kings of the earth."

SECTION HEADING: TEV "The Famous Prostitute." The wording of the title will be determined by the translation of **the great harlot** in verse 1. Other possibilities are "The prostitute and the beast"; "The woman on the beast" (NIV). Phillips, at verse 4, has the imaginative "The gorgeous mother of evil."

In this vision John sees a woman seated on a beast. She is identified as the great Babylon (verses 5,18). The seven heads of the beast are explained (verses 9-10), as are the beast's ten horns (verses 12-13). The woman and the beast are to be destroyed. The subject of the destruction of Babylon continues through 19.4.

17.1   RSV   TEV

Then one of the seven angels who had the seven bowls came and said to me, "Come, I will show you the judgment of the great harlot who is seated upon many waters,

Then one of the seven angels who had the seven bowls came to me and said, "Come, and I will show you how the famous prostitute is to be punished, that great city that is built near many rivers.

One of the seven angels who had the seven bowls: these are the angels of chapter 16.

Came: presumably the angel came from heaven down to earth, where John was.

The judgment of the great harlot: see comments on the verb "to judge," 6.10; the noun occurs also at 18.10,20; 20.4. The word for **judgment** may mean "condemnation," so that a translation can say "I will show you how God is going to condemn (or, punish) the great harlot." In translating the word for **harlot**, care should be taken not to use a vulgar or obscene term. The translation of **great** is a problem, for in English, at least, "great" refers either to size (large) or quality (excellent). Something like "notorious," or "powerful," or "infamous" will be better. Other terms for **harlot** in various languages are "woman who sells her body," "woman of the night," "woman of bad reputation," or just "bad woman."

John is speaking of "Babylon," that is, Rome (see comment at verse 18). The prophet Nahum (3.1-4) called Nineveh a whore, and Isaiah said the same of Jerusalem (1.21) and of the city of Tyre (23.15-16).

Who is seated upon many waters: this describes the city as being near rivers, which fits the city of Babylon (see Jer 51.13), not the city of Rome itself. The Greek preposition translated **upon** by RSV may mean "by" or "near" as in John 21.1, "by the Sea of Tiberias," which suits the meaning of the passage here. There may be some difficulty in maintaining the figure of a prostitute sitting near many rivers, and a translation may want to follow the lead of TEV and say "the infamous prostitute, that is, the great city that stands near many rivers."

17.2   RSV   TEV

with whom the kings of the earth have committed fornication, and with the wine of whose fornication the dwellers on earth have become drunk."

The kings of the earth practiced sexual immorality with her, and the people of the world became drunk from drinking the wine of her immorality."

RSV follows the form of the Greek text and continues the sentence to the end of verse 2. It is better in most instances to put a full stop at the end of verse 1 and begin a new sentence at verse 2, as TEV has done.

With whom the kings of the earth have committed fornication: in English **fornication** (as contrasted with adultery) implies that the woman is unmarried. Something like "sexual immorality," "immoral sexual intercourse," or even "filthy sexual practices" will be more suitable for this context. For the verb see "practice immorality," 2.14. This is a figure of idolatry, as elsewhere in the book. An alternative translation model for this sentence is "The kings (or, high chiefs) of the world committed evil (or, filthy) sexual practices with her."

With the wine of whose fornication: here the sexual immorality of the infamous prostitute is called **wine**, and the effect of her immorality (idolatry) on her partners is called drunkenness. In some languages it may be advisable not to follow literally the Greek text. A translator may follow the point of view of one commentator, that the wine was the prostitute's way of seducing her partners: "the people of the world got drunk on the wine she gave them and had sexual intercourse with her." For the noun translated **fornication** see "immorality" and comments at 2.21; 14.8.

The dwellers on earth: see 3.10.

Have become drunk: the term occurs also in 17.6. Most languages have a number of words to describe drunkenness, but few will match the English language. One word collector (Paul Dickson, *Words*) turned up 2,231 words and phrases for "drunk." However, the metaphor here refers to drunkenness from drinking wine. So translators should pick a word or phrase that means that type of drunkenness.

17.3 RSV	TEV
And he carried me away in the Spirit into a wilderness, and I saw a woman sitting on a scarlet beast which was full of blasphemous names, and it had seven heads and ten horns.	The Spirit took control of me, and the angel carried me to a desert. There I saw a woman sitting on a red beast that had names insulting to God written all over it; the beast had seven heads and ten horns.

He carried me away in the Spirit: in 1.10 and 4.2 John says "I was in the Spirit"; here and in 21.10 he describes how one of the seven angels who had the bowls carried him away **in the Spirit** (or, "spirit"). John is describing an ecstatic experience (like the one Paul talks about in 2 Cor 12.1-3). Goodspeed and Barclay use the expression "in a trance." SPCL has "Then, in the vision that the Spirit made me see, the angel took me to the desert." This is better than "in a trance." Or a translation may choose to follow TEV and TNT and say "The Spirit possessed me, and the angel carried me off." If a translation prefers to say "in the spirit" (as NRSV, REB have it), care must be taken not to say that the angel carried John's spirit off. John is talking about a vision. See 1.4,10 for comments on the translation of **Spirit**. In many languages translators may say "God's Spirit" if readers are likely to misunderstand.

A wilderness: in 12.6,14 the word is used of the desert to which the woman fled from the dragon; here it is not the same desert but some deserted place, not identified.

A scarlet beast: this beast, with **seven heads and ten horns**, is the first beast, the one that came up out of the sea (13.1). Only here is it said to be **scarlet** (in 12.3 the dragon is said to be red). Some languages distinguish between scarlet, which is a vivid red color, and ordinary red; others may not have such distinctions.

Full of blasphemous names: as in 13.1, these are words and titles that should be used only of God. Here it is not said that these names are on the beast's heads. The translation can say "it had all over it (or, over its body) names that are insulting to God."

17.4   RSV   TEV

The woman was arrayed in purple and scarlet, and bedecked with gold and jewels and pearls, holding in her hand a golden cup full of abominations and the impurities of her fornication;	The woman was dressed in purple and scarlet, and covered with gold ornaments, precious stones, and pearls. In her hand she held a gold cup full of obscene and filthy things, the result of her immorality.

Was arrayed in purple and scarlet: these are purple and scarlet clothes, or robes that she was wearing. The cloth used to make such robes was expensive and was a mark of luxury or of royalty. One may also say "The woman wore purple and scarlet (or, red) clothes."

Bedecked: this little-used English verb means "adorned" (so NRSV). The Greek text uses a verb and its related noun "gilded with gold . . . ." Something like "adorned" or "was wearing" makes for a more natural translation. In certain languages it will be necessary to say "her body and clothes were adorned" or "she had adorned (or, bedecked) her body with . . . ."

Gold and jewels and pearls: the **gold** is gold ornaments, while **jewels** may be translated "precious stones." In cultures where **pearls** are unknown, translators may use expressions such as "expensive beads named 'pearls.'" However, the focus in this context is on bodily adornments in general, not on any particular type of jewelry. Therefore it is recommended that translators in such cultures combine **jewels** and **pearls** and say, for example, "expensive stones (or, beads) of many kinds."

In her hand a golden cup: in 14.10 John speaks of the cup that is filled with the wine of God's wrath; the prostitute's gold cup is filled with the wine of her sexual immorality. Like the Old Testament prophets, John speaks of idolatry as sexual immorality and describes nations that try to lead God's people into idolatry as fornicators and whores. If it is necessary to specify which hand held the cup, it is recommended that "right hand" be said.

Full of abominations and the impurities of her fornication: this may be difficult to translate literally. The word translated **abominations** is used also in 17.5 and 21.27 (and see Luke 16.15). It means detestable things, odious, revolting, disgusting, obscene (REB "obscenities"). If the metaphor will be difficult to understand, a simile can be used: "full of the wine that represents her obscene (or, disgusting) actions and her filthy sexual practices."

Alternative translation models for this verse are:

> The woman was wearing purple and scarlet clothes. She had adorned her body with gold ornaments, precious stones, and expensive beads named "pearls." In her right hand she held a golden cup full of the wine that represents her disgusting actions and filthy sexual practices.

Or:

> . . . She had adorned her body with gold ornaments and expensive stones (or, beads) of all kinds . . . .

17.5   RSV   TEV

and on her forehead was written a name of mystery: "Babylon the great, mother of harlots and of earth's abominations."	On her forehead was written a name that has a secret meaning: "Great Babylon, the mother of all prostitutes and perverts in the world."

Was written a name of mystery: the passive **was written** does not here imply that God wrote the name; it simply says that there was a mysterious name on her forehead. As TEV shows, the phrase **a name of mystery** means "a name that has a secret meaning." In languages that do not use the passive, there are often special verbs for "written" or "inscribed" that help to avoid the passive but do not require a subject; something like the following English sentence: "On her forehead she had a name written (or, inscribed)," or "on her forehead someone had written a name." TEV's "secret meaning" may also be rendered "hidden meaning" or "meaning not known to others." See also 1.20.

Babylon the great: see 14.8. In some languages it may be necessary to make a complete sentence out of what is a title in Greek: "I am Mighty (or, Powerful) Babylon."

Mother of harlots and of earth's abominations: it is easy enough to translate **mother of harlots**, but it is more difficult to translate **mother . . . of earth's abominations**. TEV "perverts" takes this last expression to indicate people, but it is better to take it to refer to actions: "the one who is the source of all obscene (or, filthy) actions in the world." REB has "of every obscenity on earth," and NJB "all the filthy practices on earth."

An alternative translation model for this verse is:

> On her forehead she had a name inscribed that had a secret meaning. The name said, "I am great (or, powerful) Babylon, the mother of all prostitutes and the one who is the source of all obscene (or, filthy) actions in the world."

17.6   RSV   TEV

And I saw the woman, drunk with the blood of the saints and the blood of the martyrs of Jesus.

When I saw her I marveled greatly.

And I saw that the woman was drunk with the blood of God's people and the blood of those who were killed because they had been loyal to Jesus.

When I saw her, I was completely amazed.

Drunk with the blood of the saints and the blood of the martyrs of Jesus: for **saints** see 5.8. As is often the case in this book, the second group, **the martyrs**, more precisely defines the first group, **the saints**: "drunk with the blood of God's people, that is, those who had died for their faithfulness to Jesus." Here the word ordinarily translated "witness" may mean "martyr," inasmuch as the figure "the blood of" clearly indicates they have been killed. This is how NJB, FRCL, SPCL, Phps, BRCL, and TEV translate it. Some translations, however, prefer "witnesses to Jesus" (NRSV, RNAB, TNT) or "who bore testimony to Jesus" (NIV, REB). In either case the figure **the blood of** shows that these "witnesses" or **martyrs** had been killed because of their Christian faith. (See Antipas in 2.13; and see 6.9.) Other ways of translating this first sentence, then, are the following:

> And I saw (or, noticed) that the woman was drunk with the blood of God's people, the ones whom people had killed because they were faithful to (or, faithfully followed) Jesus.

Or:

> And I saw that the woman had drunk the blood of God's people, those who were killed because they were faithful to Jesus. This had made her drunk (or, intoxicated).

I marveled greatly: this translates the Greek "I marveled a great marvel," which can be expressed by "I was greatly astonished," "I was very surprised." For comments on the verb "to marvel" see 13.3.

17.7   RSV   TEV

But the angel said to me, "Why marvel? I will tell you the mystery of the woman, and of the beast with seven heads and ten horns that carries her.

"Why are you amazed?" the angel asked me. "I will tell you the secret meaning of the woman and of the beast that carries her, the beast with seven heads and ten horns.

Why marvel? "Why are you surprised (or, astonished)?" The question implies that John should have understood what he was seeing. It prepares the way for the explanation that follows. **Marvel** is expressed idiomatically in many languages; for example, "shiver in the heart (or, liver)," "be with mouth open," or "feel strange in the heart."

I will tell you the mystery: for the first time in the book, an angel interpreter appears. "I will explain the mystery to you," "I will reveal to you the secret meaning."

17.8   RSV   TEV

The beast that you saw was, and is not, and is to ascend from the bottomless pit and go to perdition; and the dwellers on earth whose names have not been written in the book of life from the foundation of the world, will marvel to behold the beast, because it was and is not and is to come.

That beast was once alive, but lives no longer; it is about to come up from the abyss and will go off to be destroyed. The people living on earth whose names have not been written before the creation of the world in the book of the living, will all be amazed as they look at the beast. It was once alive; now it no longer lives, but it will reappear.

The beast that you saw: the past tense of the verb, **saw**, may imply that the vision had disappeared. But it may simply be the writer's way of referring to the vision. TEV has not represented **that you saw**, but it is better to retain it, using the tense of the verb that indicates a completed action in the past. The beast is the one described in 13.1, which now reappears in the book. One may also say "the beast that you have just seen."

Was, and is not: this can be said "was alive once, but is now dead," "was alive, but lives no longer."

Is to ascend from the bottomless pit: see 11.7. For the auxiliary verb translated **is to**, see comments on "are about to" in 2.10. For **bottomless pit** see 9.1. This is a kind of resurrection, but the language used should not state here that the beast will be raised to life. In 13.14 this beast is described as having received a mortal wound, but it had come back to life. Here, as elsewhere in the book, the abyss is the realm of evil, destruction, and death.

Go to perdition: this is better translated "go to destruction." The translation should not imply that willingly and deliberately the beast goes off to be destroyed. The meaning is that it is destined to be destroyed (by Christ; see 19.20). In languages that do not use the passive, this may be rendered as "go off to receive destruction" or ". . . for Christ (or, God) to destroy." For the translation of **destroy** see 11.18.

The dwellers on earth: see 3.10.

Whose names have not been written in the book of life from the foundation of the world: see 3.5; 13.8. In certain languages this will be expressed as "Whose names God did not write in the book of the living before he created the world."

Will marvel to behold the beast: this is better translated "will be astonished when they see the beast" (see also comments on 13.3).

Because it was and is not and is to come: RSV has **because** as the translation of the Greek conjunction, but it may be understood as a relative, "that" (as TEV translates): "the beast that was . . ." (also REB). Others take it to mean "when they saw that the beast was alive . . . ." It is recommended that RSV not be followed here.

An alternative translation model for this verse is:

> That beast you just now saw was once alive, but lives no longer; it is about to come up out of the deep pit and will go off to receive destruction (or, for Christ [or, God] to destroy it). The people living on earth whose names God did not write in the book of the living before he created the world will all be amazed (or, have shivering hearts [livers]) as they look at the beast. It was once alive; now it no longer lives; but it will come back again.

17.9-10   RSV   TEV

RSV	TEV
9 This calls for a mind with wisdom: the seven heads are seven mountains on which the woman is seated; 10 they are also seven kings, five of whom have fallen, one is, the other has not yet come, and when he comes he must remain only a little while.	9 "This calls for wisdom and understanding. The seven heads are seven hills, on which the woman sits. They are also seven kings: 10 five of them have fallen, one still rules, and the other one has not yet come; when he comes, he must rule only a little while.

This calls for a mind with wisdom: see 13.18. The translation can say "This requires a wise thinker," ". . . wise thinking," or ". . . a person with great insight."

The seven heads are seven mountains: throughout this explanation the verb "to be" is used, as in "heads *are* mountains" and so forth. In some languages it will be better to say "represent," "stand for," or "symbolize."

Seven mountains on which the woman is seated: this is a clear reference to the city of Rome. It is to be noticed that the same verb "be seated on" is used in verses 1 and 3. In certain languages that, like English, distinguish between hills and mountains, translators should pick a term for "hills" that refers to a usually rounded natural elevation of land that is lower than a mountain. The hills referred to are generally lower than 1000 feet.

RSV and TEV differ on where verse 10 begins. RSV follows the verse division of KJV and ASV; TEV follows the UBS Greek New Testament. NRSV is now like TEV.

They are also seven kings: the fuller statement may be preferable: "the heads also represent seven kings." It is generally agreed that these seven kings were kings, or emperors, of Rome who succeeded one another; they are not kings of seven different countries. For the translation of **kings** see 1.5 and elsewhere.

Five of them have fallen: the verb "to fall" here does not necessarily mean that they were killed or deposed, but simply that they died, they no longer live. The verb (in Hebrew) is used of Abner in 2 Samuel 3.38. So the translation can say "five of them have already died."

One is: this means "one of them is now king."

The other has not yet come: this one is the last of the seven, so the translation can say "the last one is yet to appear."

When he comes he must remain only a little while: the emphasis is on the short length of his reign: "when he appears, he will be king for a little while only." As often in the New Testament, and in this book in particular, the verb translated "must" indicates God's control of human affairs (see 1.1). In that case one may say "he will be allowed to be king (or, high chief) for a little while only" or "God will let him rule for only a little while."

17.11   RSV   TEV

As for the beast that was and is not, it   And the beast that was once alive, but
is an eighth but it belongs to the seven,   lives no longer, is itself an eighth king
and it goes to perdition.   who is one of the seven and is going off
                                                   to be destroyed.

The beast that was and is not . . . is an eighth: this means that the beast that will come back from the abyss (verse 8) will become the eighth king. As stated in verse 8, he is doomed to destruction.

It belongs to the seven: the Greek seems to mean, as TEV and others translate it, that "it is one of the seven." That is, the eighth king will be one of the seven previous kings; the text does not say which one of them he will be. This explains how the seven heads can represent eight kings; one of the kings will rule twice.

17.12   RSV   TEV

And the ten horns that you saw are ten   "The ten horns you saw are ten
kings who have not yet received royal   kings who have not yet begun to rule,
power, but they are to receive authority   but who will be given authority to rule
as kings for one hour, together with the   as kings for one hour with the beast.
beast.

The ten horns . . . are ten kings who have not yet received royal power: these are ten men who will in the future become kings. These are not the same kind of kings as those represented by the seven heads; these are kings of ten different countries who will rule at the same time. The Greek "they receive authority as kings" does not indicate who will give them this authority. It is doubtful that divine activity is implied. The ten kings will rule for a very short time (**one hour**) and be under the control of the beast. And they will be destroyed when he is destroyed (19.19-21). **Hour**: in languages that do not talk about a precise period of sixty minutes, one may say "a very short period of time" or "the length of time it takes to . . ." (filling in some activity like cooking brown rice and so on)

An alternative translation model for this verse in languages that do not use the passive is:

The ten horns that you saw represent ten kings who have not yet begun to rule, but they will receive authority (or, power) to rule as kings for one hour (or, very short period of time) with the beast.

17.13   RSV   TEV

These are of one mind and give over their power and authority to the beast;	These ten all have the same purpose, and they give their power and authority to the beast.

These are of one mind and give over their power and authority to the beast: in many languages the phrase **are of one mind** will be expressed in a similar way to the Greek; for example, "put their hearts (minds) together" or "be united in their minds." It would be in keeping with the writer's style for translators to use this double statement to express one action; however, other languages may use, for example, a verb with an infinitive, as in "They will all *agree to turn over* their power and authority to the beast" or "They will all *agree to let* the beast have their . . . ." Since this is yet to take place, it is better to use the future tense. These ten kings will willingly become the beast's underlings. **Of one mind** occurs again in verse 17; for **power** see 3.8; for **authority** see "power" in 2.26.

17.14   RSV   TEV

they will make war on the Lamb, and the Lamb will conquer them, for he is Lord of lords and King of kings, and those with him are called and chosen and faithful."	They will fight against the Lamb; but the Lamb, together with his called, chosen, and faithful followers, will defeat them, because he is Lord of lords and King of kings."

They will make war on the Lamb: this includes the ten kings and the beast, so it may be better to say explicitly "the beast and they" or "the ten kings and the beast." For the verb "to make war" see 2.16.

The Lamb: see 5.6.

A comparison between RSV and TEV shows that TEV has not followed the order of the Greek text. It seems best to join the Lamb's followers to the Lamb in the statement about the Lamb's victory over the beast and the ten kings, and many translators may wish to follow TEV's model here. The text implies that they take part in the battle and share in the Lamb's victory—which RSV does not make clear. TNT has "will share his victory" at the end of the verse, which follows the order of the Greek text. And NJB translates "the Lamb will defeat them, he and his followers . . . ." However, in languages where dependent clauses always precede the main clause, it will be necessary to reorder these sentences; for example, "but the Lamb, because he is Lord of lords and King of kings, will with his called, chosen, and faithful followers defeat the beast and the ten kings."

For he is Lord of lords and King of kings: this is a way of expressing the superlative "The greatest Lord, the mightiest King," "the Lord and King of all." This is the reason why he will defeat his enemies. The same kind of language is used of God in the Old Testament (see Deut 10.17; Dan 2.47). In certain languages this will be expressed as "he is the most powerful ruler and highest chief of all." On the translation of **king** see 1.5 and elsewhere.

Those with him are called and chosen and faithful: the meaning may be expressed by "his followers are those whom God has called and chosen, and who are faithful to him." For **faithful** see 1.5; 2.10.

Alternative translation models for this verse are:

> The beast and the ten kings will attack (or, fight against) the Lamb, but the Lamb and his followers will defeat them. This is because he is the greatest Lord, the almighty King, His followers are those whom God has called and chosen, and who are faithful (or, loyal) to him.

Or:

> . . . and his followers will have the victory over them. The Lamb will defeat the beast and the ten kings because he is the most powerful ruler and highest king (or, chief) of all, and his followers . . . .

17.15   RSV   TEV

> And he said to me, "The waters that you saw, where the harlot is seated, are peoples and multitudes and nations and tongues.

> The angel also said to me, "The waters you saw, on which the prostitute sits, are nations, peoples, races, and languages.

He said to me: it is better to specify the speaker: "The angel said to me." TEV adds "also" because what follows is a continuation of the speech of the same angel in the previous verses.

The waters . . . where the harlot is seated: the translation here must be the same as in verse 1.

Are: or "represent," "stand for" (as in verses 9-10,12).

Peoples and multitudes and nations and tongues: this is the same list that appears in 5.9 and other passages, except that here **multitudes** (TEV "peoples") is used instead of "tribes" in the other passages. The explanation of **the waters** makes it clear that the powerful prostitute rules over all of the world's nations. In certain languages that do not speak about all these categories of people, this phrase will be rendered more naturally as "represent all the peoples of the world."

17.16   RSV   TEV

> And the ten horns that you saw, they and the beast will hate the harlot; they will make her desolate and naked, and

> The ten horns you saw and the beast will hate the prostitute; they will take away everything she has and leave her

devour her flesh and burn her up with fire,	naked; they will eat her flesh and destroy her with fire.

The ten horns . . . and the beast will hate: for some reason the beast and the ten kings who are his allies (verse 13) will turn against the infamous prostitute and attack her. For **hate** see 2.6.

They will make her desolate and naked: this is better translated "they will take away all her belongings, and will strip her naked" or "They will take . . . and take off all her clothes so that she is naked." If the language level allows it, the appropriate verb for **make . . . desolate** is "to despoil," "to plunder."

Devour her flesh and burn her up with fire: it must be noted that the first and the last of the four actions (**make . . . desolate** and **burn**) apply more naturally to the city (Babylon); the other two actions (**make her . . . naked, and devour her flesh**) apply to the prostitute herself. In the translation the plain meaning of all four actions should be clearly represented. For **devour her flesh** the translation can say "will devour her" (see the figure in Psa 27.2, RSV footnote; Jer 10.25; Micah 3.3). The figure is that of a wild animal that eats its victim as soon as it kills it. The statement **will . . . burn her up with fire** means to consume her body with fire. The same verb "to burn up" appears also in 18.8. This phrase may also be expressed as "they will take fire and burn her up (or, destroy her)" or "they will set her on fire . . . ."

17.17   RSV   TEV

for God has put it into their hearts to carry out his purpose by being of one mind and giving over their royal power to the beast, until the words of God shall be fulfilled.	For God has placed in their hearts the will to carry out his purpose by acting together and giving to the beast their power to rule until God's words come true.

God has put it into their hearts to carry out his purpose: the expression "to put into the heart" means to cause someone to decide, resolve, purpose. Here it is God who will make these ten kings decide to do what will actually be God's own plan, even though they are not aware of this. Without their knowing it, they will be God's instrument for achieving his purpose. So one may translate "God has caused them to decide . . . ."

Being of one mind and giving over their royal power to the beast: as in verse 13.

Until the words of God shall be fulfilled: this condition, in which the ten kings will let the beast rule over them, will last until all of God's purposes and plans are achieved. Here **the words of God** has the specific meaning of what God, through his messengers, has said will happen in the End. For the verb "fulfill" see 10.7.

Alternative translation models for this verse are:

> The ten kings will do this because God has caused them to decide to
> do what he wants them to do. And so they will all agree to surrender

their royal power to the beast. They will obey the beast until all of God's purposes are completed.

Or:

. . . and so they will all agree (or, have a united heart [mind]) and let the beast have their power to rule as kings. They will obey the beast until God has caused all his plans to be completed (or, come to fruition [bear fruit]).

17.18 RSV TEV

And the woman that you saw is the great city which has dominion over the kings of the earth."

"The woman you saw is the great city that rules over the kings of the earth."

After explaining the meaning of the beast, its seven heads and its ten horns (verses 8-12), and the meaning of the waters (verse 15), the angel now tells John explicitly that the prostitute is Rome, "the powerful city that rules over all kings of the world." It may not be possible to speak of a city having power over kings, and so it may be necessary to say "the powerful city whose king rules over the kings of all nations in the world."

18.1–19.4

RSV

TEV

The Fall of Babylon

1 After this I saw another angel coming down from heaven, having great authority; and the earth was made bright with his splendor. 2 And he called out with a mighty voice,
"Fallen, fallen is Babylon the great!
It has become a dwelling place of demons,
a haunt of every foul spirit,
a haunt of every foul and hateful bird;
3 for all nations have drunk the wine of her
impure passion,
and the kings of the earth have committed fornication with her,
and the merchants of the earth have
grown rich with the wealth of her
wantonness."
4 Then I heard another voice from heaven
saying,
"Come out of her, my people,
lest you take part in her sins,
lest you share in her plagues;
5 for her sins are heaped high as heaven,
and God has remembered her iniquities.
6 Render to her as she herself has rendered,

1 After this I saw another angel coming down out of heaven. He had great authority, and his splendor brightened the whole earth. 2 He cried out in a loud voice: "She has fallen! Great Babylon has fallen! She is now haunted by demons and unclean spirits; all kinds of filthy and hateful birds live in her. 3 For all the nations have drunk her wine—the strong wine of her immoral lust. The kings of the earth practiced sexual immorality with her, and the businessmen of the world grew rich from her unrestrained lust."
4 Then I heard another voice from heaven, saying,
"Come out, my people! Come out from
her!
You must not take part in her sins;
you must not share in her punishment!
5 For her sins are piled up as high as heaven,
and God remembers her wicked ways.
6 Treat her exactly as she has treated you;
pay her back double for all she has
done.

and repay her double for her deeds;
mix a double draught for her in the cup
she mixed.

7 As she glorified herself and played the
wanton,
so give her a like measure of torment and
mourning.
Since in her heart she says, 'A queen I sit,
I am no widow, mourning I shall never
see,'

8 so shall her plagues come in a single day,
pestilence and mourning and famine,
and she shall be burned with fire;
for mighty is the Lord God who judges
her."

9 And the kings of the earth, who committed fornication and were wanton with her, will weep and wail over her when they see the smoke of her burning; 10 they will stand far off, in fear of her torment, and say,

"Alas! alas! thou great city,
thou mighty city, Babylon!
In one hour has thy judgment come."

11 And the merchants of the earth weep and mourn for her, since no one buys their cargo any more, 12 cargo of gold, silver, jewels and pearls, fine linen, purple, silk and scarlet, all kinds of scented wood, all articles of ivory, all articles of costly wood, bronze, iron and marble, 13 cinnamon, spice, incense, myrrh, frankincense, wine, oil, fine flour and wheat, cattle and sheep, horses and chariots, and slaves, that is, human souls.

14 "The fruit for which thy soul longed has
gone from thee,
and all thy dainties and thy splendor are
lost to thee,
never to be found again!"

15 The merchants of these wares, who gained wealth from her, will stand far off, in fear of her torment, weeping and mourning aloud,

16 "Alas, alas, for the great city
that was clothed in fine linen, in purple
and scarlet,
bedecked with gold, with jewels, and with
pearls!

17 In one hour all this wealth has been laid
waste."

And all shipmasters and seafaring men, sailors and all whose trade is on the sea, stood far off 18 and cried out as they saw the smoke of her burning,

"What city was like the great city?"

19 And they threw dust on their heads, as they wept and mourned, crying out,

"Alas, alas, for the great city
where all who had ships at sea grew rich
by her wealth!
In one hour she has been laid waste.

Fill her cup with a drink twice as strong
as the drink she prepared for you.

7 Give her as much suffering and grief
as the glory and luxury she gave herself.

For she keeps telling herself:
'Here I sit, a queen!
I am no widow,
I will never know grief!'

8 Because of this, in one day she will be
struck with plagues—
disease, grief, and famine.
And she will be burned with fire,
because the Lord God, who judges
her, is mighty."

9 The kings of the earth who took part in her immorality and lust will cry and weep over the city when they see the smoke from the flames that consume her. 10 They stand a long way off, because they are afraid of sharing in her suffering. They say, "How terrible! How awful! This great and mighty city Babylon! In just one hour you have been punished!"

11 The businessmen of the earth also cry and mourn for her, because no one buys their goods any longer; 12 no one buys their gold, silver, precious stones, and pearls; their goods of linen, purple cloth, silk, and scarlet cloth; all kinds of rare woods and all kinds of objects made of ivory and of expensive wood, of bronze, iron, and marble; 13 and cinnamon, spice, incense, myrrh, and frankincense; wine and oil, flour and wheat, cattle and sheep, horses and carriages, slaves, and even human lives. 14 The businessmen say to her, "All the good things you longed to own have disappeared, and all your wealth and glamor are gone, and you will never find them again!" 15 The businessmen, who became rich from doing business in that city, will stand a long way off, because they are afraid of sharing in her suffering. They will cry and mourn, 16 and say, "How terrible! How awful for the great city! She used to dress herself in linen, purple, and scarlet, and cover herself with gold ornaments, precious stones, and pearls! 17 And in one hour she has lost all this wealth!"

All the ships' captains and passengers, the sailors and all others who earn their living on the sea, stood a long way off, 18 and cried out as they saw the smoke from the flames that consumed her: "There never has been another city like this great city!" 19 They threw dust on their heads, they cried and mourned, saying, "How terrible! How awful for the great city! She is the city where all who have ships sailing the seas became rich on her wealth! And in one hour she has lost everything!"

20 Be glad, heaven, because of her destruction! Be glad, God's people and the apostles and prophets! For God has condemned her for what

20 Rejoice over her, O heaven,
O saints and apostles and prophets,
for God has given judgment for you
against her!"
21 Then a mighty angel took up a stone like
a great millstone and threw it into the sea, saying,
"So shall Babylon the great city be
thrown down with violence,
and shall be found no more;
22 and the sound of harpers and minstrels,
of flute players and trumpeters,
shall be heard in thee no more;
and a craftsman of any craft
shall be found in thee no more;
and the sound of the millstone
shall be heard in thee no more;
23 and the light of a lamp
shall shine in thee no more;
and the voice of bridegroom and bride
shall be heard in thee no more;
for thy merchants were the great men of
the earth,
and all nations were deceived by thy
sorcery.
24 And in her was found the blood of prophets and of saints,
and of all who have been slain on
earth."

Chapter 19:
1 After this I heard what seemed to be the
loud voice of a great multitude in heaven, crying,
"Hallelujah! Salvation and glory and power belong to our God,
2 for his judgments are true and just;
he has judged the great harlot who corrupted the earth with her fornication,
and he has avenged on her the blood of
his servants."
3 Once more they cried,
"Hallelujah! The smoke from her goes up
for ever and ever."
4 And the twenty-four elders and the four living
creatures fell down and worshiped God who is
seated on the throne, saying, "Amen. Hallelujah!"

she did to you!
21 Then a mighty angel picked up a stone
the size of a large millstone and threw it into the
sea, saying, "This is how the great city Babylon will
be violently thrown down and will never be seen
again. 22 The music of harps and of human voices,
of players of the flute and the trumpet, will never
be heard in you again! No workman in any trade
will ever be found in you again; and the sound of
the millstone will be heard no more! 23 Never
again will the light of a lamp be seen in you; no
more will the voices of brides and grooms be
heard in you. Your businessmen were the most
powerful in all the world, and with your false
magic you deceived all the peoples of the world!"
24 Babylon was punished because the blood
of prophets and of God's people was found in the
city; yes, the blood of all those who have been
killed on earth.

Chapter 19:
1 After this I heard what sounded like the
roar of a large crowd of people in heaven, saying,
"Praise God! Salvation, glory, and power belong to
our God! 2 True and just are his judgments! He
has condemned the prostitute who was corrupting
the earth with her immorality. God has punished
her because she killed his servants." 3 Again they
shouted, "Praise God! The smoke from the flames
that consume the great city goes up forever and
ever!" 4 The twenty-four elders and the four living
creatures fell down and worshiped God, who was
seated on the throne. They said, "Amen! Praise
God!"

SECTION HEADING: TEV "The Fall of Babylon." "Babylon is destroyed." A noun
phrase can be used, "The destruction of Babylon," or say "God destroys the city of
Babylon." Or it may be better to be more explicit and say "A vision of the
destruction of Babylon." It may be advisable to limit this section to chapter 18 and
make of 19.1-4 a separate section with the heading "Joy in heaven over Babylon's
destruction" or "Everyone in heaven rejoices when Babylon is destroyed."
    The chapter does not actually describe Babylon's destruction but proclaims it
in a series of events: (1) An angel from heaven announces Babylon's fall (verses 1-3);
(2) a voice from heaven urges God's people to leave Babylon, and orders the forces
of destruction to do their work (verses 4-8); (3) kings lament Babylon's fall (verses

9-10); (4) businessmen from all over the world also mourn her fall (verses 11-19); (5) the writer calls upon all in heaven to celebrate Babylon's fall (verse 20); (6) a mighty angel predicts Babylon's destruction (verses 21-23); (7) the writer gives the reason why Babylon was destroyed (verse 24). In verses 9 and 18 (and implicitly in verse 15) people see Babylon being destroyed by fire.

18.1   RSV   TEV

> After this I saw another angel coming down from heaven, having great authority; and the earth was made bright with his splendor.

> After this I saw another angel coming down out of heaven. He had great authority, and his splendor brightened the whole earth.

This refers to the events immediately preceding the events in this chapter. It will be helpful in many languages to provide that information by saying "After seeing the woman who was seated on the red beast, I saw another . . . ."

Another angel coming down from heaven: this is a different angel from the one in chapter 17.

Having great authority: this describes him as a very powerful angel without saying or implying that his authority had been given him by God.

The earth was made bright with his splendor: this is better said by using the active form of the verb: "his splendor brightened the whole earth" (TEV). The verb is formed from the noun for "light" and means "to enlighten" or "to brighten"; it appears also in 21.23, "is [its] light," and in 22.5, "will be [their] light." And here the Greek word for **splendor**, usually translated "glory" (see 1.6), has the physical sense of the brilliant light that marks the angel as God's messenger. One may also translate "the bright light coming from him made the whole world bright" or ". . . lit up the whole world."

18.2   RSV   TEV

> And he called out with a mighty voice,
>   "Fallen, fallen is Babylon the
>   great!
>   It has become a dwelling place of
>   demons,
>   a haunt of every foul spirit,
>   a haunt of every foul and hateful
>   bird;

> He cried out in a loud voice: "She has fallen! Great Babylon has fallen! She is now haunted by demons and unclean spirits; all kinds of filthy and hateful birds live in her.

He called out with a mighty voice: as in 5.2; 10.3.

The announcements that follow (verses 2-3 and verses 4-8) may be rendered in poetic forms (see Section F of the introduction, "Translating the Revelation to John," pages 6 and following).

256

Fallen, fallen is Babylon the great: as in 14.8. This is what is called a "prophetic" past tense, announcing a future event as something that has already taken place.

In this verse TEV begins to use a feminine pronoun when referring to Babylon. RSV waits until the following verses to follow this pattern. Many languages cannot do this.

A dwelling place . . . a haunt: the Greek noun translated **dwelling place** appears also in Ephesians 2.22 and nowhere else in the New Testament. It is related to the verb "to dwell," used frequently in this book (see 2.13; 3.10). The word translated **haunt** usually means a guarded place, a "prison" (see 2.10; 20.7). Here it seems to mean a place where unclean spirits and disgusting birds live undisturbed; it is a refuge, a guarded sanctuary for them. **Haunt** may also be translated in English as "lair," a place where wild animals hide. Translators should attempt to find synonyms in their languages and say something like the English "It has become a refuge for . . . and the lair of . . . ," or combine the two and say "Demons and unclean (or, evil) spirits use it is as their lair."

Demons . . . every foul spirit . . . every foul and hateful bird: this is a vivid picture of a city that has been destroyed and has no one living in it. See the similar pictures drawn of Babylon (Isa 13.19-23; Jer 50.39), Edom (Isa 34.11-15), and Nineveh (Zeph 2.13-15). For **foul spirit** (that is, "unclean spirit") see 16.13; **demons** are the same as evil spirits. The **foul and hateful** birds are those birds that, according to the Law of Moses, Israelites could not eat; they were unclean (see Deut 14.12-18). The added epithet **hateful** describes these birds as disgusting, loathsome, repulsive. Perhaps the writer had bats in mind (which were classified in those days as birds).

TEXTUAL NOTE: instead of RSV (and TEV) **a haunt of every foul and hateful bird**, the UBS Greek New Testament has (following the order of words in the Greek text) "a haunt of every bird unclean [and a haunt of every beast unclean] and hateful." RSV and TEV (and most other modern translations) do not include the material within brackets. NRSV, however, has "a haunt of every foul and hateful bird, a haunt of every foul and hateful beast," which goes beyond the UBS Greek text by adding "and hateful" to "every bird."

An alternative translation model for the quotation in this verse is:

> "The great city of Babylon is finished (or, collapsed). It is completely deserted (or, no people left in it). Demons and filthy spirits are now living in it (or, have made it their lair), all kinds of unclean (or, filthy) birds live there.

18.3 RSV TEV

RSV	TEV
for all nations have drunk[k] the wine of her impure passion, and the kings of the earth have committed fornication with her, and the merchants of the earth	For all the nations have drunk her wine—the strong wine of her immoral lust. The kings of the earth practiced sexual immorality with her, and the businessmen of the world grew rich from her unrestrained lust."

> have grown rich with the
> wealth of her wantonness."

^{k} Other ancient authorities read *fallen by*

All nations have drunk the wine of her impure passion: see 14.8; 17.2.

As the RSV footnote indicates, instead of **have drunk** some Greek manuscripts and early versions have "have fallen by," that is, "have been ruined by." A few Greek manuscripts and versions have "she made all nations drink" (as in 14.8). This makes more sense in the context, and some translations prefer this form of the text; most follow the text translated by RSV and TEV.

The kings of the earth have committed fornication with her: see 17.2.

The merchants of the earth: they can be referred to as "businessmen," "traders," or "people who buy and sell goods." The word is used four times in this chapter and appears also in Matthew 13.45, and nowhere else in the New Testament.

The wealth of her wantonness: **wealth** here is literally "power, strength." The meaning can be expressed by "her excessive craving," "her unrestrained debauchery." TNT translates "excessive luxury." The noun appears only here in the New Testament. **Wantonness**: one commentator points to the use of the word in the Greek Septuagint version of 2 Kings 19.28, where it refers to the "arrogance" of the Assyrian king. This commentator believes that here it means arrogance also. But in the context of the heavy use of sexual immorality as a figure of idolatry, it seems best to keep here the idea of licentiousness, debauchery. This final sentence may also be expressed as "All the people in the world who buy and sell goods grew rich (or, gained a great amount of money) from Babylon's excessive sexual lust."

18.4   RSV   TEV

<table>
<tr><td>

Then I heard another voice from
heaven saying,
  "Come out of her, my people,
  lest you take part in her sins,
  lest you share in her plagues;

</td><td>

4 Then I heard another voice from
heaven, saying,
  "Come out, my people! Come out
    from her!
  You must not take part in her
    sins;
  you must not share in her
    punishment!

</td></tr>
</table>

Another voice from heaven: as the words **my people** clearly indicate, this is God speaking (see 16.1). So one may say "Then I heard God speak from heaven, saying . . . ."

Come out of her: it may be better to make this more complete: "Leave the city," "Come out of Babylon." See the similar command in Jeremiah 51.45.

Lest: in English, at least, it is more natural to say "so that you won't (take part)" or "to avoid (taking part)."

Take part in her sins . . . share in her plagues: God's people must leave the city in order to avoid sinning as the people of the city do. They are also to leave so that they won't be punished as the city will be. The **plagues** are God's punishment on the city (see 9.18; 15.1). So these two clauses may also be expressed as "So that you may avoid sinning as the people of Babylon do, and that God will not punish you as he will (punish) this city."

18.5   RSV   TEV

> for her sins are heaped high as   For her sins are piled up as high
>   heaven,   as heaven,
> and God has remembered her   and God remembers her wick-
>   iniquities.   ed ways.

Her sins are heaped high as heaven: the Greek verb translated **heaped** means "to glue," that is, to stick to something (see Luke 10.11, where the dust sticks to the feet); here the picture is of sins that stick to one another and keep piling up, until the pile reaches the sky. This is a vivid way of describing the large number of the sins of Babylon (see Jer 51.9). It is possible that here "sky" is more appropriate (so AT, TNT, NJB, RNAB); but **heaven** may be better, since it leads naturally to the next line. The sins have attracted God's notice.

God has remembered her iniquities: for this sense of **remembered** see 16.19; God is going to take action and punish Babylon for her sins. The noun translated **iniquities** occurs here and translated "wrongdoings" in Acts 18.14; 24.20, and nowhere else in the New Testament. It is related to the verb "to harm," "to do wrong" (see its use in 11.5; "do evil," 22.11). This sentence may also be expressed as "God has not forgotten (or, does not take his attention away from) the evil (or, harmful) things Babylon has done."

18.6   RSV   TEV

> Render to her as she herself has   Treat her exactly as she has
>   rendered,   treated you;
> and repay her double for her   pay her back double for all she
>   deeds;   has done.
> mix a double draught for her in   Fill her cup with a drink twice as
>   the cup she mixed.   strong
>   as the drink she prepared for
>   you.

It is not clear to whom God is speaking. At the beginning of verse 4 God speaks to his people in Babylon; but it does not seem likely that here God is telling his people to treat Babylon as she has treated them. So the command in this verse (repeated three times) may be directed to those who will destroy the city, either the angels or the ten kings of 17.16. But the Greek text itself gives no indication that the command in verse 6 is directed to someone else, and it would not be appropriate for a translation to add that information to the text. But the information can be given in a footnote.

259

Render to her as she herself has rendered: this means to do to her what she has done to others (the negative version of the "Golden Rule"). For this use of the verb "to give," see Romans 12.17; 1 Peter 3.9. And for the whole passage see similar expressions in Psalm 28.4; 137.8; Jeremiah 50.15,29. Another way of expressing this clause is "Whatever bad things the people of this city have done to others, you should do to them."

Repay her double for her deeds: this intensifies the command in line 1: "pay her back two times as much as she has done" (see Isa 40.2; Jer 16.18).

The third line says the same thing as the second line, using the figure of a cup filled with strong drink: "fill her cup with a drink twice as strong as the drink she gave others." The phrase **double draught** does not refer to the amount, "twice as much wine," but to its potency, "twice as strong" (see the language of 14.10).

An alternative translation model for this verse is:

> You must do bad things to Babylon just as she did to others. In fact, you should do twice as many bad things to her. You must pour wine into her cup that is twice as strong as the drink she prepared for others to drink.

18.7   RSV   TEV

> As she glorified herself and
>   played the wanton,
> so give her a like measure of tor-
>   ment and mourning.
> Since in her heart she says, 'A
>   queen I sit,
> I am no widow, mourning I shall
>   never see,'

> Give her as much suffering and
>   grief
>   as the glory and luxury she
>   gave herself.
> For she keeps telling herself:
> 'Here I sit, a queen!
>   I am no widow,
> I will never know grief!'

She glorified herself: this means "to boast": "she boasted of her greatness," "she was very vain," or "she boasted, 'I am very great.'"

Played the wanton: this is a rather quaint expression in English; the Greek means "indulged her lust," "enjoyed luxury" (see the related noun "wealth" in verse 3). NRSV has "lived luxuriously." The verb appears here and in verse 9, and nowhere else in the New Testament. These first two clauses may also be expressed as "Just as she boasted, 'I am very great,' and lived a life full of luxury (or, good things)."

A like measure of torment and mourning: for the noun translated **torment** see "torture" at 9.5; 14.11. The more general idea of "suffering" or "pain" fits the context here. The RSV sentence structure, **As she . . . so give her**, may not be the best way to translate this part of the verse; something like the TEV restructuring may be easier to follow. NJB has "Every one of her pomps and orgies is to be matched by a torture or an agony"; REB "Measure out torment and grief to match her pomp and luxury." Another way of expressing this is "You must cause her to receive extreme pain and sorrow that equals her luxurious life (or, way of life) and her pride in herself."

Since: this statement of reason will be followed by the result in verse 8, "so
. . . ." It may be better to restructure, as TEV has done, and say here "She tells
herself," "She keeps on saying to herself," "She keeps reassuring herself," or "She
keeps thinking to herself."

A queen I sit: "I am a queen, sitting on my throne." **Queen** normally refers
to the wife of a king, but in this context it means "a woman ruler" who has complete
control over her subjects. In certain languages it will sound strange to bring in a
feminine subject into the first sentence. In such a case one may say "Here I sit on
my throne, ruling with complete authority."

I am no widow, mourning I shall never see: it may not be natural to speak
of "(never) seeing mourning," so something like "I shall never mourn," "I shall
never be in mourning" may be better. This mourning is the sorrow a woman feels
when her husband dies. This boast may be stated as follows: "I am not a widow, and
I will never know the sorrow of widowhood," or "Since I have no husband, I will
never be a widow mourning her husband's death," or "I have no husband who will
die, so I will never have to weep for him." See similar language in Isaiah 47.7-9.

18.8 RSV	TEV
so shall her plagues come in a single day, pestilence and mourning and famine, and she shall be burned with fire; for mighty is the Lord God who judges her."	Because of this, in one day she will be struck with plagues— disease, grief, and famine. And she will be burned with fire, because the Lord God, who judges her, is mighty."

So: "As a result," "Because of this," or "Because Babylon boasts like this."

Her plagues: that is, the punishments that will be poured out on her (see
9.18).

In a single day: an expression for a short time; quickly or suddenly (as "one
hour" in verses 10,17,19). One may also say "Because she boasts like this, in a very
short time . . . ."

Pestilence: this translates the Greek word that ordinarily means "death" (see
6.8b).

Mourning: this is not, as such, a plague or a punishment, but the result of one;
here, then, the word may have the more restricted sense of "bereavement," that is,
the loss of her "husband" (see the language of Isa 47.8-9).

Famine: see 6.8.

She shall be burned with fire: this means she will be consumed, she will be
destroyed, by fire.

Mighty: this adjective is used of an angel in 5.2; 10.1; only here is it used of
God. It does not refer specifically to physical strength but to power in general.

For **Lord God** see 1.8; 4.8, where it is suggested that in many languages it will
be more natural to say simply "God."

Who judges her: that is, who condemns her, who punishes her (see 6.10). Other ways of saying this are "who decides how she will be punished" or "who decides how he (God) will punish her."

An alternative translation model for this verse is:

Because Babylon boasts like this, in a very short time (or, one day) God will punish her with disease, the death of a loved one, and famine. Fire will burn her up, because God, who decides how to punish her, is all powerful.

18.9　　　　　RSV　　　　　　　　　　　　　　TEV

And the kings of the earth, who committed fornication and were wanton with her, will weep and wail over her when they see the smoke of her burning;

The kings of the earth who took part in her immorality and lust will cry and weep over the city when they see the smoke from the flames that consume her.

Who committed fornication . . . with her: see verse 3; for **were wanton with her** see verse 7. One may also say "who committed evil sexual practices with her and indulged their lust (or, sexual passion)."

Will weep and wail over her: for these two verbs see 5.4,5 and 1.7. It may be better to restructure the verse and translate "When the kings . . . see the city being consumed by flames, they will cry and weep over her." The phrase **the smoke of her burning** indicates that Babylon is being destroyed by fire, and the smoke that rises from the burning city is visible a long way off. Another way of expressing this phrase is "the smoke from the fire that is burning Babylon up."

18.10　　　　　RSV　　　　　　　　　　　　　　TEV

they will stand far off, in fear of her torment, and say,
　"Alas! alas! thou great city,
　thou mighty city, Babylon!
　In one hour has thy judgment
　come."

They stand a long way off, because they are afraid of sharing in her suffering. They say, "How terrible! How awful! This great and mighty city Babylon! In just one hour you have been punished!"

They will stand far off, or "they will stand a very long distance from the city."

In fear of her torment: that is, these kings will be afraid that they will be punished with Babylon, and so they will stand a long way off. For **torment** see 9.5, "torture." This clause may also be rendered as "Because they are afraid that they will receive the extreme pain that she is suffering."

Alas! alas! This is an expression of dismay and grief. The same Greek word in 8.13 is translated "Woe." NJB here and in verses 16 and 19 translates "Mourn, mourn for this great city," an effective way of representing the meaning and feeling of the cry. TEV's model is also an effective one in modern English.

Thou great city: RSV uses the archaic pronouns **thou** and **thy**, ordinarily reserved by RSV for addressing God. It is not necessary to use the second person singular form of address, as RSV does; the third person can be used, as TEV does. NRSV has "Alas, alas, the great city, Babylon, the mighty city!"

In one hour: that is, in a short time, quickly, suddenly. See 17.12 for more information on the translation of this phrase.

Hast thy judgment come: "you have been condemned (or, punished)." For the noun see 14.7; 16.7. One may also say "In such a short time God has punished you."

18.11-13 RSV	TEV
11 And the merchants of the earth weep and mourn for her, since no one buys their cargo any more, 12 cargo of gold, silver, jewels and pearls, fine linen, purple, silk and scarlet, all kinds of scented wood, all articles of ivory, all articles of costly wood, bronze, iron and marble, 13 cinnamon, spice, incense, myrrh, frankincense, wine, oil, fine flour and wheat, cattle and sheep, horses and chariots, and slaves, that is, human souls.	11 The businessmen of the earth also cry and mourn for her, because no one buys their goods any longer; 12 no one buys their gold, silver, precious stones, and pearls; their goods of linen, purple cloth, silk, and scarlet cloth; all kinds of rare woods and all kinds of objects made of ivory and of expensive wood, of bronze, iron, and marble; 13 and cinnamon, spice, incense, myrrh, and frankincense; wine and oil, flour and wheat, cattle and sheep, horses and carriages, slaves, and even human lives.

These three verses are one sentence in Greek, as both RSV and TEV show. It is not a complicated sentence, since the goods and wares and products named in verses 12-13 are simply a list of what the businessmen have for sale.

The merchants of the earth: as in verse 3.

Cargo: the Greek word is properly a ship's cargo (see its use in Acts 21.3); here it refers to all the products, or wares, or goods that the businessmen sell. This first sentence may be also expressed as "The people on earth who buy and sell things will weep very much for Babylon, because no one buys their goods anymore."

The list that follows resembles that of Ezekiel 27.5-14. It may be broken up into smaller groups, as TEV has done, by use of descriptive phrases and of semicolons, instead of commas only, as RSV does. Six groups may be found:

(1) **gold, silver, jewels and pearls**: the gold and silver may be bullion, but are probably objects or ornaments made of gold and silver (see 17.4, which also lists jewels and pearls).

(2) **fine linen, purple, silk and scarlet**: these are cloths and clothes and may be grouped as follows: "clothes (or, cloths) made of fine linen . . ." (for **linen** see 15.5-6); **purple . . . and scarlet** are cloths dyed these two colors. Cloths with these two colors were particularly valuable (see 17.4). An alternative translation model for this group is "clothes made from beautiful white cloth named 'linen,' expensive purple cloth, soft expensive cloth named 'silk,' and scarlet colored cloth."

(3) **scented wood**: this is aromatic wood, "wood with a pleasant smell" (or else, like TEV, "rare woods"). This wood (from the citron tree) was used to make expensive furniture.

All articles of ivory . . . costly wood, bronze, iron and marble: these various artifacts may all be listed together. **Ivory** comes from the long, enlarged teeth (tusks) of elephants, which protrude out from each side of their mouths. These are used by elephants for digging, fighting, and so on. The tusks are valuable for making beautiful objects such as furniture. For **bronze** see 9.20. **Marble** is a form of limestone that can be highly polished and is often used by artists for carving sculptures. In cultures where marble is unknown, one may say "beautiful rock."

(4) Perfumes, ointments, and incenses: **Cinnamon**: a plant that produced a sweet-smelling oil, used also for burning. **Spice** was used as a perfume or ointment. **Incense**: see 5.8. **Myrrh**: an expensive ointment (see Matt 26.7,9); this may also be termed "a sweet smelling thing (or, ointment) named 'myrrh.'" **Frankincense**: also used for burning (see Matt 2.11). Where **frankincense** is unknown it may be called "a sweet smelling expensive powder named 'frankincense.'" In certain languages translators will prefer to combine all of these and say, for example, "all kinds of expensive perfumes and oils" or "all kinds of expensive sweet-smelling oils and powders."

(5) Food and drink: **wine**, **oil** (that is, olive oil, as NRSV has it), **fine flour and wheat**. **Fine flour** refers in this context to finely ground wheat flour, and **wheat** means the wheat kernels that have not yet been ground into flour. In cultures where **wheat** is unknown but other grains are cultivated, translators may use a generic term and say "finely ground flour and grain kernels."

(6) Animals and slaves: **cattle and sheep, horses and chariots**: these are not war chariots but four-wheeled carriages used for riding. **Chariots** may also be translated as "horse-pulled carts." The last item in this list of wares is **slaves, that is, human souls**. This is a possible translation of the Greek text (RNAB "and slaves, that is, human beings"; SPCL "and even slaves, who are human lives"). Most translations, however, like TEV, have "human lives" as an additional item (AT, REB, NRSV; FRCL). The trouble with this, however, is that it implies that slaves are not human beings. NIV translates "and bodies and souls of men"; NJB "their slaves, and their human cargo." GECL takes the two to mean the one thing: "and even the lives of men." The first word in Greek is "bodies," which is commonly assumed to mean slaves; the second expression is "souls (or, lives) of people." This phrase is found in the Greek Septuagint version of Numbers 31.35, meaning (female) prisoners of war, and in 1 Chronicles 5.21 of male prisoners of war. In Ezekiel 27.13 it means slaves. This usage makes it quite likely that the two here mean, as TOB translates it, "slaves and captives," that is, slaves and prisoners of war. This is the translation recommended. One may also translate these terms as "people owned by others and people captured in war."

The following information given by Beasley-Murray (page 267) should be of interest and value to the translator:

> Rome's trade was worldwide, and even this modest enumeration of its imports entails many lands. The **gold, ivory,** and **costly wood,** for example, came from North Africa, the **jewels** and **pearls** from

India, **spices** from Arabia, **cinnamon** from South China, **myrrh** from Media, **wheat** from Egypt, **horses** from Armenia, **chariots** from Gaul, and **slaves** from all areas of the world. John's double mention of the last item is revealing, since the term for slaves is "bodies," and the phrase **human souls** in ordinary speech was synonymous, but it virtually carried the meaning of human livestock.

18.14　　　RSV　　　　　　　　　　　TEV

"The fruit for which thy soul longed has gone from thee, and all thy dainties and thy splendor are lost to thee, never to be found again!"	The businessmen say to her, "All the good things you longed to own have disappeared, and all your wealth and glamor are gone, and you will never find them again!"

RSV places this verse within quotation marks, indicating that this is quoted speech; but RSV does not identify the speaker. It is better, with TEV and others, to say that the businessmen of verse 11 are the speakers.

The fruit for which thy soul longed has gone from thee: the Greek word translated **fruit** appears only here in the New Testament and means "autumn fruit," that is, ripe fruit (a related word, "late autumn," is used in Jude 12). Here the word means "all the good things," "all the pleasures." Unless **fruit** in a given language will be understood to indicate "good things," the translator should abandon the figure and state clearly what is meant by the figure. **For which thy soul longed** is literally "the desire of thy soul." The Greek noun meaning "desire" appears only here in this book. "the fruit, the desire of your soul" means "everything you longed for (or, craved)."

All thy dainties and thy splendor: in Greek there is a wordplay: *ta lipara* and *ta lampra,* which NEB represents quite well: "all the glitter and the glamour." AT and RNAB have "luxury and splendor." The first Greek word means "the fatty things," that is, delicacies, luxuries, the good things of life; the second one means "the shining things" (see its use in the phrase "bright linen" in 15.6; 19.8). This probably refers to objects that glitter, such as gold, silver, and precious stones. One possible rendering is "all the things that make you look beautiful."

Are lost to thee, never to be found again: the second part of this verse may be restructured as follows: "you have lost all your luxuries and riches, and you will never get them back again" or "you have lost all the things that make your life comfortable and all your expensive possessions, and you will never . . . ." The verbal phrase **are lost** translates the active "have left (you)"; and **(never) to be found** translates the impersonal third plural active "they will (not) find," meaning "(not) be found." In at least one language this is expressed as follows: "you will not meet the day when you will find these things again."

18.15   RSV   TEV

The merchants of these wares, who gained wealth from her, will stand far off, in fear of her torment, weeping and mourning aloud,	The businessmen, who became rich from doing business in that city, will stand a long way off, because they are afraid of sharing in her suffering. They will cry and mourn,

Almost exactly the same thing is said of the businessmen that was said of the kings in verses 9-10.

The merchants of these wares: see verses 3 and 11.

Who gained wealth from her: see verse 3.

Weeping and mourning aloud: as in verse 11. This translates the Greek "weeping and mourning, saying"; the participle "saying" is the first word of verse 16, as in TEV "and say."

18.16   RSV   TEV

"Alas, alas, for the great city that was clothed in fine linen, in purple and scarlet, bedecked with gold, with jewels, and with pearls!	and say, "How terrible! How awful for the great city! She used to dress herself in linen, purple, and scarlet, and cover herself with gold ornaments, precious stones, and pearls!

The translator should consider translating the three successive messages of doom (verses 16-17a, 19b-20, 21b-24) in poetic form (see Section F of the introduction, "Translating the Revelation to John," pages 6 and following).

Alas, alas for the great city: see verse 10.

Clothed in fine linen, in purple and scarlet: see verse 12.

Bedecked with gold, with jewels, and with pearls: see 17.4.

18.17-18   RSV   TEV

17 In one hour all this wealth has been laid waste." And all shipmasters and seafaring men, sailors and all whose trade is on the sea, stood far off 18 and cried out as they saw the smoke of her burning, "What city was like the great city?"	17 And in one hour she has lost all this wealth!" All the ships' captains and passengers, the sailors and all others who earn their living on the sea, stood a long way off, 18 and cried out as they saw the smoke from the flames that consumed her: "There never has been another city like this great city!"

In one hour: as in verse 10.

All this wealth has been laid waste: this translates the Greek verb "to make a desert," that is, to cause to disappear (see its use in 17.16, "make desolate"). A more natural way of saying this in English is "all this wealth has disappeared." In certain languages this will be expressed as "Babylon has lost all of her possessions."

Shipmasters and seafaring men, sailors and all whose trade is on the sea: this list intends to include all people who make their living in maritime trade. **Shipmasters** can mean "steersmen, pilots," or as RSV translates it in Acts 27.11, "captain"; here it means the ships' captains. The "captain" is the one who commands the ship or gives commands to the sailors. The second phrase, translated **seafaring men** by RSV, is a curious one, and no exact parallel to it has been found. Literally it says "everyone who sails to a place." Most take it to mean, quite generally, "voyagers," "seafarers," "all who travel by ship" (REB, NRSV, NIV); the specific sense "passengers" is preferred by TEV, TNT, FRCL, BRCL. Some take it to mean the merchants who went with their goods aboard the ship (the Greek equivalent of the Latin *vectores*). Either "those who travel on the sea," "passengers," or "people who pay to travel on the ship" seems to be the best option. Sailors may be expressed as "people who make the boat go" or "people who work under the captain (or, boss) of the ship." In land-bound cultures where only small fishing boats are known, it is important to designate "ships" as "large boats that travel on the sea (or, ocean)." The fourth group are "those who earn their living on the sea." This does not include fishermen; it means people engaged in maritime commerce.

They saw the smoke of her burning: as in verse 9.

What city was like the great city? This is a rhetorical question meaning "There has never been a city as great as this one!" See a similar rhetorical question in 13.4.

18.19 RSV	TEV
And they threw dust on their heads, as they wept and mourned, crying out, "Alas, alas, for the great city where all who had ships at sea grew rich by her wealth! In one hour she has been laid waste.	They threw dust on their heads, they cried and mourned, saying, "How terrible! How awful for the great city! She is the city where all who have ships sailing the seas became rich on her wealth! And in one hour she has lost everything!"

They threw dust on their heads: a sign of grief (see Ezek 27.30). So one may translate "They threw dust on their heads to show their grief (or, how sorry they were)."

Wept and mourned: as in verses 11 and 15.

Alas, alas for the great city: as in verses 10 and 16.

Where all who had ships at sea grew rich by her wealth: "all seafaring traders became rich from her wealth (or, prosperity)" or "all shipowners who travel on the sea to buy and sell gained many possessions from Babylon's wealth." The Greek word translated **wealth** is the superlative form of the adjective "valuable" (see its use in verse 12, "costly wood"), and appears only here in the New Testament.

In one hour she has been laid waste: see the similar expression in verse 17.

18.20   RSV   TEV

Rejoice over her, O heaven,   Be glad, heaven, because of her
O saints and apostles and proph-   destruction! Be glad, God's people and
    ets,   the apostles and prophets! For God has
for God has given judgment for   condemned her for what she did to you!
    you against her!"

RSV (also NIV, RNAB) includes this verse in the lament of the seafaring people, but this seems most unlikely. TEV does not indicate who the speaker is. Some believe it is the voice that speaks in verse 4; others take it to be the angel of verse 1; and others take it to be the writer of the book. TEV intends the verse to be read as the writer's words.

Rejoice over her, O heaven: this is a command for all heavenly beings to rejoice over Babylon's downfall. See a similar command in 12.12. For the translation of **Rejoice** see 11.10.

O saints and apostles and prophets: they are also exhorted to be glad; for **saints** see 5.8; for **prophets** see 10.7. Here **apostles** probably are the twelve apostles of Jesus (as in 21.14). In certain languages this will be expressed as "Christ's chief messengers."

It is uncertain whether these **saints and apostles and prophets** are thought of as being in heaven, that is, that they are martyrs (see 17.6 and the references there), or whether they are alive. Commentators are divided on the subject. But the statement that follows seems to indicate that they are martyrs, for it compares what God is doing to Babylon with what Babylon had done to them. The statement can be translated "by condemning her, God has vindicated your cause," or "God has judged in your favor by condemning her," or "God has imposed on her the sentence she passed on you." The last one seems preferable; it conforms to the requirement of Deuteronomy 19.16-19, that the same punishment be meted out to a guilty person which that person inflicted on the victim—the so-called *lex talionis*, "the law of revenge." For ways to translate **has given judgment**, see comments on the verb "judge" at 6.10.

An alternative translation model for this verse is:

> You who live in Heaven, be glad (or, let your heart [liver] be bright), because God has destroyed Babylon. God's people, along with Christ's chief messengers (or, apostles) and those who proclaim God's message should rejoice. For God has condemned Babylon for the things that she has done to you.

18.21   RSV   TEV

Then a mighty angel took up a   Then a mighty angel picked up a
stone like a great millstone and threw it   stone the size of a large millstone and
into the sea, saying,   threw it into the sea, saying, "This is
    "So shall Babylon the great city   how the great city Babylon will be vio-
        be thrown down with vio-   lently thrown down and will never be

lence,   seen again.
and shall be found no more;

A mighty angel: see 5.2; 10.1.

A stone like a great millstone: "a stone that was as big as a large millstone." This refers to the large upper stone, turned by an animal to grind grain. Where **millstone** is unknown the translation can be "a very large stone."

The sea: see 10.2.

So shall Babylon the great city be thrown down with violence: the Greek word translated **violence** means "with an impulsive rush," like that of an unruly crowd or a herd of pigs, and appears only here in the New Testament. In languages where "to throw down" does not apply naturally to the destruction of a city, the translation may have to say "With violence like this the mighty city Babylon will be destroyed" or "This is how God will use great violence to destroy the great city Babylon."

Shall be found no more: see the similar expression in verse 14: "will never reappear," "will be gone forever," or "people will never see this city again."

In verses 22-23 the angel addresses the city, using the second person singular. It may be well to do the same here in verse 21, as follows: "Babylon, you mighty city, this is how you will be violently destroyed! Mighty city, you will disappear forever!" or in languages that do not use the passive, "Babylon, you mighty city, this is how God will destroy you with great force! Mighty city . . . ."

18.22 RSV	TEV
and the sound of harpers and minstrels, of flute players and trumpeters, shall be heard in thee no more; and a craftsman of any craft shall be found in thee no more; and the sound of the millstone shall be heard in thee no more;	The music of harps and of human voices, of players of the flute and the trumpet, will never be heard in you again! No workman in any trade will ever be found in you again; and the sound of the millstone will be heard no more!

The sound of harpers . . . shall be heard in thee no more: this can be said more naturally: "No one will ever again hear harpists (or, people) playing their harps in your streets" or "No one will ever again hear in your streets the music of harps." For **harpers** see 14.2.

Minstrels: in current American English this word does not mean "musicians" or "singers," which are better terms. The Greek word means "skilled in the arts," especially music.

Flute players and trumpeters: flutes and trumpets are wind instruments. This phrase can be more naturally expressed by "those who play flutes and those who play trumpets" or "those who blow flutes and those who blow trumpets."

A craftsman of any craft: this refers to skilled workers as opposed to common laborers (see Acts 19.24,38).

The sound of the millstone shall be heard in thee no more: this is a way of saying that mills won't be grinding any grain (because there will be no grain to grind).

Alternative translation models for this verse are:

> Never again, Babylon, will there be music in your streets, the music of harps and of singers, the music of flutes and of trumpets. All your skilled workers will disappear, and your mills will have no grain to grind.

Or:

> . . . no one will hear people plucking strings of a harp, or people singing, or people blowing flutes or trumpets. All . . . .

18.23   RSV   TEV

RSV	TEV

and the light of a lamp
   shall shine in thee no more;
and the voice of bridegroom and
   bride
   shall be heard in thee no
   more;
for thy merchants were the great
   men of the earth,
   and all nations were deceived
   by thy sorcery.
	Never again will the light of a lamp be seen in you; no more will the voices of brides and grooms be heard in you. Your businessmen were the most powerful in all the world, and with your false magic you deceived all the peoples of the world!"

The angel continues, saying that no lamps will ever be lit in Babylon again (for **lamp** see comments on "lampstand" in 1.12), nor will there be any more weddings, because there will be no one in the city to light a lamp or to get married; the city will be deserted. One may also translate "Never again will people see the light of a lamp shining in you; never again will they hear the voices of a man and woman getting married."

Thy merchants were the great men of the earth: this and what follows in this verse is an explanation given by the angel to Babylon, telling her why she will be destroyed. Babylon (Rome) was the most powerful financial center in the world, and the businessmen were the richest and most powerful. For **merchants** see 18.3.

All nations were deceived by thy sorcery: for **deceived** see comments on "beguiling" in 2.20. For **sorcery** (or, "magic") see 9.21. There is no justification for TEV "false (magic)."

18.24   RSV   TEV

> And in her was found the blood
>   of prophets and of saints,
> and of all who have been slain
>   on earth."

>   Babylon was punished because the
> blood of prophets and of God's people
> was found in the city; yes, the blood of
> all those who have been killed on earth.

RSV prints this verse as part of the angel's statement (also NIV, TNT, RNAB, AT, Mft, Brc). This may well be correct despite the change from the second person of address in verses 22-23 to the third person here in verse 24; verse 21 also has the third person. TEV (and FRCL, SPCL, Phps, REB) attributes this verse to the writer. No one can be dogmatic. However, it is probably best to interpret this as a statement by the writer.

In her was found the blood of prophets and of saints: this is a vivid way of saying "she is guilty of killing the prophets and God's people" (see 16.6; 17.6).

All who have been slain on earth: the speaker includes others, as well as Christians, who have been slaughtered in Rome and elsewhere. This is like Jesus' words about Jerusalem in Matthew 23.35-36. For **slain** see 5.6; 6.9.

An alternative translation model for this verse is:

> God punished Babylon because she (or, it [the city]) was guilty of killing the people who proclaimed God's message, and all the other people who belong to God. Yes, Babylon is guilty of killing people all over the world.

19.1   RSV   TEV

>   After this I heard what seemed to
> be the loud voice of a great multitude in
> heaven, crying,
>   "Hallelujah! Salvation and glory
>   and power belong to our God,

>   After this I heard what sounded
> like the roar of a large crowd of people
> in heaven, saying, "Praise God! Salva-
> tion, glory, and power belong to our
> God!

SECTION HEADING: a translator should consider the possibility of making 19.1-4 a separate section, with its own section heading; see the suggestion at the beginning of chapter 18.

After this: many translators will wish to make clear what **this** refers to and say, for example, "After the mighty angel had finished speaking."

What seemed to be the loud voice: the writer avoids saying explicitly that he heard the actual voice of a large crowd in heaven. Perhaps these are the angels mentioned in 5.11, in which case TEV "of people" is not appropriate. Some commentators take the Greek adverb "like" or "as" (RSV **what seemed to be**) to be a way of reminding the readers that a vision is being described, not an actual event. However, in many languages translators have to say what the huge crowd was composed of. If a translator feels it's "people," then TEV's model may be followed. However, it is also possible to say "a great number of heavenly beings shouting."

Crying: this is better translated "shouting" or even "singing."

271

The praise that follows may be rendered in poetic form (see Section F of the introduction, "Translating the Revelation to John," pages 6 and following).

Hallelujah: this represents the command in Hebrew "Praise Yah"; Yah is a shortened form of Yahweh. This expression, in its transliterated form, has entered several European languages. Where it is not known as an expression of praise or thanksgiving, the translation can be "Praise God," "Praise the Lord" or "Let us praise God." (See verse 5, below.)

Salvation and glory and power belong to our God: see similar language in 7.10; 12.10. For **salvation** see 7.10; **glory**, 1.6; **power**, 3.8. A possible way of translating this is "God is our Savior! He is majestic (or, glorious) and powerful!"

19.2

RSV	TEV
for his judgments are true and just; he has judged the great harlot who corrupted the earth with her fornication, and he has avenged on her the blood of his servants."	True and just are his judgments! He has condemned the prostitute who was corrupting the earth with her immorality. God has punished her because she killed his servants."

His judgments are true and just: see 16.7.

He has judged the great harlot: for the verb **judged** see 6.10; here it means "he has condemned (the infamous prostitute)" or "he has decided how he will punish."

Who corrupted the earth with her fornication: the writer is talking about idolatry but continues to use the language of sexual immorality. The verb **corrupted** means "to ruin," here in a moral and spiritual sense of leading into sin, specifically the sin of idolatry. For **fornication** see 17.2. An alternative translation model for this clause is "who caused the people of the earth to do evil by committing evil sexual practices with her."

He has avenged on her the blood of his servants: see the same language in 6.10, where the same Greek verb "to avenge" is used. Here **the blood** means the slaughter, the killing of God's servants. For **servants** see 1.1.

19.3

RSV	TEV
Once more they cried, "Hallelujah! The smoke from her goes up for ever and ever."	Again they shouted, "Praise God! The smoke from the flames that consume the great city goes up forever and ever!"

Once more they cried may be also rendered as "Once more the huge crowd of people cried."

The smoke from her goes up for ever and ever: in 18.9,18 we read of the smoke of the fire that destroys Babylon. Here the heavenly crowd celebrates the fact that the fire that consumes Babylon will never stop burning. See similar language in Isaiah 34.10.

19.4   RSV   TEV

And the twenty-four elders and the four living creatures fell down and worshiped God who is seated on the throne, saying, "Amen. Hallelujah!"

The twenty-four elders and the four living creatures fell down and worshiped God, who was seated on the throne. They said, "Amen! Praise God!"

The twenty-four elders: see 4.4.
The four living creatures: see 4.6-8.
Fell down and worshiped God who is seated on the throne: see 4.10.
Amen: see 1.6.

19.5-10

RSV   TEV
                                                 The Wedding Feast of the Lamb

5 And from the throne came a voice crying,
    "Praise our God, all you his servants,
    you who fear him, small and great."
6 Then I heard what seemed to be the voice of a great multitude, like the sound of many waters and like the sound of mighty thunderpeals, crying,
    "Hallelujah! For the Lord our God the Almighty reigns.
7   Let us rejoice and exult and give him the glory,
    for the marriage of the Lamb has come,
    and his Bride has made herself ready;
8   it was granted her to be clothed with fine linen, bright and pure"—
for the fine linen is the righteous deeds of the saints.
    9 And the angel said to me, "Write this: Blessed are those who are invited to the marriage supper of the Lamb." And he said to me, "These are true words of God." 10 Then I fell down at his feet to worship him, but he said to me, "You must not do that! I am a fellow servant with you and your brethren who hold the testimony of Jesus. Worship God." For the testimony of Jesus is the spirit of prophecy.

    5 Then there came from the throne the sound of a voice, saying, "Praise our God, all his servants and all people, both great and small, who have reverence for him!" 6 Then I heard what sounded like a crowd, like the sound of a roaring waterfall, like loud peals of thunder. I heard them say, "Praise God! For the Lord, our Almighty God, is King! 7 Let us rejoice and be glad; let us praise his greatness! For the time has come for the wedding of the Lamb, and his bride has prepared herself for it. 8 She has been given clean shining linen to wear." (The linen is the good deeds of God's people.)
    9 Then the angel said to me, "Write this: Happy are those who have been invited to the wedding feast of the Lamb." And the angel added, "These are the true words of God."
    10 I fell down at his feet to worship him, but he said to me, "Don't do it! I am a fellow servant of yours and of your brothers, all those who hold to the truth that Jesus revealed. Worship God!"
    For the truth that Jesus revealed is what inspires the prophets.

SECTION HEADING: TEV "The Wedding Feast of the Lamb"; an alternative heading can be "In praise of the Lamb and his Bride," "The Lamb marries," or "The Lamb takes a Bride." This section does not have an account of the wedding of the Lamb but an announcement of that coming event.

    TEV, following the UBS Greek New Testament, has verse 5 as the first verse of this section. It is better, however, to place verse 5 as the last verse of the previous

273

section, and to begin this section with verse 6. The text itself makes this most likely: "Then I heard" in verse 6 begins a new section, as "After this I heard" in verse 1 begins the previous section.

19.5   RSV   TEV

And from the throne came a voice crying,
 	
    "Praise our God, all you his servants,
    you who fear him, small and great."
	Then there came from the throne the sound of a voice, saying, "Praise our God, all his servants and all people, both great and small, who have reverence for him!"

From the throne came a voice: this is not God speaking, as the words **our God** indicate. Perhaps the speaker is one of the four living creatures, who were nearest the throne. Other instances of an unidentified voice speaking are: 6.6, from among the four living creatures; 9.13, from among the four horns of the altar; 16.1,7, from the temple. In 21.3 there is once more a voice coming from God's throne. Translators in many languages will need to render this clause as "Then I heard someone calling from the throne, saying . . . ."

The translator should consider rendering this song of praise and the one in verses 6b-8 as poetry (see Section F of the introduction, "Translating the Revelation to John," pages 6 and following).

Praise our God: this is the equivalent of "Hallelujah" in verse 1.

His servants, you who fear him: these are not two groups but one: "you who serve him, who have reverence for him." For **fear him, small and great**, see 11.18. The command is given to God's people on earth.

Alternative translation models for this verse are:

> Then (or, After that) I heard someone calling from the throne, saying, "You must praise our [inclusive] God, all people, both weak and powerful, who serve him and revere him."

Or:

> . . . "All you people, both weak and powerful, who have reverence for God must say to him, 'We give honor to you.'"

19.6   RSV   TEV

Then I heard what seemed to be the voice of a great multitude, like the sound of many waters and like the sound of mighty thunderpeals, crying,
    "Hallelujah! For the Lord our
    God the Almighty reigns.
	Then I heard what sounded like a crowd, like the sound of a roaring waterfall, like loud peals of thunder. I heard them say, "Praise God! For the Lord, our Almighty God, is King!

I heard what seemed to be the voice: as in verse 1, this cry of praise comes from people on earth. One may also translate "Then I heard what sounded like a great number of people shouting."

Like the sound of many waters: as in 1.15; 14.2.

Like the sound of mighty thunderpeals: see 6.1; 14.2. **Mighty** in this context means "very loud."

Hallelujah: see verse 1.

The Lord our God the Almighty reigns: see similar statements in 11.15,17; for the title of God see also 1.8; 4.8; 15.3.

An alternative translation model for this verse is:

> Then I heard what sounded like a great number of people shouting. It was loud like the sound of a giant waterfall (or, the waves of the sea) and like the roar of thunder (or, the sound of the sky roaring). They said, "Let us praise God! For our all-powerful God is king (or, rules over all)."

19.7   RSV   TEV

RSV	TEV
Let us rejoice and exult and give him the glory, for the marriage of the Lamb has come, and his Bride has made herself ready;	Let us rejoice and be glad; let us praise his greatness! For the time has come for the wedding of the Lamb, and his bride has prepared herself for it.

Let us rejoice and exult and give him the glory: this kind of self-exhortation, or command in the first person plural, may be expressed by "We must all . . . ." For **rejoice** see 11.10; the Greek verb translated **exult** appears only here in Revelation. Translators should look for synonyms in their languages that refer to great joy. For **give him the glory** see 11.13; 14.7.

The marriage of the Lamb has come: this is more naturally expressed by saying "The time has come for the Lamb to get married." The bride of the Lamb is the church; the wedding is the perfect union between Christ and his church, which is one of the events of the End.

His Bride has made herself ready: the Greek noun translated **Bride** (NRSV "bride") is simply "woman." In English the word "bride" is applied to a woman at the time of her wedding and for a short time thereafter. Some languages may not have a specialized term and may have to refer to the bride as "the woman the Lamb is going to marry." For the verb translated **made . . . ready**, compare 8.6, where it similarly means "prepared."

An alternative translation model for the last part of this verse is:

> . . . For the time has come for the Lamb to take a wife (or, a woman), and she has prepared herself to receive him.

19.8   RSV   TEV

it was granted her to be clothed   She has been given clean shining linen
with fine linen, bright and   to wear." (The linen is the good deeds of
pure"—   God's people.)
for the fine linen is the righteous deeds
of the saints.

It was granted her: for the passive use of the verb "to give," indicating God
as the actor, see 6.4a. Implicit is the idea of "right" or "privilege." Thus a translation
may choose to say "God has given her . . . ," or ". . . has given her the right . . . ,"
or ". . . has allowed her . . . ."

Fine linen, bright and pure: see 15.6. The Greek word there translated
"linen" is different from the one used here, but there is no difference in meaning
other than that this term emphasizes the **fine** quality of the cloth. The one used here
appears also in 18.12,16; 19.14.

For the fine linen is the righteous deeds of the saints: by use of quotation
marks and a dash after **pure**, RSV indicates that this is a comment from the writer.
TEV does the same by placing this explanatory comment within parentheses. Here,
as elsewhere, **is** means "represents," "signifies"; **righteous deeds** are the kind that
God requires of his people; for **saints** see 5.8.

An alternative translation model for this verse is:

God has given her clothes made of clean, shining linen to wear."
(The linen represents the good deeds that God's people do.)

19.9   RSV   TEV

And the angel said[1] to me, "Write   Then the angel said to me, "Write
this: Blessed are those who are invited   this: Happy are those who have been
to the marriage supper of the Lamb."   invited to the wedding feast of the
And he said to me, "These are true   Lamb." And the angel added, "These
words of God."   are the true words of God."

[1] Greek *he said*

The angel said to me: the RSV footnote shows that the Greek text says only
"he said to me." The words that follow clearly indicate it is an angel speaking,
probably the one of chapter 17.

Blessed: see 1.3.

Those who are invited to the marriage supper of the Lamb: the Greek verb
translated **invited** is simply "called"; the use of the perfect tense here suggests that
"who have been invited" (TEV) is a better translation. In terms of a wedding, "feast"
or "banquet" is more appropriate than **supper**. In certain languages one may say,
for example, "the feast (or, fiesta) to celebrate the marriage of the Lamb" or "the
feast to celebrate the Lamb taking a wife."

The Destruction of Babylon and Defeat of the Enemies 19.10

These are true words of God: the Greek is ambiguous, and the meaning may be "These words of God are true," "These are true words from God," or "These true words come from God." Perhaps the second option is to be preferred, stated differently: "This is a true message from God" (note Brc, "This is a genuine message from God"). And to what it refers is also in doubt; it may be specifically what the angel says in this verse, or the song in verses 6-8, or more generally the whole book. Perhaps the song in verses 6-8 is what the angel refers to (see also 21.5; 22.6). However, since it is uncertain what the word **These** refers to, translators should keep their translations ambiguous.

19.10 RSV	TEV
Then I fell down at his feet to worship him, but he said to me, "You must not do that! I am a fellow servant with you and your brethren who hold the testimony of Jesus. Worship God." For the testimony of Jesus is the spirit of prophecy.	I fell down at his feet to worship him, but he said to me, "Don't do it! I am a fellow servant of yours and of your brothers, all those who hold to the truth that Jesus revealed. Worship God!" For the truth that Jesus revealed is what inspires the prophets.

I fell down at his feet to worship him: see 1.17; 4.10.

You must not do that! "Don't worship me!" In more colloquial English this would be said "You can't do that!"

I am a fellow servant with you and your brethren: instead of a noun phrase, a sentence with a finite verb may be better: "Like you and your fellow believers, I also serve God (or, am a servant of God)" or "I serve God just as you and your fellow believers do."

Who hold to the testimony of Jesus: the phrase is the same as in 1.2; 12.17, and probably means the same, as expressed by TEV: "who are faithful to the truth revealed by Jesus." This takes the genitive phrase **the testimony of Jesus** to be a subjective genitive, "the testimony given by Jesus," not an objective genitive, "the testimony given about Jesus."

Worship God: this can be said more emphatically, "God is the one you must worship." For **worship** see 4.10 and elsewhere.

For the testimony of Jesus is the spirit of prophecy: commentaries and translations are divided over whether or not these words are spoken by the angel or are the writer's own comment. NRSV, NIV, REB, TNT, AT, and RNAB attribute it to the angel; RSV, TEV, Mft, Phps, NJB, FRCL, SPCL, and BRCL take it to be the writer's comment. The Greek text, of course, gives no hint on the subject. There is no decisive factor to determine which is correct; the decision rests with the translator.

The genitive phrase **the testimony of Jesus** must mean here what it does in the earlier part of the verse; it would be inconceivable that here it means something different. In favor of the objective genitive, "the testimony given about Jesus," are Phps, REB, RNAB. REB provides a dynamic equivalent translation: "For those who bear witness to Jesus have the spirit of prophecy." In favor of the subjective genitive, "the testimony given by Jesus," are TEV, Mft, AT, NJB, NIV, SPCL, FRCL, TNT. FRCL provides a good rendering: "For the truth revealed by Jesus is what inspires the

277

prophets." A translator must decide on one or the other; simply to reproduce formally the genitive phrase **the testimony of Jesus** is not translation. A translator should take into account the way in which this phrase is rendered in 1.2,9; 6.9; 12.17; 20.4.

As for **the spirit of prophecy,** it seems best to take it to mean "inspiration," that is, the power that inspires the prophets, that enables them to proclaim the Christian message. In this context that power is "the truth revealed by Jesus," as TEV has it. Some take **spirit** here to mean God's Spirit and translate "For it is the Spirit that enables God's people to proclaim the truth revealed by Jesus." This is possible but does not seem as likely as the other. Another translation model for this final sentence is "This truth that Jesus revealed is what enables people to (or, gives them the power to) proclaim God's message."

An alternative translation model for this verse is:

> Then I prostrated myself before his feet (or, in front of him) to give him honor, but he said to me, "Don't do that! I serve God just as you and your fellow believers do. They are the ones who follow the truth that Jesus revealed. So God is the one you should worship."

For the truth that Jesus revealed is what enables (or, empowers) people to proclaim God's message.

19.11-21

RSV	TEV
	The Rider on the White Horse

11 Then I saw heaven opened, and behold, a white horse! He who sat upon it is called Faithful and True, and in righteousness he judges and makes war. 12 His eyes are like a flame of fire, and on his head are many diadems; and he has a name inscribed which no one knows but himself. 13 He is clad in a robe dipped in blood, and the name by which he is called is The Word of God. 14 And the armies of heaven, arrayed in fine linen, white and pure, followed him on white horses. 15 From his mouth issues a sharp sword with which to smite the nations, and he will rule them with a rod of iron; he will tread the wine press of the fury of the wrath of God the Almighty. 16 On his robe and on his thigh he has a name inscribed, King of kings and Lord of lords.	11 Then I saw heaven open, and there was a white horse. Its rider is called Faithful and True; it is with justice that he judges and fights his battles. 12 His eyes were like a flame of fire, and he wore many crowns on his head. He had a name written on him, but no one except himself knows what it is. 13 The robe he wore was covered with blood. His name is "The Word of God." 14 The armies of heaven followed him, riding on white horses and dressed in clean white linen. 15 Out of his mouth came a sharp sword, with which he will defeat the nations. He will rule over them with a rod of iron, and he will trample out the wine in the wine press of the furious anger of the Almighty God. 16 On his robe and on his thigh was written the name: "King of kings and Lord of lords."
17 Then I saw an angel standing in the sun, and with a loud voice he called to all the birds that fly in midheaven, "Come, gather for the great supper of God, 18 to eat the flesh of kings, the flesh of captains, the flesh of mighty men, the flesh of horses and their riders, and the flesh of all men, both free and slave, both small and great." 19 And I saw the beast and the kings of the earth with their armies gathered to make war against him who sits upon the horse and against his army.	17 Then I saw an angel standing on the sun. He shouted in a loud voice to all the birds flying in midair: "Come and gather together for God's great feast! 18 Come and eat the flesh of kings, generals, and soldiers, the flesh of horses and their riders, the flesh of all people, slave and free, great and small!" 19 Then I saw the beast and the kings of the earth and their armies gathered to fight

20 And the beast was captured, and with it the false prophet who in its presence had worked the signs by which he deceived those who had received the mark of the beast and those who worshiped its image. These two were thrown alive into the lake of fire that burns with sulphur. 21 And the rest were slain by the sword of him who sits upon the horse, the sword that issues from his mouth; and all the birds were gorged with their flesh.

against the one who was riding the horse and against his army. 20 The beast was taken prisoner, together with the false prophet who had performed miracles in his presence. (It was by those miracles that he had deceived those who had the mark of the beast and those who had worshiped the image of the beast.) The beast and the false prophet were both thrown alive into the lake of fire that burns with sulfur. 21 Their armies were killed by the sword that comes out of the mouth of the one who was riding the horse; and all the birds ate all they could of their flesh.

SECTION HEADING: TEV "The Rider on the White Horse." Other possible headings are "The Messiah defeats the beast," "God's promised Savior defeats the beast," or "The defeat and destruction of the beast and the false prophet."

Here begin the events of the End, the final defeat of evil, and the reign of God and his Messiah. In this section (19.11-21) John sees first the rider of the white horse, as the rider sets out with his armies to fight (verses 11-16). Then John sees an angel who summons the birds to come to the sumptuous feast that will soon be ready for them—the corpses of the defeated forces (verses 17-18). And then John sees the beast, the false prophet, and their armies gathered to fight the Messiah; their soldiers are all killed, and the beast and the false prophet are thrown alive into hell (verses 19-21). A good division of this material can follow this outline, each section beginning with the statement "And I saw" (verses 11,17,19).

19.11   RSV   TEV

Then I saw heaven opened, and behold, a white horse! He who sat upon it is called Faithful and True, and in righteousness he judges and makes war.

Then I saw heaven open, and there was a white horse. Its rider is called Faithful and True; it is with justice that he judges and fights his battles.

I saw heaven opened: see 4.1; 11.19; 15.5.
Behold: an exclamation of surprise (see 1.7).
A white horse: see 6.2. White is the color of victory.
He who sat upon it: better, "Its rider" (see 6.2).
Faithful and True: in 3.14 Jesus is called "the faithful and true witness"; and see "the true one" in 3.7. This is a name and should be kept as concise as possible. In this context translators in certain languages will need to combine these two adjectives and say "The Trustworthy One" or "The One who Serves God Faithfully."
In righteousness he judges and makes war: it is for a righteous cause, or governed by righteous principles, that he judges, that is, condemns, and makes war (see Isa 11.3-5). For **judges** see 6.10; and for **makes war** see 2.16. So one may also render this clause as "He uses right (or, correct) principles when he condemns people and fights against his enemies."

19.12   RSV   TEV

His eyes are like a flame of fire, and on   His eyes were like a flame of fire, and
his head are many diadems; and he has   he wore many crowns on his head. He
a name inscribed which no one knows   had a name written on him, but no one
but himself.   except himself knows what it is.

Eyes . . . like a flame of fire: this describes his eyes as shining like fire (see
1.14; 2.18).
Diadems: see 12.3; 13.1.
A name inscribed: the text does not say where the name was written;
presumably it was on his forehead. Nor is there any intimation as to who wrote it;
it is a way of saying that he had a name on him. In certain languages it will be
necessary to translate "He had a name written on his body," and in other languages
"They (unknown subjects or agents) had written a name on him (or, his body)."
No one knows but himself: see 2.17.
In verses 12-13, 15-16 RSV uses the present tense of the verbs (following the
Greek), whereas TEV continues using the past tense, which is more suitable for the
narrative (see 13.12).
An alternative translation model for this verse is:

> His eyes shone (or, blazed) like fire, and on his head he had (or,
> wore) many crowns (or, chiefs' hats). They had written a name on
> his body, but only he knows what it is.

19.13   RSV   TEV

He is clad in a robe dipped in[m] blood,   The robe he wore was covered with
and the name by which he is called is   blood. His name is "The Word of God."
The Word of God.

[m] Other ancient authorities read *sprinkled with*

He is clad: in the narrative the present tense here is strange. For the verb "to
wear (clothes)" see comments on "wrapped in a cloud" in 10.1.
A robe dipped in blood: it may be that the robe, by having been dipped in
blood, was blood-red in color; or it may be that the robe was actually dripping blood,
from having been dipped in it. The latter seems preferable; the translation can be "a
robe soaked with blood." As the RSV footnote indicates, some Greek manuscripts
and early versions have "sprinkled" or "spattered." The evidence for the text
translated by RSV and TEV is stronger. The blood that stains his robe is the blood of
slaughtered enemies. For **robe** see 1.13. Another possible rendering for this sentence
is "He was wearing a robe (or, long cloth outer garment) that was covered (or, dirty)
with blood."
The name by which he is called: either "his name is" or "the name he is
known by." This name, **The Word of God**, is not the name known only to himself;

it is the name by which he is addressed (see the other two names in verses 11 and 16).

19.14   RSV   TEV

And the armies of heaven, arrayed in   The armies of heaven followed him,
fine linen, white and pure, followed him   riding on white horses and dressed in
on white horses.   clean white linen.

The armies of heaven: at first glance it seems that these are angels; but the fact that they are dressed in fine linen, white and pure (see verse 8), indicates that these are the victorious martyrs (see similar descriptions in 3.5; 7.14). And in 17.14 the soldiers of the conquering Lamb are his faithful followers. Like their leader, they also ride white horses.

19.15   RSV   TEV

From his mouth issues a sharp sword   Out of his mouth came a sharp sword,
with which to smite the nations, and he   with which he will defeat the nations.
will rule them with a rod of iron; he will He will rule over them with a rod of
tread the wine press of the fury of the   iron, and he will trample out the wine in
wrath of God the Almighty.   the wine press of the furious anger of
                                           the Almighty God.

From his mouth issues a sharp sword: see 1.16; 2.12,16.
To smite the nations: this means "to conquer, to punish, to defeat the nations." This verb is used also in 11.6.
He will rule them with a rod of iron: see 2.27; 12.5.
He will tread the wine press: see 14.19-20.
The fury of the wrath of God the Almighty: see 16.19. For the title see verse 6 and also 1.8.

19.16   RSV   TEV

On his robe and on his thigh he has a   On his robe and on his thigh was writ-
name inscribed, King of kings and Lord   ten the name: "King of kings and Lord
of lords.   of lords."

On his robe and on his thigh: some suggest that this means "on the part of the robe that covered his thigh," which is a reasonable assumption, as the writer would have clearly seen this name. If it was on his thigh, it would have been hidden. But only Mft follows this: "and on his robe, upon his thigh . . . ." If a translation has to specify which leg the writer is talking about, probably the right leg should be chosen.

A name inscribed: as in verse 12.
King of kings and Lord of lords: see 17.14.

19.17   RSV   TEV

Then I saw an angel standing in   Then I saw an angel standing on
the sun, and with a loud voice he called   the sun. He shouted in a loud voice to
to all the birds that fly in midheaven,   all the birds flying in midair: "Come
"Come, gather for the great supper of   and gather together for God's great
God,   feast!

An angel standing in the sun: many times John has seen an angel (5.2; 7.2;
10.1; 14.6,8,9; 14.15,17,18; 18.1; 20.1), but this is the only one described as standing
in or on the sun. The Greek preposition normally means "in," and this is how most
translations render it. But "on" seems more appropriate.
All the birds that fly in midheaven: "all the birds flying high in the air" (see
8.13; 14.6). These are carrion birds, that is, birds that eat dead bodies, and in certain
languages it will be necessary to designate them this way.
Come, gather for the great supper of God: they are to gather together for
the feast that God will provide for them. Instead of the literal **great supper of God**,
it may be better to translate "the bountiful feast (or, fiesta) that God is going to
prepare."

19.18   RSV   TEV

to eat the flesh of kings, the flesh of   Come and eat the flesh of kings, gener-
captains, the flesh of mighty men, the   als, and soldiers, the flesh of horses and
flesh of horses and their riders, and the   their riders, the flesh of all people, slave
flesh of all men, both free and slave,   and free, great and small!"
both small and great."

To eat the flesh of: it should be quite clear that these are dead bodies. The
angel reads the menu:
Of kings . . . of captains . . . of mighty men: the **captains** are army officers;
see in 6.15 "military chiefs" (TEV); **mighty men** are soldiers, or warriors. It is not
necessary, as RSV does, to repeat **the flesh of** before each item.
The flesh of horses and their riders: this can be said "of horses and the
soldiers who ride them."
The flesh of all men, both free and slave: this includes everybody, slave or
free. In English the order "slave and free" (TEV) is more natural. For **free and
slave** see 6.15.
Both small and great: see 11.18. Again, the order "great and small" (TEV) is
more natural in English.
For verses 17-18 see Ezekiel 39.17-20.

19.19 RSV TEV

And I saw the beast and the kings of the earth with their armies gathered to make war against him who sits upon the horse and against his army.

Then I saw the beast and the kings of the earth and their armies gathered to fight against the one who was riding the horse and against his army.

The beast: the first beast, the one that came out of the sea (13.1-10; 17.11-14).

The kings of the earth with their armies: they are referred to in 16.14.

Gathered: this passive form reflects the account in 16.14,16, where the three foul spirits bring the kings together for the final battle.

Against him who sits upon the horse: as in the frequent description of God as "the one who sits on the throne" (see 4.2-3,9,10; 5.1,7,13; 6.16; 7.15), so here the conquering Messiah is referred to by the phrase used to describe him in verse 11.

An alternative translation model for this verse is:

> Then I saw the beast and all the kings (high chiefs) of the world, along with their soldiers (or, fighting men), gathering together to fight against the one who was riding on the horse and against his soldiers.

19.20 RSV TEV

And the beast was captured, and with it the false prophet who in its presence had worked the signs by which he deceived those who had received the mark of the beast and those who worshiped its image. These two were thrown alive into the lake of fire that burns with sulphur.

The beast was taken prisoner, together with the false prophet who had performed miracles in his presence. (It was by those miracles that he had deceived those who had the mark of the beast and those who had worshiped the image of the beast.) The beast and the false prophet were both thrown alive into the lake of fire that burns with sulfur.

Was captured: he was taken prisoner by the conquering Messiah. In languages that do not use the passive, one may say, for example, "The Messiah (or, God's Savior) captured the beast . . . ."

The false prophet: see 16.13.

In its presence had worked the signs . . . worshiped its image: see 13.13-17; 14.9,11; 16.2. The double phrase **those who had received the mark of the beast and those who worshiped its image** does not refer to two different groups but to the same people, who had received the mark and worshiped the statue of the beast. The same language should be used here that is used in the other passages cited.

Were thrown alive: by the conquering Messiah.

The lake of fire that burns with sulphur: this is Gehenna, but it is not called by that name in Revelation. In some languages it will be called "place full of fire that burns with sulfur" or "the place of torture that is like being burned by flaming sulfur." For **sulphur** see 14.10. NJB and NIV provide a good translation: "the fiery lake of burning sulfur."

19.21

RSV	TEV
And the rest were slain by the sword of him who sits upon the horse, the sword that issues from his mouth; and all the birds were gorged with their flesh.	Their armies were killed by the sword that comes out of the mouth of the one who was riding the horse; and all the birds ate all they could of their flesh.

The rest were slain: that is, all their soldiers were killed; none escaped alive. In certain languages this will be expressed as "The Messiah killed all their soldiers."

By the sword of him who sits upon the horse: the text speaks only of the Messiah killing the enemy forces. The text does not say explicitly that his soldiers engaged in the fighting and killing (see 17.14). So this sentence may be translated as follows: "The one who was sitting on the horse used the sword that was protruding from his mouth to . . . ."

All the birds were gorged with their flesh: the birds ate their fill of the bountiful feast.

20.1-6

RSV	TEV
	The Thousand Years
1 Then I saw an angel coming down from heaven, holding in his hand the key of the bottomless pit and a great chain. 2 And he seized the dragon, that ancient serpent, who is the Devil and Satan, and bound him for a thousand years, 3 and threw him into the pit, and shut it and sealed it over him, that he should deceive the nations no more, till the thousand years were ended. After that he must be loosed for a little while.	1 Then I saw an angel coming down from heaven, holding in his hand the key of the abyss and a heavy chain. 2 He seized the dragon, that ancient serpent—that is, the Devil, or Satan—and chained him up for a thousand years. 3 The angel threw him into the abyss, locked it, and sealed it, so that he could not deceive the nations any more until the thousand years were over. After that he must be set loose for a little while.
4 Then I saw thrones, and seated on them were those to whom judgment was committed. Also I saw the souls of those who had been beheaded for their testimony to Jesus and for the word of God, and who had not worshiped the beast or its image and had not received its mark on their foreheads or their hands. They came to life, and reigned with Christ a thousand years. 5 The rest of the dead did not come to life until the thousand years were ended. This is the first resurrection. 6 Blessed and holy is he who shares in the first resurrection! Over such the second death has no power, but they shall be priests of God and of Christ, and they shall reign with him a thousand years.	4 Then I saw thrones, and those who sat on them were given the power to judge. I also saw the souls of those who had been executed because they had proclaimed the truth that Jesus revealed and the word of God. They had not worshiped the beast or its image, nor had they received the mark of the beast on their foreheads or their hands. They came to life and ruled as kings with Christ for a thousand years. 5 (The rest of the dead did not come to life until the thousand years were over.) This is the first raising of the dead. 6 Happy and greatly blessed are those who are included in this first raising of the dead. The second death has no power over them; they shall be priests of God and of Christ, and they will rule with him for a thousand years.

SECTION HEADING: TEV "The Thousand Years." This can also be "The Devil is bound for one thousand years," or "They tie the Devil up for one thousand years"; "The one thousand years reign of Christ," or "Christ reigns for one thousand years."

This section can go through verse 10 instead of verse 6, and the heading can be "The defeat and destruction of Satan." But it may be better to keep the one thousand years' imprisonment of Satan as a separate section, since this is the only passage in the Bible that speaks of a thousand years.

In the first vision (verses 1-3) John sees the Devil being chained and thrown into the abyss. In the second vision (verses 4-6) he sees the resurrected martyrs ruling with Christ during the one thousand years of Satan's imprisonment.

20.1	RSV	TEV

Then I saw an angel coming down from heaven, holding in his hand the key of the bottomless pit and a great chain.

Then I saw an angel coming down from heaven, holding in his hand the key of the abyss and a heavy chain.

Then: as with the first sentence of many of the chapters in Revelation, the writer indicates that the events that he is seeing in the present chapter follow immediately after events in the previous chapter. In many languages it will be helpful to tie this verse in with what happened in 19.19-21 and say, for example, "After the Messiah conquered the beast, the false prophet, and their soldiers, I saw . . . ."

An angel coming down from heaven: as in 18.1 and elsewhere.

Holding in his hand: if necessary the translation can say "in his right hand." There is no verb in Greek, which says only "in his hand."

The key of the bottomless pit: see 9.1; 17.8.

A great chain: this may be said "a heavy chain," "a thick chain." It is assumed to be made of metal. In cultures where metal chains are unknown, one may say something like "a big (or, thick) rope," or else employ some other material that is used for tying up people.

20.2-3	RSV	TEV

2 And he seized the dragon, that ancient serpent, who is the Devil and Satan, and bound him for a thousand years, 3 and threw him into the pit, and shut it and sealed it over him, that he should deceive the nations no more, till the thousand years were ended. After that he must be loosed for a little while.

2 He seized the dragon, that ancient serpent—that is, the Devil, or Satan—and chained him up for a thousand years. 3 The angel threw him into the abyss, locked it, and sealed it, so that he could not deceive the nations any more until the thousand years were over. After that he must be set loose for a little while.

Seized: this verb is better translated "overcame" (NJB), "subdued" (SPCL), "overpowered," or "captured." It's not that the angel just grabbed him, but that he overpowered him.

The dragon, that ancient serpent, who is the Devil and Satan: see 12.9.

Bound him for a thousand years, and threw him into the pit: the reader should not understand the text to say that the angel tied the Devil up with the chain for a thousand years and then threw him into the abyss. What is meant, of course, is that the angel overcame the devil, bound him with the chain, and threw him into the abyss, where he stayed, bound, for a thousand years.

The pit: this is the abyss (see 9.1 and verse 1, above).

Shut it and sealed it over him: this assumes that there is an entrance, a door, to the pit, and it may be necessary for a translation to say so explicitly. With the key that he was carrying, the angel locked the door and then sealed it. So instead of translating **shut** (the door), as RSV does, it is better to say "locked (the door)," as TEV does. As in Matthew 27.66, the sealing would be the use of some device to show that the door was not to be opened. The seal shows that the pit has been closed by God's command. For **seal** one may also say "put a device on the door to make sure it stayed closed."

He should deceive the nations no more: see in 12.9 "the deceiver of the whole world."

Were ended: the same verb that is used in 15.1,8.

He must be loosed: this is part of God's plan, as the verb translated **must** shows (see 1.1). The Devil must be set free for a short period of time before his destruction. It is probable that the one who frees Satan is the angel who tied him up in the pit, so in languages that do not use the passive, one may say "After that, the angel will set him free for a short time." However, if translators feel that the subject here is ambiguous, one may say "After that, they will set . . . ."

Alternative translation models for verses 2-3 are:

> The angel overpowered the dragon, that ancient serpent also known as the Devil, or Satan, and bound him with the chain. Then he threw him into the abyss, and locked and sealed the door of the abyss. The Devil must stay there for a thousand years, and during that time he will not be able to deceive the nations of the world. After the one thousand years are over, he must be set loose for a little while.

Or:

> The angel captured the dragon, that serpent (or, snake) from ancient times whom they also call the Devil or Satan. He took the chain and tied the Devil up. Then he threw him into the deep pit. With the key that he was holding he locked the door of the pit and sealed it. The Devil must stay there for a thousand years, and during that time he will not be able to deceive the people on the earth. After the one thousand years are over, the angel will free him for a short time.

20.4   RSV   TEV

Then I saw thrones, and seated on them were those to whom judgment was committed. Also I saw the souls of those who had been beheaded for their testimony to Jesus and for the word of God, and who had not worshiped the beast or its image and had not received its mark on their foreheads or their hands. They came to life, and reigned with Christ a thousand years.

Then I saw thrones, and those who sat on them were given the power to judge. I also saw the souls of those who had been executed because they had proclaimed the truth that Jesus revealed and the word of God. They had not worshiped the beast or its image, nor had they received the mark of the beast on their foreheads or their hands. They came to life and ruled as kings with Christ for a thousand years.

Then I saw thrones: although the text does not specify it, these thrones are in heaven, not on earth.

Seated on them: this translates the third person plural active "they sat on them," the equivalent in the Greek of an impersonal passive. Another way to state this is "The ones sitting on them."

Those to whom judgment was committed: "those to whom God had given the right to rule." Often in the Bible the verb "to judge" and the noun "judgment" mean "to rule" and "rule." As the end of the verse makes clear, they were given the right to rule with Christ for a thousand years. They are not appointed judges but rulers, kings (see Matt 19.28; Luke 22.30).

Also I saw the souls of those who had been beheaded: this begins a lengthy description of the martyrs (see 6.9 "the souls of those who had been slain"). The Greek verb translated **beheaded** (appearing only here in the New Testament) indicates that an ax was used in their execution. For **souls** see 6.9. This clause may also be rendered as "Also I saw the souls of those people whom others had beheaded (cut their heads off)."

It should be clear that **the souls of those who had been beheaded**, that is, the martyrs, are precisely the ones who were sitting on the thrones. The Greek text says (quite literally) "I saw thrones, and they sat on them, and power to rule was given them, and the souls . . . hands." The clause beginning "and the souls" is in apposition to the unnamed subject of the verb "they sat." Neither RSV nor TEV is satisfactory, since neither one clearly shows the connection between the two parts of the passage. A more satisfactory rendering, then, of the first part of this verse is "Then I saw thrones (kings' chairs), and the ones seated on them were those whom God had given the right to rule. They were the souls of those people . . . ."

For their testimony to Jesus: see comments, 1.2,9; 12.17; 19.10.

For the word of God: see comments at 1.2,9; 6.9.

Had not worshiped the beast or its image: see 13.12,15; 14.9.

Had not received its mark on their foreheads or their hands: see 13.16; 14.9.

They came to life: they came back to life at the same time that the Devil was thrown into the abyss. Other ways of rendering this are "They returned to life," "They received life again," or even "God caused them to live again."

Reigned with Christ: "they ruled as kings with Christ." The Greek text here has the definite article with "Christ," so that it probably should be translated as the title "the Messiah" and not as a proper noun. The name "Christ" appears in Revelation as part of the name "Jesus Christ" in 1.1,2,5; it appears with the Greek definite article here and in verse 6; and, following "God," it appears with the definite article and the possessive "his" ("his Messiah") in 11.15; 12.10. Both here and in verse 6 it is recommended that it be translated as the title, "the Christ," "the Messiah," or "God's Chosen Savior," and not as a proper noun.

An alternative translation model for this verse is:

> And then I saw some thrones, on which sat those who had been beheaded because they had proclaimed the message of Jesus and the word of God. These people had not worshiped the beast or its statue, and they had not received the mark of the beast on their foreheads or their hands. They came back to life and sat on the thrones. God gave them the right to rule, and they reigned with the Messiah for a thousand years.

20.5   RSV   TEV

The rest of the dead did not come to life until the thousand years were ended. This is the first resurrection.	(The rest of the dead did not come to life until the thousand years were over.) This is the first raising of the dead.

The rest of the dead . . . were ended: only after the one thousand years do all the other dead people, Christians and non-Christians, come back to life. This bit of information interrupts the narrative, which is why TEV places it within parentheses. This is intended to make clear to the reader that the rest of the verse is linked directly to verse 4. One may also translate "All the other people who had died . . . ."

This is the first resurrection: that is, the resurrection of the martyrs in verse 4 is the first resurrection (as verse 6 makes clear). It is possible to render this clause as "This is the first time that God will raise people from death" or ". . . will cause people to come back to life."

20.6   RSV   TEV

Blessed and holy is he who shares in the first resurrection! Over such the second death has no power, but they shall be priests of God and of Christ, and they shall reign with him a thousand years.	Happy and greatly blessed are those who are included in this first raising of the dead. The second death has no power over them; they shall be priests of God and of Christ, and they will rule with him for a thousand years.

Blessed and holy: for **Blessed** see 1.3; **holy** here has the meaning of being completely dedicated to God, belonging entirely to him. Neither RSV nor TEV has done an adequate job of representing the meaning in this context. SPCL translates

"Happy are those who participate in the first resurrection, for they belong to the holy people." And Brc has "God's joy will come to the man who has a share in the first resurrection! He is one of God's dedicated people." These two translations are better.

He who shares in the first resurrection: the gender-inclusive plural should be used in languages where the singular excludes any women, "those who experience this first resurrection," or "those who are raised from death at this time," or "those whom God raises from death at this time," or "those whom God causes to come back to life at this time."

Over such the second death has no power: only at verse 14 is the reader told precisely what **the second death** is. It is better not to give that information here; and the mention of **the first resurrection** makes it possible for the reader to get some idea of what **the second death** means. But if the literal phrase **the second death** carries no meaning or carries the wrong meaning, then a translation can say "Those who take part in the first resurrection will not experience the second death, that is, eternal death in the lake of fire."

They shall be priests of God and of Christ, and they shall reign: "they shall serve as priests of God and the Messiah, and they will rule as kings." See 1.6; 5.10.

Alternative translation models for this verse are:

> Those who are included among the ones who will be raised from death at this time are happy indeed; they are God's own people. They will not die the second time, but they will be priests in the service of God and of the Messiah, and they will reign with him for one thousand years.

Or:

> Those whom God raises from death at this time are happy indeed; they are his own people. They will not be destroyed in the lake of fire like dying a second time, but they will serve God and his Chosen Savior as priests, and will rule . . . .

20.7-10

RSV

The Defeat of Satan

7 And when the thousand years are ended, Satan will be loosed from his prison 8 and will come out to deceive the nations which are at the four corners of the earth, that is, Gog and Magog, to gather them for battle; their number is like the sand of the sea. 9 And they marched up over the broad earth and surrounded the camp of the saints and the beloved city; but fire came down from heaven and consumed them, 10 and the devil who had deceived them was thrown into the lake of fire and sulphur where the beast and the false prophet

7 After the thousand years are over, Satan will be set loose from his prison, 8 and he will go out to deceive the nations scattered over the whole world, that is, Gog and Magog. Satan will bring them all together for battle, as many as the grains of sand on the seashore. 9 They spread out over the earth and surrounded the camp of God's people and the city that he loves. But fire came down from heaven and destroyed them. 10 Then the Devil, who deceived them, was thrown into the lake of fire and sulfur, where the beast and the

were, and they will be tormented day and night for ever and ever.

false prophet had already been thrown; and they will be tormented day and night forever and ever.

SECTION HEADING: TEV "The Defeat of Satan," or "The final conflict," or "Fire destroys God's enemies."

Satan and his forces are defeated, not by the Messiah, as were the beast and the false prophet and their armies (19.19-21), but by fire from heaven. Satan is thrown alive into the lake of burning sulfur, and there he and the beast and the false prophet suffer forever.

20.7-8   RSV   TEV

7 And when the thousand years are ended, Satan will be loosed from his prison 8 and will come out to deceive the nations which are at the four corners of the earth, that is, Gog and Magog, to gather them for battle; their number is like the sand of the sea.

7 After the thousand years are over, Satan will be set loose from his prison, 8 and he will go out to deceive the nations scattered over the whole world, that is, Gog and Magog. Satan will bring them all together for battle, as many as the grains of sand on the seashore.

Are ended: as in verse 3, "were ended."

Satan will be loosed from his prison: if the passive verb must be changed to the active form, either "God" or "an angel" will be the subject. Since it was an angel who imprisoned Satan, it is probably an angel that will release him from prison. So one may translate "An angel will release . . . ." The phrase **from his prison** may be rendered as "from where he is tied up (or, chained)."

Will come out to deceive: Satan will continue his activity as the deceiver (see 12.9). Here **come** represents the right perspective: Satan will "come" and not "go" from the abyss to earth's surface, as TEV translates.

The nations which are at the four corners of the earth: this does not mean only the nations located at the four corners of the earth (see 7.1), but all nations on earth (TEV).

That is, Gog and Magog: these two names are from Ezekiel 38–39, where Gog is the chief ruler in the land of Magog. Here they are symbolic names for the nations themselves. It is possible that they are meant to be Satanic beings, but it seems more likely they are names of the nations. The translation can say "these nations are known as Gog and Magog" or "they call these nations (or, groups of people) Gog and Magog."

To gather them for battle: in 16.14 this is done by the three foul spirits that came out of the mouths of the dragon, the beast, and the false prophet. Here it is Satan himself who brings them together for battle.

Their number is like the sand of the sea: this is a way of saying that they are too many to be counted, an expression frequently used in the Bible (see Gen 32.12; Jer 15.8; Rom 9.27; Heb 11.12). It should be clear that the antecedent of **their** is not the nations as such, but the people who will fight against God's people. If the figure **like the sand of the sea** makes no sense, it can be abandoned and the literal meaning "too many to be counted" or something similar can be said.

An alternative translation model for this verse is:

> When the thousand years come to an end, the angel will release (or, set free) Satan from where he is tied up, and he will come out to deceive the nations (or, groups of people) who are scattered all over the world. These nations are called Gog and Magog. Satan will bring them all together to the place where they will fight. There will be so many of them that one cannot count them.

20.9   RSV   TEV

And they marched up over the broad earth and surrounded the camp of the saints and the beloved city; but fire came down from heaven[n] and consumed them,	They spread out over the earth and surrounded the camp of God's people and the city that he loves. But fire came down from heaven and destroyed them.

[n] Other ancient authorities read *from God, out of heaven,* or *out of heaven from God*

Both RSV and TEV follow the Greek in changing from the future tense of the verbs in verses 7-8 to the past tense in verses 9-10. Beckwith comments that in verses 7-8 John speaks as a prophet, and in verses 9-10 he reports what he had seen in a vision. If the change of tense causes too much trouble, a translator can use the future tense in verses 9-10; but the past tense should be kept, if at all possible.

They marched up over the broad earth: it is possible that the Greek word translated **earth** means here "land," that is, the land of Israel. But "earth" is how most translations render the word. The Greek verb translated **they marched up** is "they went up," in the sense of spreading out all over the earth's surface. Another way of expressing this is "they went out everywhere over the earth."

Surrounded the camp of the saints and the beloved city: the two expressions refer to only one place, not two: "they surrounded the city that God loves, where his people were living." The Greek word translated **camp** may mean: (1) a military camp; (2) a "stopping place," like the camps where the Hebrews stopped on their way from Egypt to Canaan; or (3) "army," as in Hebrews 11.34. In Hebrews 13.11-13 the word is used of the Hebrews' camping place, and then, by extension, it is used to refer to the city of Jerusalem, outside of which Jesus was crucified. Here it seems that **camp** means city, without the specific idea of a military camp. The phrase **the beloved city** can be translated "the city that God loves." The city is Jerusalem, but the name should not appear in the translation. For **city** compare 11.2. Alternative translation models for this first sentence are "They went out over the whole earth and surrounded the city that God loves, where his people were living" or ". . . and surrounded the place where God's people were living; that is the city that he loves."

Fire came down from heaven and consumed them: as in Ezekiel 38.22; and for the verb **consumed** see 11.5. It is God who sends the fire down, and as the RSV footnote shows, some Greek manuscripts and early versions include the name of God. It is recommended that the Greek text represented in RSV and TEV be followed; if, however, a translator prefers to include God as the one who sent the fire down, there is no harm done.

20.10   RSV   TEV

and the devil who had deceived them was thrown into the lake of fire and sulphur where the beast and the false prophet were, and they will be tormented day and night for ever and ever.

Then the Devil, who deceived them, was thrown into the lake of fire and sulfur, where the beast and the false prophet had already been thrown; and they will be tormented day and night forever and ever.

The devil . . . was thrown into the lake of fire and sulphur: he joins the beast and the false prophet in the place of eternal punishment (see 19.20).

They will be tormented day and night for ever and ever: for the verb **be tormented** see 14.10; and for the expression indicating eternity, see 14.11.

An alternative translation model for languages that do not use the passive is the following:

> Then they threw the Devil, who deceived all these people, into the place that burns with fiery sulfur, where they had already thrown the beast and the false prophet. The fire will torment all of them day and night for ever.

C-7. The Final Judgment, the New Heaven, the New Earth, and the New Jerusalem
(20.11–22.5)

20.11-15

RSV   TEV

The Final Judgment

11 Then I saw a great white throne and him who sat upon it; from his presence earth and sky fled away, and no place was found for them. 12 And I saw the dead, great and small, standing before the throne, and books were opened. Also another book was opened, which is the book of life. And the dead were judged by what was written in the books, by what they had done. 13 And the sea gave up the dead in it, Death and Hades gave up the dead in them, and all were judged by what they had done. 14 Then Death and Hades were thrown into the lake of fire. This is the second death, the lake of fire; 15 and if any one's name was not found written in the book of life, he was thrown into the lake of fire.

11 Then I saw a great white throne and the one who sits on it. Earth and heaven fled from his presence and were seen no more. 12 And I saw the dead, great and small alike, standing before the throne. Books were opened, and then another book was opened, the book of the living. The dead were judged according to what they had done, as recorded in the books. 13 Then the sea gave up its dead. Death and the world of the dead also gave up the dead they held. And all were judged according to what they had done. 14 Then death and the world of the dead were thrown into the lake of fire. (This lake of fire is the second death.) 15 Whoever did not have his name written in the book of the living was thrown into the lake of fire.

SECTION HEADING: TEV "The Final Judgment." Another way to render this is "God judges the world for the final time."

In this vision John sees God seated on a large white throne, with all people assembled before him. They are all judged according to what they have done. The created universe disappears, and Death and Hades are destroyed.

20.11	RSV	TEV

Then I saw a great white throne and him who sat upon it; from his presence earth and sky fled away, and no place was found for them.

Then I saw a great white throne and the one who sits on it. Earth and heaven fled from his presence and were seen no more.

A great white throne: as in 1.4; 4.2; here it is a very large throne, and it is white. God is referred to, as in the earlier instances, as **him who sat upon it**. The translation can say "Then I saw God sitting on a large white throne."

From his presence: there is something about God's expression that causes the created universe to disappear; see similar language in Psalm 114.7.

Earth and sky fled away, and no place was found for them: here it seems better to translate "earth and heaven," or "heaven and earth," which is a familiar (biblical) way of referring to the whole universe (see 21.1, which speaks of a new universe replacing the old one). **Sky** doesn't seem to fit as well in English, but in many other languages it will be quite natural. Note NRSV "the earth and the heaven," and REB "earth and heaven." The statement **no place was found for them** means that they disappeared. They were never seen again (see also 12.8).

Alternative translation models for this second sentence are:

> When he appeared, earth and sky (or, heaven) disappeared and no one saw them anymore.

Or:

> When he appeared, the universe disappeared forever.

20.12	RSV	TEV

And I saw the dead, great and small, standing before the throne, and books were opened. Also another book was opened, which is the book of life. And the dead were judged by what was written in the books, by what they had done.

And I saw the dead, great and small alike, standing before the throne. Books were opened, and then another book was opened, the book of the living. The dead were judged according to what they had done, as recorded in the books.

The dead, great and small: this means all who have died, including important and common people (see 11.18; 13.16; 19.5,18). These are "the rest of the dead" of verse 5, that is, all the rest of humanity in addition to the resurrected martyrs. As verse 5 makes clear, these dead people have been raised to life for this final judgment; but the text here does not explicitly say they have been resurrected. The text also says nothing of any persons who are alive at the time of the Final Judgment.

Books were opened: presumably the attending angels opened these books, the ones in which the actions of all people are recorded. In some languages it will be necessary to say "they (unknown subjects) opened the books."

Another book . . . the book of life: see 3.5; 13.8.

Were judged by what was written in the books, by what they had done: this can be stated "were judged according to what they had done, as recorded (or, written) in the books." For **by what they had done**, compare "as your works deserve" in 2.23. In languages that do not use the passive, one may say "God judged them according to what (or, the things) they had done, as he had recorded it in the books."

Beginning with **books were opened** the translation can read as follows:

> . . . and the books in which the actions of all people had been recorded were opened. And then another book was opened, the book containing the names of those who will live forever with God. All the dead were judged according to what they had done, as recorded (or, written) in the books.

Or:

> . . . they opened the books in which God had recorded the actions of all people. Then they opened another book. This book contained the names of those people who will live forever with God. He judged all the dead people according to what they had done, as he had recorded it in the books.

20.13   RSV   TEV

And the sea gave up the dead in it, Death and Hades gave up the dead in them, and all were judged by what they had done. | Then the sea gave up its dead. Death and the world of the dead also gave up the dead they held. And all were judged according to what they had done.

The sea gave up the dead in it: here **the sea** (see 10.2) is pictured as a living being, allowing the dead it held to go and stand with the others before God's throne. Those who had died at sea were not thought of as going to Sheol, the world of the dead, but as remaining there in the depths of the water. If this kind of statement is not possible in some languages, the translation can say "Then the dead in the sea also went to be judged by God" or "Then . . . for God to judge them." The same can be done for the next statement, **Death and Hades gave up the dead in them**. For **Death and Hades** see 1.18; 6.8. They are also spoken of as living beings (as in 6.8).

An alternative translation model for this verse is:

Then the people who had died in the sea went for God to judge them. Death and the world of the dead gave up the dead people in them, and God judged them all according to their deeds (or, the things they had done).

20.14-15	RSV	TEV

14 Then Death and Hades were thrown into the lake of fire. This is the second death, the lake of fire; 15 and if any one's name was not found written in the book of life, he was thrown into the lake of fire.

14 Then death and the world of the dead were thrown into the lake of fire. (This lake of fire is the second death.) 15 Whoever did not have his name written in the book of the living was thrown into the lake of fire.

Death and Hades were thrown into the lake of fire: they suffer the same fate as that of the beast and the false prophet (19.20; 20.10).

This is the second death, the lake of fire: for comments on **the second death**, see 2.11; 20.6; for comments on **the lake of fire**, see 19.20. The expression "the first death" is not used; it is clear from the context in which **the second death** appears that it is the final, eternal death of the wicked, as opposed to the temporal death of all living beings. A translation may choose to say "final death" if this should prove easier to understand.

If any one's name was not found written in the book of life, he: in many languages it is better to use the gender-inclusive plural form, "all those whose names were not written . . . were thrown," or else the singular indefinite "anyone whose name was not found written . . . was thrown" (NRSV).

21.1-8

RSV	TEV
	The New Heaven and the New Earth

1 Then I saw a new heaven and a new earth; for the first heaven and the first earth had passed away, and the sea was no more. 2 And I saw the holy city, new Jerusalem, coming down out of heaven from God, prepared as a bride adorned for her husband; 3 and I heard a loud voice from the throne saying, "Behold, the dwelling of God is with men. He will dwell with them, and they shall be his people, and God himself will be with them; 4 he will wipe away every tear from their eyes, and death shall be no more, neither shall there be mourning nor crying nor pain any more, for the former things have passed away."

5 And he who sat upon the throne said, "Behold, I make all things new." Also he said, "Write this, for these words are trustworthy and true." 6 And he said to me, "It is done! I am the Alpha and the Omega, the beginning and the end. To the thirsty I will give from the fountain of the

1 Then I saw a new heaven and a new earth. The first heaven and the first earth disappeared, and the sea vanished. 2 And I saw the Holy City, the new Jerusalem, coming down out of heaven from God, prepared and ready, like a bride dressed to meet her husband. 3 I heard a loud voice speaking from the throne: "Now God's home is with mankind! He will live with them, and they shall be his people. God himself will be with them, and he will be their God. 4 He will wipe away all tears from their eyes. There will be no more death, no more grief or crying or pain. The old things have disappeared."

5 Then the one who sits on the throne said, "And now I make all things new!" He also said to me, "Write this, because these words are true and can be trusted." 6 And he said, "It is done! I am the first and the last, the beginning and the end. To anyone who is thirsty I will give the right to

water of life without payment. 7 He who conquers shall have this heritage, and I will be his God and he shall be my son. 8 But as for the cowardly, the faithless, the polluted, as for murderers, fornicators, sorcerers, idolaters, and all liars, their lot shall be in the lake that burns with fire and sulphur, which is the second death."

drink from the spring of the water of life without paying for it. 7 Whoever wins the victory will receive this from me: I will be his God, and he will be my son. 8 But cowards, traitors, perverts, murderers, the immoral, those who practice magic, those who worship idols, and all liars—the place for them is the lake burning with fire and sulfur, which is the second death."

SECTION HEADING: TEV "The New Heaven and the New Earth." This can be expressed as "The new universe," "The new world."

In this vision (which goes to 22.5) John sees the new universe, which replaces the old one that has disappeared (20.11). The greater part of the vision is taken up with the description of the new Jerusalem (21.9–22.5).

In this section (21.1-8) messages are heard from heaven (verses 3-4) and from God, sitting on his throne (verses 5-8), announcing that human history has run its course, that God's plan has been realized, and that the union between God and humanity is now complete and will last forever.

21.1   RSV   TEV

Then I saw a new heaven and a new earth; for the first heaven and the first earth had passed away, and the sea was no more.

Then I saw a new heaven and a new earth. The first heaven and the first earth disappeared, and the sea vanished.

Then I saw: this marks a new vision (see 20.1,4,11). **Then**: as with the initial verses of other chapters, translators may include information from verses 11-14 of the previous chapter and say, for example, "After the vision of the final judgment, I saw . . ." or "After the vision of God judging everyone, I saw . . . ."

A new heaven and a new earth: the words emphasize the fact that the old universe has not been renewed but has been replaced. A new creation has taken place (see Isa 65.17; 2 Peter 3.13). In some languages it will be more natural to say something like "a new sky and a new earth," or even "a new universe."

The first heaven and the first earth had passed away: see 20.11. TEV "disappeared" is wrong; it should be "had disappeared."

The sea was no more: in 20.11 nothing is said or implied about the sea. In other passages (see 5.13; 10.6; 14.7) the sea is explicitly mentioned, together with heaven and earth, but not in 20.11. There is no sea (new or old) in the new universe. The translation can be "the sea no longer exists," "there is no more sea (or, ocean)."

An alternative translation model for this verse is:

> After the vision of God judging everyone, I saw a new universe, for
> the first universe had disappeared, and the sea (or, ocean) no longer
> existed.

21.2   RSV   TEV

| And I saw the holy city, new Jerusalem, coming down out of heaven from God, prepared as a bride adorned for her husband; | And I saw the Holy City, the new Jerusalem, coming down out of heaven from God, prepared and ready, like a bride dressed to meet her husband. |

The holy city, new Jerusalem: it may be necessary to join the two phrases in a more explicit fashion, "the holy city (or, God's city), which is the new city of Jerusalem." Reference has already been made in 3.12 to the new Jerusalem; there "the city of my God" expresses what is said here by the phrase **the holy city** (see 11.2 and "the beloved city" in 20.9).

Out of heaven from God: God sends the city, which is in heaven, down to earth. So the translation may be "coming down out of heaven, sent by God" or ". . . from the presence of God."

Prepared as a bride adorned for her husband: here **prepared** translates the same Greek verb translated "made . . . ready" in 19.7. The verb translated **adorned** appears also in 21.19, with reference to the precious stones in the foundation of the city. For the use of the verb in a context similar to this one, see 1 Timothy 2.9. In the context of a bride and groom, the verb would include the bride's clothing, headdress, and jewelry. The words **for her husband** may not be entirely satisfactory (nor TEV "like a bride dressed to meet her husband"), since the setting is obviously that of a wedding. A better translation may be "The city was like a woman dressed for her wedding, ready to join the man she is going to marry."

21.3   RSV   TEV

| and I heard a loud voice from the throne saying, "Behold, the dwelling of God is with men. He will dwell with them, and they shall be his people,° and God himself will be with them;ᵖ | I heard a loud voice speaking from the throne: "Now God's home is with mankind! He will live with them, and they shall be his people. God himself will be with them, and he will be their God. |

° Other ancient authorities read *peoples*
ᵖ Other ancient authorities add *and be their God*

I heard a loud voice from the throne: see 19.5.

The translator should consider the possibility of translating as poetry the message that follows in verses 3-4 (see Section F of the introduction, "Translating the Revelation to John," pages 6 and following).

Behold: see 1.7.

The dwelling of God is with men: "from now on God will live with humankind," "and now God will have his home among people." The noun **dwelling** and the verb **dwell** translate the same Greek noun and verb used in 13.6 (and see 7.15 "shelter").

They shall be his people: "they will all belong to him" or "they will all worship (or, obey) him." As the RSV footnote shows, instead of the singular **people** (RSV and TEV), some Greek manuscripts, including the older ones, and a few early versions have the plural "peoples" (many more versions have the singular). Following a very common rule of textual criticism, the plural "peoples" has greater claim to be the original text than the singular "people," since the plural form is obviously more difficult. Of the translations consulted, however, only NRSV and TOB have the plural. It is recommended that the plural form be translated. In languages where no distinction exists between the singular "people" and the plural "people," the most natural term should be used.

God himself will be with them: here **will be** means "remain," reinforcing what was said before, that he "will live with them." As the RSV footnote shows, a number of Greek manuscripts and early versions add at the end of the verse "(and be) their God." This is then literally "God himself with them will be their God." Some, like TEV, translate this "and he will be their God"; others, "(God himself will be with them) as their God" or "and he will be the God who is with them" (TOB); and others take this as the equivalent of a title, "and 'God-with-them' will be their God." If, following TEV, this phrase is included, the translation can be "and God himself, their own God, will be (or, stay) with them."

21.4   RSV   TEV

| he will wipe away every tear from their eyes, and death shall be no more, neither shall there be mourning nor crying nor pain any more, for the former things have passed away." | He will wipe away all tears from their eyes. There will be no more death, no more grief or crying or pain. The old things have disappeared." |

He will wipe away every tear from their eyes: as in 7.17 translators should attempt to keep this vivid picture.

Death shall be no more, neither shall there be mourning nor crying nor pain any more: here bodily death is meant: "death will no longer exist" or "people will never die," "no one will ever die." For **mourning** see 18.7,8, where it has the sense of "bereavement" or "sorrow." **Crying** here has the specific sense of "weeping," as it does in Hebrews 5.7; in other passages in the New Testament where the Greek word occurs, it has the meaning of "outcry," "clamor." And for **pain** see 16.10,11, where it is translated "anguish" and "pain" in those two verses. Instead of noun phrases, verbal phrases may be used: "No one will ever die, no one will ever again grieve or weep or suffer."

For the former things are passed away: this means that the old mode of existence, in which death, mourning, weeping, and pain were an inescapable part of the human situation, will be replaced by a new manner of life that does not include them. "The old world (or, universe) will no longer exist" (see 2 Cor 5.17). God's promise in verse 5 is realized.

An alternative translation model for this verse is:

He will wipe away every tear from their eyes. No one will ever die. No one will ever feel sorrowful or weep or experience pain anymore, for the old world (or, universe) no longer exists.

21.5

RSV	TEV
And he who sat upon the throne said, "Behold, I make all things new." Also he said, "Write this, for these words are trustworthy and true."	Then the one who sits on the throne said, "And now I make all things new!" He also said to me, "Write this, because these words are true and can be trusted."

He who sat upon the throne said: now God speaks. So in many languages it will be helpful to say "God, who sits on the throne, said . . . ."

Behold: see 1.7.

I make all things new: this is the counterpart of the last statement in verse 4. It is probably better to translate, as do NJB, NIV, NRSV, "I am making all things new."

Also he said, "Write this . . .": the Greek text does not say that he was speaking to John, but the context makes this quite clear, and the translation should make it specific, as does TEV: "He also said to me" (see 14.13; 19.9; compare 10.4).

Write this: **this** probably refers only to verses 1-4, not to the whole book, and may be expressed in certain languages as "the things I have just told you."

For: this is how most translations render the Greek conjunction; some, however, take it to mean "that": "Write that these words are . . . ." However, **for** or "because" are more likely.

These words are trustworthy and true: for **trustworthy** see "faithful" at 1.5; for **true** see 3.7. If the passive implicit in **trustworthy** is difficult to express, it may be better to translate "everyone can believe these words; they are true." Brc translates "You can believe what I am saying, for it is true." See similar statements in 15.3; 16.7; 19.2; 22.6; and in 19.9 "These are true words of God."

21.6

RSV	TEV
And he said to me, "It is done! I am the Alpha and the Omega, the beginning and the end. To the thirsty I will give from the fountain of the water of life without payment.	And he said, "It is done! I am the first and the last, the beginning and the end. To anyone who is thirsty I will give the right to drink from the spring of the water of life without paying for it.

It is done! See 16.17. In Greek the verb here is plural, "They are done," as contrasted with the singular in 16.17. The antecedent is probably "these words," and the translation can be "All these things are now done (or, accomplished)," "I have done all these things," or "I have caused all these things to happen."

I am the Alpha and the Omega, the beginning and the end: see 1.8; 1.17; 22.13. The two declarations mean the same: "I am the first and the last; I am the beginning and the end." In this context perhaps "I begin all things and bring all things to an end" will be more natural in many languages.

To the thirsty I will give: it may be better to follow the normal order, "I will give to anyone who is thirsty" or "I will give to all who are thirsty," or in certain languages, "I will give to anyone who craves water."

From the fountain of the water of life: "I will give the water that comes from the fountain of life-giving water" or "I will give them water to drink from a place where water is flowing that gives life." See similar language in 7.17; 22.17.

Without payment: it should be clear that it is the one who drinks the water who will not have to pay. "I will give them, free of charge, water" (see 7.17). The last sentence in this verse may be translated as follows: "I will give to all who are thirsty water to drink from the fountain of life-giving water, and they will not have to pay for it" or "I will give water to all who are thirsty. This water comes from a place where water is flowing that gives life. They do not have to give anything in return."

21.7	RSV	TEV
	He who conquers shall have this heritage, and I will be his God and he shall be my son.	Whoever wins the victory will receive this from me: I will be his God, and he will be my son.

He who conquers: this is the expression found at the end of the seven letters in chapters 2–3 (2.7,11,17,26; 3.5,12,21).

Shall have this heritage: the Greek verb can mean to inherit something from one's parents or their estate. But here, as often in the New Testament, it means to receive as a gift. Here, as elsewhere, the words **heritage** or "inheritance" are not very satisfactory, since they imply the death of the donor. See the same terms used in connection with the Kingdom of God (Matt 25.34), eternal life (Mark 10.17), the promise (Heb 6.12), the blessing (Heb 12.17). The word **this** translates the plural "these things" in Greek and refers back to the blessings and privileges described in verses 1-6. So the translation can be "will receive these things from me" or "I will give him these things."

I will be his God and he shall be my son: see 2 Samuel 7.14. To make this inclusive of men and women, the plural forms may have to be used, "I will give all these things to those who win the victory, and I will be their God and they will be my children (or, people)."

21.8	RSV	TEV
	But as for the cowardly, the faithless, the polluted, as for murderers, fornicators, sorcerers, idolaters, and all liars, their lot shall be in the lake that burns with fire and sulphur, which is the second death."	But cowards, traitors, perverts, murderers, the immoral, those who practice magic, those who worship idols, and all liars—the place for them is the lake burning with fire and sulfur, which is the second death."

In this verse eight different kinds of people are listed who will be thrown into the lake of burning sulfur. It is not implied that all are exclusive categories; what is meant is that any person guilty of any one or more of these sins will suffer **the second death**. For a similar list see 22.15.

Cowardly: people who were not courageous and constant in their Christian witness. To express the idea of **cowardly**, many languages use vivid idiomatic expressions; for example, "white-eyed people" (Thai).

Faithless: apostates, those who had renounced, or given up, their Christian faith. This may be expressed in many languages as "stopped believing in Jesus" or "turned their backs on Jesus."

Polluted: this refers to those who were guilty of gross sins or heathen worship; in Greek it is the passive participle of the verb meaning "to make foul"; the related noun "pollution," "abomination," is used in 17.4,5; 21.27. Other ways to express this are "people who have made themselves dirty (or, unclean) through worshiping idols" or "people who have committed foul (or, dirty) sins."

Murderers: those who deliberately kill others, not in warfare.

Fornicators: those who indulge in immoral sexual activity; the word occurs again in 22.15. It is probable that here the word carries its normal meaning and is not a figure for idolatry.

Sorcerers: see comments on "sorceries" in 9.21; 18.23. These are people who regular do "sorcery."

Idolaters: see "worshiping . . . idols" in 9.20; the word appears also in 22.15.

All liars: as in 21.27 and 22.15, those who lie are condemned to hell. See also 3.9.

Their lot shall be in the lake: here **lot** means destiny, which is condemnation and punishment. "They will be condemned to the lake," or "they will be punished by being thrown into the lake," or "I will punish them by throwing them into the lake."

The lake that burns with fire and sulphur: see 19.20; 20.10.

The second death: see 20.14.

21.9–22.5

RSV

TEV

The New Jerusalem

9 Then came one of the seven angels who had the seven bowls full of the seven last plagues, and spoke to me, saying, "Come, I will show you the Bride, the wife of the Lamb." 10 And in the Spirit he carried me away to a great, high mountain, and showed me the holy city Jerusalem coming down out of heaven from God, 11 having the glory of God, its radiance like a most rare jewel, like a jasper, clear as crystal. 12 It had a great, high wall, with twelve gates, and at the gates twelve angels, and on the gates the names of the twelve tribes of the sons of Israel were inscribed; 13 on the east three gates, on the north three gates, on the south three gates, and on the west three gates. 14 And the wall of the city had twelve

9 One of the seven angels who had the seven bowls full of the seven last plagues came to me and said, "Come, and I will show you the Bride, the wife of the Lamb." 10 The Spirit took control of me, and the angel carried me to the top of a very high mountain. He showed me Jerusalem, the Holy City, coming down out of heaven from God 11 and shining with the glory of God. The city shone like a precious stone, like a jasper, clear as crystal. 12 It had a great, high wall with twelve gates and with twelve angels in charge of the gates. On the gates were written the names of the twelve tribes of the people of Israel. 13 There were three gates on each side: three on the east, three on the south, three on the north, and three

foundations, and on them the twelve names of the twelve apostles of the Lamb.

15 And he who talked to me had a measuring rod of gold to measure the city and its gates and walls. 16 The city lies foursquare, its length the same as its breadth; and he measured the city with his rod, twelve thousand stadia; its length and breadth and height are equal. 17 He also measured its wall, a hundred and forty-four cubits by a man's measure, that is, an angel's. 18 The wall was built of jasper, while the city was pure gold, clear as glass. 19 The foundations of the wall of the city were adorned with every jewel; the first was jasper, the second sapphire, the third agate, the fourth emerald, 20 the fifth onyx, the sixth carnelian, the seventh chrysolite, the eighth beryl, the ninth topaz, the tenth chrysoprase, the eleventh jacinth, the twelfth amethyst. 21 And the twelve gates were twelve pearls, each of the gates made of a single pearl, and the street of the city was pure gold, transparent as glass.

22 And I saw no temple in the city, for its temple is the Lord God the Almighty and the Lamb. 23 And the city has no need of sun or moon to shine upon it, for the glory of God is its light, and its lamp is the Lamb. 24 By its light shall the nations walk; and the kings of the earth shall bring their glory into it, 25 and its gates shall never be shut by day—and there shall be no night there; 26 they shall bring into it the glory and the honor of the nations. 27 But nothing unclean shall enter it, nor any one who practices abomination or falsehood, but only those who are written in the Lamb's book of life.

Chapter 22:

1 Then he showed me the river of the water of life, bright as crystal, flowing from the throne of God and of the Lamb 2 through the middle of the street of the city; also, on either side of the river, the tree of life with its twelve kinds of fruit, yielding its fruit each month; and the leaves of the tree were for the healing of the nations. 3 There shall no more be anything accursed, but the throne of God and of the Lamb shall be in it, and his servants shall worship him; 4 they shall see his face, and his name shall be on their foreheads. 5 And night shall be no more; they need no light of lamp or sun, for the Lord God will be their light, and they shall reign for ever and ever.

on the west. 14 The city's wall was built on twelve foundation stones, on which were written the names of the twelve apostles of the Lamb. 15 The angel who spoke to me had a gold measuring stick to measure the city, its gates, and its wall. 16 The city was perfectly square, as wide as it was long. The angel measured the city with his measuring stick: it was fifteen hundred miles long and was as wide and as high as it was long. 17 The angel also measured the wall, and it was 216 feet high, according to the standard unit of measure which he was using. 18 The wall was made of jasper, and the city itself was made of pure gold, as clear as glass. 19 The foundation stones of the city wall were adorned with all kinds of precious stones. The first foundation stone was jasper, the second sapphire, the third agate, the fourth emerald, 20 the fifth onyx, the sixth carnelian, the seventh yellow quartz, the eighth beryl, the ninth topaz, the tenth chalcedony, the eleventh turquoise, the twelfth amethyst. 21 The twelve gates were twelve pearls; each gate was made from a single pearl. The street of the city was of pure gold, transparent as glass.

22 I did not see a temple in the city, because its temple is the Lord God Almighty and the Lamb. 23 The city has no need of the sun or the moon to shine on it, because the glory of God shines on it, and the Lamb is its lamp. 24 The peoples of the world will walk by its light, and the kings of the earth will bring their wealth into it. 25 The gates of the city will stand open all day; they will never be closed, because there will be no night there. 26 The greatness and the wealth of the nations will be brought into the city. 27 But nothing that is impure will enter the city, nor anyone who does shameful things or tells lies. Only those whose names are written in the Lamb's book of the living will enter the city.

Chapter 22:

1 The angel also showed me the river of the water of life, sparkling like crystal, and coming from the throne of God and of the Lamb 2 and flowing down the middle of the city's street. On each side of the river was the tree of life, which bears fruit twelve times a year, once each month; and its leaves are for the healing of the nations. 3 Nothing that is under God's curse will be found in the city.

The throne of God and of the Lamb will be in the city, and his servants will worship him. 4 They will see his face, and his name will be written on their foreheads. 5 There shall be no more night, and they will not need lamps or sunlight, because the Lord God will be their light, and they will rule as kings forever and ever.

302

SECTION HEADING: TEV "The New Jerusalem."

Now comes an extended description of the new creation, the new holy city in which God's people will live in peace and happiness forever and ever. As verse 10 indicates, this new city will be on earth, the new earth.

21.9 RSV	TEV
Then came one of the seven angels who had the seven bowls full of the seven last plagues, and spoke to me, saying, "Come, I will show you the Bride, the wife of the Lamb."	One of the seven angels who had the seven bowls full of the seven last plagues came to me and said, "Come, and I will show you the Bride, the wife of the Lamb."

One of the seven angels: see 15.6-7 and chapter 16. It is not certain that this is the same angel who spoke to John in 17.1.

Come, I will show you: as in 17.1. In certain languages this sentence will be rendered as "Let us go, I will show you."

The Bride, the wife of the Lamb: this is the new Jerusalem, not, as in 19.7, God's people. If in a given language **the Bride, the wife** is an impossible combination, it is enough to say "the Bride of the Lamb" or "the woman who will be the Lamb's wife." The marriage has not yet taken place.

21.10 RSV	TEV
And in the Spirit he carried me away to a great, high mountain, and showed me the holy city Jerusalem coming down out of heaven from God,	The Spirit took control of me, and the angel carried me to the top of a very high mountain. He showed me Jerusalem, the Holy City, coming down out of heaven from God

In the Spirit he carried me away: as in 17.3. Translators may choose to say "The Spirit (or, God's Spirit) possessed (or, took control of) me, and the angel carried me to . . . ."

To a great, high mountain: "to the top of a very high mountain." It should be made clear that the writer was carried to the top of the mountain (as TEV renders it).

The holy city Jerusalem coming down out of heaven from God: as in verse 2. In both passages **holy** has the basic meaning of "belonging to God," "God's own city." For **city** see 3.12; 11.2, and elsewhere.

An alternative translation model for this verse is:

> God's Spirit took control of me, and the angel carried me to the top of a very high mountain. There he showed me God's city Jerusalem coming down out of heaven from the presence of God.

21.11   RSV   TEV

having the glory of God, its radiance like a most rare jewel, like a jasper, clear as crystal.	and shining with the glory of God. The city shone like a precious stone, like a jasper, clear as crystal.

Having the glory of God: meaning "shining with the light of the presence of God" (compare Ezek 43.5). For **the glory of God** see 15.8 (also comments at 1.6). One may also translate "It was shining (or, glowing) with the brilliant light that comes from God."

Its radiance like a rare jewel: this **radiance** is a fuller description of the light that shines from the city: "It was shining like a precious (or, expensive) stone." The adjective **rare** translates the Greek superlative form of the adjective "precious, costly," as in the phrase "costly wood" in 18.12.

A jasper, clear as crystal: for **jasper** see 4.3; for **crystal** see 4.6a; 22.1. TNT translates "crystal-clear jasper." In cultures where these stones are unknown, one may say, for example, "with a beautiful green and red light, just like clear transparent glass."

21.12-13   RSV   TEV

12 It had a great, high wall, with twelve gates, and at the gates twelve angels, and on the gates the names of the twelve tribes of the sons of Israel were inscribed; 13 on the east three gates, on the north three gates, on the south three gates, and on the west three gates.	12 It had a great, high wall with twelve gates and with twelve angels in charge of the gates. On the gates were written the names of the twelve tribes of the people of Israel. 13 There were three gates on each side: three on the east, three on the south, three on the north, and three on the west.

A great, high wall: this can be translated "a very high wall" or "a strong, high wall." It may be necessary to say "It had a very high wall around it." In many cultures **high wall** will be expressed as "high fence."

Twelve gates ... twelve angels ... the names of the twelve tribes: it should be clear in the translation that there was one angel standing guard at each of the twelve gates, and one name on each gate. In many languages it will be necessary to say "at each of the gates there was an angel on guard (or, watching it)."

The twelve tribes of the sons of Israel: this can be more simply said "the twelve tribes of Israel." The whole sentence may be expressed as "On the gates they had written the names of the twelve tribes of Israel, one name on each gate."

Commentators note the rather unusual sequence of the points of the compass: east, north, south, west (as in Ezek 42.16-19). In Ezekiel 48.30-34 the order is north, east, south, west, and in 1 Chronicles 9.24 it is east, west, north, south. Some try to find a hidden meaning in the order followed; if there is such a meaning, it is not obvious to the reader. Some languages have a fixed sequence that is followed, such as English "north, south, east, and west." A translator should feel free to follow such a sequence in the language into which the translation is being done.

21.14   RSV   TEV

And the wall of the city had twelve foun-   The city's wall was built on twelve foundations, and on them the twelve names   dation stones, on which were written the
of the twelve apostles of the Lamb.   names of the twelve apostles of the
                                         Lamb.

The wall . . . had twelve foundations: these are "foundation stones" (TEV).
The picture seems to be that of large stones, each one of which reaches from one
gate to the next, twelve in all; or else there is a foundation stone under each of the
twelve gateways. In any case, the foundation stones are partly above ground, since
the name of the twelve apostles of Christ can be seen written on them. The phrase
the twelve apostles of the Lamb presumably refers to the twelve disciples of Jesus,
as listed in the Gospels. For **apostles** see 18.20. It should be clear in translation
(which it is not in RSV or TEV) that there is one name per stone. NJB makes this
quite explicit: "each one of which bore the name of one of the apostles of the
Lamb." "Foundation stones" in some languages will be expressed as "root stones"
or "basic stones."
    Alternative translation models for this verse are:

    They had built the wall (or, fence) of the city on top of twelve large
    stones. The name of one of the twelve apostles of the Lamb was
    written on each stone.

Or:

    . . . Each stone had the name of one of the twelve chief messengers
    of the Lamb written on it.

21.15   RSV   TEV

    And he who talked to me had a   The angel who spoke to me had a gold
measuring rod of gold to measure the   measuring stick to measure the city, its
city and its gates and walls.   gates, and its wall.

He who talked to me: "the angel who was talking with me" or, simply, "The
angel."
    A measuring rod of gold: this is like the measuring rod John was given in
11.1, except that this one is made of gold.
    To measure the city and its gates and walls: this seems to be a comprehen-
sive way of saying "to measure the whole city, including its gates and walls." What
seems to be implied is that the measuring is to be done on the outside of the wall
that surrounds the city.
    An alternative translation model for this verse is:

    The angel who had been speaking to me held a gold stick for
    measuring the size of things. He was going to measure the city . . . .

21.16   RSV   TEV

The city lies foursquare, its length the   The city was perfectly square, as wide as
same as its breadth; and he measured   it was long. The angel measured the city
the city with his rod, twelve thousand   with his measuring stick: it was fifteen
stadia;[q] its length and breadth and   hundred miles long and was as wide and
height are equal.   as high as it was long.

[q] About fifteen hundred miles

The city lies foursquare: this is more naturally said "The city was a square,"
with the following explanation: "its width and its length were the same." In some
languages one may say "all four sides were the same length" or ". . . were of equal
length."

He measured the city: as explained in verse 15, the picture seems to be that
of the angel measuring the wall that surrounds the city.

Twelve thousand stadia: for **stadia** see 14.20. NRSV, like TEV, has in the text
"fifteen hundred miles." This is equal to twenty-four hundred kilometers. What
seems implied, though not stated explicitly, is that each of the four sides of the wall
that surrounded the city was 1,500 miles long. The city was a perfect cube, as high
as it was wide and long. Some commentators point out that this measure could also
apply to a structure in the form of a pyramid, but the figure of a cube seems more
likely.

21.17   RSV   TEV

He also measured its wall, a hundred   The angel also measured the wall, and it
and forty-four cubits by a man's mea-   was 216 feet high,[g] according to the
sure, that is, an angel's.   standard unit of measure which he was
                                              using.[h]

[g] high; *or* thick.
[h] *In verses 16 and 17 the Greek text
speaks of "12,000 furlongs" and "144
cubits" which may have symbolic significance.*

Its wall, a hundred and forty-four cubits: TEV takes this distance (216 feet)
to be the height of the wall (also NJB, REB, FRCL, Phps). It may, however, refer to
its thickness (NIV, BRCL). Some commentators make the point that, for a city that is
1,500 miles tall, a wall only 216 feet (66 meters) tall is so small that it seems foolish.
But it is also pointed out that the wall, in this case, is not for the protection of the
city (inasmuch as the gates stay open all the time) but for its demarcation. In any
case, the notion of height is preferable to that of thickness. A translation should opt
for one or the other; simply to say, as RSV and others say, **a hundred and forty-four
cubits** (or, 216 feet, or 66 meters), without indicating that this is the height, does not

qualify as a translation. An alternative translation model is "He also determined the height (or, thickness) of the wall (or, fence). It was 216 feet (or, 66 meters)."

A man's measure, that is, an angel's: the meaning here is that the measurement used by the angel was the normal one used at that time; it was not a special angelic measurement. NRSV now has "by human measurement, which the angel was using"; RNAB "according to the standard unit of measurement the angel used"; NJB "by human measurements." Or the translation can be "according to the way people measure things."

The purpose of the footnote at the end of verse 17 in TEV is to allow the reader to appreciate the fact that the numbers 12,000 and 144, in verses 16 and 17, may have symbolic value, since they are both multiples of twelve (12 x 1000; 12 x 12), a number in the Bible that indicates completeness. This fact can be carried over into translation by using the biblical terms **stadia** and **cubits**; but neither of them, in English at least, is in current usage. But the two can be used, and in footnotes the modern equivalents may be given. One translation has tried to represent the text by saying "12,000 kilometers . . . 144 arm's lengths" (an "arm's length" in that language is a standard measure). This may be possible in other languages.

21.18	RSV	TEV

The wall was built of jasper, while the city was pure gold, clear as glass.	The wall was made of jasper, and the city itself was made of pure gold, as clear as glass.

Jasper: see verse 11 and 4.3.

The city was pure gold: this includes the streets and the buildings. One may also say "everything in the city was made out of pure gold."

Clear as glass: this seems to indicate very pure gold, of the highest quality. The light of the city seems to shine through the gold (**clear as glass**). An alternative model for this final sentence is "Everything in the city was made out of gold, so pure that light seemed to shine through it just like glass."

21.19-20	RSV	TEV

19 The foundations of the wall of the city were adorned with every jewel; the first was jasper, the second sapphire, the third agate, the fourth emerald, 20 the fifth onyx, the sixth carnelian, the seventh chrysolite, the eighth beryl, the ninth topaz, the tenth chrysoprase, the eleventh jacinth, the twelfth amethyst.	19 The foundation stones of the city wall were adorned with all kinds of precious stones. The first foundation stone was jasper, the second sapphire, the third agate, the fourth emerald, 20 the fifth onyx, the sixth carnelian, the seventh yellow quartz, the eighth beryl, the ninth topaz, the tenth chalcedony, the eleventh turquoise, the twelfth amethyst.

The foundations of the wall of the city: "The foundation stones of the wall around the city," "The stones upon which the wall around the city was built," or, more simply, ". . . of the wall."

Adorned with every jewel: the Greek verb translated **adorned** is the same one used of the bride in verse 2. Here **every** means, more generally, "of all kinds," "of different kinds." **Every jewel** may also be expressed as "all kinds of beautiful (or, expensive) stones."

The first was jasper: it is not certain whether the Greek text means "the first foundation stone was adorned with jasper" or "the first foundation stone was made of jasper." The majority of commentaries and translations take the Greek to mean that the first foundation stone was a jasper, that is, that each foundation stone was a single huge precious stone. This involves an apparent inconsistency, but it is not different in kind or degree from other such inconsistencies in this book. So one may translate "the first foundation stone was made of jasper" or "the first stone was made of a green and blue material."

There is considerable uncertainty over some of the twelve stones named, and modern translations differ. A comparison of ten translations in English (RSV, NRSV, NEB, REB, RNAB, TNT, NJB, NIV, AT, TEV) shows that seven of the translations agree almost unanimously on eight of the twelve stones (NJB is markedly different from the others). RSV and TEV differ on the names of three of the stones.

If the names of all the stones are not readily available in a given language, the best thing to do is to identify the stone by its color; for example, "a precious blue stone," or the like. In some languages, however, it will be difficult, if not impossible, to name this many different colors. In some instances it may be necessary to transliterate the foreign names, "a precious stone called 'jasper.'" The translator should consult the illustrations in Bible dictionaries, such as *The Interpreter's Dictionary of the Bible,* volume 3, facing page 472.

Jasper: see 4.3. NJB and SPCL have "diamond."

Sapphire: a precious stone, usually blue.

Agate: a semiprecious stone of various colors; perhaps green is indicated here.

Emerald: see 4.3 (the emerald is a superior variety of beryl).

Onyx: a semiprecious stone, of various colors; perhaps here a red stone. Here a number of translations have "sardonyx," which is a variety of onyx.

Carnelian: see 4.3; it is a variety of chalcedony.

Chrysolite: in today's terminology this is a peridot, a transparent yellowish-green silicate of magnesium. The biblical gem was probably a gold-colored stone; so TEV "yellow quartz," and NJB "gold quartz."

Beryl: usually bluish-green, but of other colors as well.

Topaz: usually yellow.

Chrysoprase: the modern stone is an apple-green chalcedony, but there is uncertainty about the meaning of the Greek term (**chrysoprase** is a transliteration of the Greek).

Jacinth: or "hyacinth." This is a reddish-orange variety of zircon. TEV and REB have "turquoise," which is blue or bluish-green.

Amethyst: purple or violet.

21.21   RSV   TEV

And the twelve gates were twelve pearls,   The twelve gates were twelve pearls;
each of the gates made of a single pearl,   each gate was made from a single pearl.
and the street of the city was pure gold,   The street of the city was of pure gold,
transparent as glass.   transparent as glass.

The twelve gates were twelve pearls: here **gates** probably means the
gateways, or else the watch towers above the gateways. For **pearls** see 17.4.
The street of the city: as in 11.8, either the broad main street or a collective
term for all the streets (also 22.2); probably the main street.
Pure gold, transparent as glass: similar to the phrase in verse 18.

21.22   RSV   TEV

And I saw no temple in the city,   I did not see a temple in the city,
for its temple is the Lord God the Al-   because its temple is the Lord God Almighty and the Lamb.   mighty and the Lamb.

No temple: this can be said "no place for worship" or "no building (or, house)
in which to worship God."
Its temple is the Lord God the Almighty and the Lamb: a temple is a special
place for worshiping the God who is in heaven. In the new Jerusalem God and Jesus
Christ are always present in the whole city, and no separate place for worshiping
them is needed. In some languages one will say, for example, "Because the Lord God
Almighty and the Lamb take the place of a temple."
Lord God the Almighty: see 1.8; 4.8; 11.17; 15.3; 16.7.

21.23   RSV   TEV

And the city has no need of sun or   The city has no need of the sun or the
moon to shine upon it, for the glory of   moon to shine on it, because the glory
God is its light, and its lamp is the   of God shines on it, and the Lamb is its
Lamb.   lamp.

Has no need of sun or moon to shine upon it: the city does not depend on
the sun or the moon for its light; its light comes from a different source.
The glory of God is its light: for **glory** see verse 11 and comments at 1.6.
Its lamp is the Lamb: this involves a formal contradiction, inasmuch as all the
light the city needs comes from God's glory shining on it. The use of the word **lamp**
is not to give the Lamb an inferior function; it is a way of saying that the Lamb also
supplies light. For **lamp** see comments on "lampstand" in 1.12. God and the Lamb
provide all the light needed all the time, so there is no need of sun, or moon, or
lamps.
An alternative translation model for the final part of this verse is:

Because the brilliant light of God shines on it and the Lamb lights
it up just as a lamp does.

21.24   RSV   TEV

By its light shall the nations walk; and   The peoples of the world will walk by its
the kings of the earth shall bring their   light, and the kings of the earth will
glory into it,   bring their wealth into it.

By its light shall the nations walk: here, as elsewhere in the Bible, "to walk"
means "to live," "to carry on one's activities." The meaning here is "All the peoples
of the world will live in the light that shines forth from the city." See Isaiah 60.3.

The kings of the earth shall bring their glory into it: here **glory** stands for
that which brings fame or honor to someone, namely riches, valuable possessions. So
TEV and others have "their wealth," "their riches." See Psalm 72.10.

21.25   RSV   TEV

and its gates shall never be shut by   The gates of the city will stand open all
day—and there shall be no night there;   day; they will never be closed, because
                                                 there will be no night there.

Its gates shall never be shut by day: this says only that the gates stay open
all day long. But in light of what follows, **and there shall be no night there**, it is
clear that the text means the gates will stay open all the time, twenty-four hours a
day (see Isa 60.11), because in the new Jerusalem there will be no nighttime, when
city gates are closed. There will be light a full twenty-four hours every day.

21.26   RSV   TEV

they shall bring into it the glory and the   The greatness and the wealth of the
honor of the nations.   nations will be brought into the city.

They shall bring: as it stands in RSV, the subject of this verb is "the kings" of
verse 24. This is possible, but in light of the fact that in Greek the verb here is in the
future tense, whereas in verse 24 it is in the present tense, it is possible that this
third person plural active form of the verb is the equivalent of a passive, "will be
brought in," with no indication of who the actor is. Following this interpretation the
translation can be "the people of the world will bring" (NRSV "People will bring
. . ."). However, in languages that do not use the passive, translators will need to
express this clause in a way similar to RSV, using the pronoun **they** to refer to
unknown subjects.

The glory and the honor: these two abstract nouns stand for concrete objects:
"their treasure and their wealth" (NJB, RNAB); REB has "splendour and wealth."

An alternative translation model for this verse is:

They will bring all the beautiful things and possessions of the people of the world into the city.

21.27   RSV   TEV

But nothing unclean shall enter it, nor any one who practices abomination or falsehood, but only those who are written in the Lamb's book of life.	But nothing that is impure will enter the city, nor anyone who does shameful things or tells lies. Only those whose names are written in the Lamb's book of the living will enter the city.

Nothing unclean: the use of the neuter "no thing" in the Greek seems to imply vessels or other objects used in worship; but in light of the following masculine, literally "the one who does abomination and lie," the initial **nothing unclean** probably includes people as well as objects. Here **unclean** means ceremonially impure, profane as opposed to sacred. In certain languages this will be expressed as "taboo objects" or "objects with bad taboo."

Anyone who practices abomination or falsehood: for **abomination** see 17.4,5; and see "polluted" and comments in 21.8. In the Old Testament both terms are used to indicate the worship of idols, and that may be the meaning here.

Those who are written in the Lamb's book of life: see 3.5; 13.8; 17.8; 20.12,15.

22.1   RSV   TEV

Then he showed me the river of the water of life, bright as crystal, flowing from the throne of God and of the Lamb	The angel also showed me the river of the water of life, sparkling like crystal, and coming from the throne of God and of the Lamb

Then: as in other chapters this word indicates that the events in this verse immediately follow what happens in chapter 21. Some translators will wish to say "After the angel showed me the new city, he showed . . . ."

He showed me: it is better to make the subject explicit, "the angel showed me" (as NRSV has done); see 21.9.

The river of the water of life: the genitive phrase **water of life** is better translated "life-giving water" (see 21.6 "the fountain of the water of life").

Bright as crystal: see expressions with a similar meaning in 4.6; 21.11.

Flowing from the throne of God and of the Lamb: as 3.21 and 22.3 make clear, God and the Lamb sit on the same throne, not on two different thrones. The idea of **flowing from** can be expressed by "flowing from under."

through the middle of the street of the city; also, on either side of the river, the tree of life[r] with its twelve kinds of fruit, yielding its fruit each month; and the leaves of the tree were for the healing of the nations.	and flowing down the middle of the city's street. On each side of the river was the tree of life, which bears fruit twelve times a year, once each month; and its leaves are for the healing of the nations.

[r] Or *the Lamb. In the midst of the street of the city, and on either side of the river, was the tree of life,* etc.

Through the middle of the street of the city: as the RSV footnote shows, it is possible to end verse 1 with a full stop and begin verse 2 with "Through the middle . . ." joined to the following "was the tree of life." So SPCL translates "In the middle of the main street of the city, and on each side of the river, grew the tree of life." Most translations, however, divide and punctuate as RSV and TEV do. TEV has used the two verbs "coming (from)" and "flowing (down)," instead of the one verb **flowing** (RSV) of the Greek text in verse 1. For **the street of the city** see 21.21.

On either side of the river, the tree of life: both RSV and TEV (and other translations as well) translate quite literally **the tree of life**, and so portray one single tree that grows in two different places, that is, on both sides of the river. This is an impossible statement, but the language may be explained by the fact that in the Old Testament there is the one tree of life-giving fruit (Gen 2.9; 3.22; see also Rev 2.7; 22.14,19), and the writer wants to preserve this figure. But it is possible to take the singular **the tree** to be a collective term, "the trees of life" (see Ezek 47.12). Beckwith, who favors this interpretation, comments "there are multitudes of trees." It is recommended that translators choose the plural form.

Tree of life: "life-giving trees," or "trees that bear life-giving fruit," or "trees that bear fruit that causes people to live."

Its twelve kinds of fruit, yielding its fruit each month: it is most improbable that the Greek text means that the tree bears a different fruit each month; rather it means, as TEV and others have it, "which bears fruit twelve times a year, once each month" (so NJB, RNAB, REB, SPCL, FRCL).

The leaves . . . were for the healing of the nations: "the leaves . . . are used to heal the wounds of all peoples" or "all peoples of the world use the leaves to heal their wounds (or, to cure their diseases)."

An alternative translation model for verses 1 and 2 is:

> After the angel showed me the new city, he showed me the river full of water that gives life. It sparkled with a beautiful green and red light, like the clear transparent glass named "crystal." The river flowed out from under the throne of God and the Lamb, and went through the wide road (or, big street) of the city. On each side of the river stood life-giving trees that bear fruit twelve times a year, once each month. The people of the world use their leaves for healing wounds (or, curing disease).

22.3   RSV   TEV

There shall no more be anything ac-   Nothing that is under God's curse will
cursed, but the throne of God and of   be found in the city.
the Lamb shall be in it, and his servants   The throne of God and of the
shall worship him;   Lamb will be in the city, and his ser-
                                                vants will worship him.

There shall no more be anything accursed: the text may mean, as RSV
translates it, that anything or any person under God's curse will exist no more. In the
context, however, it is preferable to translate, with TEV and others, "Nothing under
God's curse will be in the city." The precise sense of the Greek neuter noun
translated **accursed** (used only here in the New Testament) is a person or a thing
that God declares unacceptable. Such a person or thing is put under the ban, that is,
is banished, condemned to destruction. In the translation it should be quite clear that
this "curse" is God's judgment, not that of a person. Other ways to translate this
clause are "Nothing that is unacceptable to God is allowed in the city" or "No person
or thing that God declares unacceptable (or, taboo) may stay in the city."

But the throne of God and of the Lamb shall be in it: see verse 1. This
reads rather strangely in RSV, which connects it with what precedes. It is better to
place a full stop at the end of the previous statement (as NRSV does) and begin a
new sentence here, without the adversative conjunction **but** (which NRSV retains);
the Greek *kai* here means simply "and."

His servants shall worship him: or "his servants will serve him." The Greek
verb usually means "to serve as priest" (see its use in 7.15, where TEV translates
"serve"). The singular **him** here and "his face . . . his name" in verse 4 refer to God,
as verse 5 makes clear. Here **his servants** are all the inhabitants of the new
Jerusalem. An alternative translation model for the final part of this verse is "The
throne of God and the Lamb will be in the city, and God's servants will serve him."

22.4   RSV   TEV

they shall see his face, and his name   They will see his face, and his name will
shall be on their foreheads.   be written on their foreheads.

They shall see his face: "they will see God face to face." What has always
been impossible (see Exo 33.20; 1 Tim 6.16) will then be possible (see Matt 5.8;
1 John 3.2).

His name shall be on their foreheads: that is, the name of God (see 14.1).

22.5   RSV   TEV

And night shall be no more; they need   There shall be no more night, and they
no light of lamp or sun, for the Lord   will not need lamps or sunlight, because
God will be their light, and they shall   the Lord God will be their light, and
reign for ever and ever.   they will rule as kings forever and ever.

Night shall be no more: or, as in 21.25, "there shall be no night there."

They need no light of lamp or sun: as in 21.23.

The Lord God will be their light: the Greek verb translated **will be their light** (literally "will shine on them") is used in the passive voice in 18.1, "was made bright." Here the Lamb is not included, as he is in 21.23, as the source of light in the new Jerusalem.

They shall reign for ever and ever: see similar statements about their reign in 5.10; 20.6. On **for ever and ever**, see comments on 1.6, and compare 11.15. Their reign is eternal, as eternal as God's.

Here end the visions in Revelation.

D. Epilogue

(22.6-21)

22.6-17

RSV

6 And he said to me, "These words are trustworthy and true. And the Lord, the God of the spirits of the prophets, has sent his angel to show his servants what must soon take place. 7 And behold, I am coming soon."

Blessed is he who keeps the words of the prophecy of this book.

8 I John am he who heard and saw these things. And when I heard and saw them, I fell down to worship at the feet of the angel who showed them to me; 9 but he said to me, "You must not do that! I am a fellow servant with you and your brethren the prophets, and with those who keep the words of this book. Worship God."

10 And he said to me, "Do not seal up the words of the prophecy of this book, for the time is near. 11 Let the evildoer still do evil, and the filthy still be filthy, and the righteous still do right, and the holy still be holy."

12 "Behold, I am coming soon, bringing my recompense, to repay every one for what he has done. 13 I am the Alpha and the Omega, the first and the last, the beginning and the end."

14 Blessed are those who wash their robes, that they may have the right to the tree of life and that they may enter the city by the gates. 15 Outside are the dogs and sorcerers and fornicators and murderers and idolaters, and every one who loves and practices falsehood.

16 "I Jesus have sent my angel to you with this testimony for the churches. I am the root and the offspring of David, the bright morning star."

17 The Spirit and the Bride say, "Come." And let him who hears say, "Come." And let him who is thirsty come, let him who desires take the water of life without price.

TEV

The Coming of Jesus

6 Then the angel said to me, "These words are true and can be trusted. And the Lord God, who gives his Spirit to the prophets, has sent his angel to show his servants what must happen very soon."

7 "Listen!" says Jesus. "I am coming soon! Happy are those who obey the prophetic words in this book!"

8 I, John, have heard and seen all these things. And when I finished hearing and seeing them, I fell down at the feet of the angel who had shown me these things, and I was about to worship him. 9 But he said to me, "Don't do it! I am a fellow servant of yours and of your brothers the prophets and of all those who obey the words in this book. Worship God!" 10 And he said to me, "Do not keep the prophetic words of this book a secret, because the time is near when all this will happen. 11 Whoever is evil must go on doing evil, and whoever is filthy must go on being filthy; whoever is good must go on doing good, and whoever is holy must go on being holy."

12 "Listen!" says Jesus. "I am coming soon! I will bring my rewards with me, to give to each one according to what he has done. 13 I am the first and the last, the beginning and the end."

14 Happy are those who wash their robes clean and so have the right to eat the fruit from the tree of life and to go through the gates into the city. 15 But outside the city are the perverts and those who practice magic, the immoral and the murderers, those who worship idols and those who are liars both in words and deeds.

16 "I, Jesus, have sent my angel to announce these things to you in the churches. I am descended from the family of David; I am the bright morning star."

17 The Spirit and the Bride say, "Come!"

> Everyone who hears this must also say,
> "Come!"
> Come, whoever is thirsty; accept the water
> of life as a gift, whoever wants it.

SECTION HEADING: TEV "The Coming of Jesus," or else "Jesus promises to come soon."

The book comes to a close with Jesus' repeated promise to come soon (verses 7,12,20). There are warnings and exhortations, and a solemn assurance that the book is authentic and true. TEV places the last four verses (verses 18-21) in a separate section, but they may be included in this section. If this is done, the title for the whole section may be "The ending of the book" or "Epilogue" (as NJB has it).

Beckwith's summary of this chapter, which he calls "Epilogue," is worth quoting (pages 771–72). He compares it with the Prologue (1.1-8), as follows:

> In both alike the revelation is authenticated in the most solemn manner; it comes from God himself (22.6, 1.1), and from Jesus (22.16, 1.1), through angelic agency (22.6,16, 1.1). It is a message of genuine prophecy, 22.6,9,10,18f., 1.3. The author of the book is the John well known to the seven churches, 22.8, 1.1,4,9, but duly commissioned as a prophet, 22.8f.,10, 1.1,9-11. The book, given with these most certain sanctions, is to be read in the churches, 22.18,16, 1.3,11. Its messages encourage the faithful with the promise of sure reward, 22.7,12,14, 1.3, and warn the unfaithful and unbelieving of impending retribution, 22.11f.,18f., 1.7. The coming of the Lord is near, 22.7,10,12,20, 1.3. The central divine figure is he who was known in the historic Jesus, but is to come in the majesty of the ascended Christ, 22.16,12f., 1.5,7.

22.6

RSV	TEV
And he said to me, "These words are trustworthy and true. And the Lord, the God of the spirits of the prophets, has sent his angel to show his servants what must soon take place.	Then the angel said to me, "These words are true and can be trusted. And the Lord God, who gives his Spirit to the prophets, has sent his angel to show his servants what must happen very soon."

He said to me: the speaker is the angel who came to John in 21.9 (see 21.15; 22.1).

These words are trustworthy and true: see 21.5. The reference here is probably to the whole book, so one may translate "All these words are . . . ," or even "All the words that you have heard are . . . ."

And the Lord, the God of the spirits of the prophets: some take this sentence to be the words of the author, not the angel. There is no translation, however, that separates this from the first sentence in this verse. The meaning is that God inspires the spirits of his prophets. This may be translated "And the Lord God, who inspires the prophets" (so TNT, NJB, REB) or, as TEV has it, "the Lord God, who gives his Spirit to the prophets." This statement is related to the one in 19.10. The meaning here is that Christian prophets (see 10.7) are inspired, or controlled, by the Holy Spirit as they proclaim their messages. The RSV rendering, **the Lord, the God of . . . ,**" follows the punctuation of the Greek text; most translations, however, are like TEV "the Lord God," and it is recommended that translators follow this rendering. For **prophets** see 10.7. Another way to render this phrase is "For God, who causes his Spirit to empower those who preach his message . . . ."

Has sent his angel to show his servants what must soon take place: see 1.1. There the text says that he sent his angel to John. This may be implied here, but it is better not to add this to the text. As in 1.1, this is a reference to all the visions and revelations in the book. **Show his servants** may be expressed as "to make known to all those who serve him" or "to cause all those who serve him to see."

His servants: either the prophets (see 10.7; 11.18) or else all believers (see 2.20; 7.3; 19.5; 22.3). The latter is preferable.

22.7	RSV	TEV

And behold, I am coming soon."	"Listen!" says Jesus. "I am com-
Blessed is he who keeps the words	ing soon! Happy are those who obey the
of the prophecy of this book.	prophetic words in this book!"

And behold, I am coming soon: see 3.11; for **behold** see 1.7. RSV prints this statement as part of the direct speech beginning in verse 6. This means that RSV probably takes the speaker in verse 6 to be Jesus, not the angel, for it is Jesus who promises to come soon (see verses 12,20). Some translations are like RSV; it is better, however, to take the speaker in verse 6 as the angel, and Jesus as the speaker in verse 7a. NRSV has closing quotation marks at the end of verse 6 and opening quotation marks at the beginning of verse 7. This indicates two different speakers, but in neither case does NRSV specify who is the speaker. FRCL and BRCL, like TEV, identify the speaker here as Jesus.

A translation like TEV, that translates "Listen!" (instead of RSV's outmoded **Behold**), will have a problem if, like Portuguese, Spanish, French, and other languages, there are separate forms for the singular and the plural of the verb. If a translation chooses to say "Listen" or "Pay attention," or something similar, and has to be specific as to whether the command is in the singular or the plural form, it is better to use the plural (as BRCL does), since the words are not addressed solely to John but to all believers, to all the readers (and hearers) of this book. In some languages it will be necessary to say "All of you must listen" or "Listen, all of you!"

Blessed: see 1.3.

He who keeps the words of the prophecy of this book: see 1.3. The reference to **this book** seems to imply that it is John himself who says this. So it is better to follow RSV (and NRSV) and make verse 7b a separate paragraph. For the verb "to keep," meaning "to obey," see 1.3; 3.8; 12.17; 14.12. **The prophecy of this book** may also be expressed as "the words of this book that tell about present and future events" or "what this book tells will happen now and later (or, in the future)."

317

To repeat what has been said about the speakers in verse 6-7: in verse 6a the speaker is the angel; in verse 6b the speaker may be John, but this is not certain; in verse 7a Jesus speaks; in verse 7b the writer of the book is the speaker.

An alternative translation model for this verse is:

> Jesus says, "You [plural] must listen! I am coming soon."
> Happy are those people who obey all the things that are said in this book about what will happen now and later.

22.8

RSV	TEV
I John am he who heard and saw these things. And when I heard and saw them, I fell down to worship at the feet of the angel who showed them to me;	I, John, have heard and seen all these things. And when I finished hearing and seeing them, I fell down at the feet of the angel who had shown me these things, and I was about to worship him.

I John am he who heard and saw these things: "I am John, the one who heard and saw all these things." The readers know who he is, and he assures them that he himself had all these visions and revelations from God.

And when I heard and saw them: it is better to follow TEV and say something like "And after hearing and seeing them all, I . . . ."

I fell down to worship at the feet of the angel: it should be clear that this means that John was about to worship the angel. So the statement should be "I fell down at the angel's feet to worship him" (see 19.10). Another way to say this is "I prostrated myself before the feet of the angel to give him honor." See also comments on **worship** at 4.10.

The angel who showed them to me: here John identifies this angel (verse 6) as the one who showed him everything he saw in his visions. For **showed** see 1.1; 4.1.

22.9

RSV	TEV
but he said to me, "You must not do that! I am a fellow servant with you and your brethren the prophets, and with those who keep the words of this book. Worship God."	But he said to me, "Don't do it! I am a fellow servant of yours and of your brothers the prophets and of all those who obey the words in this book. Worship God!"

The angel's response is very much like the response given in 19.10.

A fellow servant with you and your brethren the prophets: "I serve God, just as you and your brothers, the prophets, do" or "Like you and your fellow prophets, I am only a servant of God."

And with those who keep the words of this book: the angel adds that this group, "all who obey the messages in this book," are also his fellow servants; like them, he also serves God.

Worship God: see 19.10.

22.10   RSV   TEV

And he said to me, "Do not seal   And he said to me, "Do not keep the
up the words of the prophecy of this   prophetic words of this book a secret,
book, for the time is near.   because the time is near when all this
                                       will happen.

Do not seal up the words of the prophecy of this book: "Do not seal this book of prophetic messages" (see the opposite of this in Dan 12.4,9). For the sense of the verb "to seal," see 10.4. The angel commands John not to stamp "Top Secret," as it were, on the book, but to leave it open and make its message available to all readers. If the verb "to seal" is difficult or impossible to represent, the translation can be "Do not keep the prophetic messages of this book a secret," or "Don't hide from people the prophetic messages of this book," or "Don't prevent people from knowing the . . . ." For **prophecy of this book** see verse 7 and 1.3.

The time is near: everything that has been announced in the book will happen soon (see 1.3).

22.11   RSV   TEV

Let the evildoer still do evil, and the   Whoever is evil must go on doing evil,
filthy still be filthy, and the righteous and whoever is filthy must go on being
still do right, and the holy still be holy." filthy; whoever is good must go on doing
                                           good, and whoever is holy must go on
                                           being holy."

This rather strange command is explained by the fact that the End will come soon, and there is no time left for people to change their way of living. This situation can be clearly expressed by beginning the verse "In the meantime" or "Meanwhile."

Let: this is the way of expressing a third-person command in English. "Those who are evil are to go on being evil." Or it can be stated as a concession, "And so, the person who is evil may keep on doing evil" (see Dan 12.10, for a parallel).

The parallel pairs are not meant to describe two different kinds of bad people (**evildoers** and **filthy**) and two different kinds of good people (**righteous** and **holy**). Rather, this is an emphatic way of contrasting the bad and the good. The noun **evildoer** translates the Greek present participle of the verb "to do evil," and **do evil** translates the aorist imperative of the same verb. For its use in the sense of "harm," "injure," "wound," see 2.11; 9.10,19.

Filthy: this is used in a moral and spiritual sense, not a physical sense; "immoral," "corrupt," "sinful." The Greek adjective is used also in James 2.2 in a literal sense, of "shabby" clothing; the Greek verb is used only here in the New

Testament. Other ways of saying this are: "minds (or, hearts) dirty from immorality" or "people who do filthy or immoral practices."

The righteous still do right: "whoever is righteous (or, good) must keep on doing what is right." For the adjective **righteous** see "just" in 15.3; 16.5; for the noun **right** (or, "righteousness") see 19.11.

The holy still be holy: for **the holy** see comments on "saints" in 5.8; the verb "to be holy" occurs only here in Revelation. The idea may be the primary one of being dedicated to God, belonging exclusively to God. So Brc translates "the man who is dedicated to God must continue in his dedication"; or **holy** may have here the idea of spiritual purity, of being free from sin. SPCL translates "Whoever is holy must keep on sanctifying himself"; in the context this may be the meaning intended, or one may express this clause as "whoever is holy must refrain from doing evil" or "whoever does not sin must remain free from sin."

An alternative translation model for this verse is:

> And so all people who do evil must (or, should) keep on doing evil, and all those who practice immorality must continue doing filthy immoral things. And all those who do good must continue doing what is right, and all who are holy must refrain from doing evil.

22.12   RSV   TEV

"Behold, I am coming soon, bring-   "Listen!" says Jesus. "I am coming my recompense, to repay every one   ing soon! I will bring my rewards with
for what he has done.   me, to give to each one according to
                                            what he has done.

Behold, I am coming soon: for **Behold** see 1.7; and see comment at verse 7, above. By its use of quotation marks, RSV intends to show that someone other than the writer is speaking. It is better to indicate that Jesus is the speaker, as TEV, FRCL, and BRCL do.

Bringing my recompense, to repay every one: this applies to all, the righteous and the evil alike. So **my recompense** may be reward (see 11.18) or it may be punishment (see 18.6). Another way of expressing this is "I am coming to either reward or punish all people for what they have done."

For what he has done: see 2.23, "as your works deserve"; 20.12,13.

22.13   RSV   TEV

I am the Alpha and the Omega, the first   I am the first and the last, the begin-
and the last, the beginning and the   ning and the end."
end."

I am the Alpha and the Omega: see 1.8; 21.6; **the first and the last**: see 1.17; 2.8; **the beginning and the end**: see 21.6. All three phrases proclaim the same basic truth in three different ways.

320

22.14   RSV   TEV

   Blessed are those who wash their robes,⁵ that they may have the right to the tree of life and that they may enter the city by the gates.

   Happy are those who wash their robes clean and so have the right to eat the fruit from the tree of life and to go through the gates into the city.

⁵ Other ancient authorities read *do his commandments*

Blessed: see 1.3.

Those who wash their robes: see 7.14. Here nothing is said about "in the blood of the Lamb," as in 7.14. It is implied, of course, that this washing makes the robes clean, and this may be expressly stated, "those who wash their robes clean" (TEV). For **robes** see 6.11.

As the RSV footnote indicates, instead of **who wash their robes**, some Greek manuscripts have "who do his commandments" (see 12.17; 14.12). The text translated by RSV and TEV is to be preferred.

That: this appears to indicate purpose; and by placing a comma after **robes**, RSV seems to connect **that** with **Blessed**. It is possible to take the Greek conjunction translated **that** to express purpose and connect it with the verbal phrase **wash their robes**: "those who wash their robes in order to . . . ." But it seems better to take the conjunction as final, indicating result: "and as a result they have . . . ." So NRSV "so that they will have the right . . . ."

Have the right to the tree of life: that is, have the right to eat the fruit of the tree (see 22.2).

Enter the city by the gates: this is somewhat strange, for it seems to imply that others will have to enter by some other way. The force of this statement may be what would be expressed in English by "the right to enter the city freely," "full and free access to the city." Since **the tree of life** is inside the city, it may be desirable to reverse the two actions as follows: "And so they will have the right to go through the gates into the city and eat the fruit from the tree of life."

22.15   RSV   TEV

Outside are the dogs and sorcerers and fornicators and murderers and idolaters, and every one who loves and practices falsehood.

But outside the city are the perverts and those who practice magic, the immoral and the murderers, those who worship idols and those who are liars both in words and deeds.

Outside are: this means that they will not be allowed to enter the city: "They will be kept outside the city" or "The following people will not be allowed to enter the city."

In 21.8 all of these, except **the dogs**, are included among those destined to the lake of burning sulfur.

The dogs: as commentators point out, this was an expression that was applied by Jews to Gentiles (see Psa 22.16,20; Matt 15.26,27). And in Philippians 3.2 it is used of those who were trying to impose Jewish laws on Christians. It is difficult to say what, precisely, the word means here; perhaps it means much the same as the "polluted" in 21.8, that is, "filthy heathens." Some suggest that this is a general term, further defined by the following terms. Alternative translation models for this phrase are "people who have made themselves dirty (or, unclean) through worshiping idols" or "people who have committed the following foul (or, dirty) sins."

Sorcerers . . . fornicators . . . murderers . . . idolaters: see 21.8.

Every one who loves and practices falsehood: "all who love to lie and do it all the time" (see "all liars" in 21.8).

22.16   RSV   TEV

RSV	TEV
"I Jesus have sent my angel to you with this testimony for the churches. I am the root and the offspring of David, the bright morning star."	"I, Jesus, have sent my angel to announce these things to you in the churches. I am descended from the family of David; I am the bright morning star."

Have sent my angel to you: in English this appears to say the same thing, in direct speech, that is said in narrative in 1.1, that is, **you** is John, the writer of the book. But in Greek **you** here is plural and means the believers, the readers of the book. So TEV has "to announce these things to you in the churches," and SPCL translates "declare all of this to the churches." Some take the plural **you** here to mean the prophets as a group, of whom John is one (see verse 9); this is possible but does not seem likely. **The churches** are the seven churches of chapters 2–3. See 1.11 for information on the translation of "churches."

With this testimony: this translates the Greek infinitive "to testify" (see the same verb in verses 18 ("I warn") and 20). Instead of the precise sense of "testify," the more general meaning of "declare," "announce" is intended here.

I am the root and the offspring of David: the phrase **root and offspring** means "descendant." Here **root** is used in the sense of what comes from the root, that is, a shoot (see 5.5; Isa 11.10; Rom 15.12 "a root of Jesse"). And the word translated **offspring** is used also in Acts 17.28-29, "we are indeed his offspring" (TEV "we are God's children"). If the figurative language of **root** or "shoot" can be kept in translation, it should be done. But if this is not a natural way of speaking of a descendant, the translation should say "the descendant of" or "the one who descends from." This is not merely genealogical information; it is the assertion that he is the Messianic King, "the Son of David." For "descendant of David" or "Root of David" see 5.5.

The bright morning star: this also seems to have messianic overtones (see Num 24.17). See the use of the phrase "the morning star" in 2.28. As the morning star announces the day, Jesus is the sign and evidence of the coming of God's new Day. One may also say "the one who is like the star that shines at sunrise."

An alternative translation model for this verse is:

"I, Jesus, have sent my messenger (or, angel) to announce these things to you [plural] who are in the groups of God's people. I am the descendant of King David; I am the one who is like the star that appears (or, shines) at sunrise."

22.17 RSV	TEV
The Spirit and the Bride say, "Come." And let him who hears say, "Come." And let him who is thirsty come, let him who desires take the water of life without price.	The Spirit and the Bride say, "Come!" Everyone who hears this must also say, "Come!" Come, whoever is thirsty; accept the water of life as a gift, whoever wants it.

The translator should consider the possibility of presenting this verse in poetic form, as a stanza of three or four lines (see Section F of the introduction, "Translating the Revelation to John," pages 6 and following).

The Spirit and the Bride say, "Come": the command, or request, is addressed to Christ, asking him to come at once to the world. Here the Spirit is speaking together with **the Bride**, the people of God (19.7). It may be that the Spirit is speaking through the prophet, but the text does not imply this. It may be necessary to indicate explicitly to whom they speak: "The Spirit and the Bride say to Jesus . . ." or ". . . say, 'Come, Lord Jesus!'" (see verse 20). For **Bride** see 19.7. In this context another way of expressing this is "the wife of the Lamb."

Let him who hears say: "and all those who hear this are also to say." The assembled believers, as they hear this book being read to them (1.3 and comments), are to repeat the prayer of the Spirit and the Bride.

Him who is thirsty . . . him who desires: the plural form can be used, in order to avoid being exclusive: "All who are thirsty and who want water (or, want water to drink)."

Come . . . take the water of life without price: "Come . . . and drink the life-giving water, without having to pay for it" (see 21.6). This invitation is addressed to those who are thirsty and want water.

An alternative translation model for this verse is:

The Spirit (or, God's Spirit) and the Wife of the Lamb say to Jesus, "You [singular] must come." Everyone who hears this must also say, "Come!" Whoever is thirsty must come and accept the water that gives life.

22.18-21

RSV	TEV *Conclusion*
18 I warn every one who hears the words of the prophecy of this book: if any one adds to	18 I, John, solemnly warn everyone who hears the prophetic words of this book: if anyone

them, God will add to him the plagues described in this book, 19 and if any one takes away from the words of the book of this prophecy, God will take away his share in the tree of life and in the holy city, which are described in this book.

20 He who testifies to these things says, "Surely I am coming soon." Amen. Come, Lord Jesus!

21 The grace of the Lord Jesus be with all the saints. Amen.

adds anything to them, God will add to his punishment the plagues described in this book. 19 And if anyone takes anything away from the prophetic words of this book, God will take away from him his share of the fruit of the tree of life and of the Holy City, which are described in this book.

20 He who gives his testimony to all this says, "Yes indeed! I am coming soon!"

So be it. Come, Lord Jesus!

21 May the grace of the Lord Jesus be with everyone.

SECTION HEADING: TEV "Conclusion." This can also be "Final warning and promise," "John warns the readers of the book," or "Jesus promises to return."

The book closes with a solemn warning to all not to add to or delete anything from the contents of the book. Once more Jesus promises to come soon, a promise to which believers respond with a fervent prayer, "Come, Lord Jesus!" The book ends with a benediction.

22.18   RSV   TEV

I warn every one who hears the words of the prophecy of this book: if any one adds to them, God will add to him the plagues described in this book,

I, John, solemnly warn everyone who hears the prophetic words of this book: if anyone adds anything to them, God will add to his punishment the plagues described in this book.

I warn every one who hears the words of the prophecy of this book: the verb translated **warn** is the same one translated "to witness" in verse 16. Here the verb carries an explicit threat, which justifies the translation **warn**. The warning is made by the writer himself, and it is addressed to believers assembled for worship who are listening to the book being read to them. It should be clear that the speaker here is John. For **the words of the prophecy of this book**, see verses 7 and 10. **Warn** (TEV "solemnly warn") may also be expressed as "tell everyone who hears to listen carefully." **This book** may be rendered as "this book I have written."

If any one adds to them: the warning is against any alteration in the contents of the book, either adding material to it or deleting something from it (see Deut 4.2; 12.32). Such additions or deletions would change the message and would therefore bring punishment from God. John is a prophet and his message comes from God.

Add . . . the plagues described in this book: these are the plagues of chapters 15 and 16. The language **add to him the plagues** may be difficult to express, and it may be better to translate "God will punish him with the plagues" or "God will add to his punishment the plagues" (TEV). One may also say "God will also punish this person with the seven plagues." Of course a form including both men and women should be used, to make the warning apply to everyone.

An alternative translation model for this verse is:

I, John, solemnly warn every person who listens to the message about things that are happening now and in the future, which I have written in this book: if anyone adds anything to this message, God will add to your punishment. He will punish you with the seven plagues that I have described in this book.

22.19   RSV   TEV

and if any one takes away from the words of the book of this prophecy, God will take away his share in the tree of life and in the holy city, which are described in this book.

And if anyone takes anything away from the prophetic words of this book, God will take away from him his share of the fruit of the tree of life and of the Holy City, which are described in this book.

If any one takes away: this may be translated "Whoever deletes," or "omits," or "subtracts."

The words of the book of this prophecy: RSV formally represents the different form and word order of the Greek, but the meaning is the same as in verses 7,10,18. See also comments at 1.3.

Take away his share in the tree of life and in the holy city: for the Greek noun translated **share**, see 20.6, "he who shares in," meaning "who has a right to participate in"; see also 21.8, "their lot" in a negative sense of having a share of punishment. The meaning of this statement is "take away his right to eat the fruit of the tree of life and to enter the holy city" (see verse 14). Or else, taking the words in a more literal sense, the idea may be that God has given each believer a share of the fruits of the tree of life and a place to live in the new Jerusalem: "God will take away from him his share of the fruits of the tree of life and his place in the holy city." For **the holy city** see 21.2,10.

An alternative translation model for verses 18-19 is:

> I, John, solemnly warn all who hear the reading of the prophetic messages that I have written in this book: if you add anything to them, God will add to your punishment. God will punish you with the seven plagues described in this book. And if you take out anything from the prophetic messages of this book, God will take away from you the blessings described in this book. God will take away your right to eat the fruit of the tree of life and to live in the holy city.

22.20   RSV   TEV

He who testifies to these things says, "Surely I am coming soon." Amen. Come, Lord Jesus!

He who gives his testimony to all this says, "Yes indeed! I am coming soon!"

So be it. Come, Lord Jesus!

He who testifies to these things: the same verb "to testify," used in verses 16 and 18, here has the sense of "announce," "proclaim." The speaker is Jesus, and

these things are the visions and revelations that he has proclaimed and that are recorded in this book. The meaning may be expressed by "He who declares these messages."

Surely I am coming soon: as in verses 7 and 12.

Amen. Come, Lord Jesus! The initial **Amen** may be translated "So be it" or "May it be so" (see 1.6). The speaker is John, the writer of the book. **Come, Lord Jesus** is the Greek equivalent of the Aramaic *Marana tha* (1 Cor 16.22, "Our Lord, come!").

22.21 RSV TEV

The grace of the Lord Jesus be with all the saints.[t] Amen.

May the grace of the Lord Jesus be with everyone.[i]

[t] Other ancient authorities omit *all;* others omit *the saints*

[i] everyone; *some manuscripts have* God's people; *others have* all of God's people.

The grace of the Lord Jesus: this is the usual benediction Paul uses to close his letters (see Rom 16.20; 1 Cor 16.23; Gal 6.18). The only other place in Revelation that the Greek word translated **grace** is used is in the standard phrase "Grace and peace" in 1.4. The prayer here may be translated "May the Lord Jesus show his great love" or "May the Lord Jesus give his richest blessings."

All the saints: this means "all of God's people" (see 5.8). TEV follows another Greek text, "everyone" (or, "all of you"). In this context this reading means the same as **all the saints** of the text translated by RSV. As the TEV and RSV footnotes show, there is still another variant text, "the saints."

Amen: see comments at 1.6. The Greek text followed by TEV does not have this final word. There is no harm in including it in translation, but it is better to omit it and perhaps mention it in a footnote.

Selected Bibliography

Bible Texts and Versions Cited

Texts

The Greek New Testament. 3rd edition, corrected, 1983. K. Aland, M. Black, C.M. Martini, B.M. Metzger, and A. Wikgren, editors. Stuttgart: United Bible Societies. (Cited as UBS Greek New Testament.)

Novum Testamentum Graece. 26th edition, 1979; corrected, 1981. Erwin Nestle and Kurt Aland, editors. Stuttgart: Deutsche Bibelgesellschaft.

Septuaginta: Id est Vetus Testamentum graece iuxta LXX interpretes. 1935. Edited by Alfred Rahlfs. Stuttgart: Württembergische Bibelanstalt. (Cited as Septuagint.)

Versions

Die Bibel in heutigem Deutsch: Die Gute Nachricht des Alten und Neuen Testaments. 1982. Stuttgart: Deutsche Bibelgesellschaft. (Cited as GECL, German common language version.)

The Bible: A New Translation. 1926. James Moffatt, translator. London: Hodder & Stoughton. (Cited as Mft.)

La Bible en français courant. 1986. Paris: Alliance Biblique Universelle. (Cited as FRCL, French common language version.)

A Bíblia na Linguagem de Hoje. 1988. São Paulo: Sociedade Bíblica do Brasil. (BRCL, Brazilian common language version.)

The Complete Bible: An American Translation, 1923, 1927, 1948. The Old Testament translated by J.M. Powis Smith and others; the Apocrypha and the New Testament translated by Edgar J. Goodspeed. Chicago: University of Chicago Press. (Cited as AT.)

Dios Habla Hoy: La Biblia con Deuterocanónicos. Versión Popular. 1966, 1970, 1979. New York: Sociedades Biblicas Unidas. (Cited as SPCL, Spanish common language version.)

The Good News Bible: The Bible in Today's English Version. 1976, 1979. New York: American Bible Society. (Cited as TEV.)

The Holy Bible (Authorized or King James Version). 1611. (Cited as KJV.)

The Holy Bible: Newly Edited by the American Revision Committee. 1901. New York: Thomas Nelson & Sons. (Cited as ASV.)

The Holy Bible: Revised Standard Version. 1952, 1971, 1973. New York: Division of Christian Education of the National Council of the Churches of Christ in the United States of America. (Cited as RSV.)

The Holy Bible: Translated from the Latin Vulgate (Douay-Rheims Version). 1609. (Cited as Douay.)

The New American Bible New Testament: Revised Edition. 1986. New York: Catholic Book Publishing Co. (Cited as RNAB.)

The New English Bible. Second edition, 1970. London: Oxford University Press and Cambridge University Press. (Cited as NEB.)

The New Jerusalem Bible. 1985. Garden City, NY: Doubleday. (Cited as NJB.)

The New Revised Standard Version. 1989. New York: Oxford University Press. (Cited as NRSV.)

The New Testament: A New Translation. Volume 2, *The Letters and the Revelation.* 1969. Translated by William Barclay. London: Collins. (Cited as Brc.)

The New Testament in Modern English. 1972. Translated by J.B. Phillips. New York: Macmillan. (Cited as Phps.)

The NIV Study Bible: New International Version. 1985. Grand Rapids: Zondervan. (Cited as NIV.)

The Revised English Bible. 1989. London: Oxford University Press and Cambridge University Press. (Cited as REB.)

Traduction œcuménique de la Bible. 1972, 1975, 1977. Paris: Société biblique française et Éditions du Cerf. (Cited as TOB.)

The Translator's New Testament. 1973. London: British and Foreign Bible Society. (Cited as TNT.)

Lexicons

Arndt, William F., and F. Wilbur Gingrich. 1979. *A Greek-English Lexicon of the New Testament and Other Early Christian Literature.* Second edition, revised and augmented by F. Wilbur Gingrich and Frederick W. Danker. Chicago and London: The University of Chicago Press. (Cited as Arndt and Gingrich Lexicon.)

Louw, Johannes P. and Eugene A. Nida. 1988. *Greek-English Lexicon of the New Testament: Based on Semantic Domains.* 2 vols. New York: United Bible Societies.

Commentaries

Beasley-Murray, George R. 1978 (revised edition). *The Book of Revelation* (New Century Bible Commentary). Grand Rapids, Michigan: Eerdmans; London: Marshall, Morgan & Scott.

Beckwith, Isbon T. 1919. *The Apocalypse of St. John.* New York: Macmillan.

Bratcher, Robert G., and Eugene A. Nida. 1961. *A Handbook on The Gospel of Mark* (UBS Handbook Series). New York: United Bible Societies.

Bratcher, Robert G., and William D. Reyburn. 1991. *A Handbook on The Book of Psalms* (UBS Handbook Series). New York: United Bible Societies.

Caird, George B. 1966. *A Commentary on the Revelation of St. John the Divine* (Harper's New Testament Commentaries). New York, London: Harper & Row.

Charles, R.H. 1920. *A Critical and Exegetical Commentary on The Revelation of St. John* (International Critical Commentary). Edinburgh: T & T Clark.

Clark, David J., and Norm Mundhenk. 1982. *A Handbook on The Books of Obadiah and Micah* (UBS Handbook Series). New York: United Bible Societies.

Collins, Adela Yarbro. 1990. "The Apocalypse (Revelation)." In *The New Jerome Biblical Commentary,* pages 996–1016. Edited by Raymond E. Brown, Joseph A. Fitzmyer, and Roland E. Murphy. Englewood Cliffs, New Jersey: Prentice Hall.

Newman, Barclay M., and Philip C. Stine. 1988. *A Handbook on The Gospel of Matthew* (UBS Handbook Series). New York: United Bible Societies.

Péter-Contesse, René, and John Ellington. 1990. *A Handbook on Leviticus* (UBS Handbook Series). New York: United Bible Societies.

Sweet, John P.M. 1990. *Revelation* (TPI New Testament Commentaries). London: SCM Press; and Philadelphia: Trinity Press International.

Swete, H.B. 1906. *The Apocalypse of St. John.* London: Macmillan.

de Waard, Jan, and William A. Smalley. 1979. *A Handbook on The Book of Amos* (UBS Handbook Series). New York: United Bible Societies.

Other Studies

Buttrick, G.A., ed. 1962. *The Interpreter's Dictionary of the Bible.* 4 vols. Nashville: Abingdon.

Crim, Keith, ed. 1976. *The Interpreter's Dictionary of the Bible.* Supplementary Volume. Nashville: Abingdon.

Fauna and Flora of the Bible. 1972. London: United Bible Societies.

Robert G. Hall. "Living creatures in the midst of the throne: another look at Revelation 4.6." *New Testament Studies* 36:4 (October 1990), pages 609-613.

Glossary

This Glossary contains terms that are technical from an exegetical or a linguistic viewpoint. Other terms not defined here may be found in a Bible Dictionary.

ABSTRACT refers to terms that designate the qualities and quantities (that is, the features) of objects and events but which are not objects or events themselves. For example, "red" is a quality of a number of objects but is not a thing in and of itself. Typical abstracts include "goodness," "beauty," "length," "breadth," and "time."

ABSTRACT NOUN is one that refers to a quality or characteristic, such as "beauty" or "darkness."

ACTIVE. See **VOICE.**

ACTOR. See **AGENT.**

ADJECTIVE is a word which limits, describes, or qualifies a noun. In English, "red," "tall," "beautiful," and "important" are adjectives.

ADVERB is a word which limits, describes, or qualifies a verb, an adjective, or another adverb. In English, "quickly," "soon," "primarily," and "very" are adverbs.

ADVERSATIVE describes something opposed to or in contrast with something already stated. "But" and "however" are adversative conjunctions.

AGENT is one who accomplishes the action in a sentence or clause, regardless of whether the grammatical construction is active or passive. In "John struck Bill" (active) and "Bill was struck by John" (passive), the agent in either case is John.

ALLEGORY is a story in which persons (or other figures) and actions are used to symbolize spiritual forces, truths, human conduct, experience, etc. **ALLEGORICAL** interpretation of Scripture sees similar symbolic meaning in the historical parts of the Bible.

ALLUSION in discourse is an implicit reference to another object or event.

AMBIGUOUS (AMBIGUITY) describes a word or phrase which in a specific context may have two or more different meanings. For example, "Bill did not leave because

331

John came" could mean either (1) "the coming of John prevented Bill from leaving" or (2) "the coming of John was not the cause of Bill's leaving." It is often the case that what is ambiguous in written form is not ambiguous when actually spoken, since features of intonation and slight pauses usually make clear which of two or more meanings is intended. Furthermore, even in written discourse, the entire context normally serves to indicate which meaning is intended by the writer.

ANCIENT VERSIONS. See **VERSIONS.**

ANTECEDENT describes a person or thing which precedes or exists prior to something or someone else. In grammar, an antecedent is the word, phrase, or clause to which a pronoun refers.

AORIST refers to a set of forms in Greek verbs which denote an action completed without the implication of continuance or duration. Usually, but not always, the action is considered as completed in past time.

APPOSITION is the placing of two expressions together so that they both refer to the same object, event, or concept; for example, "my friend, Mr. Smith." The one expression is said to be the **APPOSITIVE** of the other.

ARAMAIC is a language that was widely used in Southwest Asia before the time of Christ. It became the common language of the Jewish people in Palestine in place of Hebrew, to which it is related.

ARTICLE is a grammatical class of words, often obligatory, that indicate whether the following word is definite or indefinite. In English the **DEFINITE ARTICLE** is "the," and the **INDEFINITE ARTICLE** is "a" or "an."

AUXILIARY is a word which combines closely with another word and which serves to specify certain important aspects of meaning. The term **AUXILIARY** is normally employed in referring to auxiliaries to verbs; for example, "shall," "will," "may," or "ought."

BORROWING, to BORROW, is the process of using a foreign word in another language. For example, "matador" is a Spanish word that has been **BORROWED** by English speakers for "bullfighter."

CANONICAL is a word used to describe books or parts of the Bible which are included in the **CANON** of the Old or New Testament. The **CANON** is the list of books which are accepted as inspired Scripture, with religious authority.

CAUSATIVE (CAUSAL) relates to events and indicates that someone or something caused something to happen, rather than that the person or thing did it directly. In "John ran the horse," the verb "ran" is a causative, since it was not John who ran, but rather it was John who caused the horse to run.

CLAUSE is a grammatical construction, normally consisting of a subject and a predicate. The **MAIN CLAUSE** is that clause in a sentence which could stand alone as a complete sentence, but which has one or more dependent or subordinate clauses related to it. A **DEPENDENT CLAUSE** is a clause in a sentence which is dependent upon or embedded within the sentence. For example, "if he comes" is a dependent clause in the sentence "If he comes, we'll have to leave." A **SUBORDINATE CLAUSE** is dependent on the main clause, but it does not form a complete sentence.

CLIMAX (CLIMACTIC) is the point in a discourse, such as a story or speech, that is the most important, or the turning point, or the point of decision.

COLLECTIVE refers to a number of things (or persons) considered as a whole. In English, a collective noun is considered to be singular or plural, more or less on the basis of traditional usage; for example, "The crowd is (the people are) becoming angry."

COMMAND. See **IMPERATIVE.**

COMMON LANGUAGE TRANSLATION is one that uses only that portion of the total resources of a language that is understood and accepted by all as good usage. Excluded are features peculiar to a dialect, substandard or vulgar language, and technical or highly literary language not understood by all.

COMPONENTS are the parts or elements which go together to form the whole of an object. For example, the components of bread are flour, salt, shortening, yeast, and water. In a similar way, the phrases, words, and other elements in a sentence may be considered its components; and the meaning of a word regularly consists of a set of components that fit together to form the meaning.

COMPOUND refers to forms of words or phrases consisting of two or more parts.

CONCRETE refers to the reality or experience of things or events, particularly in contrast to **ABSTRACT.** The term "child," for example, is concrete, but "childhood" is an abstraction. See **ABSTRACT.**

CONDITIONAL refers to a clause or phrase which expresses or implies a condition, in English usually introduced by "if."

CONJUNCTIONS are words that serve as connectors between words, phrases, clauses, and sentences. "And," "but," "if," and "because" are typical conjunctions in English.

CONNOTATION involves the emotional attitude of a speaker (or writer) to an expression he or she uses, and the emotional response of the hearers (or readers). Connotations may be good or bad, strong or weak, and they are often described in such terms as "colloquial," "taboo," "vulgar," "old-fashioned," and "intimate."

CONSTRUCTION. See **STRUCTURE.**

CONTEXT (CONTEXTUAL) is that which precedes and/or follows any part of a discourse. For example, the context of a word or phrase in Scripture would be the other words and phrases associated with it in the sentence, paragraph, section, and even the entire book in which it occurs. The context of a term always affects its meaning, so that a word does not mean exactly the same thing in one context that it does in another context.

CONTINUATIVE means continuing. The term is used of certain adverbs ("now," "then," "still," etc.) and of certain verb tenses or aspects ("used to do," "are running," "will be enjoying," etc.).

COPYISTS were people who made handwritten copies of books, before the invention of printing. See **MANUSCRIPTS.**

CULTURAL EQUIVALENT is a kind of translation in which certain details from the culture of the source language are changed because they have no meaning or may even carry a wrong meaning for speakers of the receptor language. Cultural equivalent translation should be used only when absolutely necessary for conveying the intended meaning, and it may be important to add an explanatory note. See **CULTURE.**

CULTURE (CULTURAL) is the sum total of the beliefs, patterns of behavior, and sets of interpersonal relations of any group of people. A culture is passed on from one generation to another, but undergoes development or gradual change.

DECLARATIVE refers to forms of a verb or verb phrase which indicate statements assumed to be certain; for example, "prepared" in "She prepared a meal." Such a statement is declarative rather than imperative or interrogative.

DEFINITE ARTICLE. See **ARTICLE.**

DEMONSTRATIVE PRONOUN refers to one or more specific persons, things, events, or objects by indicating or singling out what is referred to. "That," "this," and "those" are demonstrative pronouns in English.

DEPENDENT CLAUSE. See **CLAUSE.**

DESCRIPTIVE is said of a word or phrase which characterizes or describes another term.

DIMINUTIVE is a word form indicating primarily smallness of size, but also familiarity, endearment, or (in some cases) contempt.

DIRECT DISCOURSE, DIRECT SPEECH. See **DISCOURSE.**

DIRECT OBJECT is the goal of an event or action specified by a verb. In "John hit the ball," the direct object of "hit" is "ball."

DISCOURSE is the connected and continuous communication of thought by means of language, whether spoken or written. The way in which the elements of a discourse are arranged is called DISCOURSE STRUCTURE. DIRECT DISCOURSE (or, DIRECT SPEECH) is the reproduction of the actual words of one person quoted and included in the discourse of another person; for example, "He declared 'I will have nothing to do with this man.' " INDIRECT DISCOURSE (or, INDIRECT SPEECH) is the reporting of the words of one person within the discourse of another person, but in an altered grammatical form rather than as an exact quotation; for example, "He said he would have nothing to do with that man."

DIVINE PASSIVE is the use of the passive form of a verb in order to avoid mentioning God or the name of God. For example, "You will be blessed" uses the passive "be blessed" but may be understood to mean "God will bless you." See also VOICE, PASSIVE.

DOXOLOGY is a hymn or other expression of praise to God, typically in a heightened or poetic literary form.

DYNAMIC EQUIVALENCE is a type of translation in which the message of the original text is so conveyed in the receptor language that the response of the receptors is (or, can be) essentially like that of the original receptors, or that the receptors can in large measure comprehend the response of the original receptors, if, as in certain languages, the differences between the two cultures are extremely great. In recent years the term FUNCTIONAL EQUIVALENCE has been applied to what is essentially the same kind of translation.

EMPHASIS (EMPHATIC) is the special importance given to an element in a discourse, sometimes indicated by the choice of words or by position in the sentence. For example, in "Never will I eat pork again," "Never" is given emphasis by placing it at the beginning of the sentence.

EPEXEGETIC (EPEXEGETICAL) refers to the addition of a word or words to explain the word or words that precede. For example, one meaning of "the gift of the Spirit" can be that "of the Spirit" is used epexegetically to mean "the gift that is the Spirit."

EQUIVALENCE (EQUIVALENT): a very close similarity in meaning, as opposed to similarity in form; see DYNAMIC EQUIVALENCE, which contrasts with FORMAL EQUIVALENCE.

ESCHATOLOGICAL refers to the end of the world and the events connected with it. In this connection, the "world" is understood in various ways by various persons.

EXCLUSIVE first person plural excludes the person(s) addressed. That is, a speaker may use "we" to refer to himself and his companions, while specifically excluding the person(s) to whom he is speaking. See **INCLUSIVE**.

EXCLUSIVE AND INCLUSIVE LANGUAGE are terms that apply to certain uses in languages such as English, where a term that includes only a portion of a group is used to refer to the entire group. For example, "brothers" is appropriate as an **EXCLUSIVE** term if indeed the intended meaning of the text does exclude sisters; however, when "brothers" designates, for example, fellow believers who are both male and female, it is far better to use an **INCLUSIVE** expression such as "fellow Christians" or "believers." Of course, in languages where the term for "brother" already includes both male and female, there will be no such problem.

EXEGESIS (EXEGETICAL) is the process of determining the meaning of a text (or the result of this process), normally in terms of "who said what to whom under what circumstances and with what intent." A correct exegesis is indispensable before a passage can be translated correctly.

EXHORTATION is the verbal act of encouraging, attempting, or urging, to make someone change a course of action or a matter of belief. "Do your best to encourage one another!" is an **EXHORTATION**.

EXPLICIT refers to information which is expressed in the words of a discourse. This is in contrast to **IMPLICIT** information. See **IMPLICIT**.

EXPOSITION is the act of systematically setting forth an idea or concept; it means to explain, define, clarify.

FEMININE is one of the Greek genders. See **GENDER**.

FIGURE, FIGURE OF SPEECH, or **FIGURATIVE EXPRESSION** involves the use of words in other than their literal or ordinary sense, in order to bring out some aspect of meaning by means of comparison or association. For example, "raindrops dancing on the street," or "his speech was like thunder." **METAPHORS** and **SIMILES** are figures of speech.

FINITE VERB is any verb form which distinguishes person, number, tense, mode, or aspect. It is usually referred to in contrast to an **INFINITIVE** verb form, which indicates the action or state without specifying such things as agent or time. See **INFINITIVE**.

FIRST PERSON. See **PERSON**.

FOCUS is the center of attention in a discourse or in any part of a discourse.

FORMAL EQUIVALENCE is a type of translation in which the features of form in the source text have been more or less mechanically reproduced in the receptor language.

FULL STOP is a marker indicating the end of a sentence; the marker is usually a period.

FUTURE TENSE. See **TENSE.**

GENDER is any of three grammatical subclasses of Greek nouns and pronouns (called **MASCULINE, FEMININE,** and **NEUTER**), which determine agreement with and selection of other words or grammatical forms.

GENERAL. See **GENERIC.**

GENERIC has reference to a general class or kind of objects, events, or abstracts; it is the opposite of **SPECIFIC.** For example, the term "animal" is generic in relation to "dog," which is a specific kind of animal. However, "dog" is generic in relation to the more specific term "poodle."

GENITIVE case is a grammatical set of forms occurring in many languages, used primarily to indicate that a noun is the modifier of another noun. The genitive often indicates possession, but it may also indicate measure, origin, characteristic, separation, or source, as in "child's toy," "pound of flour," "Jesus of Nazareth," "people of God," or "Garden of Eden."

GRAMMATICAL refers to grammar, which includes the selection and arrangement of words in phrases, clauses, and sentences.

GREEK is the language in which the New Testament was written. It belongs to the Indo-European family of languages and was the language spoken in Achaia, which is Greece in modern times. By the time of Christ Greek was used by many of the people living in the eastern part of the Roman empire, so that early Christians could speak and write to one another in Greek, even though they were born in different countries.

HEBREW is the language in which the Old Testament was written. It belongs to the Semitic family of languages. By the time of Christ many Jewish people no longer used Hebrew as their common language. The **HEBREWS** originally included people who did not belong to the twelve tribes of Israel, but after the Israelites settled in Canaan, the term generally was used to refer to the people of the twelve tribes, who had their own Hebrew language and culture.

IDEOPHONE is a vocal expression, often one that does not fit into the usual grammatical pattern of a language, yet expresses such things as an emotion, a quality, or a movement, and may sometimes mark or emphasize a feature of discourse. Ideophones are especially common in African languages, where their use and definition vary greatly.

337

IDIOM, or **IDIOMATIC EXPRESSION,** is a combination of terms whose meanings cannot be understood by adding up the meanings of the parts. "To hang one's head," "to have a green thumb," and "behind the eightball" are American English idioms. Idioms almost always lose their meaning or convey a wrong meaning when translated literally from one language to another.

IMPERATIVE refers to forms of a verb which indicate commands or requests. In "Go and do likewise," the verbs "Go" and "do" are imperatives. In most languages imperatives are confined to the grammatical second person; but some languages have corresponding forms for the first and third persons. These are usually expressed in English by the use of "must" or "let"; for example, "We must not swim here!" or "They must work harder!" or "Let them eat cake!"

IMPERFECT TENSE is a set of Greek verb forms designating an uncompleted or continuing kind of action, especially in the past.

IMPERSONAL VERB is a usage of the verb which denotes an action by an unspecified agent. It may involve the use of the third person singular, as in "It is raining" or "One normally prefers cake," or in some languages the use of the third person plural, as in "They say . . . ," or in still other languages the use of the first person plural, as in "We cook this way," meaning "People cook this way." Such use of a pronoun is sometimes referred to as the **INDEFINITE** pronoun.

IMPLICIT (IMPLIED) refers to information that is not formally represented in a discourse, since it is assumed that it is already known to the receptor, or evident from the meaning of the words in question. For example, the phrase "the other son" carries with it the implicit information that there is a son in addition to the one mentioned. This is in contrast to **EXPLICIT** information, which is expressly stated in a discourse. See **EXPLICIT.**

IMPLY. See **IMPLICIT, IMPLIED.**

INCLUSIVE first person plural includes both the speaker and the one(s) to whom that person is speaking. See **EXCLUSIVE.**

INCLUSIVE LANGUAGE. See **EXCLUSIVE AND INCLUSIVE LANGUAGE.**

INDEFINITE article or pronoun. See **IMPERSONAL VERB.**

INDIRECT DISCOURSE. See **DISCOURSE.**

INFINITIVE is a verb form which indicates an action or state without specifying such factors as agent or time; for example, "to mark," "to sing," or "to go." It is in contrast to **FINITE VERB** form, which often distinguishes person, number, tense, mode, or aspect; for example "marked," "sung," or "will go." See **FINITE VERB.**

INJUNCTION may refer in a general way to the act of urging or encouraging someone to do something, or to the more restricted sense of an authoritative order or command which must be obeyed.

INSTRUMENT is the object used in accomplishing an action. In the sentence "John opened the door with a key," the "key" is the instrument. See also **AGENT**.

INTERJECTIONS are exclamatory words or phrases, invariable in form, usually used to express emotion. "Hey!" or "Oh!" and "Indeed!" are examples of interjections.

INTERPRETATION of a text is the exegesis of it. See **EXEGESIS**.

LEVEL refers to the degree of difficulty characteristic of language usage by different constituencies or in different settings. A translation may, for example, be prepared for the level of elementary school children, for university students, for teen-agers, or for rural rather than urban people. Differences of level also are involved as to whether a particular discourse is formal, informal, casual, or intimate in nature.

LITERAL means the ordinary or primary meaning of a term or expression, in contrast with a figurative meaning. A **LITERAL TRANSLATION** is one which represents the exact words and word order of the source language; such a translation is nearly always unnatural or awkward in the receptor language.

LITURGICAL refers to liturgy, that is, public worship; more particularly to the prayers, responses, etc. which are often expressed in traditional or archaic language forms.

LOAN WORD is a foreign word that is used in another language. See **BORROWING**.

MAIN CLAUSE. See **CLAUSE**.

MANUSCRIPTS are books, documents, or letters written or copied by hand. A **COPYIST** is one who copies a manuscript. Thousands of manuscript copies of various Old and New Testament books still exist, but none of the original manuscripts. See **TEXT**.

MASCULINE is one of the Greek genders. See **GENDER**.

METAPHOR is likening one object, event, or state to another by speaking of it as if it were the other; for example, "flowers dancing in the breeze" compares the movement of flowers with dancing. Metaphors are the most commonly used **FIGURES OF SPEECH** and are often so subtle that a speaker or writer is not conscious of the fact that he or she is using figurative language. See **SIMILE**.

MIDDLE VOICE. See **VOICE**.

MODE, MODAL refers to forms of verbs in certain languages which indicate the attitude of a speaker to what he or she is saying; for example, wish, hesitancy, command, etc. The various categories of modal verb forms are called modes or moods. In English they are expressed by such auxiliary verbs as "can," "do," "may," "shall," etc.

MODIFY is to affect the meaning of another part of the sentence, as when an adjective modifies a noun, or an adverb modifies a verb.

NARRATIVE DISCOURSE is a text consisting of a series of successive and related events.

NEUTER is one of the Greek genders. See **GENDER**.

NOMINATIVE CASE in Greek and certain other languages is the case which indicates the subject of a finite verb.

NOUN is a word that names a person, place, thing, or idea, and often serves to specify a subject or topic of discussion.

NOUN PHRASE. See PHRASE.

OBJECT of a verb is the goal of an event or action specified by the verb. In "John hit the ball," the object of "hit" is "ball." See **DIRECT OBJECT**.

OBJECTIVE GENITIVE is a grammatical form commonly used in Greek and which occurs when a noun showing action is directed to another noun that is affected by the action; the affected noun is in the genitive form. For example, "fear of God" does not mean that God possesses the fear, but that the fear is directed to God as the object of fear. See also **GENITIVE**.

PAPYRI (singular **PAPYRUS**) are, in the context of this Handbook, those texts of the Scriptures which were written originally on papyrus (an early form of paper) and which are representative of the earliest forms of the Greek text.

PARAGRAPH is a distinct segment of discourse dealing with a particular idea, and usually marked with an indentation on a new line.

PARALLEL, PARALLELISM, generally refers to some similarity in the content and/or form of a construction; for example, "The man was blind, and he could not see." The structures that correspond to each other in the two statements are said to be parallel.

PARAPHRASE is a restatement of a meaning in a different form. Paraphrases are of two principal types: (1) grammatical (for example, "John hit the man" and "the man was hit by John") and (2) lexical (for example, "the man refuses to work" and "he declines all employment").

PARENTHETICAL STATEMENT is a statement that interrupts a discourse by departing from its main theme. It is frequently set off by marks of parenthesis ( ).

PARTICIPIAL indicates that the phrase, clause, construction, or other expression described is governed by a **PARTICIPLE**.

PARTICIPLE is a verbal adjective, that is, a word which retains some of the characteristics of a verb while functioning as an adjective. In "singing children" and "painted house," "singing" and "painted" are participles.

PARTICLE is a small word whose grammatical form does not change. In English the most common particles are prepositions and conjunctions.

PARTICULAR is the opposite of **GENERAL**. See **GENERIC**.

PASSAGE is the text of Scripture in a specific location. It is usually thought of as comprising more than one verse, but it can be a single verse or part of a verse.

PASSIVE. See **VOICE**.

PAST TENSE. See **TENSE**.

PERFECT TENSE is a set of verb forms that indicate an action completed before the time of speaking or writing. For example, in "John has finished his task," "has finished" is in the perfect tense. The perfect tense in Greek also indicates that the action, or else the result of the action, continues into the present, as in "Christ has arisen." See also **TENSE**.

PERSON, as a grammatical term, refers to the speaker, the person spoken to, or the person or thing spoken about. **FIRST PERSON** is the person(s) speaking (such as "I," "me," "my," "mine," "we," "us," "our," or "ours"). **SECOND PERSON** is the person(s) or thing(s) spoken to (such as "thou," "thee," "thy," "thine," "ye," "you," "your," or "yours"). **THIRD PERSON** is the person(s) or thing(s) spoken about (such as "he," "she," "it," "his," "her," "them," or "their"). The examples here given are all pronouns, but in many languages the verb forms have affixes which indicate first, second, or third person and also indicate whether they are **SINGULAR** or **PLURAL**.

PERSONAL PRONOUN is one which indicates first, second, or third person. See **PERSON** and **PRONOUN**.

PHRASE is a grammatical construction of two or more words, but less than a complete clause or a sentence. A phrase is usually given a name according to its function in a sentence, such as "noun phrase," "verb phrase," or "prepositional phrase."

PLURAL refers to the form of a word which indicates more than one. See **SINGULAR**.

341

POINT OF VIEW, or viewpoint, is the place or situation or circumstance from which a speaker or writer presents a message. If, for example, the viewpoint place is the top of a hill, movement in the area will be described differently from the way one would describe it from the bottom of a hill. If the viewpoint person is a priest, he will speak of the temple in a way that differs from that of a common person.

POSSESSIVE refers to a grammatical relationship in which one noun or pronoun is said to "possess" another ("John's car," "his son," "their destruction"). In Greek this relation is generally marked by the **GENITIVE CASE.** See **GENITIVE CASE.**

POSSESSIVE PRONOUNS are pronouns such as "my," "our," "your," or "his," which indicate possession.

PREPOSITION is a word (usually a particle) whose function is to indicate the relation of a noun or pronoun to another noun, pronoun, verb, or adjective. Some English prepositions are "for," "from," "in," "to," and "with."

PRESENT TENSE. See **TENSE.**

PRONOUNS are words which are used in place of nouns, such as "he," "him," "his," "she," "we," "them," "who," "which," "this," or "these."

PROPER NOUN is the name of a unique object, as "Jerusalem," "Joshua," "Jordan." However, the same name may be applied to more than one object; for example, "John" (the Baptist or the Apostle) and "Antioch" (of Syria or Pisidia).

PROSE is the ordinary form of spoken or written language, without the special forms and structure of meter and rhythm which are characteristic of poetry.

PURPOSE CLAUSE designates a construction which states the purpose involved in some other action; for example, "John came in order to help him," or "John mentioned the problem to his colleagues, so that they would know how to help out."

QUALIFY (QUALIFICATION) is to limit the meaning of a term by means of another term. For example, in "old man," the term "old" qualifies the term "man."

QUOTATION is the reporting of one person's speech by another person. See **DISCOURSE, DIRECT DISCOURSE.**

READ, READING. See **TEXT, TEXTUAL.**

RECEPTOR is the person(s) receiving a message. The **RECEPTOR LANGUAGE** is the language into which a translation is made. For example, in a translation from Hebrew into German, Hebrew is the source language and German is the receptor language.

REDUNDANT (REDUNDANCY) refers to anything which is entirely predictable from the context. For example, in "John, he did it," the pronoun "he" is redundant. A feature may be redundant and yet may be important to retain in certain languages, perhaps for stylistic or for grammatical reasons.

REFERENT is the thing(s) or person(s) referred to by a pronoun, phrase, or clause.

RELATIVE CLAUSE is a dependent clause which describes the object to which it refers. In "the man whom you saw," the clause "whom you saw" is relative because it relates to and describes "man."

RENDER means translate or express in a language different from the original. **RENDERING** is the manner in which a specific passage is translated from one language to another.

RESTRUCTURE. See **STRUCTURE.**

RHETORICAL refers to forms of speech which are employed to highlight or make more attractive some aspect of a discourse. A **RHETORICAL QUESTION**, for example, is not a request for information but is a way of making an emphatic statement.

RHYTHM is the periodic pattern of accented syllables in a line of poetry.

SECOND PERSON. See **PERSON.**

SEMITIC refers to a family of languages which includes Hebrew, Aramaic, and Arabic. Greek belongs to quite another language family, with a distinct cultural background. In view of the Jewish ancestry and training of the writers of the New Testament, it is not surprising that many Semitic idioms and thought patterns (called Semitisms or Hebraisms) appear in the Greek writings of the New Testament.

SENTENCE is a grammatical construction composed of one or more clauses and capable of standing alone.

SEPTUAGINT is a translation of the Hebrew Old Testament into Greek, begun some two hundred years before Christ. It is often abbreviated as LXX.

SIMILE (pronounced SIM-i-lee) is a **FIGURE OF SPEECH** which describes one event or object by comparing it to another, using "like," "as," or some other word to mark or signal the comparison. For example, "She runs like a deer," "He is as straight as an arrow." Similes are less subtle than metaphors in that metaphors do not mark the comparison with words such as "like" or "as." See **METAPHOR.**

SINGULAR refers to the form of a word which indicates one thing or person, in contrast to **PLURAL,** which indicates more than one. See **PLURAL.**

SPECIFIC refers to the opposite of **GENERAL, GENERIC.** See **GENERIC.**

STRUCTURE is the systematic arrangement of the elements of language, including the ways in which words combine into phrases, phrases into clauses, clauses into sentences, and sentences into larger units of discourse. Because this process may be compared to the building of a house or bridge, such words as **STRUCTURE** and **CONSTRUCTION** are used in reference to it. To separate and rearrange the various components of a sentence or other unit of discourse in the translation process is to **RESTRUCTURE** it.

STYLE is a particular or a characteristic manner in discourse. Each language has certain distinctive **STYLISTIC** features which cannot be reproduced literally in another language. Within any language, certain groups of speakers may have their characteristic discourse styles, and among individual speakers and writers, each has his or her own style. Various stylistic devices are used for the purpose of achieving a more pleasing style. For example, synonyms are sometimes used to avoid the monotonous repetition of the same words, or the normal order of clauses and phrases may be altered for the sake of emphasis.

SUBJECT is one of the major divisions of a clause, the other being the predicate. In "The small boy walked to school," "The small boy" is the subject. Typically the subject is a noun phrase. It should not be confused with the semantic **AGENT,** or **ACTOR.**

SUBORDINATE CLAUSE. See **CLAUSE.**

SUPERLATIVE refers to the form of an adjective or adverb that indicates that the object or event described possesses a certain quality to a greater degree than does any other object or event implicitly or explicitly specified by the content. "Most happy" and "finest" are adjectives in the superlative degree.

SYMBOL (SYMBOLIC) is a form, whether linguistic or nonlinguistic, which is arbitrarily and conventionally associated with a particular meaning. For example, the word "cross" is a linguistic symbol, referring to a particular object. Similarly, within the Christian tradition, the cross as an object is a symbol for the death of Jesus.

SYNONYMS are words which are different in form but similar in meaning, such as "boy" and "lad." Expressions which have essentially the same meaning are said to be **SYNONYMOUS.** No two words are completely synonymous.

SYNOPTIC GOSPELS are Matthew, Mark, and Luke, which share many characteristics that are not found in John.

SYNTAX is the selection and arrangement of words in phrases, clauses, and sentences.

TABOO refers to something set apart as sacred by religious custom and is therefore forbidden to all but certain persons or uses (positive taboo), or something

344

which is regarded as evil and therefore forbidden to all by tradition or social usage (negative taboo).

TENSE is usually a form of a verb which indicates time relative to a discourse or some event in a discourse. The most common forms of tense are past, present, and future.

TEXT, TEXTUAL, refers to the various Greek and Hebrew manuscripts of the Scriptures. A **TEXTUAL READING** is the form in which words occur in a particular manuscript (or group of manuscripts), especially where it differs from others. **TEXTUAL EVIDENCE** is the cumulative evidence for a particular form of the text. See also **MANUSCRIPTS**.

THEME is the subject of a discourse.

THIRD PERSON. See **PERSON**.

TRANSITION in discourse involves passing from one thought-section or group of related thought-sections to another.

TRANSLATION is the reproduction in a receptor language of the closest natural equivalent of a message in the source language, first, in terms of meaning, and second, in terms of style.

TRANSLITERATE (TRANSLITERATION) is to represent in the receptor language the approximate sounds or letters of words occurring in the source language, rather than translating their meaning; for example, "Amen" from the Hebrew, or the title "Christ" from the Greek.

UNAMBIGUOUS indicates that a word or phrase is clearly understood in only one way. See **AMBIGUOUS**.

VERBS are a grammatical class of words which express existence, action, or occurrence, such as "be," "become," "run," or "think."

VERBAL has two meanings. (1) It may refer to expressions consisting of words, sometimes in distinction to forms of communication which do not employ words ("sign language," for example). (2) It may refer to word forms which are derived from verbs. For example, "coming" and "engaged" may be called verbals, and participles are called verbal adjectives.

VERSIONS are translations. The **ANCIENT VERSIONS**, or early versions, are translations of the Bible, or of portions of the Bible, made in early times; for example, the Greek Septuagint, the ancient Syriac, or the Ethiopic versions.

VOCATIVE indicates that a word or phrase is used for referring to a person or persons spoken to. In "Brother, please come here," the word "Brother" is a vocative.

VOICE in grammar is the relation of the action expressed by a verb to the participants in the action. In English and many other languages, the **ACTIVE VOICE** indicates that the subject performs the action ("John hit the man"), while the **PASSIVE VOICE** indicates that the subject is being acted upon ("The man was hit"). The Greek language has a **MIDDLE VOICE,** in which the subject may be regarded as doing something to or for himself (or itself); for example, "He washed," meaning "He washed himself."

VULGATE is the Latin version of the Bible translated and/or edited originally by Saint Jerome. It has been traditionally the official version of the Roman Catholic Church.

WORDPLAY in a discourse is the use of the similarity in the sounds to produce a special effect.

Index

This index includes concepts, key words, and terms for which the Handbook contains a discussion useful for translators. Greek and Hebrew words that are included are listed according to transliterated English alphabetical order.

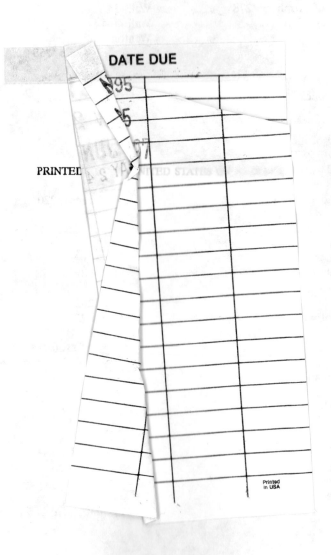

DATE DUE

Printed
in USA